# RECONCILABLE DIFFERENCES

### A History of Canada-US Relations

## STEPHEN AZZI

OXFORD
UNIVERSITY PRESS

# OXFORD
UNIVERSITY PRESS

Oxford University Press is a department of the University of Oxford.
It furthers the University's objective of excellence in research, scholarship,
and education by publishing worldwide. Oxford is a registered trade mark of
Oxford University Press in the UK and in certain other countries.

Published in Canada by
Oxford University Press
8 Sampson Mews, Suite 204,
Don Mills, Ontario  M3C 0H5 Canada

www.oupcanada.com

Copyright © Oxford University Press Canada 2015

The moral rights of the author have been asserted

Database right Oxford University Press (maker)

First Edition published in 2015

**Library and Archives Canada Cataloguing in Publication**

Azzi, Stephen, 1965-, author
Reconcilable differences : a history of Canada-US relations
/ Stephen Azzi.

(Living history series)
Includes bibliographical references and index.
ISBN 978-0-19-544707-1 (pbk.)

1. Canada--Relations—United States—Textbooks. 2. United
States—Relations—Canada--Textbooks. I. Title.

FC249.A99 2014          327.71073          C2014-902171-2

Cover image: Library and Archives Canada/C-090217

Oxford University Press is committed to our environment.
This book is printed on Forest Stewardship Council® certified paper
and comes from responsible sources.

Printed and bound in Canada

2 3 4 — 19

*for Julia and Mark*

# Contents

Chapter 10 ✦ Resilience, 1968–1984: The Rise and Fall of Canadian Nationalism   181

Chapter 11 ✦ Reconciliation, 1984–1993: The Political and Economic Partnership of the Mulroney Years   211

## Chapter 12 ✢ Unipolarity, since 1993: The United States and Canada after the Cold War   228

# Figures

# Foreword to the *Living History* Series

Canadian history is as fascinating as it is diverse. Over the past two centuries alone, Canada has participated in a number of major international conflicts and developed one of the world's strongest economies. Political action and social movement activism have transformed Canada's approaches to gender, class, sexual orientation, Aboriginal issues, and racial and ethnic diversity. While there has been much compromise and cooperation in Canada's history, there have also been many clashes and conflicts.

Certainly there is no shortage of vital stories to tell about the rich history of this complex land. The *Living History* series aims to explore and analyze these histories in greater depth than can be done in broad Canadian history survey courses and texts. To ensure this level of analysis, I have worked with Oxford University Press Canada to select leading Canadian scholars to share their perspectives on major themes that echo through Canada's past—themes such as Native–newcomer interactions, Canada–US relations, politics and power, national identity, regional tensions, language and culture, family life, race and ethnicity, and environmental issues. Through vibrant stories and detailed analyses, the books in this series will bring Canada's diverse and intertwined histories to life, and they will undoubtedly inspire many readers to pursue further study or work in this highly captivating field.

Matthew Hayday
Series Editor, *Living History* Series
Associate Professor, University of Guelph

# Preface

———⁂———

On the border between St Stephen, New Brunswick, and Calais, Maine, the War of 1812 was not much of a war at all. "Not one dollar's worth of property was taken by violence from any man on the lines," local resident Duncan M'Coll later recalled, "neither was there any killed, wounded, or taken prisoner amongst us."[1]

M'Coll was the Methodist pastor for St Stephen, making him the spiritual leader for the largest denomination in the area, but his congregation did not stop at the Canada–US border. He counted among his parishioners the Methodists of Calais. When the war broke out between Britain and the United States in 1812, prominent residents of the two towns, under M'Coll's leadership, created a committee of public safety to prevent the outbreak of hostilities in the area. M'Coll moved freely across the border, urging both British and American troops to respect the friendship that had long existed between the two communities. When the war ended in 1814, M'Coll was jubilant: peace and order had been maintained.

Four lessons from this episode provide the backbone for this book, the first being that the Canada–US border has always been porous. Individuals, families, ideas, and beliefs have crossed easily from one country to the other. In addition to distinct Canadian and American national experiences, the people of the two countries have shared a transnational one—a product of common values and similar responses to the challenges of the North American environment. When we understand that the border did not stop the forces of history—when we seek to engage the Canadian and American past beyond the national context—we better understand both countries. "The historian of the United States who is ignorant of Canadian history is ignorant of his own history," American historian Robin Winks said several decades ago. The reverse is also true: "Canadians cannot understand their history without understanding American history." This book rejects both those American historians who exaggerate the uniqueness of the United States and the Canadian scholars who see the US as primarily a negative influence on their country's development. Nor should we be taken in by the romanticism of continentalists who laud the "special relationship" between the two countries. The goal is a balanced approach that does not ignore or exaggerate the influence of the two countries on each other.

The second lesson of Maine and New Brunswick's War of 1812 is that the Canadian–American relationship differs from region to region. Canada and the United States were at war in the Niagara peninsula and along the St Lawrence River from 1812 to 1814, and American forces burned York (now Toronto) in 1813. Yet the residents of New Brunswick and Maine experienced a much different reality, never witnessing any fighting. There are countless other instances throughout history where different regions have a profoundly different view of the Canadian–American connection. In the late nineteenth century, many Ontarians saw close ties to the United States as a form of treason, but Western Canadians saw things differently. There was much for them to copy from the American example because conditions were similar on each side of the border. For Westerners in both Canada and the United States, history was marked by conflicts with Aboriginal peoples, the building of railways, the struggle to farm in arid regions, and the growth of resentment toward the moneyed interests "back east." Even in our times, the Canadian attitude toward the United States and the American attitude toward Canada vary widely across the continent.

The third lesson is that the Canadian–American relationship is not easily summarized. Yes, the War of 1812 was a brutal affair, but that is only part of the story. Even in the midst of war, cooperation between the two countries continued along the Maine–New Brunswick border and elsewhere. Simple descriptions of the Canada–US connection (e.g., Canada is an American colony) often conceal as much as they reveal, as do lazy comparisons of the two countries (e.g., Canada is more peaceful and tolerant than the United States).

Our fourth lesson: political developments have been crucial to the history of the Canadian–American relationship, but understanding deepens when we move beyond politics. From 1812 to 1814, the United States was at war with Britain and the British colonies that would become Canada, a conflict born of high politics. Yet war was not the reality everywhere—certainly not in St Stephen and Calais. We see a different story when we look not just at politicians and soldiers, but also at communities and individuals struggling to survive. Knowing the Canada–US connection requires the study of governments, but also of regions, social movements, economics, and culture.

This book's subject is the interplay of Canada and the United States from the birth of the two countries until the present day. It considers how Ottawa interacted with Washington, how Canadians dealt with the overwhelming presence of American culture, how protest movements developed simultaneously in the two countries, how ideas flowed across the boundary, how Aboriginal people dealt with a border they often did not recognize, how Canadians tried to benefit from American prosperity without joining the United States, and how public opinion shaped the relationship. Successive chapters grapple with the key scholarly debates in the field: Were Canada and the United States distinct societies founded on fundamentally different values? Did Liberal governments destroy Canada's relationship with Britain and prepare Canada for absorption by the US? Has Canada's independence been threatened by strong economic ties to the United States? Have Canadian and American values been converging or diverging over time? There are no easy answers to any of these questions, but confronting them helps us move toward a greater understanding of Canada and the United States—and the long and complex relationship between them.

# Further Reading

There are several books on Canadian–American relations. The best overview is Norman Hillmer and J.L. Granatstein's elegant and authoritative work, *For Better or For Worse: Canada and the United States into the Twenty-First Century*, 2nd ed. (Toronto: Thomson Nelson, 2007). Robert Bothwell's lively book, *Canada and the United States: The Politics of Partnership* (Toronto: University of Toronto Press, 1992), is strongest on the period after 1945. The meticulous *An Introduction to Canadian–American Relations*, 2nd ed. (Scarborough, Ontario: Nelson, 1989), by Edelgard E. Mahant and Graeme S. Mount, is unsurpassed on nineteenth-century developments. Social and cultural factors play a larger role in John Herd Thompson and Stephen Randall, *Canada and the United States: Ambivalent Allies*, 4th ed. (Montreal and Kingston: McGill–Queen's University Press, 2008), a work that suggests that Canada has been reduced to a colony of the United States.

More specialized sources are worthwhile. Lawrence Martin provides an engaging study of national leaders in *The Presidents and the Prime Ministers, Washington and Ottawa Face to Face: The Myth of Bilateral Bliss, 1867–1982* (Toronto: Doubleday, 1982). In *Dispersed Relations: Americans and Canadians in Upper North America* (Washington: Woodrow Wilson Center Press; Baltimore: Johns Hopkins University Press, 2007), Reginald C. Stuart offers a transnational perspective, focussing on recent economic, political, social, and cultural developments. On anti-Americanism in Canada, see J.L. Granatstein's fast-paced account, *Yankee Go Home? Canadians and Anti-Americanism* (Toronto: HarperCollins, 1996).

The finest overview history of US foreign policy is George C. Herring's monumental work, *From Colony to Superpower: US Foreign Relations since 1776* (Oxford: Oxford University Press, 2008). For examinations of US policy toward Canada, see Edelgard Mahant and Graeme S. Mount, *Invisible and Inaudible in Washington: American Policies toward Canada* (Vancouver: UBC Press, 1999); and Gordon T. Stewart, *The American Response to Canada since 1776* (East Lansing: Michigan State University Press, 1992).

General works on Canadian foreign policy devote much of their attention to Canada's relationship with its southern neighbour: Norman Hillmer and J.L. Granatstein, *Empire to Umpire: Canada and the World into the Twentieth Century* (Toronto: Thomson Nelson, 2008); Robert Bothwell, *Alliance and Illusion: Canada and the World, 1945–1984* (Vancouver: University of British Columbia Press, 2007); and C.P. Stacey, *Canada and the Age of Conflict: A History of Canadian External Policies*, 2 vols. (Toronto: University of Toronto Press, 1984). Useful and often forgotten are the biennial volumes in the *Canada in World Affairs* series (Toronto: Oxford University Press, 1941–85), which covered the period from the 1930s to 1965, and 1971 to 1973. Since 1984, the *Canada Among Nations* series (various publishers) has issued a volume almost every year, each containing cutting-edge work by leading scholars.

# Acknowledgements

This book would not exist were it not for Matthew Hayday and Norman Hillmer. As editor of Oxford University Press's Living History series, Matthew invited me to write a book on Canadian–American relations and later provided valuable commentary on the manuscript. Norman convinced me to take up the project and he read each chapter, saving me from errors of fact, weaknesses in interpretation, and lapses in style. He inspired me to live up to his very high standards.

Many students helped with the research for this book and shared their insights with me. I am particularly indebted to Tim Greenough, Eric Harding, Victoria Malpass, Amber McCarthy, Rebecca Malpass, Samantha Crawford, Chaé Robidas, Kaleigh Bradley, Alana Bowles, Matthew Fron, Ian Wereley, and Aaron Goldstein-Storseth.

I have been fortunate to work with talented editors at Oxford University Press: Caroline Starr, Mary Wat, Meg Patterson, Leah-Ann Lymer, and Maria Jelinek.

Colleagues at Laurentian University and Carleton University provided support. Todd Webb taught me much of what I know about the period before the 1860s and reviewed the book's early chapters. Sara Burke, Linda Ambrose, David Leeson, Ariel Beaujot, and Patrick Cavaliere gave me sound advice, as did Graeme Mount, a pioneer in the field of Canadian–American relations. Librarians proved indispensable, no one more so than Christine Taylor at Carleton and Ashley Thomson at Laurentian.

Several scholars generously responded to my pleas for assistance. Patricia Roy, Philippe Lagassé, Patrick Harrigan, and Hector Mackenzie all read large portions of the manuscript and provided valuable insight and guidance. Philippe also kindly shared with me the results of research he had yet to publish, as did Dawn Flood. John English, J.R. Miller, Julian Gwyn, J.M. Bumsted, Andrew Burtch, Greg Donaghy, Chris Dornan, Dwight Mason, Janice Cavell, and Richard Clippingdale graciously answered my many questions, helping fill in the gaps in my knowledge. David Ratz of Lakehead University and Dan Bousfield of Western University read the entire manuscript, pointed out weaknesses, and offered helpful advice.

I benefitted from informal talks with Rarihokwats, Dave Noble, Lt.-Gen. (ret'd) Ken Pennie, and Lt.-Gen. (ret'd) Charles Bouchard. Libby Jones and Frank A. Tinker provided information on their father, Frank Tinker. Gen. (ret'd) Ray Henault kindly read over a key portion of the manuscript on defence policy.

I am fortunate to be sharing my life with Adriana Gouvêa, who is always patient, encouraging, and supportive. This book is dedicated, with all my love, to my children, Julia and Mark.

## CHAPTER 1

# Loyalties, 1763–1814

## *The American Revolution, Loyalism, and the War of 1812*

## Introduction

Loyalty was not a simple matter for William Smith. He was thoroughly American, born in New York City in 1728, and educated at Yale College, before becoming a prosperous lawyer and influential politician in his hometown. In the 1760s, he gained the nickname "Patriotic Billy" for his strenuous objections to new taxes that London had imposed upon the American colonies without their consent. Smith said the people of New York should refuse to transact any business requiring them to pay the taxes created by the 1765 Stamp Act, a measure he said had "lost Great Britain the affection of all her colonies."[1] As the conflict with Britain pushed the North American colonies toward revolution, Smith urged Britain to withdraw its troops from New York and Boston to avoid clashes between soldiers and local residents. But as much as Smith condemned British blundering and wanted the colonies to exert a greater degree of self-government, he implored his fellow Americans to act with moderation and caution. After fighting broke out in 1775, Smith tried to maintain neutrality, finding fault on the part of both the British and the Americans.

Ultimately forced to choose sides, Smith came out against American independence in 1778. Yet he continued to believe that more political power should be in the hands of the colonists and that they, not the British government, should decide their own taxation. As a reward for his loyalty, the British made Smith the chief justice of New York in 1780. When the Revolutionary War ended in 1783, he considered remaining in New York, but knew his property would be confiscated and he would have to endure verbal and perhaps physical abuse from the victorious Patriots. He fled to England, but eventually returned to North America. Settling in the British colony of Quebec, he became chief justice, a member of the colonial council, and the closest adviser to the governor, Lord Dorchester (Guy Carleton).

Although few residents of British North America were, like Smith, members of the colonial elite, most shared his ambivalence about the revolution. The Revolutionary War was not, as often portrayed, a straightforward fight between two clearly drawn sides: the British and the American colonists. The sympathies of most residents of British North America were difficult to pin down, both before and during the uprising. The conflict was a revolution, but it was also a civil war, one that pitted neighbour against neighbour, rebellious Americans against those who fought for the British Crown. The majority of Americans opposed the taxes Britain had forced upon the colonies, but most were also wary about resorting to violence.

## Prelude to Revolution

In the 1770s and 1780s, 13 rebellious British colonies formed the United States, but others remained loyal to Britain. Historians often cloak these events with the aura of inevitability, emphasizing the differences between the colonies that rebelled and those that did not. But at the time, the situation was complex. Each British colony in North America was unique in its own way, with distinctive cultural patterns, attitudes, and accents. There were strong bonds and similarities between some of the rebellious colonies and those that remained in the British Empire. Nova Scotia, which did not join the revolution, had much in common with the colonies of New England. Massachusetts had stronger links with Nova Scotia than it did with the colonies to the south.

Although diverse, the British holdings in North America were in many ways alike. The majority of the population in each colony had been born on the Continent. The Congregationalist faith predominated in New England and Nova Scotia, while the Church of England was the established religion in the South. Catholics and Jews faced discrimination throughout the colonies. Women were also subjected to prejudice and inequality virtually everywhere: men often considered women inferior, believing that their role was to serve their husbands, care for their children, and maintain their households by tending to the garden, caring for livestock, and making clothing. In most places, women could not vote, hold office, attend public schools, sign contracts, or own property. Cities and towns remained small by today's standards, as most people lived and worked on farms, ranches, or plantations. All colonies depended on exports, meaning they had volatile economies. Still, the period before the revolution was an era of prosperity throughout British North America. Colonists were generally better off than residents of the British Isles, though wealth was not evenly distributed,

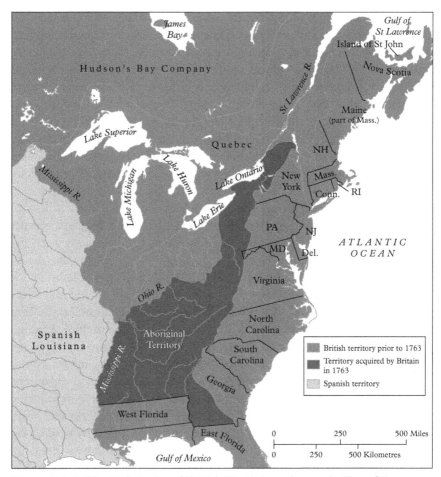

**Figure 1.1** ⊹ The 18 Colonies of British North America on the Eve of the American Revolution

On the eve of the American Revolution, Britain had 18 diverse colonies in North America, 13 of which would rebel. Nova Scotia had much in common with the neighbouring colonies in New England.

Source: Adapted from Murrin's *Liberty, Equality, Power* 4e, p. 162 (Wadsworth, 2004).

being concentrated in the hands of a growing class of merchants and land-owners. In most colonies, including Nova Scotia, this elite dominated the elected assemblies. Politicians everywhere pushed to increase the power of the assemblies and to decrease the authority of the governor and other officials appointed by the British government.

Nova Scotia's most important ties—those of society, culture, and economy—were with New England. After failing to lure immigrants to Nova Scotia from Britain and continental Europe, the British had encouraged New Englanders to settle in Nova Scotia, giving them free land, often taken from the French-speaking Acadians who were brutally expelled between 1755 and 1763. In 1759, Nova Scotia's governor, Charles Lawrence, issued a proclamation reassuring potential settlers that his colony was much like New England: "The government of Nova Scotia is constituted like those of the neighbouring colonies. . . . The courts of justice are also constituted in like manner with those of the Massachusetts, Connecticut and other northern colonies."[2] The population of Nova Scotia was not homogenous and included Scots, Irish, Germans, and Acadians, but the largest group were the New Englanders who dominated the colony, as they set out to create a new New England. In 1775, on the eve of revolution, the population of the colony was 20,000, three-quarters of whom were Planters, as the New Englanders called themselves, using a now-archaic English word for *colonists*.

The Planters arrived in Nova Scotia with their New England accents and outlook. Most were Congregationalists, whose religious views were distinctly more American than British. Theirs was the evangelical Christianity of New England, with its democratic impulse. They saw little need for clergymen with formal theological training, instead emphasizing individual conversion and a person's direct relationship with God. Churches in Nova Scotia, as in New England, forbade working on Sunday, gambling, dancing, playing cards, using the devil's name, smiling in church, and a wide range of other apparently frivolous activities. Planters built homes similar to those they had inhabited before moving to Nova Scotia. Like New Englanders, most Planters were farmers or fishers, and some were artisans. After moving north, they maintained their family and business ties in New England. Nova Scotia's communities were on the coast and were not linked by road to the capital, Halifax. Their trade was by ship, and was mostly with New England, which provided supplies and bought Nova Scotia's produce. The Planters were a majority on the appointed provincial council (which functioned as both an executive and legislative body) and in the elected assembly. They were commonly called "Nova Scotia's Yankees" and inhabited a colony that historian John Bartlet Brebner described as "New England's Outpost."[3]

The Planters' political views had a New England pedigree. The earliest arrivals convinced the governor to create an elected assembly in 1758. They also pushed unsuccessfully for the right to elect their own town officials. In 1762, residents of Liverpool, Nova Scotia, asserted their right to self-government, employing the language common in New England. They "were born in a country of liberty" and thus claimed the "right and authority" to choose their own officials. Any attempt by the governor of Nova Scotia to interfere with this would be "encroaching on our freedom and liberty and depriving us of a privilege that belongs to no body of people but ourselves."[4]

While most of Nova Scotia was connected to New England, Halifax had stronger ties to Britain. As home to a British naval base, the city was pro-British in sentiment, as were all the areas of North America where the mother country maintained a strong military presence. In 1764, there were almost as many military personnel in Halifax as civilians. As a second-generation colony, one developed later than most of the others in North America, Nova Scotia was similar to Georgia in its strong links with Britain. Both colonies were heavily dependent on Britain to help cover the costs of their administration and both were largely run by officials appointed by London. The two capitals, Halifax and Savannah, were frontier outposts, less established than Boston and other colonial centres.

Predominantly French-speaking and Roman Catholic, Quebec had little in common with the other British possessions. The British had won a large chunk of New France in the 1763 Treaty of Paris at the end of the Seven Years' War, which had pitted Britain against France and Spain. Most French colonists lived in the St Lawrence valley, which now became the British colony of Quebec. Officials set out to impose British law on Quebec and populate the area with English-speakers. British legislation discriminated against Roman Catholics, preventing them from working in the public service, holding military office, sitting in the legislature, practising law, or serving on juries. As a result, the Catholic Church in Quebec lost its official status and most Quebeckers were denied the rights available to British subjects. British officials assumed that large numbers of English-speakers would move to Quebec and overwhelm the French, who would eventually be assimilated. Several hundred American merchants did settle there, but they were still greatly outnumbered by the French population, which totalled 70,000 in 1765.

The first British governor of Quebec quickly realized that French Canadians would not be easily assimilated. James Murray came to sympathize with the majority and refused to create an elected assembly, which would have represented only a few hundred Protestants and not the tens of thousands of Catholics who were denied the vote. He allowed Catholics to practise law and serve on juries, and re-established the French civil code while maintaining British criminal law. He recognized the tithe, the mandatory payments that Catholics made to the church, and preserved the seigneurial system, a form of feudalism. Murray's replacement, Guy Carleton, convinced the British to formalize Murray's policies. In the Quebec Act of 1774, London confirmed many of the features that had distinguished New France from British North America.

# Revolution

Conflict between Britain and its North American colonies grew gradually from the 1760s until revolution broke out in 1775. In 1763, the British had won the Seven Years' War over France and Spain, a conflict fought in North

America, the Caribbean, and Europe. In the Treaty of Paris of that year, France surrendered all territory in continental North America. To Britain went Canada (renamed Quebec), while Spain gained Louisiana from France and gave up Florida to the British.

Britain had incurred enormous debts during the war and now sought to pay them off. The British came to believe that the American colonies should pay a larger share of the cost of running the empire. Britain's national debt had doubled during the Seven Years' War, a conflict fought in part to defend the interests of the colonies, which had long clashed with the French and Spanish in North America. By 1765, residents of the British Isles were paying taxes averaging 26 shillings per person per year, while colonists were paying around one shilling.[5] The British government imposed new taxes on the American colonies to make sure they paid a fair share for their own defence.

Suffering the effects of a global depression and used to a large degree of self-government, the colonists deeply resented having new taxes forced upon them. Americans questioned London's right to tax them, pointing out that the British Parliament did not include representatives from the colonies. Across British North America, colonists protested against the taxes, particularly the levy on all printed material, called the stamp tax because the law required that newspapers, legal instruments, and other documents be printed on paper that had been embossed (or stamped) to show that the tax had been paid. In Halifax, the tax collector, known as the stamp master, received an anonymous death threat, and he and the devil were hanged in effigy on the public gallows. A ship's captain destroyed stamped newspapers found on board his vessel. *The Halifax Gazette* reported that people were waiting "with great impatience to hear the happy news of the Stamp Act being repealed."[6] In Liverpool, on Nova Scotia's South Shore, residents burned a copy of the Stamp Act. When the sheriff of Lunenburg arrived in Liverpool in pursuit of a schooner whose captain had violated the tax laws, a gang of 50 men threatened the lawman's life and ordered him to drop the matter. Yet the protests in Nova Scotia were mild compared to those in the colonies to the south. The Nova Scotia assembly did not object and did not even consider sending delegates to the Stamp Act Congress in New York, where colonial representatives met to discuss the tax and other grievances against Britain. Nova Scotia would have opposed the Stamp Act more vigorously "had it not been for the military force always kept up in that province," according to John Penn, governor of Pennsylvania.[7]

When a new government took office in London in 1766, Parliament repealed the Stamp Act, but at the same time reasserted its authority over the colonies "in all cases whatsoever."[8] The British government claimed it had as much right to tax the colonists as it did the residents of the British Isles. New levies, the Townshend duties, were imposed in 1767, reigniting the controversy. When the Massachusetts House of Representatives tried to coordinate the growing protests over the taxes, the colony's British governor responded by dissolving the assembly. Some colonists began boycotting British goods, causing imports from Britain to drop by about 40 per cent.[9] Increasingly, colonists argued that the British government was plotting against American liberties.

In 1770, the Townshend duties were repealed, except for the tax on tea, which, for Americans, became a symbol of British oppression. In the 1773 Boston Tea Party, protestors boarded a ship and dumped tea into the harbour. In Portsmouth, New Hampshire, shipments of tea were turned back. In Halifax, the reaction was milder: some merchants refused to handle tea from the East India Company, which had a monopoly over the export of the product to British North America. In 1774, John Fillis and William Smith, both Halifax merchants born in New England, called a public meeting to protest the arrival of a shipment of tea. After a magistrate declared the gathering illegal, the organizers backed down. The governor, Francis Legge, learned of other protest meetings in the colony, which he considered "contrary to the public good," and ordered that residents "refrain from all such meetings and assemblies."[10]

Britain responded to the Boston Tea Party with the Coercive Acts of 1774, known in the colonies as the Intolerable Acts. Until the tea was paid for, the port of Boston was closed to all products, except food and firewood. Legislation replaced the elected council with an appointed one and allowed military officers to commandeer homes and other private buildings to quarter their troops. Colonists were also upset with the Quebec Act of 1774, which they considered one of the Intolerable Acts, because it gave Quebec the area north of the Ohio River and east of the Mississippi, territory that many of the other colonies were hoping to expand into. The Quebec Act seemed designed to prevent the growth of the colonies. Colonists were further outraged that the measure provided for French civil law in Quebec and for government by an appointed council, rather than an elected one, as was common in British North America.

Until 1774, most colonists remained loyal to Britain, assuming the conflict could be settled within the British Empire. The situation began to change that year with the First Continental Congress, which met in response to the Intolerable Acts. Delegates from 12 of the colonies met in Philadelphia to define their grievances and agree on a course of action. Not included were those on the periphery: Quebec, Nova Scotia, the Island of St John (later Prince Edward Island), Georgia, and East and West Florida. The congress demanded repeal of the Coercive Acts and a commitment that London would not levy taxes or send troops to the colonies without their consent. The delegates pledged to create committees of observation to oversee a boycott of British goods. At the local level, colonists challenged British authority. Patriots, as the revolutionaries called themselves, prevented courts from sitting and established elected conventions, which began acting like governments by collecting taxes and organizing militia units.

Hostilities broke out in Lexington, Massachusetts, in April 1775, and on 4 July 1776, the Second Continental Congress approved a Declaration of Independence. In the colonies, reaction to these events was mixed. Support for the Revolutionaries was strong in Massachusetts and Pennsylvania, but weaker the farther one moved from the Revolutionary centre. In Nova Scotia, Maine, Vermont (part of New York until 1777), and Georgia, there was only limited support for a revolution. East and West Florida did not rebel at all. Quebec observed the revolution from the perspective of a curious outsider. In Brebner's words, "The fires of imminent revolution may have been glowing fiercely in a number of places near the geographical centre, but the heat grew less as it radiated outward to the margins."[11] The Aboriginal peoples were also divided. The six nations of the Iroquois Confederacy split, with the Mohawk, Cayuga, and Seneca fighting on the British side, while the other three nations tried to maintain neutrality. Eventually the Oneida and Tuscarora sided with the Patriots, and the Onondaga went to the British.

Historians have often asked why Nova Scotia did not join the American Revolution, a question that encourages an emphasis on, or even an exaggeration of, differences between Nova Scotia and the other colonies. A more neutral question, one less likely to distort the record, would ask simply about Nova Scotian attitudes toward the rebellion. In 1774, Nova Scotia's loyalties were not at all clear. Most Nova Scotians were uncommitted, concerned primarily with their own survival. Outside of Halifax, there was considerable sympathy for the rebels. Residents of Sunbury County declared their support for the Patriots. The people of Onslow and Truro refused to take the oath of allegiance to the British Crown. Other communities in the west of the province, including Yarmouth, Barrington, and Liverpool, continued to trade with the rebellious colonies, even after the revolution was well underway.

As in New England, Congregationalist ministers in Nova Scotia often favoured rebellion. Three came close to being charged with making treasonous statements. Pastor Seth Noble convinced the people of Maugerville to sign a document siding with New England. They saw "no shadow of justice" in the British position and asserted that "tyranny ought to be resisted in its first appearance."[12] When a British warship arrived in 1777, Maugerville residents renewed their allegiance to the Crown, but Noble refused to take the oath, instead fleeing to New England where he enlisted in the Revolutionary army. When fighting began, most of the Congregationalist clergy acted as Noble had, leaving Nova Scotia to head south.

In Halifax, a few acts of sabotage revealed some support for the revolution. In 1775, an unexplained fire destroyed a shipment of hay destined for the British military in Boston. Twice Patriots tried to burn the Halifax dockyard. Still, the colony had a financial interest in British success, as Nova Scotians sold supplies to the British military. Throughout the colony, there was opposition to British policies, but it was more diffuse than in other colonies and was more easily suppressed by the authorities, who banned public meetings and criminalized political protest.

One measure of Nova Scotian opinion on the revolution was the popular response to efforts to create a militia that would defend against a possible invasion from the south. In the fall of 1775, the Nova Scotia assembly passed one law that created a militia and assigned one-fifth of the soldiers to defend Halifax and another to impose a new tax to cover the militia's costs. Governor Legge faced widespread, almost universal, opposition to the plan. Residents in Cumberland signed a petition calling the Militia Act "the greatest piece of cruelty." After having been invited to move to Nova Scotia from New England, they were now being compelled "to march . . . in arms against their friends and relatives."[13] The residents of Yarmouth asked Legge to allow them to remain neutral: "We are almost all of us born in New England, and we have fathers, brothers, and sisters in that country." Divided between the "affection to our nearest relations" and loyalty to king and country, the petitioners wanted to know if they would be allowed to live in peace, taking no side in the struggle.[14] Sent by Legge to report on the situation in the Annapolis Valley, Captain John Stanton reported that "nineteen out of twenty are natives of New England" and asked Legge "what dependence or reliance" the governor could have in a militia raised from their ranks. "To put a confidence in such fellows," Stanton feared, "would be acting like the man who cherished a snake in his bosom, till heated with the warmth of his blood it bit him to death."[15] Only some of the militia turned out, and none agreed to serve in Halifax, so Legge suspended both the tax and the Militia Act in January 1776.

In the western part of Nova Scotia, a small minority sought to take up arms against the British. The leaders, Jonathan Eddy and John Allan, were both members of the assembly. In February 1776, Eddy led a delegation that set out to meet the Revolutionary general George Washington and to ask him to invade Nova Scotia. In a March 1776 discussion at Harvard College in Cambridge, Massachusetts, Washington encouraged the Nova Scotians to talk with the Continental Congress in Philadelphia. They arrived in Philadelphia in April, but could not convince the Congress to divert troops north. Instead, it authorized Eddy to organize his own military action. In Boston, the Massachusetts Council gave Eddy permission to recruit men for an attack on Fort Cumberland, Nova Scotia, and provided him with munitions and food. Eddy recruited small numbers in Machias, Maine; Maugerville, Nova Scotia; and other settlements along the Saint

John River. His plan depended on Aboriginal support, but the Penobscot of Maine remained neutral, the Maliseet of the Saint John Valley provided a token contingent of 16 men, and the Mi'kmaq sent only a handful of their 500 warriors. In all, about 80 men travelled to Cumberland, where another 100 joined Eddy's cause. They laid siege to Fort Cumberland from late October to late November 1776, trying to capture it twice, until British reinforcements drove them away. Allan had refused to take part in the Eddy Rebellion, which he considered futile. Instead, he organized his own military action. He visited General Washington in December 1776 and met with the Continental Congress the next month. Congress authorized the Massachusetts Council to raise and pay up to 3,000 men for an expedition to Nova Scotia, but Allan recruited fewer than 100. With supplies provided by Massachusetts, they marched to Saint John, where British troops forced their retreat to Maine.

Most of the Nova Scotia Yankees might well have welcomed an American army of liberation, but did not want to participate in an independent insurrection. As a result, the majority remained neutral, actively supporting neither side. In 1770, Nova Scotia's population was less than 15,000, tiny compared to the 235,000 in Massachusetts, the centre of Revolutionary sentiment in New England. Potential rebels were scattered across Nova Scotia in isolated settlements, cut off from each other. In Halifax, the presence of the Royal Navy prevented any possible insurrection, and the interests of local merchants remained with Britain. They believed that after the revolution they could take over New England's trade with the West Indies, as British law prevented foreign countries from doing business with its colonies in the Caribbean. In short, the areas outside Halifax were not apolitical, but neutral, taking a wait-and-see approach, often sympathetic to rebels, but too sparsely populated and isolated to take up arms. Halifax was loyal because of its commercial interests and the presence of the Royal Navy.

In Quebec, reaction to the revolution was mixed, with both pro-British and pro-Patriot sentiment visible in the colony. George Washington believed French Canadians might well join the revolution. In a proclamation, he invited them to "unite with us in an indissoluble union" and asked them to provide supplies to the American forces he had sent to defeat the British in Quebec.[16] Washington's words had little impact on the French-Canadian elite, who generally supported Britain. The church and the landed gentry (known as seigneurs) feared losing their privileged place in society, which had been guaranteed under the Quebec Act, and worried that a revolution would mean the creation of an elected assembly, which would diminish their own power. The peasants, called *habitants*, cared primarily about their own survival. At first, they appeared sympathetic to the revolution. They sold food to the American invaders when the Revolutionary army occupied part of the colony over the winter of 1775–6, but then hid their grain when the Americans ran out of cash. Perhaps 500 joined the American army, but an equal number supported Britain by enlisting in the militia.

The Revolutionary War came to an end when British forces surrendered in 1781. In the 1783 Treaty of Paris, Britain recognized the independence of the United States of America, promised to remove British troops from US soil, and agreed that Americans could fish in the Gulf of Saint Lawrence and off the coast of Newfoundland. The two countries pledged themselves to "firm and perpetual peace." The treaty did not clearly define the northern boundaries of the new United States, creating a series of problems for future diplomats.

Neither side was satisfied with the outcome. The Americans imagined that the remaining British colonies would one day be part of the United States. The Articles of Confederation, which functioned as the first constitution of the United States, contained a clause allowing Canada automatic admission to the union. For their part, the British and their Loyalist supporters were convinced that the Revolutionary experiment could not last and that North America would be British again. No one thought that upper North America could remain permanently divided between Britain's colonies and the United States. The conflict was far from over.

## Loyalism

The American Revolution was a struggle between the British and their American colonies, but it was also a North American civil war that pitted colonist against colonist. Estimates suggest that 40 per cent of the white population in the rebellious colonies supported the revolution, 20 per cent preferred a peaceful resolution—one that would have the colonies stay British—and 40 per cent were either neutral or leaned to whichever side seemed to be prevailing. Many Americans agonized over which position to take, and some changed positions during the course of the revolution.

Of approximately 500,000 Americans who sided with Britain, an estimated 60,000 to 100,000 fled the rebellious colonies during or shortly after the revolution, mostly in the period from 1781 to 1784. These refugees moved to different parts of the Empire: about half went to Quebec or Nova Scotia, while most of the rest travelled to Britain or the Caribbean. The majority went to places where they could own land. By far the largest contingent, 30,000 to 35,000, settled in Nova Scotia, while 6,000 to 10,000 moved to present-day Ontario, mostly in the Niagara peninsula and the area near Kingston. Fewer than 1,000 went to the Island of Saint John (later Prince Edward Island), with a similar number settling in Newfoundland, a British possession that did not yet have colonial status.

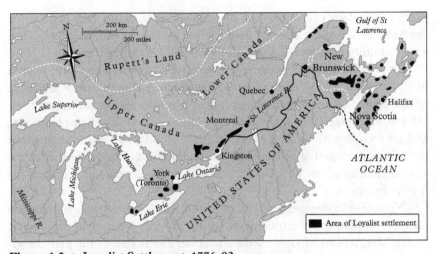

**Figure 1.2** ✤ **Loyalist Settlement, 1776–92**

From 1776 to 1792, Loyalists settled in Quebec and Nova Scotia, particularly in areas that became Upper Canada (today's Ontario) and New Brunswick.

Source: Adapted from Cartographica Inc.

Records are incomplete, making it difficult for a historian to define the Loyalists who settled in present-day Canada. From limited documents, we can make certain generalizations. Above all, we know that the Loyalists were not a homogenous group. About half of them were from the British army: disbanded soldiers who were mostly American-born, though others came from England, Scotland, Ireland, and Germany. The other half were civilians: men, women, and children of European descent, but also large numbers of blacks (perhaps 3,000) and Aboriginal people (about 2,000, mostly Iroquois). Roughly half the Loyalists had fled New York, and almost all the rest came from New England. The overwhelming majority, more than 80 per cent, were farmers, but the Loyalist ranks did include some professionals, merchants, artisans, and tradesmen.

The Loyalists were heavily dependent on the British government. The mother country provided transportation to Nova Scotia or Quebec for many of the Loyalists, as well as farmland at little or no cost, tools and provisions, and compensation for loss of property in the Loyalists' original colonies. The British built flourmills and sawmills to make Loyalist communities viable and kept taxes low throughout British North America. In 1794, property in Upper Canada (today's Ontario) was taxed at one-fifth the rate of property in New York State. When the poor grain harvest caused hunger in 1789, Britain supplied food to its colonies, while the governments of the northeast American states provided little.

For a generation after the revolution, large numbers of Americans continued to flow into Canada. Until 1798, Upper Canada classified these migrants as Loyalists. Lord Sydney, the British home secretary, defined them as not just those who had been loyal to Britain during the American Revolution, but anyone who had suffered "under the ruinous and arbitrary laws and constitution of the United States."[17] The so-called Late Loyalists received free land, but not the provisions and tools that had gone to the first wave of refugees. By 1812, Americans were the largest single immigrant group in British North America and composed about 80 per cent of the Upper Canadian population.

The Loyalists had an immense impact on the history of Canada and Canadian–American relations. The Loyalist influence was strongest in those areas where they overwhelmed the existing population. Loyalists doubled the population of the Nova Scotia peninsula and quadrupled that in the rest of the mainland, the area that became New Brunswick. Their presence was strong in Cape Breton and Upper Canada, but less pronounced in Lower Canada (today's Quebec) and negligible in Prince Edward Island and Newfoundland.

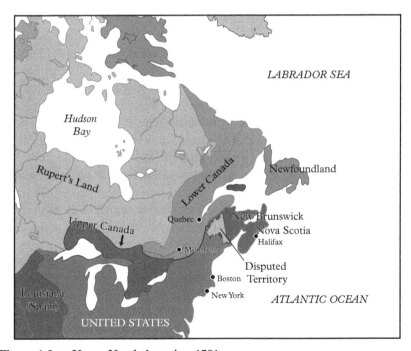

**Figure 1.3** ✤ **Upper North America, 1791**

The Treaty of Paris of 1783 set the boundary between British North America and the new United States. Largely because of the Loyalist migration, the British separated New Brunswick from Nova Scotia and split Quebec into Upper and Lower Canada.

Source: Adapted from Canadiana.org, at http://www.canadiana.ca/citm/imagepopups/bna-1791_e.html.

The Loyalists forced a political reorganization of British North America. Conflict between Loyalists and earlier inhabitants resulted in both Nova Scotia and Quebec being split. New Brunswick and Cape Breton broke away from Nova Scotia in 1784, as their inhabitants felt distant and isolated from the capital at Halifax. (Cape Breton was reunited with Nova Scotia in 1820.) For years after, the Loyalists dominated political life in New Brunswick, holding most of the key offices. In Nova Scotia, Loyalists in the assembly helped break the control of Halifax over the province. In 1791, Quebec was split into Upper and Lower Canada, because the Loyalists insisted upon a province of their own, instead of being outnumbered by French Canadians. Unlike Lower Canada, Upper Canada would have an elected assembly and would use British common law instead of the French civil code. Throughout British North America, Loyalists pushed to limit the power of governors and other appointed officials, and to give more power to elected assemblies, trying to reproduce the political systems of pre-Revolutionary New York and New England.

The Loyalists found honour in their defeat. They could not define themselves as the Americans who had lost the revolution. Instead, they identified with Britain, even if most Loyalists had been born in North America and many had come from families that had lived for generations on North American soil. They made enthusiastic demonstrations of their devotion to the Crown and showed contempt for the American republican form of government. They exalted the British emphasis on order, hierarchy, and authority. Dependent on British officials for land and supplies, they accepted a large role for government, unlike Americans, who often distrusted political power. Yet, at the same time that the Loyalists were constructing a British identity, they remained American in outlook and lifestyle. Many still had strong personal ties with the United States, and some built strong economic links as well.

Slowly, the Loyalists built societies remarkably similar to those they had fled. They spoke with American, not British, accents and vocabulary. Their religious patterns followed those of the United States. Like New Yorkers and New Englanders, the overwhelming majority of Loyalists were evangelical Christians, particularly Methodists or Baptists, unlike the British who were more likely to belong to the Church of England. The Loyalists created an education system that owed more to the United States than to Britain. In New England, the law required towns to provide community-run schools to teach reading and writing, in contrast to Britain where the dominant educational institution at the primary level was the proprietary school, which charged tuition and was owned and operated privately by a teacher or schoolmaster. Although there were some proprietary schools in Upper Canada and New Brunswick, common schools on the American model took root in the 1790s, eventually evolving into today's public schools. The Loyalists also adopted the American freehold tenure system of land ownership, which allowed farmers to own their land, rejecting the British system under which most were tenants. In Nova Scotia and Upper Canada, Loyalists built farmhouses that closely resembled those in New York State and New England, using the same wood-frame construction. On Nova Scotia's Atlantic coast, the Cape Cod house was as common as it was in Maine and Massachusetts. Even Loyalist gravestones were similar to those in the United States, constructed in similar styles and displaying similar motifs.

Loyalist views on race were complicated, and mirrored the conflict over the issue in the United States. Many of the Loyalists supported slavery, and some brought their slaves, numbering more than 1,000, with them as they fled. But, as with the residents of New York and New England, the majority of Loyalists opposed slavery. British North America refused to extradite fugitive slaves to the United States, even those who had broken the law while escaping. Loyalists were pleased when Upper Canada passed a 1793 law that gradually abolished slavery by banning the import of slaves and providing that children born to slaves would become free at age 25. The measure was virtually identical to the gradual emancipation law passed in 1784 in Connecticut and was similar to others adopted in New England and New York in the 1780s and 1790s.

Yet, opposing slavery, whether in British North America or the United States, did not mean favouring racial equality. Blacks faced discrimination on both sides of the border. Few black Loyalists received land, and those who did had much smaller, poorer-quality plots than the white Loyalists. Blacks were not allowed to vote and were denied the right to trial by jury. They were segregated from whites and had trouble finding work. Most became day-labourers, indentured servants, or tenant farmers who were required to give a large share of their crop to the landlord. In the words of one observer, these sharecroppers lived, "in short, in a state of slavery."[18] In the summer of 1784, a mob of unemployed white veterans assaulted blacks and destroyed their homes in Shelburne and Birchtown, Nova Scotia. The situation was so dire that about half of Nova Scotia's blacks, about 1,200 in all, left in 1792 to go to Sierra Leone in Africa.

Despite their frequently avowed British identity, the Loyalists accepted many of the political principles of the United States, including the American emphasis on liberty, equality, and individual rights. Americans had expanded on the British notion of self-government, rejecting Britain's aristocracy and class system. Since most Americans were not members of the Church of England, they also rejected the idea of an established church. Loyalists fought a proposal to give the Church of England a privileged position in Upper Canada, as it had in Britain. By 1790, some British officials in Nova Scotia considered the Loyalists subversive republicans because their views so closely mirrored those of the Americans. In 1792, Upper Canada's surveyor general, David W. Smith, noted that the members of the House of Assembly had "violent levelling tendencies," meaning a desire to end social hierarchies, and that they followed American "patterns and models."[19] There were even some similarities in the American and Loyalist perspectives on pre-Revolutionary British policy. The Loyalists agreed with their fellow Americans that many British leaders were incompetent and that Britain had mistreated the colonies. The difference between the two groups was that the Revolutionaries believed British policy was tyrannical and justified the resort to violence; the Loyalists thought the British were inept and that differences could be worked out politically and peacefully.

American in many ways, the Loyalists were also anti-American. They nursed prejudices against the United States, and for good reason. The American Revolution had been one of the bloodiest civil wars in history. About 25,000 American men had died in the conflict, and the economic cost had been enormous. Some Loyalists had been imprisoned; others were subjected to mob violence and vigilante justice, with several being literally tarred and feathered. Their property was confiscated and they were often fined or compelled to pay taxes two or three times. Many lost family members in the fighting. As a result, in the words of political scientist David Bell, the Loyalists had a "sense of indignation bordering on rage."[20] They had been loyal to the Crown, but had lost a war, fled their homes, and settled in a cold, often-uninhabited land. They directed their bitterness toward the United States and constructed myths to help them dignify their loss.

Loyalists magnified the subtle dissimilarities between themselves and Americans. The father of psychoanalysis, Sigmund Freud, identified "the narcissism of small differences," the tendency of individuals to create an identity by exaggerating their tiny disparities with others. This concept could be applied to the Loyalists' attitude toward the United States. They were not so much distinct from Americans as they thought they were distinct. They considered themselves more conservative than Americans, less individualistic, and more concerned with the community's best interests. They believed that they stood for "true liberty," in contrast to the Americans, whose form of democracy was, in the Loyalist mind, the equivalent of mob rule and a threat to liberty.

In short, the Loyalists suffered from an identity crisis. Within Loyalism was a tension between their American heritage and their constructed anti-American ideology. They had to reconcile their American ideas with their desire to be different from Americans. As a result, they became obsessive about comparing British North America to the United States in ways that demonstrated their own superiority. They might have lost the revolution, but they comforted themselves in knowing they were the better people: more law-abiding, peaceful, and free.

# Seymour Martin Lipset's *Continental Divide*

Seymour Martin Lipset's 1990 book, *Continental Divide: The Values and Institutions of the United States and Canada*, was a seminal work on Canadian–American relations. Lipset (1922–2006) was a professor at several major US universities and author or co-author of some 20 books and countless articles. He was one of the most highly regarded academics in the world, and his work had influence far beyond his own discipline of sociology. Lipset studied Canada to help him understand his own country, particularly those factors that made the United States unique. "He who knows only one country, knows none," he frequently told his students.[21]

Lipset advanced his ideas on the differences between the two countries in several books and articles, but most fully in *Continental Divide*, which became a bestseller in Canada, a rare feat for an academic book. In a frequently quoted line, Lipset began by asserting that "two nations, not one, came out of the American Revolution."[22] The United States developed as the country of revolution: individualistic, populist, and egalitarian. The Loyalists fled north because their values were not in tune with the ideology of the new country, and as a result Canada developed as the country of counter-revolution—more conservative, more deferential.

Lipset argued that subsequent differences between Canada and the United States could be traced to the Loyalists. They rejected revolution, which is why Canada slowly evolved into independence from Britain, rather than suddenly declaring it, as the Americans had done. Following their Loyalist heritage, Canadians distrust direct democracy, rejecting the American practices of holding referenda and of voting for the head of government, senators, and minor officials. The Loyalist dependence on the British government provided a foundation for the Canadian willingness to accept a larger role for the state. For Lipset, this explained why Canada adopted a universal, publicly funded health insurance system, while the Americans long rejected universality and still have a mixed public–private system. It also accounted for the Canadian tendency to be more deferential and law-abiding, more willing to control gun ownership, and more likely to hold the police in high regard.

Lipset's analysis of the American Revolution oversimplifies a complex history. The rupture that created Canada and the United States was not as sudden or as complete as he would have us believe. Allegiance was not easy to define: Americans could not be neatly divided into two categories and labelled *Patriots* or *Loyalists*. Many Americans, perhaps 40 per cent, had sought neutrality during the conflict, committing to neither side. More importantly, the majority of those who opposed the revolution, perhaps 80 per cent, remained in the US afterward, and many others returned after having fled to Quebec or Nova Scotia. Of the original members of the New York City Chamber of Commerce, one-third were Loyalists. As a Philadelphia newspaper commented in 1813, "There are some in America whose souls are perfectly British."[23] Lipset exaggerated the differences between the Loyalists and the Patriots, ignoring the very close similarities in their views on issues such as equality and freedom of religion. He also failed to notice that the Loyalists were quickly outnumbered by Late Loyalists, often looking for affordable land and not escaping from the American government.

Lipset's description of long-term trends should also be viewed with a critical eye. For example, the government has not always been more active in Canada than in the United States. Canadian social programs surpassed their American counterparts in the 1960s and 1970s, when the public health-care system, the Canada Pension Plan, the Canada Student Loans program, and other measures were established. But from the 1930s to the 1960s, the American government was more involved in people's lives than the Canadian government. Lipset's comparison of Canada and the United States was bound to emphasize the differences between the two countries. Adding a third nation to the mix, Britain perhaps, would have highlighted many of the similarities between the North American neighbours.

## From the Revolution to the War of 1812

Revolutions are turbulent and chaotic. The American Revolution ushered in a period of political confusion and cultural ferment that lasted on both sides of the border until at least the War of 1812. The revolution had severed political links and disrupted (but not broken) social ties between the rebellious 13 colonies and the British Empire, but new patterns had yet to solidify.

After the revolution, the population of British North America, with the exception of Quebec, remained similar to that of the northern United States. The border was porous, without customs or immigration posts; Americans could migrate north, and British North Americans could move south, without a passport or visa. John Graves Simcoe, lieutenant-governor of Upper Canada, actively recruited American immigrants, offering 200 acres of land to every family for a minimal fee. From 1791 to 1812, Upper Canada's population grew from 14,000 to 75,000, thanks primarily to American settlers. By 1812, the Late Loyalists were 60 per cent of the Upper Canadian population, outnumbering both the original Loyalists and British immigrants. For the Americans, what mattered was land, not ideology: most were not fleeing the US political system, but looking to establish a homestead. When they arrived in Upper Canada, they did not suddenly change their identity, and some even continued to celebrate the American Independence Day every Fourth of July. Upper Canadians might have considered these immigrants traitors or enemies, but never foreigners.

Although the populations continued to mingle, tensions existed between the United States and British North America. The Treaty of Paris of 1783 had ended the Revolutionary War and promised perpetual peace in upper North America, but did not prevent a series of disputes from arising. The two sides could not agree on the border between Maine and New Brunswick. Some Americans thought they should be compensated for slaves the British army had helped to flee north during the revolution. The British failure to evacuate forts on the American northwest frontier, as the treaty required, irritated the US government, which blamed the British for conflict in the area between Americans and Aboriginal people.

Americans particularly resented British actions toward both US merchant ships and British-born sailors who had taken American citizenship. Britain and its continental allies fought against France in the French Revolutionary and Napoleonic Wars, which began in 1792. The US declared its neutrality and claimed the right to sell non-military goods to either side. Britain had hoped to use its control of the seas to stop French ships and to starve France until it surrendered, a plan the Americans were undermining by selling large amounts of food to France. In response, Britain's Royal Navy began seizing American vessels en route to Europe. These actions ran headlong into the American concept of freedom of the seas, the notion that the high seas were open to all and could not be controlled by one nation or group of nations.

When stopping American ships, the British were not only after goods headed to France; they were also searching for British subjects who could be forced into service in the Royal Navy. This practice, known as impressment, caused a bitter conflict between the two countries, in part because of different definitions of citizenship. For Britain, anyone born a British subject was a British subject for life. For the Americans, an immigrant could take US citizenship and renounce previous loyalties. Many of the men forcibly conscripted into the Royal Navy were Brits according to the British definition, but US citizens in the eyes of the United States. In US port cities, Americans released their anger by attacking British sailors.

Jay's Treaty of 1794, named after the US negotiator, Chief Justice John Jay, settled several of these disputes. The British agreed to evacuate the frontier forts by 1796 and to pay damages for seizing American ships and cargo. For its part, the United States pledged to pay pre-Revolutionary debts that Americans owed to the British and agreed that Britain could seize food and war *matériel* on American ships travelling to France. British subjects,

American citizens, and Aboriginal people could "pass and repass" the border without restriction and were free to "carry on trade and commerce with each other" without paying duties. The two sides referred the Maine–New Brunswick boundary issue to an arbitration commission, which eventually ruled in Britain's favour. The treaty said nothing about impressment, the most divisive of the disputes between the two countries, or about compensation for runaway slaves.

# War of 1812

A Loyalist serving in the Glengarry Light Infantry during the War of 1812 was performing sentry duty when an American rifleman shot one of his fellow militiamen. The Canadian returned fire, killing the enemy, and then went to pillage the dead man's belongings. He quickly realized that he had just taken the life of his own brother. The War of 1812, like the American Revolution, was both an Anglo–American conflict and a North American civil war. It was a fight that pitted brother against brother. Loyalty remained difficult to define, as the United States and Britain, in the words of historian Alan Taylor, still "competed for the allegiance of the peoples in North America."[24]

Bitterness between Britain and the United States remained after Jay's Treaty. The British evacuated their forts in the Northwest, but an alliance of Aboriginal nations, led by the Shawnee chief Tecumseh, resisted the westward expansion of the US into Aboriginal territory, and American officials suspected Britain of helping them. At sea, the Royal Navy began enforcing a blockade of continental Europe, systematically stopping and searching neutral ships, including American merchant vessels. The British seized any ships carrying cargo that might aid the French, taking about 1,000 American vessels by 1812. The British also continued with impressment. The Royal Navy needed about 12,000 new sailors every year to replace those lost through death, desertion, wounds, and illness. Recruiters faced two challenges: a shortage of healthy, military-age men in Britain and competition from the growing American merchant marine, which offered lucrative wages to sailors of any nationality, sometimes as much as five times the pay in the Royal Navy.[25] Only about half the sailors on American merchant ships were born in the US; most of the rest came from the British Isles. Documents were easily forged, and the British frequently rejected proof that an individual was born in the US. As a result, the majority of those taken from US ships were American-born. From 1803 to 1812, between 3,000 and 8,000 US citizens were impressed, which Americans saw as an insult to their national sovereignty. The US tried a variety of tactics to end the practice, including negotiations and embargo on trade with Britain, but to no avail. Finally, in June 1812, the US declared war on Britain.

The conflict was "uncomfortably like a civil war," to use the words of one British officer.[26] During the war, there were countless families split in their allegiance and many individuals whose loyalty was suspect. William Elliott, who had been born in Maryland, had served in the US infantry, and had received an honourable discharge. He had become disgruntled with the United States, moved to Upper Canada, married, took the oath of allegiance to the king, and served as a militia captain during the war, but his two brothers remained behind, serving in the US army and navy. Another example was an Irishman named Boyle, whose first name has been lost to history. He had settled in North America and served in US army, but then deserted and moved to Amherstburg, Upper Canada. In 1812, Canadian officials suspected his loyalties and demoted him from his rank of sergeant major in the militia—all because he was friendly to Americans.

In the US, there was no consensus on the war. President James Madison and most Democratic–Republicans in Congress supported war, while most Federalists opposed American participation. Opposition was particularly strong in New England, New Jersey, and New York, the areas closest to the border with British North America. In several New England communities, flags flew at half-staff after the United States declared war. Massachusetts clergymen condemned the American declaration of war, one of them urging his flock to "proclaim an honourable neutrality."[27] The governor of Massachusetts, Caleb Strong, spoke publicly against the war and, along with the governors of Rhode Island and Connecticut, refused a request to provide militiamen to serve under federal command. The governor of Vermont, Jonas Galusha, supported the war and provided militiamen for the US government, but then lost the 1813 election to Martin Chittenden, who tried to withdraw his state's troops from the field. Throughout the war, New Englanders lent money and sold supplies to the British. Near the end of the conflict, the British commander reported that two-thirds of his men were eating American beef, mostly from Vermont and New York.[28] By then, some New Englanders were seriously considering secession from the United States.

Opinion was also split in Upper Canada. Most US-born residents supported the British, but a minority did not. Historian Gerald Craig described their behaviour as "disaffection, treason, or neutralism."[29] Some returned to the US, others joined the American side when US forces invaded Upper Canada, and still others declared themselves neutral and refused to join the local militias. A few businessmen hoped for an American victory that would allow Canada to join the United States. Yet most Upper Canadians were interested in their family, friends, and farms, not in wars and high politics.

The war left a bitter legacy. American forces occupied York (now Toronto), the capital of Upper Canada, and razed the Parliament and other public buildings. After US troops burned Newark (now Niagara-on-the-Lake), the British retaliated by setting fire to Buffalo. Later, British forces captured the American capital, Washington, and torched several government buildings, including the presidential mansion, the White House. The British launched attacks on New Orleans, Washington, Baltimore, and other key targets, while US forces invaded Upper and Lower Canada. The British army, supplemented by local militia and Aboriginal allies, pushed Americans back. As in the American Revolution, the Aboriginal peoples were divided. Some sided with the British, most notably the Iroquois under Tecumseh, but other First Nations, particularly those in US territory, maintained neutrality or allied themselves with the US. Protected by British sea power, the Atlantic colonies did not see combat.

After Napoleon lost the Battle of Waterloo and abdicated on 11 April 1814, Britain's war with France came to an end. The British dropped the blockade of Europe and stopped seizing US ships and American soldiers. With the causes of war gone, Britain and the United States made peace. In December 1814, the two powers signed the Treaty of Ghent, which restored the pre-war status quo. There was no agreement on the key issues of impressment, freedom of the seas, and the trading rights of neutral powers. No borders were changed, and neither side provided compensation to the other. A joint commission was established to settle outstanding boundary disputes. The War of 1812, the second and final phase of the American Revolution, was now over and both sides resigned themselves to the permanent division of upper North America.

## Summary

On the eve of the American Revolution, Britain's North American colonies were each distinct, but neighbouring colonies—with the exception of Quebec—had much in common. A knowledgeable observer could not have easily divided the colonies into two categories: the 13 that would rebel and the rest that would not. Even after the revolution broke out, the situation was complex. There were supporters and opponents of revolution in every colony, and large numbers of people everywhere who avoided taking sides. As result, the revolution took on the character of a civil war. When Britain lost, a significant number of the revolution's opponents fled to Quebec and Nova Scotia, where they pushed for the creation of new colonies, Upper Canada and New Brunswick. With a contradictory identity—at once American and anti-American—they laid the foundations for Canada's ambivalent relationship with its southern neighbour. The War of 1812, in many ways another civil war, confirmed the result of the American Revolution: upper North America would be permanently divided into the United States and the areas that would eventually form Canada.

# Beyond the Book

1. Compare the reaction to the American Revolution in Nova Scotia and Quebec to that in the other British North American colonies.
2. Assess the arguments that Seymour Martin Lipset advanced in *Continental Divide*.
3. To what extent can it be said that the Loyalists were both American and anti-American?

# Further Reading

On pre-Revolutionary Nova Scotia, see Margaret Conrad, ed., *They Planted Well: New England Planters in Maritime Canada* (Fredericton, New Brunswick: Acadiensis Press, 1988). The best source on the colony's response to the American Revolution remains John Bartlet Brebner's *The Neutral Yankees of Nova Scotia: A Marginal Colony during the Revolutionary Years* (1937; Toronto: McClelland and Stewart, 1969). Maurice W. Armstrong emphasizes the importance of religion in "Neutrality and Religion in Revolutionary Nova Scotia," *New England Quarterly* 19, no. 1 (March 1946): 50–62. Gordon Stewart and George Rawlyk expand on Armstrong's argument, adding the idea of a "missing decade," in *A People Highly Favoured of God: The Nova Scotia Yankees and the American Revolution* (Toronto: Macmillan, 1972). One particularly effective response to Stewart and Rawlyk is Donald Desserud, "Nova Scotia and the American Revolution: A Study of Neutrality and Moderation in the Eighteenth Century," in *Making Adjustments: Change and Continuity in Planter Nova Scotia, 1759–1800*, edited by Margaret Conrad (Fredericton, New Brunswick: Acadiensis Press, 1991), 89–112. Ernest Clarke describes the Eddy Rebellion in detail in *The Siege of Fort Cumberland, 1776: An Episode in the American Revolution* (Montreal and Kingston: McGill–Queen's University Press, 1995).

On Quebec's reaction to the revolution, three older sources remain valuable: Hilda Neatby, *Quebec: The Revolutionary Age, 1760–1791* (Toronto: McClelland and Stewart, 1966); Gustave Lanctot, *Canada and the American Revolution, 1774–1783*, translated by Margaret M. Cameron (Toronto: Clarke Irwin, 1967); and George F.G. Stanley, *Canada Invaded, 1775–1776* (Toronto: Hakkert, 1973). On the Iroquois Confederacy, see Barbara Graymont, *The Iroquois in the American Revolution* (Syracuse, New York: Syracuse University Press, 1972).

The best introduction to the Loyalists is Wallace Brown and Hereward Senior, *Victorious in Defeat: The Loyalists in Canada* (Toronto: Methuen, 1984). David V.J. Bell analyzes their complex impact in "The Loyalist Tradition in Canada," *Journal of Canadian Studies* 5, no. 2 (May 1970): 22–33. Jane Errington provides a subtle and sophisticated analysis in *The Lion, the Eagle, and Upper Canada: A Developing Colonial Ideology* (Montreal and Kingston: McGill–Queen's University Press, 1987), as does Neil MacKinnon in *This Unfriendly Soil: The Loyalist Experience in Nova Scotia, 1783–1791* (Montreal and Kingston: McGill–Queen's University Press, 1986). In *Liberty's Exiles: American Loyalists in the Revolutionary World* (New York: Knopf, 2011), Maya

Jasanoff emphasizes the Loyalists' American roots. L.F.S. Upton tells William Smith's story in *The Loyal Whig: William Smith of New York and Quebec* (Toronto: University of Toronto Press, 1969). In *Whig–Loyalism: An Aspect of Political Ideology in the American Revolutionary Era* (Rutherford, New Jersey: Fairleigh Dickinson University Press, 1969), William Allen Benton examines the ideas of Smith and other Americans who "turned against the revolution they had helped to start." Although some of the language is out of date, the best source on black Loyalists remains James W. St G. Walker's *The Black Loyalists: The Search for a Promised Land in Nova Scotia and Sierra Leone, 1783–1870* (1976; Toronto: University of Toronto Press, 1992). A superb overview of the American immigrant experience in Canada can be found in J.M. Bumsted's essay on "Americans" in the *Encyclopedia of Canada's Peoples*, edited by Paul Robert Magocsi (Toronto: University of Toronto Press, 1999), 183–99 (available at www.multiculturalcanada.ca/ecp).

Seymour Martin Lipset's views are expounded in *Continental Divide: The Values and Institutions of the United States and Canada* (New York: Routledge, 1990) and rebutted in Edward Grabb, James Curtis, and Douglas Baer, "Defining Moments and Recurring Myths: Comparing Canadians and Americans after the American Revolution," *Canadian Review of Sociology and Anthropology* 37, no. 4 (November 2000): 373–419.

On the War of 1812, the best source is Alan Taylor's *The Civil War of 1812: American Citizens, British Subjects, Irish Rebels, and Indian Allies* (New York: Alfred A. Knopf, 2010), which is exhaustively researched and a superb example of the new borderlands history. Also valuable are George Sheppard, *Plunder, Profit, and Paroles: A Social History of the War of 1812 in Upper Canada* (Montreal and Kingston: McGill–Queen's University Press, 1994); and Richard Buel, Jr., *America and the Brink: How the Political Struggle over the War of 1812 Almost Destroyed the Young Republic* (New York: Palgrave Macmillan, 2005).

## CHAPTER 2

# Identities, 1814–1860

## *Building a Distinctive Canada after the War of 1812*

## Introduction

Elijah Leonard was one American immigrant who should have been above suspicion. In the 1830s, Leonard was an ironworker and a businessman, a loyal and hardworking citizen of St Thomas, Upper Canada. Later, in the 1850s, he began a successful political career, serving as mayor of London, a member of the pre-Confederation legislature, and a senator in post-Confederation Canada. But when rebellions broke out in Upper and Lower Canada in 1837, neighbours immediately distrusted Leonard because he had been born in the United States and had only moved to Canada as a teenager. He was called a spy and was arrested four times on frivolous charges. He later remembered that his accusers knew him well and "should have been well aware that I could not be in any way interested in the rebellion." It seemed to Leonard that his accusers were the kind of people who "took every occasion to flaunt their 'loyalty'."[1]

Leonard's treatment reflected the tensions in Upper and Lower Canada after the War of 1812. The American Revolution had split English-speaking North America into two: the new United States and the remaining British North America, colonies that would eventually become Canada. The War of 1812 confirmed the outcome of the revolution, and widened the gap between the United States and the future Canada. Afterward, British officials worked to reduce American influences within the colonies and distance them from the United States.

# Impact of the War of 1812

In Upper Canada, where much of the War of 1812 had been fought, people nurtured bitter memories of the conflict, remembering homes that had been burned and fathers, husbands, or sons who had been killed. People remained certain that the United States coveted Upper Canada and would invade again. Many were sure that Americans did not really believe in freedom: why else were they the only people to ally themselves with Napoleon, a bloody tyrant? This judgment was unfair. Americans had been troubled by Napoleon's dictatorship and declared war on Britain in defence of American interests, not to side with the French emperor. Still, Upper Canadians were convinced that the war proved American hypocrisy.

Upper Canadians constructed a distinctive mythology around their memories of the war. They came to believe that the conflict had been won because of the strength and discipline of the common people, those who had joined and supported local militias, and not because of the professional skill of the British regular army, which in fact had done the majority of the fighting. For the next one hundred years and more, Upper Canadians and then Ontarians celebrated their heroes of the war. They honoured Laura Secord, the woman who had overheard American soldiers talking of an attack on Beaver Dams, near Niagara Falls, and walked 30 kilometres to warn the British. At Queenston Heights, Upper Canadians constructed an imposing monument to Sir Isaac Brock, the British general considered the saviour of Upper Canada. They wrote poems to honour the Shawnee war chief Tecumseh, a British ally who won a decisive battle against the Americans. That Tecumseh was fighting for the interests of his own people and cared little about Britain or British North America did not stop Upper Canadians from thinking of him as one of their heroes.

Upper Canadians also created myths about their earlier history. They convinced themselves that Loyalists had been the colonial elite in pre-Revolutionary America, that they had suffered greatly for their loyalty, and that they had been British—even though most of the original Loyalists were born in North America and had distinctly American values.

In the Maritimes, the War of 1812 had considerably less impact on the identity of the people, largely because the war had not been fought there and the US military threat to the region was less pronounced. Anti-Americanism was less evident in Nova Scotia, New Brunswick, and Prince Edward Island, where a more open attitude toward the United States prevailed and where a close relationship with New England was left largely untouched by the conflict. In fact, many Maritimers constructed their own myths of the War of 1812—myths that emphasized a cross-border friendship continuing in the face of war. In southwest New Brunswick, the legend spread that the residents of St Stephen had given British gunpowder to their neighbours in Calais, Maine, so the Americans could make fireworks for their Fourth of July celebration. The story is still widely believed—and was repeated by Prime Minister Stephen Harper in 2010—though it most certainly never happened.[2] (See this book's preface for a description of the amicable but tense wartime relationship between St Stephen and Calais.)

In Upper Canada, the political elite, composed mostly of British-born officials, cultivated the myths about the War of 1812 and the colony's Loyalist history. Troubled by American sentiment in the colony, they worked to create a national identity to distinguish Canada from the United States and emphasize British North America's Britishness. As a first step, officials created a hostile environment for Americans in Upper Canada. Those who had openly sympathized with the US during the war were expelled from Upper Canada or harassed until they left of their own accord. Lieutenant-Governor Francis Gore ordered local magistrates not to administer the oath of allegiance to American immigrants, preventing them from becoming British subjects, which in turn meant they could not own land, vote, or hold public office.

At the same time, London encouraged immigration from Britain to its North American colonies. After the Napoleonic Wars, the British government helped demobilized soldiers to settle in Upper Canada, convincing many to live close to the US border and provide a buffer against the American presence. The veterans received free transportation to Canada, land, and food until they were settled, as well as farming implements at reduced cost. Still others left the British Isles because of an economic recession, travelling to Canada in search of opportunities. In excess of 50,000 Irish arrived in British North America from 1825 to 1829, far more than the estimated 2,000 American immigrants who arrived during the longer period from 1821 to 1830.[3] By 1851, Britain's resettlement policy had succeeded. The census showed that Americans were only a tiny portion of the population of Upper Canada (then known officially as Canada West), greatly outnumbered by those born in British North America or the British Isles. (See Figure 2.1.)

It was not enough to promote British immigration and drive out the Americans. The Upper Canadian government undertook extensive efforts to shift the colony from a North American identity to a British one. The education system was purged of the American teachers and textbooks that had once been widespread. The Common School Act of 1846 created a provincial board of education, which would make a list of acceptable texts, rather than leaving it to local boards or individual teachers, who often favoured American books. The act also prevented foreigners from becoming teachers, though the chief superintendent of education explained that this

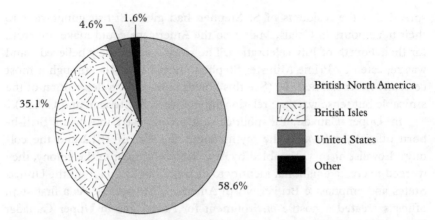

**Figure 2.1** ✦ Birthplaces of the Residents of Upper Canada (Canada West), 1851

Source: Data provided by Canada, Department of Agriculture, *Censuses of Canada, 1608–1876*, vol. 5 (Ottawa: Department of Agriculture, 1878), 24–5.

did not apply to Europeans, meaning that the law banned only Americans from teaching in Upper Canadian schools. Yet, at the same time, the legislation demonstrated the common values that united the English-speaking parts of North America. The law assumed that education was a right for all children and that local boards should exercise considerable control over schools—ideas widely accepted in the United States but not in Britain, where education was still a private matter and where most schools were funded through tuition fees.

The struggle over American influences could be seen in religion as well. In the nineteenth century, Methodism was the fastest-growing denomination in both the United States and Upper Canada. Although it had begun in Britain, Methodism had taken on a distinctly New-World form in North America, becoming a more powerful force than it ever had been in the Old World. Until the War of 1812, the Methodist church in Upper and Lower Canada had no independent existence of its own but was an offshoot of the Methodist Episcopal church in the United States. Yet, as Todd Webb has shown, after the war, Upper Canadian Methodists tried to distance themselves from their American roots and embraced a British outlook and British practices. Upper Canadian Methodists officially broke with the American church in 1828. For most of the next 50 years, the Canadian Methodist church was united with the British church, and the leader in Canada was appointed in Britain. Once common, American-born itinerant Methodist preachers became increasingly rare in Upper Canada.

Despite official efforts to build a distinctive British identity in the lands north of the United States, similarities between the English-speaking peoples on both sides of the border remained. Visitors from abroad commented frequently on the common lifestyle, behaviour, and speech. French politician and philosopher Alexis de Tocqueville toured North America in the 1830s, observing that the population of Upper Canada and the Maritimes was "identical to that of the United States." Similarly, when Patrick Shirreff, a Scot, visited the Niagara region in the same decade, he found that "the manners and customs of the people were essentially Yankee, with less intelligence, civility, and sobriety." An Irishman, John R. Godley, reported in the 1840s that Upper Canadians were "neither British nor American," but proximity to the United States meant that they were less British and "more American than they believe themselves to be, or would like to be considered."[4]

Fear of another American invasion remained common among members of the Upper Canadian public, the colonial administration, and British officials in London. Large expenditures were made to protect against the US military. In the Rush–Bagot Agreement of 1817, Britain and the United States agreed to restrict the number of warships on the Great Lakes. This limited arms-reduction agreement did not signify the beginnings of an undefended border between the two sides. Instead, both continued to build and strengthen fortifications on the lakes. In the late 1820s and early 1830s, the Royal Engineers created the Rideau Canal to allow ships to move from Montreal to Kingston without having to use the St Lawrence River, where they would be within range of American guns. The canal cost £1 million, making it the most expensive military construction project in the history of British North America. In the same period, the British built large fortresses, or citadels, in Quebec City and Halifax. In Kingston, they erected another citadel, Fort Henry, and four round, stone fortifications, called Martello towers.

The Americans, too, prepared for the possibility of war, building new forts along the border, including one at Rouse's Point, New York. Construction was well along when surveyors discovered an error: the Americans were building their fort in Lower Canada. Work was abandoned, but recommenced in 1840s after the British agreed to cede the land to the United States as part of a treaty designed to settle several outstanding disputes between the two countries. By the time Fort Montgomery was completed 30 years later, it was no longer needed, but to this day the Canadian–American border bends north at Lake Champlain to keep Rouse's Point in the United States.

In the years after the War of 1812, the main political debate in Upper Canada was over the Alien Question: should those born in the United States be considered British subjects if they had settled in Canada after 1783, when Britain recognized the independence of the United States, or were they foreigners (or *aliens* in the language of the day)? A majority in Upper

Canada's elected Legislative Assembly, Reformers believed that the immigrants should be considered British subjects and should enjoy all the rights associated with citizenship. The British-born writer and political activist Robert Gourlay travelled through western Upper Canada a few years after the war and reported that "the very best people were those called Yankees": they were "active, intelligent, friendly" and skilled in "the art of settlement." The American immigrants had been loyal to Britain during the war, so there was no justification for the "absurd" decision to discriminate against them.[5] In contrast, the Tories, who controlled the government and the appointed Legislative Council, believed that the Americans were foreigners. The case was ultimately taken to London, where the British government instructed Upper Canada to recognize the rights of the American-born. The controversy ended with the passage of Upper Canada's Naturalization Act of 1828, which recognized American-born residents as British subjects if they arrived before 1820 or if they naturalized by taking the oath of allegiance after seven years of residence.

With the Alien Question settled, it became possible for Americans to assume a prominent role in Upper Canadian life. In the 1830s, 1840s, and 1850s, American entrepreneurs arrived in Canada in search of wealth. In the Ottawa valley, Americans developed the lumber industry—harvesting timber, building sawmills, and buying steamboats and barges to move their products to market. Many were active in the political and social lives of their community. Born in Vermont, Joseph Merrill Currier made his fortune in the lumber business and later served on the Ottawa city council, in the pre-Confederation legislature, and in the House of Commons after Confederation. After establishing a successful company to transport produce and lumber on the St Lawrence and adjoining waterways, Moss Kent Dickenson of New York became mayor of Ottawa and served in the House of Commons. In Hamilton, Americans established the city's first foundry and built a carriage factory. In Oil Springs, near Sarnia, James Miller Williams of New Jersey was the first person to drill successfully for oil in North America. He was active, too, in banking, railways, and life insurance, as well as serving in the colonial legislature.

# Thomas Chandler Haliburton and Sam Slick

Popular culture provides a window into a society's attitudes. Many of the values of English-speaking North America were revealed in the works of Thomas Chandler Haliburton, the best-read British North American writer of the nineteenth century and the first internationally renowned writer from the area that would become Canada. Ernest Hemingway once said there was only one Canadian writer of the first rank, Haliburton, who was in the same tier as literary titans Joseph Conrad and James Joyce. A Nova Scotian, Haliburton was descended from both Loyalists and Planters. He worked as a judge, but became famous for creating the character Sam Slick, a clock-maker from Connecticut. Slick first appeared in short stories that Haliburton published in a Nova Scotia newspaper in 1835. The tales were popular, and Haliburton published 11 volumes of them over the next two decades.

Sam Slick embodied British North America's love–hate relationship with the United States. Slick is a stereotypical American, and the caricature reveals the smug sense of superiority that many British North Americans felt toward the United States. Slick is a braggart, proclaiming in his New England accent that the Stars and Stripes is the "first flag in the univarse now," a dig at the British who, with good reason, still believed their country to be the world's pre-eminent power. He carries with him the American distrust for intellectuals, arguing that "books only weaken your understandin' as water does brandy." And he repeatedly shows himself corrupt and unprincipled, even arguing at one point that it is wrong to steal a watch, but "honest and legal" to cheat a person out of one.[6] Yet Slick has many positive traits: he is energetic, enterprising, friendly, intelligent, and—in the end—likeable. Throughout the stories, Haliburton reveals his admiration for Yankee entrepreneurship and his belief that British North Americans could improve their economic lot through hard work and innovation, as the Americans had. Haliburton seemed to believe Nova Scotia could thrive only by combining a British government with an American economy.

The stories were distinctly Nova Scotian, but it says much about British North America that they could be, at the same time, characteristically American. Haliburton broke with European literary traditions, writing with an American irreverence. His main character spoke with a New England accent and used the colloquialisms of his time and place, which might explain why the books were popular in the United States. In fact, the American writer Artemus Ward is said to have called Haliburton "the father of American humor."[7] As a boy, Mark Twain carried *The Clockmaker* with him everywhere he went, even to church, laughing out loud as he read this first volume of Sam Slick stories.

# Rebellions of 1837–8

By the early 1830s, Upper and Lower Canada were being torn apart, pulled in opposite directions by a colonial government determined that Canada should be ruled according to the British model and by reformers who demanded American-style democracy. The 1829 election of Andrew Jackson as president of the United States created an earthquake, not only in American politics but also in British North America. The movement he inspired, Jacksonian Democracy, aimed to break the economic and political power of the establishment. In the United States, this translated into universal suffrage for white males, government positions filled through election instead of appointment, and the abolition of the central bank, thought to benefit mainly the interests of the rich. In British North America, reformers were influenced by Jackson, but faced different problems that required different solutions. Above all, they wanted responsible government, meaning that the political executive would be answerable to the people's elected representatives.

Democracy was slow in coming to British North America. Although the Loyalists had brought with them many American political ideals, the government remained in the hands of appointed officials, mostly British-born, who resisted efforts to turn power over to the people. In Upper Canada, a small elite group of Tories, known as the Family Compact, controlled the government; the Château Clique, a similar group, ruled in Lower Canada. In both places, the appointed colonial governments increasingly came into conflict with the elected assemblies, which sought a greater level of democracy. Reformers in Upper Canada and members of the Parti patriote in Lower Canada wanted the colonies to remain part of the British Empire, but aimed for a government responsible to the people, rather than to the British government in London.

In Lower Canada, the rebellion was led by Louis-Joseph Papineau, a politician, lawyer, and seigneur (a member of the landed gentry), who was influenced by Jacksonian Democracy. In 1834 Papineau and his party drafted a list of grievances, the 92 Resolutions, calling for responsible government. The colony would stay in the British Empire and would retain a British parliamentary system, but would borrow elements from the American model. Representation in the legislature would be based on population, and government posts would go to individuals of virtue and talent, not to those born into influential families. Disenchanted by the poverty he saw in England and the socio-economic problems in Lower Canada, Papineau later became convinced that annexation to the United States was preferable to staying in the British Empire.

The Reform leader in Upper Canada, William Lyon Mackenzie, travelled a similar intellectual journey. A Scottish-born newspaper editor and politician, Mackenzie's attitude toward the United States was at first ambivalent. He admired American democracy, but he also respected Britain and abhorred the practice of slavery in the US South. Yet his ideas began to change as Jacksonian Democracy transformed the US. When he visited the United States in 1829, he was impressed by American prosperity and by President Jackson, whom he met. Mackenzie campaigned with growing zeal for responsible government and began attacking the Bank of Upper

Canada for representing the interests of the elites rather than the public. Reformers won a majority in the Assembly in 1834, the year Mackenzie was also elected first mayor of Toronto, but his efforts at reform were stifled when the appointed upper house (known as the Legislative Council) refused to approve bills passed by the Assembly.

Lieutenant-Governor Francis Bond Head thought he was engaged in a "moral war" to keep Canada British and out of the hands of the Americans. The lines were drawn "between those who were for British institutions, against those who were for soiling the empire by the introduction of democracy."[8] Head broke the impasse between the government and the Assembly by calling an election in 1836, campaigning openly for the Tories, and condemning Reformers as rebels and traitors. To ensure a Tory victory, Head condoned the use of violence and bribery, both particularly effective in the days before the secret ballot. The Reformers were roundly defeated at the polls, Mackenzie himself losing his seat. As it became clear that the Reformers could not implement their agenda under the existing political system, Mackenzie turned increasingly to the American example. In August 1837, the Reformers of Toronto issued a declaration of grievances, which borrowed heavily, in some places verbatim, from the American Declaration of Independence. Their draft constitution for Upper Canada, issued in November, also used phrases lifted directly from the American original. It called for a system patterned on the American model, with a bicameral legislature and direct election of the head of government.

Tensions finally exploded in 1837. Violence broke out first in Lower Canada in November. After rioting erupted in Montreal, officials issued warrants for the arrest of Patriote leaders on the charge of high treason. They fled to the countryside, where plans for a rebellion quickly took shape. About 5,000 Patriotes took up arms against the government, but the British army was able to crush them, killing 300 rebels in several battles and skirmishes. Inspired by initial reports of the uprising in Lower Canada, Mackenzie began an armed rebellion in Toronto with a mixed group of insurgents, one-third of them American immigrants. Although he led between 500 and 700 men, they scattered when they encountered 200 volunteers and militiamen. Three days later, government forces marched to Mackenzie's headquarters and drove out the few hundred remaining rebels. Near Brantford, Dr Charles Duncombe got word from Toronto that an uprising was underway, and attempted his own rebellion with 500 men, 200 of whom, including Duncombe himself, were American-born. They too fled at the appearance of the militia. The rebellions crushed, Papineau, Mackenzie, Duncombe, and other leaders escaped to the United States. In both Upper and Lower Canada a majority may well have favoured responsible government, but rejected violence as a means to that end.

Mackenzie tried to continue the fight from the United States. With between 150 and 200 rebels, he crossed back into Canada, seizing Navy Island on the Niagara River. He then declared the creation of a provisional government for the Republic of Upper Canada and began planning an invasion of the mainland. Mackenzie's forces were supplied from the US by the steamboat *Caroline*. In late December 1837, at Fort Schlosser, New York, British forces seized the ship and set fire to it. The episode destroyed Mackenzie's republic, which could not survive without supplies.

The *Caroline* incident heightened tensions between Canada and the United States. When the rebellion broke out, the US government had declared itself neutral. Congress set aside $625,000 for the defence of the northern border, but neither Congress nor the president, Martin Van Buren, did anything to help the rebels. But after the *Caroline* incident, Americans were outraged that Britain had violated their sovereignty by seizing an American ship in US waters and that a US citizen had died in the incident. Van Buren demanded reparations from Britain and called up the militia. In later years, Americans strengthened their defences along the border. The forts at Niagara and Oswego were improved, and new ones were constructed at Detroit (Fort Wayne) and Buffalo (Fort Porter).

In the border states, Americans followed these events closely, seeing the rebels as a latter-day version of their own Revolutionary heroes. The US government might have been neutral, but private citizens supported the rebellion in the hopes of pushing Britain out of North America. Secret clubs, known as Hunters' Lodges, were created in northern states to liberate Canada from British control. Some members were motivated by a desire to free Canada, while others were out of work and hoping to win land or loot if an invasion succeeded. In late 1838, they carried out assaults on Prescott and Sandwich in Upper Canada, attacks easily repelled by local militias. Afterward, Upper Canadian officials executed several of the invaders.

Britain responded to the rebellions by dispatching an experienced politician, Lord Durham, to become governor general of British North America and to prepare a report on the political situation in the colonies. His instructions from the British government suggested that the problem in Canada was the negative influence of American political ideas. Durham disagreed. He praised the American systems of education and municipal government, and spoke highly of the consistent and efficient way the US dealt with public land, in contrast to the haphazard approach in Lower and Upper Canada. The United States was more prosperous than Canada, Durham noted, in part because Americans had a "perfectly free and eminently responsible government." Two measures would help prevent future unrest in the colonies. First, French Canadians had to be assimilated. This could be accomplished by uniting Upper and Lower Canada (and, if possible, all of British North America) to weaken the power of the French. Union would have the added benefit of strengthening the colony, making it better able to resist the growing influence of the United States. Second, said Durham, the colony should have responsible government. Not only would this satisfy public demands for more democracy but it also would diminish American hostility toward British North America and help Canada build a "nationality," so that Upper and Lower Canadians could resist absorption into the US.[9]

The British government eventually accepted the recommendations. Upper and Lower Canada were merged into the United Province of Canada, though this would not have the desired effect of assimilating French Canadians, who defended their own interests with vigour within the larger colony. After some delay, British North America moved to responsible government, first in Nova Scotia in 1848, and then in the other colonies, a move that helped bring stability to the border between the United States and British North America.

# Normalizing the Status Quo

Despite the tumultuous nature of the half century following the War of 1812, the United States and British North America slowly settled their outstanding disputes, laying the foundation for the peaceful Canadian–American relationship of the twentieth century. Relations improved, despite both anti-American sentiment north of the border and efforts by colonial officials to reduce American influences. Britain was losing interest in North America, and anti-British sentiment in the United States was on the decline, providing the opportunity to resolve longstanding problems.

Most of the Canadian–American border was settled in the period from 1818 to 1842, always through negotiation and arbitration. Although haphazard, this process was highly effective. Few international boundaries have proven as resilient as the one between Canada and the United States, precisely because it was set gradually and through mutual agreement rather than by war. In 1807, British and American officials agreed that the 49th parallel would be the northern border of the United States from the crest of the Rocky Mountains to the Lake of the Woods near the centre of the continent, but tensions with Britain during the Napoleonic Wars prevented the US from ratifying the agreement. With the end of the wars, the two sides sat down again, and in the Convention of 1818 agreed to that same boundary. The area west of the Rockies, known as Oregon Territory (present-day British Columbia, Washington, Idaho, and Oregon, as well as parts of Montana and Wyoming), would be jointly occupied by the two countries for up to 10 years while they discussed how to divide it.

Although the boundary on the eastern half of the continent had been settled by the 1783 Treaty of Paris, many conflicts remained. The treaty's description of the border between Maine and New Brunswick was inadequate because it did not match the terrain. At one point, for instance, the boundary was to be the St Croix River, but it was not clear which river was the St Croix. Was it the one also known as the Schoodic, or the one called the Magaguadavic? In 1830, the two sides placed the issue in the hands of a neutral third party (King William I of the Netherlands), who came to a compromise solution, giving the US two-thirds of the disputed territory. The British accepted the ruling, but the United States refused to ratify it. Tensions flared late in the decade, with each side sending troops to the disputed areas and arresting "trespassers."

The conflict continued to escalate until the Aroostook War of 1839. Maine militiamen sparked the war by arresting New Brunswick lumberjacks and seizing their equipment. Some of the lumbermen retaliated, capturing three American officials and taking them back to Fredericton, New Brunswick's capital, where they were jailed. The governor of Maine declared that his state had been invaded and pledged to send further troops. The state legislature authorized the call-up of a 10,000-man militia and the expenditure of $800,000. After the American prisoners were released, the lieutenant-governor of New Brunswick called on Maine to withdraw its militia, threatening to send British troops if Maine did not immediately comply. At that point, Congress became involved, setting aside $10 million for the conflict and empowering the president to call up 50,000 troops. "I do not see how this can terminate without a general war," wrote Upper Canada's lieutenant-governor George Arthur, watching from Toronto.[10] With war imminent, President Van Buren turned to General Winfield Scott, a skilled military commander and tactful diplomat. "If you want *war*," Scott told the president, "I need only look on in silence. The Maine people will make it for you fast and hot enough. . . . But if *peace* be your wish, I can give no assurance of success. The difficulties will be formidable." Van Buren responded that he wanted "peace with honor," and dispatched Scott to the area.[11] The general convinced both sides to pull back from the brink. The Aroostook War ended without a single death. The boundary issue was put before a commission, which was unable to solve the dilemma.

The northeastern border was not finally settled until the Webster–Ashburton Treaty of 1842, which also cleared up several other disagreements. The US would get about 60 per cent of the disputed territory in Maine and New Brunswick, and the border south of Montreal would be adjusted so that Fort Montgomery on Rouse's Point could be built on US soil. The treaty provided for the extradition of those accused of committing serious crimes, putting an end to the longstanding problem of criminals

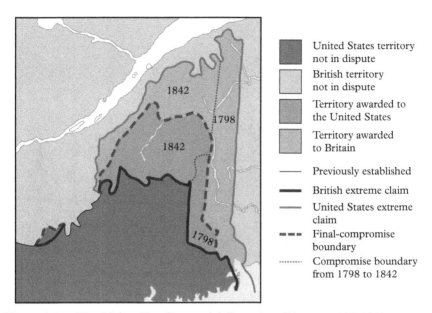

United States territory
not in dispute

British territory
not in dispute

Territory awarded to
the United States

Territory awarded
to Britain

—— Previously established

▬▬ British extreme claim

—— United States extreme
claim

▬ ▬ ▬ Final-compromise
boundary

········ Compromise boundary
from 1798 to 1842

**Figure 2.2** ✦ **The Maine–New Brunswick Boundary Dispute, 1798–1842**

Some vague wording in the Treaty of Paris of 1783 left the border between Maine and
New Brunswick in dispute. In the southern and eastern portions of the disputed territory, the matter was settled in 1798, but no agreement could be reached over the north-
western portion. Tensions grew throughout the 1830s until the two sides were on the
verge of war. Finally, the 1842 Webster–Ashburton Treaty settled the issue.

Source: Adapted from R. Louis Gentilcore, ed., *Historical Atlas of Canada*, vol. 2, *The Land Transformed,
1800–1891* (Toronto: University of Toronto Press, 1993), plate 21.

evading justice by fleeing across the border. Britain was careful that the
treaty's extradition terms were drafted so as not to require British North
America to return fugitive slaves to the United States. In a separate note,
Britain gave a convoluted apology for the sinking of the *Caroline* in 1837.
Britain's envoy, Lord Ashburton, and US Secretary of State Daniel Webster
could also have settled the boundary west of the Rocky Mountains, but
decided to put it off. Ashburton found the summer heat and humidity of
Washington unbearable, complaining that he was in an oven where he could
not work during the day or sleep at night.

The boundary west of the Rockies was set in the Oregon Treaty of 1846,
with the two countries agreeing to extend the line along the 49th parallel to
the Strait of Georgia. From 1857 to 1862, surveyors working for a joint international commission fixed the border's location on land from the West Coast
to the crest of the Rocky Mountains, marking it with stone cairns, bundles
of logs, or earth mounds spaced one to three miles apart, depending on the
terrain. After the American Civil War, the work resumed. Canadian and
American boundary commissions worked together from 1872 to 1876,

**Photo 2.1** ✢ **Sappers at a 49th parallel boundary mound**

Sappers of the North American Boundary Commission mark the 49th parallel with a mound of earth in the summer of 1873. (Source: Library and Archives Canada, C-073304.)

running the border along the 49th parallel from the Lake of the Woods to the Rockies.

The boundary's location through the Strait of Georgia was less clear. Different readings of the treaty put the ownership of several islands in dispute. One of them, San Juan Island, was settled by both Americans and British subjects. The Hudson's Bay Company ran a sheep ranch near a tiny farm owned by an American, Lyman Cutler. One of the company's pigs repeatedly dug up Cutler's potatoes. Enraged that the company did nothing to stop this, despite repeated complaints, Cutler shot and killed the animal, the only casualty of what became known as the Pig War of 1859. Cutler offered $10 compensation for the pig, but company officials threatened to have him arrested if he did not pay $100, an exorbitant amount in those days. The commander of the US army in the Northwest, Brigadier General William S. Harney, who happened to be in the area, received a formal request from the Americans on San Juan to provide a company of soldiers to protect them. Brash and anti-British, Harney sent more than 60 men. When they arrived, their commander announced that only US law would be in force on the island. James Douglas, the governor of the British colony of Vancouver Island, responded by asking the Royal Navy to dispatch a warship. A British frigate arrived with orders to prevent the Americans from landing more troops.

In the end, the crisis was resolved by General Winfield Scott, the same man who had defused the Aroostook War of 1839. Until the matter could be settled permanently, the two sides agreed to joint occupation, with the American troops moving to one side of the island. The US government recalled General Harney before he could do further damage. In 1871, Britain and the United States agreed to put the matter in the hands of the German emperor, who ruled in favour of the United States in 1872.

# Annexationism

The sense of identity in British North America could never be separated from economic considerations. The United States was developing as an economic dynamo, while British North Americans puzzled over whether they could share in American prosperity without joining the United States or becoming an American economic colony. These issues were pushed to the fore in the 1840s. In 1846, Britain began a move toward free trade with all countries by repealing the Corn Laws, its tariff on imported grain. British North American products had previously been admitted to the British market at a much lower tariff than goods from outside the Empire, but now all imports to Britain would be subject to the same tariff, meaning that British North American products would no longer receive preferential treatment in the British market. British North America had been selling significant amounts of timber and food to Britain, exports that now declined. A global depression hit Canada in 1846, exacerbating the problem. Shipments to Britain from Montreal, Canada's political and commercial capital, were cut in half, causing half the trading firms in the city to go bankrupt. Although the problems were mainly a result of the depression, Montreal's economic elite became convinced that Britain's trade policy was ruining them. It seemed the Canadian economy could only be saved by increasing exports to the United States to offset the loss of markets in Britain. Canada sought freer trade with the United States, but the US Senate blocked a bill to lower tariffs on some Canadian products. Now it seemed that the only way to increase access to American markets was to join the United States.

The thorny relationship between French-speaking and English-speaking Montrealers further complicated the situation. Before the rebellions of 1837, Lower Canada had been controlled by the colony's anglophone minority. With the coming of responsible government, the colonial government became answerable to the Canadian Legislative Assembly, in which francophones had a significant share of the seats. Many anglophones felt that their power was ebbing and that Britain had abandoned them to the French. When the legislature approved a measure to compensate those who had lost property in Lower Canada during the 1837 and 1838 rebellions, including many of the rebels themselves, Montreal's English community embarked on two days of rioting, throwing stones at the governor general, ransacking the homes of Reform Party leaders, and setting the Parliament buildings on fire. After order was restored, the government decided to move the capital to another city, and Montreal anglophones began to flirt with the idea of annexation to the United States.

The Annexation Manifesto of October 1849 was an act of desperation by Montreal's political and business establishment. The initial declaration, "Address to the People of Canada," was published in the *Montreal Gazette* and signed by 325 prominent Montrealers, including John Abbott (later prime minister of Canada), Alexander Tilloch Galt (later Canada's first minister of finance), Antoine-Aimé Dorion (later federal minister of justice), and John and William Molson (whose brewery would later become a national symbol). More than 1,000 signed a petition in support of the declaration. Annexation was justified on economic grounds: joining the US would allow American capital to flow into Canada, open the US market to Canadian products, and let US-manufactured goods enter Canada without a costly tariff.

The annexation movement had the overwhelming support of the anglophone elite in Canada East (the former Lower Canada), but never won over a majority in British North America. Francophones worried that their community would lose its identity in the United States, as had the French in Louisiana. The Catholic Church opposed annexation for fear that it would be stripped of its privileged position in Canada East, where it was responsible for francophone education and could legally compel Catholics to pay the tithe, a form of tax to support the church. In Nova Scotia and Prince Edward Island there was not much sympathy, though some in New Brunswick were interested in annexation, perhaps because the province's timber trade had been particularly hard hit by the depression. In Canada West (the former Upper Canada), annexationists were considered traitors. Writers and politicians denounced the United States for allowing slavery and its expansionist foreign policy, the Americans having recently annexed Texas and much of the present-day western United States. Some in Canada West even condemned the republican form of government as ungodly: after all, God ruled over the Kingdom of Heaven, not the Republic of Heaven.

Many Americans, particularly in the border states, were interested in annexing Canada. French Canadians had settled in New England, and they were eager that their friends and relatives be part of the same country. The legislatures of Vermont and New York passed resolutions supporting annexation, but the federal government kept its distance, lest it upset the delicate political balance in the United States between the North and South over the defining issue of the age, slavery. In 1849, the states were evenly divided between the 15 in the South that allowed slavery and the remaining 15 that outlawed it. It was all but politically impossible for a president to pursue openly the annexation of Canada, which would tip the balance toward the North. Most politicians said little about the subject, no doubt sharing the view of the *Toledo Blade* that Canada would join the United States eventually, in its own time: "When the fruit is fully ripe it will fall into our lap without any exertion on our part."[12]

# Reciprocity

Born of economic desperation, the annexation movement declined in 1850 when the Canadian economy began to recover. Still, Britain had learned a lesson from Montreal's brief flirtation with annexation. Governor General Lord Elgin warned London that Britain might lose its North American colonies if it did not agree to a reciprocity treaty, an agreement between the United States and British North America to reduce or abolish their tariffs on a large number of each other's products. Canada would be content within the British Empire so long as it enjoyed the same level of prosperity as the United States, but if Britain did not arrange a trade agreement, Elgin wrote, "The worst I fear will come, and at no distant day."[13] For Lord Elgin and other British officials, reciprocity was not a first step to annexation; rather, it was a way of preventing annexation.

After years of negotiations, Lord Elgin and US Secretary of State William L. Marcy signed the Reciprocity Treaty in June 1854. The agreement provided for free trade in most natural products between the United States and all of British North America except Newfoundland. Each side would have access to the other's Atlantic fisheries north of the 36th parallel (roughly north of North Carolina). Lake Michigan, the one Great Lake wholly within the United States, would be opened to the British, and Americans would have access to the canals and waterways of British North America. The treaty would run initially for 10 years and could be ended by either party with one year's notice.

Both sides benefitted from the agreement, which remained in effect until March 1866. Not only did it lessen tensions between British North America and the United States, but it also resulted in a dramatic increase in trade between them. Maine, for example, was able to import coal, lumber, flaxseed, stone, and wool more easily from British North America than from its more distant traditional American sources. And the British colonies benefitted from an impressive increase in exports.

The precise impact of the treaty has long been debated. Many scholars have attributed the growth in trade to factors other than reciprocity, such as the American need for grain, horses, and timber to fight the US Civil War (1861–5). Yet the exponential increase of British North American

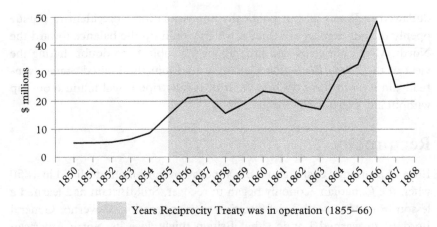

Years Reciprocity Treaty was in operation (1855–66)

**Figure 2.3** ❖ Exports from British North America to the United States, 1850–68

Source: Data provided by Canada. Parliament. *Sessional Papers*, 7th Parliament, 1st Session, vol. 11 (Ottawa: Parliament, 1891), p. xxxiv.

exports to the United States began shortly after the treaty came into force and long before the Civil War broke out, suggesting a close relationship between reciprocity and trade growth. By removing tariffs, the Reciprocity Treaty substantially reduced the cost of American goods in British North America and British North American products in the United States, which no doubt increased their sales. The growth in trade was too substantial and coincided too closely with the period that reciprocity was in force for the figures to be dismissed, as some have tried, as a simple result of a fluctuating business cycle.

## Summary

The half century following the War of 1812 was crucial in solidifying the break between the United States and the British colonies that would become Canada. Fearful of losing more territory to the United States, colonial officials worked to reduce American influences in British North America and to foster a British identity. They portrayed American political ideas as treasonous and put down violent uprisings in 1837 and 1838. Knowing that many British North Americans were drawn to the prosperity of the United States, Britain negotiated a trade agreement that allowed the colonists to find a greater market south of the border for many of their products. The British worked to finalize the boundary between British North America and the United States. This not only sharpened the separation between the two peoples, but it also laid the groundwork for a future friendship between them. Good fences made for good neighbours.

# Beyond the Book

1. What was the impact of the War of 1812 on Canadian attitudes toward the United States? To what extent are Canadian attitudes today similar to those in the years after 1814?
2. Why was the border between Canada and the United States so difficult to resolve? Why does it not run straight? Why has it proven so resilient?
3. What was the relationship between economic considerations and attitudes toward the United States in 1840s Montreal? Is there still a connection between the economics and politics of the Canadian–American relationship?

# Further Reading

A thorough overview of Upper Canada in the years after the War of 1812 can be found in Gerald M. Craig's *Upper Canada: The Formative Years, 1784–1841* (Toronto: McClelland and Stewart, 1963). Also valuable is Craig's "The American Impact on the Upper Canadian Reform Movement before 1867," *Canadian Historical Review* 29, no. 4 (December 1948): 333–52. Jane Errington explores the shaping of Upper Canadian identity in her path-breaking and nuanced book, *The Lion, the Eagle, and Upper Canada: A Developing Colonial Ideology* (Montreal and Kingston: McGill–Queen's University Press, 1987). Paul Romney's "Re-Inventing Upper Canada: American Immigrants, Upper Canadian History, English Law, and the Alien Question" is a concise but important study of the Alien Question, the most important political issue in 1820s Upper Canada. Romney's piece can be found in Roger Hall, William Westfall, and Laurel Sefton MacDowell, eds., *Patterns of the Past: Interpreting Ontario's History* (Toronto: Dundurn Press, 1988), 78–107. One of Canada's leading young historians is Todd Webb, whose cutting-edge work on Methodism is best captured in *Transatlantic Methodists: British Wesleyanism and the Formation of an Evangelical Culture in Nineteenth-Century Ontario and Quebec* (Montreal and Kingston: McGill–Queen's University Press, 2013).

On the 1837 rebellions, see Michel Ducharme, *Le concept de liberté au Canada à l'époque des révolutions atlantiques, 1776–1838* (Montreal: McGill–Queen's University Press, 2010); Allan Greer, *The Patriots and the People: The Rebellion of 1837 in Rural Lower Canada* (Toronto: University of Toronto Press, 1993); Allan Greer, "1837–38: Rebellion Reconsidered," *Canadian Historical Review* 76, no. 1 (1995), 1–18; J.E. Rea, "William Lyon Mackenzie—Jacksonian?" *Mid-America: An Historical Review* [Chicago] 50, no. 3 (1968), 223–35; and Colin Read, *The Rising in Western Upper Canada, 1837–8: The Duncombe Revolt and after* (Toronto: University of Toronto Press, 1982).

Of the many studies of Haliburton and Sam Slick, the best is Richard A. Davies, *Inventing Sam Slick: A Biography of Thomas Chandler Haliburton* (Toronto: University of Toronto Press, 2005).

Francis M. Carroll provides a thorough and well-researched account of the settling of the Canadian–American border in *A Good and Wise Measure: The Search for the Canadian–American Boundary, 1783–1842* (Toronto: University of Toronto Press, 2001). Reginald C. Stuart ably analyzes US policy in *United States Expansionism and British North America, 1775–1871* (Chapel Hill: University of North Carolina Press, 1988). Scott Kaufman's *The Pig War: The United States, Britain, and the Balance of Power in the Pacific Northwest, 1846–72* (Lanham, Maryland: Lexington Books, 2004) is the best source on that comical episode.

On economic issues, older works prevail. Donald F. Warner's *The Idea of Continental Union: Agitation for the Annexation of Canada to the United States, 1849–1893* (Lexington: University of Kentucky Press, 1960) has held up well over the years. Donald C. Masters, *The Reciprocity Treaty of 1854* (1937; Toronto: McClelland and Stewart, 1963) is very old and very dull but still the single best overview on reciprocity. Marilyn Gerriets and Julian Gwyn add nuance in "Tariffs, Trade and Reciprocity: Nova Scotia, 1830–1866," *Acadiensis* 25, no. 2 (Spring 1996): 62–82.

## CHAPTER 3

# Havoc, 1860–1871

## *Slavery, the American Civil War, and Canadian Confederation*

## Introduction

For George Brown, slavery in the American South was not just a problem for the United States, but for all of North America. "We are in the habit of calling the people of the United States 'the Americans'," he explained, "but we too are Americans; on us, as well as on them, lies the duty of preserving the honour of the continent." After all, slavery was a "leprosy" that affected "all around it."[1] Brown was editor of Toronto's *Globe*, the highest-circulation newspaper in British North America. From the ages of 18 to 24, he had lived in New York, an experience that strengthened both his opposition to slavery and his belief in the superiority of the British political system. For him, Canadians were Americans with two crucial differences: a monarch and a parliamentary democracy.

Like many liberals, Brown sided with the North during the American Civil War. When tensions between Canada and the United States caused many Canadians to turn against the Union in favour of the Southern Confederacy, Brown refused to change his loyalties. Slavery was a disgrace that justified the use of force to end it. But he was troubled by what would happen after the North had won the war. Would the US attack Canada? Would Canada's southern neighbour continue its westward expansion into territories that Brown considered as rightfully belonging to Canada? The solution, it seemed to Brown, was for British North America to unite into one country, which would eventually extend to the Pacific. Political deadlock in Canada spurred Brown to action. He put aside his longstanding enmity for conservative leader John A. Macdonald and proposed the creation of a coalition government to work toward the union of Canada and the Maritimes. Although the idea had been around for years, it was Brown's initiative that started the negotiations toward what he termed "a new nationality" and what would become modern Canada.[2]

# Slavery and the Underground Railroad

The American struggle over slavery is often seen as an experience that distinguished the United States from Canada. Simply put, the United States permitted slavery, while Canada did not; the United States fought a bloody civil war over the issue, while Canada handled racial issues peacefully. In fact, the story of slavery and the Civil War is one that links as much as divides the two societies. Canada had its own history of slavery and continued to discriminate against blacks long after emancipation. In this, Canada was remarkably similar to the Northern United States.

By the mid-nineteenth century, Canadians seemed to have erased their own history of slavery. "Slavery never had an existence in Canada," the *Globe* claimed in 1849.[3] Subsequent generations of Canadians came to believe that their national story was devoid of prejudice and that they were more decent than Americans. Yet, slavery existed in Canada: among the Aboriginal people before they had contact with Europeans and afterward under both the French and British regimes. Some Loyalists brought slaves with them when they fled the United States for Quebec or Nova Scotia. Yet most Loyalists came from the Northern states and shared the racial attitudes of New England and New York. They might not have seen blacks as equal to whites, but they did find slavery morally repugnant.

In 1793, Upper Canada passed legislation to abolish slavery gradually, but this did not put Canadians ahead of Americans. Six of the fifteen US states had already passed similar laws, and Upper Canada's was closely patterned after Connecticut's 1784 statute. When it came to slavery, Upper Canada was just another Northern US state. In the rest of British North America, slavery slowly died out by the early 1820s, without legislative action. It was formally abolished in the British Empire on 1 August 1834, after it had already been banned or was being phased out in all 12 Northern US states. The British Empire's measure predated President Abraham Lincoln's Emancipation Proclamation by less than 30 years.

People in both British North America and the United States were part of an international campaign to abolish slavery that had begun in the late eighteenth century. After slavery was outlawed in Canada and the Northern states, abolitionists in those places, both whites and freed blacks, continued to push for emancipation in the US South. Canada's first abolitionist organization, the Upper Canada Anti-Slavery Society, was founded in Toronto in

1837. It was ineffective and short-lived, doing little beyond passing resolutions condemning slavery.

The US Fugitive Slave Act had a profound impact on the abolition movement on both sides of the border. Passed into law in 1850, the measure was aimed to prevent slaves from escaping and to return those who did. Anyone who helped a slave flee, even by providing food or shelter, could suffer stiff penalties, including imprisonment. Everyone, even a bystander, was obliged to help capture fugitive slaves or face heavy fines. To recover a slave, the owner merely had to present a sworn statement to a judge or commissioner. No warrant was necessary for arrest, and suspected slaves had no right to a jury trial. Even free blacks now felt threatened, as anyone could swear an affidavit claiming them as runaway slaves. Escaping to the Northern US was no longer an option. To be guaranteed freedom, a slave had to make it to Canada to get beyond the reach of American law. As a result, thousands of blacks fled to Canada in the winter of 1850–1.

Many of the fugitives escaped on the Underground Railroad. Not literally underground and not a railroad, it was an ad hoc network of abolitionists who helped blacks flee to the Northern states, Mexico, the Bahamas, or Canada. Though long celebrated by Canadians as a key part of their history, the Underground Railroad was a transnational enterprise. Indeed, it was more American than Canadian. Fugitive slaves needed a friendly destination, which Upper Canada provided by offering them asylum, but the means of escape was primarily on US territory and was mostly run by Americans. In short, the railroad was American; only some of the terminals were Canadian. It is impossible to say with certainty how many slaves fled to Canada: There were no immigration posts at the border to count the fugitives entering Canada, and many blacks were not counted in the Canadian census. Two historians have undertaken rigorous examinations of the question, but have come up with widely divergent numbers. Robin Winks has suggested that 40,000 blacks fled to British North America from 1840 to 1860. In contrast, Michael Wayne estimated there were around 20,000 blacks in Upper Canada in 1861.[4]

In reaction to the Fugitive Slave Act, the Anti-Slavery Society of Canada was born in Toronto in early 1851. The organization ran a night school in Toronto for fugitives and worked to find them employment. Several prominent Torontonians were active in the organization, including *Globe* editor George Brown and Toronto's mayor. From the beginning, the society was closely affiliated with the abolition movement in the United States. The speaker at the April 1851 meeting was Frederick Douglass, the best-known black abolitionist in the United States, who addressed a crowd of 1,200.

If the abolition movement had a bible, it was *Uncle Tom's Cabin*, the 1852 novel by Harriet Beecher Stowe. The book's title character is a slave,

**Figure 3.1** ✛ Routes of the Underground Railroad

The Underground Railroad brought slaves from the Southern United States to freedom in the Northern states or Canada.

Source: Adapted from Mary Ellen Snodgrass, *The Underground Railroad: An Encyclopedia of People, Places, and Operations* (Armonk, NY: M.E. Sharpe Inc., 2008), vol. 1, p. xxxv.

separated from his wife and children when his master sells him. Eventually, he ends up as the property of Simon Legree, one of the great villains of American literature. The book ends when Tom is beaten to death on Legree's orders, but not before the slave forgives his owner. In the United States, Stowe's work strengthened the abolitionist cause by awakening Americans to the evil of slavery, but it had a profound impact in Canada too, selling well in both English- and French-language editions. The first Canadian edition sold out in three weeks. Excerpts were published in Toronto's *Globe*, and the novel was serialized in *The Maple Leaf*, a Montreal magazine. While a law student at McGill University, the future Canadian prime minister

Wilfrid Laurier read the book, an experience he later said made him into "an anti-slavery man."[5] *Uncle Tom's Cabin* was the most popular American book among Canadian high-school students into the 1930s, and continued to sell well in Toronto until the 1950s.

The book had a Canadian connection. Stowe knew Montreal, having visited several times, and in the novel two of the slaves escape to that city. Canadians came to believe that Uncle Tom himself was patterned on Josiah Henson, a slave who fled to Upper Canada in 1830 at the age of 41, becoming a leader among local blacks. Canadians liked to say that the real Uncle Tom had not died at the feet of Simon Legree, but had found safety by fleeing to Canada, a myth that confirmed the Canadian sense of superiority over Americans. Henson's home, near Dresden, Ontario, is still preserved as Uncle Tom's Cabin Historic Site.

As in the Northern states, there were several efforts to create settlements for blacks in Upper Canada. Most were farming communities that were home to a few hundred blacks. Cursed with weak leadership, they generally failed because of problems with money and organization. Only Buxton (also known as the Elgin Settlement) was truly successful. Established south of Chatham by an Irish minister, William King, the community had more than 700 residents at its peak in the 1860s. At one time, it had four churches, a post office, a general store, a hotel, and a bank. Residents worked on the farm or in the brickyard, sawmill, or flourmill, or in the blacksmith, carpenter, or shoe shops. The quality of Buxton's three schools could be seen in the success that many of the former pupils achieved after returning to the United States following the Civil War. Their numbers included a US senator, a member of the House of Representatives, and a Mississippi judge. Still others became doctors, lawyers, and teachers.

That a large number of fugitives went back to the United States after the abolition of slavery says much about the welcome they received in Canada. They were free in Canada, but faced constant racism, much as they would have in the Northern states. Indeed, George Brown thought that prejudice against blacks was stronger in Canada than south of the border. Many blacks agreed; they might have had greater legal rights in Canada, but they faced more bigotry than in the Northern US.[6] In Canada, as in the US North, people believed blacks were inferior, often subjecting them to verbal abuse and refusing them both lodging at hotels and service in restaurants. Many property owners would not sell to blacks, and, though usually colour-blind, the government occasionally discriminated against them. Blacks were not allowed to serve on juries or in public office in the Maritimes, were forced into segregated units in the New Brunswick militia, and had to send their children to segregated schools in many places throughout British North America. This racism had legal sanction well into the twentieth century. In 1940, for instance, the Supreme Court of Canada ruled that a pub could refuse to serve a black man on the basis of his skin colour.

Osborne Perry Anderson was one of many blacks who encountered racism on both sides of the Canadian–American border. By one account, he was "well educated, a man of natural dignity, modest, simple in character and manners."[7] Born free in Pennsylvania in 1830, Anderson attended Oberlin College in Ohio before moving to Canada in 1850, the year of the Fugitive Slave Act. He settled in Chatham, where he became active in the abolition movement and worked as a printer for a black newspaper, the *Provincial Freeman*. His life changed in 1858, when he met John Brown.

Brown was an American activist determined to do away with slavery by any means necessary. In 1858, he began planning and fundraising for a slave revolt. Brown met with abolitionists in many places in Upper Canada, including Ingersoll, Hamilton, and Toronto. In St Catharines in April, he met with Harriet Tubman, an escaped slave and the best-known organizer of the Underground Railroad, often called Moses for her efforts to help blacks escape bondage. She agreed to help Brown recruit men to fight at his side. In May, Brown travelled to Chatham, home to the largest concentration of blacks in Canada, where he held a meeting to make general plans for a rebellion. There he encountered Osborne Anderson, who acted as recording secretary at some of Brown's meetings. Anderson pledged his life to Brown's cause and was elected a member of the provisional congress that would form the government in the South after the revolt.

Brown's plans were set in motion in October 1859. With 18 followers, he seized the US arsenal at Harpers Ferry, Virginia. US troops took back the fort, killing 10 of Brown's men. Convicted of treason and hanged with six others, Brown became a hero to abolitionists. Anderson survived the revolt, evaded capture, and made his way via the Underground Railroad back to Canada. In Chatham, he wrote the only eyewitness account of the raid. During the Civil War, he returned to the United States, where he enlisted in the Northern army.

## The American Civil War

The American Civil War was not just a conflict within the United States, but an event that caused upheaval across the continent. It not only forced the end of slavery in the US, but also put pressure on Britain's North American colonies to unite.

After Abraham Lincoln won the presidential election of November 1860, the Southern states feared that the new president and his Republican Party would abolish slavery. Eleven states seceded to form the Confederate States of America. In April 1861, Confederate forces bombarded Fort

Sumter, South Carolina, marking the beginning of the bloodiest war in American history. More Americans died in the Civil War than in the Revolutionary War, the War of 1812, the First World War, the Second World War, the Korean War, and the Vietnam War combined.

Canadian opinion on the war was divided. On the one hand, many conservatives were anti-American, which translated into pro-Confederate sentiment. They hoped the South would win, thus splitting the US in two. Not only would this mean a weaker United States on Canada's border, but it also would be a form of just retribution: much as the United States had once seceded from the British Empire, the South was now seceding from the United States. When the North lost the first major battle of the war, the Battle of Bull Run in July 1861, Canadian conservatives celebrated with champagne, raising three cheers to the Confederacy in the Legislative Assembly in Quebec City. On the other hand, Canadian liberals tended to be highly critical of slavery, which led them to sympathize with the Union. Yet growing fear of a US invasion of Canada, coupled with a series of incidents that set the US against Britain, sapped support for the North, even among its former sympathizers in British North America.

The Civil War soured relations between British North America and the United States. The British Empire officially declared its neutrality one month after the outbreak of hostilities, but many British North Americans took up arms, usually on the side of the North. At the same time, thousands of deserters and draft evaders from the Northern army sought refuge in Canada and the Maritimes. Halifax and Saint John were home to blockade runners, ships that evaded the Northern naval blockade of the South, often delivering both arms to the Confederacy and Southern cotton to its overseas markets. Maritime ports were also home to sea raiders, private ships that stopped Northern merchant vessels and seized their cargos, at the cost of millions of dollars to Northern shipping. Britain's actions, too, helped to elevate tensions between the United States and British North America. Many in the North interpreted Britain's neutrality as support for the South. The US government was particularly incensed that British companies sold ships to the Confederacy, including the *Alabama*, a vessel that captured or destroyed more than 60 Northern vessels.

The *Trent* affair, which pushed Britain and the United States to the brink of war, was the first of three crises that embittered relations between the two countries during the Civil War. The British steamship *Trent* was travelling to Europe in November 1861 when it was stopped in international waters by a US Navy frigate. American sailors boarded the *Trent*, arrested two Confederate diplomats, and returned them to the mainland, where they were held by American authorities. The British viewed this as a violation of their sovereignty and sent an ultimatum to the US, demanding the release of the diplomats. Britain stopped exporting arms to the United States and dispatched 11,000 troops to Canada. "I fear war is upon us," wrote Lord Newcastle, Britain's secretary of state for the colonies.[8] In late December 1861, the United States released the Confederate officials, which ended the war scare but did not ease relations between Britain and the United States.

The second major incident, the *Chesapeake* affair, also revolved around the issue of sovereignty at sea. In December 1863, 16 Confederate sympathizers, most of whom were New Brunswickers, hijacked the Northern steamship *Chesapeake*. In the process, they wounded two crew members, and shot and killed one of the ship's engineers, whose body they threw overboard. A US Navy ship trapped the *Chesapeake* off the coast of Nova Scotia and turned it over to the authorities in Halifax. The hijackers fled before capture, except one, who managed to escape when he was brought to shore in Halifax. Four of the hijackers were later arrested in New Brunswick, but a judge refused to extradite them to the US, dismissing the charges against them. Both sides were angry—the British that the American ship had entered British waters, and the Americans that the miscreants had not been extradited to be tried as pirates.

The St Albans raid was the third and best known of the events that strained relations between Britain and the United States. In October 1864, 26 Confederate soldiers entered St Albans, Vermont, from Canada, robbed three banks, and rushed back over the border, in the process killing one man and wounding another. Thirteen of the robbers were arrested in Canada, but they were released two months later when a judge ruled that there was no basis for holding them. Americans reacted with outrage. The *New York Times* suggested that a repeat performance might lead to war: "If the Canadians persist in allowing these murderous incursions into our territory, we *must* protect ourselves, whatever the consequence."[9]

The US government did not contemplate war but it did take action against British North America. In November, one month after the raid, the US gave notice of its intent to terminate the Rush–Bagot Agreement, which limited warships on the Great Lakes. In December, the State Department began requiring foreigners, "especially" British North Americans, to carry passports when entering the United States. As passports were expensive and not easy to obtain, this greatly reduced the number of people who could cross the US border. In January 1865, the US Congress instructed the president to give notice that the US would cancel the Reciprocity Treaty. The US later thought better of the first two measures, allowing the Rush–Bagot agreement to continue and rescinding the passport requirement, but the Reciprocity Treaty did not survive the animosity of the Civil War years.

Tensions between British North America and the United States persisted, despite the end of the Civil War with a Northern victory in April 1865. Tens of thousands of unemployed veterans joined the US branch of the Fenian Brotherhood, an Irish nationalist group created in the 1850s with the intent of using force to advance the cause of Irish independence from Britain. In 1866, the Fenians carried out a series of ineffective raids on targets in British North America. They destroyed bridges, cut telegraph wires, damaged or stole private property, and engaged in combat against local militias. Officials in British North America were outraged that the United States had neither prevented these raids nor put the leaders on trial. The skirmishes increased public support for a union of the colonies to offer them greater security. Scholars have often been dismissive of the Fenian threat, but the raids had a profound psychological impact on British North America and helped to unite the colonies.

# Confederation

The union of Canada and the Maritimes—turning scattered colonies into a country—had long been a topic of after-dinner speeches. It would be easier to link British North America with a railway if there were one colonial government instead of several. One large colony would be stronger economically than four smaller ones. Uniting with the Maritimes would help Canada break the deadlock in the Legislative Assembly between conservatives and liberals. Yet, the main reasons for colonial union were not domestic. The poet of Confederation, politician Thomas D'Arcy McGee, pointed south to explain why Canada and the Maritimes had to come together: "Look around you in this age of earthquake . . . look around you to the valley of Virginia, look around you to the mountains of Georgia, and you will find reasons as thick as blackberries."[10] The American threat was on everyone's mind in 1864, when British North American politicians met in Charlottetown and Quebec City to negotiate the terms of Confederation.

The United States gave British and colonial politicians a sense of urgency. The Americans had cancelled the Reciprocity Treaty, weakening the British North American economy. In the Civil War, a Northern victory was within sight, particularly after the fall of Atlanta, which took place on the second day of the Charlottetown Conference. The United States had the largest army in the world and was antagonistic to Britain, leaving the colonies vulnerable. A sense of anxiety was reinforced by Britain's faltering commitment to North America. The British were increasingly worried about the situation in continental Europe in the 1860s, a time of tension and frequent war. London pushed the colonies to unite so they could better defend themselves, which would allow Britain to withdraw troops from North America for a possible European conflict. No military expert imagined that a united Canada could withstand an invasion by the American army, but many politicians believed that the Americans were less likely to attack a united, self-governing, semi-sovereign entity than a group of scattered, small British colonies.

The Fenians played a crucial role. After the terms of Confederation were negotiated, Britain insisted that each colonial government had to accept them. An obstacle emerged in New Brunswick, which had an anti-Confederation government after 1865. The Fenian raids in New Brunswick in the spring of 1866 convinced many voters to seek the security of a larger union, and in that year's election, they returned a pro-Confederation government, which allowed the project to proceed. In Canada, too, the Fenian attacks highlighted the colony's military weakness and reinforced support for Confederation.

The westward growth of the United States was a further concern. Americans had come to accept the concept of manifest destiny, the idea that the United States had a mission to expand over much or all of North America. Minnesota had become a state in 1858, and Oregon in 1859. With the Civil War coming to an end, it was natural to expect that American expansionist impulses would again find an outlet in the West, including the Northwest. The American frontier was extending farther and farther, ever closer to the Hudson's Bay Company's territory in the interior. John A. Macdonald, the driving force behind Confederation, said that he was willing to leave the area "a wilderness for the next half century," but he feared that "if Englishmen do not go there, Yankees will."[11] The Americans were also expanding into the Far West. In the 1860s, large numbers of American prospectors had travelled to British Columbia in search of gold, and the United States was eying Alaska, then a Russian colony. The Russians had first offered to sell it to the United States in 1859, and succeeded in doing so in 1867.

On 1 July 1867, Canada, New Brunswick, and Nova Scotia were united into one country, which took the name Canada. Under the terms of Canada's constitution, the British North America Act, there would be one Canadian government, headquartered in Ottawa, but also a provincial government for each of the four provinces, Nova Scotia, New Brunswick, Ontario, and Quebec. Three other provinces would soon join: Manitoba in 1870, British Columbia in 1871, and Prince Edward Island in 1873. Canada's status was ambiguous: It would be a new creature—a *dominion*— neither a colony nor completely independent. The British monarch continued as head of state. In Ottawa, the queen's duties were discharged by a governor general, appointed by the British government. Canada could neither amend its constitution nor pursue a distinctive foreign policy, but otherwise Canada was able to, and did, govern itself.

The proximity of the United States had pushed the colonies toward union and shaped the nature of Confederation itself. Colonial politicians sought to emulate the best of the United States, while avoiding the weaknesses of the American system, particularly those that had led to the Civil War. The US constitution was "one of the most skilful works which human intelligence ever created," in Macdonald's view. "[It] is one of the most perfect organizations that ever governed a free people."[12] Thus, the fathers of Confederation adopted a federal system, with power divided between Ottawa and the provincial capitals, a system the Americans had pioneered. Unlike their British counterparts, Canadian members of Parliament would be paid, as were American representatives. Electoral districts would be redistributed every decade to take account of shifting populations, again mirroring the practice in the United States, but not in Britain. Yet, the Canadian constitution would give much greater power to the central government to avoid the regional struggles that had culminated in the Civil War. Macdonald had read about the creation of the US constitution and had been influenced by the writings of Alexander Hamilton, a founding father who had argued the US should have a strong national government. Hamilton's colleagues had rejected several of his proposals, but Macdonald now picked them up and slotted them into Canada's constitution. As a result, Canadian senators would serve for life, the federal government would have the power to disallow provincial legislation, and the federal government would hold the residual powers (i.e., any powers not specifically assigned to the provinces)—all ideas that came to Canada courtesy of the debates at the American Constitutional Convention of 1787.

## The Treaty of Washington

Macdonald travelled to Washington in February 1871 with grave misgivings. Canada's first prime minister knew he had to be at the table, as a member of the British delegation, when Britain settled its remaining disputes with the United States. He hoped he could convince the Americans to restore the Reciprocity Treaty, which they had cancelled in anger at the British during the Civil War. At the same time, he was convinced that Britain, worried about Germany's growing strength in Europe, was determined to buy friendship with the Americans, even at the cost of Canada's interests. If the resulting treaty proved unpopular at home, Macdonald would be blamed. "I contemplate my visit to Washington with a good deal of anxiety," he told a friend. "If things go well, my share of the kudos will be but small, and if anything goes wrong I will be made the scapegoat at all events so far as Canada is concerned."[13]

Alongside the other delegates, Macdonald signed the Treaty of Washington on 8 May 1871. Under its terms, Britain apologized for the damage done to Northern shipping during the Civil War by the *Alabama* and other British-built Confederate ships, agreeing to pay compensation in an amount to be determined by a tribunal. (In 1872, the amount was set at $15.5 million.) Canada sought but did not receive reparations for damages done by the Fenians. Macdonald also failed to win a reciprocity agreement to provide for free trade in a wide range of products. The Treaty of Washington did allow for free trade in fish and fish products between Canada and the United States. Canadians and other British subjects would be allowed free access to Lake Michigan, and Americans to the St Lawrence River. For the next 10 years, Americans would be given the right to fish in Canadian waters, and British subjects (including Canadians) given the right to fish in the less abundant American waters north of the 39th parallel (roughly north of Delaware). An international commission would decide how much the United States should pay for the right to fish in Canadian waters. (In 1877, the commission set the amount at $5.5 million.) "Well, here go the fisheries," Macdonald said as he signed the treaty.[14]

The treaty marked the beginning of a new era in Canadian–American relations. No longer would the relationship be characterized by the hostility and the threats of war that had long been typical. Instead, the two would embark on a sustained period of peace and friendship.

# Summary

Despite the tensions that frequently pushed the two sides to the edge of war, there had always been basic underlying similarities between the people of Canada and the United States. Canadian myths, which endure to this day, portray Canada as avoiding the struggle over race that ripped the United States apart in the mid-nineteenth century. But as abolitionists at the time knew, Canada was not so different. Upper Canada abolished slavery at the same time and in the same way as the Northern states, and, like their brothers and sisters across the border, Canadians continued to discriminate against blacks long after emancipation.

The American Civil War was a reminder of the closely intertwined nature of Canadian and US history. As part of the British Empire, Canada and the Maritimes were officially neutral, but the conflict had a profound impact on them. Thrust close to war and subjected to American retaliation, such as the ending of the Reciprocity Treaty, British North America clearly saw its vulnerability to the United States. Urged along by Britain, colonial politicians negotiated the union of British North America into the country we now know as Canada. Still, events south of the border did not just push the colonies together. They also influenced the nature of Canada's constitution, as the colonial politicians strove to create a better America—a country that would enjoy the freedom and prosperity of the United States, while avoiding the sectionalism that had led to the Civil War. In 1871, the Treaty of Washington put an end to an epoch of conflict unleashed by the American Revolution. It finally confirmed that there would be two countries in upper North America: Canada and the United States.

# Beyond the Book

1. Why were there tensions between the United States and British North America during the Civil War?
2. How did events south of the border affect the timing of Canadian Confederation?
3. In what ways did the Canadian fathers of Confederation work to copy the strengths and avoid the weaknesses of the US constitution? Did they succeed?

# Further Reading

The best overview of the black experience in British North America in the nineteenth-century is Robin W. Winks, *The Blacks in Canada: A History*, 2nd ed. (Montreal and Kingston: McGill–Queen's University Press, 1997), a work that is particularly insightful on the Underground Railroad. Allen P. Stouffer shows both the high level of racism in Canada West and the lack of public interest in efforts to do away with slavery in his well-researched book, *The Light of Nature and the Law of God: Antislavery in Ontario, 1833–1877* (Montreal and Kingston: McGill–Queen's University Press, 1992). William H. Pease and Jane H. Pease tell of the efforts to create communities in Upper Canada for fugitive blacks in *Black Utopia: Negro Communal Experiments in America* (Madison: State Historical Society of Wisconsin, 1963). For George Brown's role in the anti-slavery movement, see J.M.S. Careless's classic biography, *Brown of the Globe*, 2 vols. (Toronto: Macmillan, 1959, 1963).

Robin W. Winks, *The Civil War Years: Canada and the United States*, 4th ed. (Montreal and Kingston: McGill–Queen's University Press, 1998), is a superb transnational history of the American Civil War that shows the conflict's impact on politics and identity in British North America. Also valuable is John A. Williams, "Canada and the Civil War," in *Heard Round the World: The Impact Abroad of the Civil War*, edited by Harold Hyman (New York: Alfred A. Knopf, 1969), 257–98; and Amanda Foreman's monumental *A World on Fire: Britain's Crucial Role in the American Civil War* (New York: Random House, 2012).

P.B. Waite's *Life and Times of Confederation: Politics, Newspapers, and the Union of British North America* (Toronto: University of Toronto Press, 1962; Toronto: Robin Brass Studio, 2001) is now more than 50 years old, but remains the best narrative source on Confederation. On the Fenians, see David A. Wilson's tour-de-force, *Thomas D'Arcy McGee*, vol. 2, *The Extreme Moderate, 1857–1868* (Montreal and Kingston: McGill–Queen's University Press, 2011); and Peter Vronsky's superb *Ridgeway: The American Fenian Invasion and the 1866 Battle that Made Canada* (Toronto: Allen Lane, 2011).

## CHAPTER 4

# Wests, 1860–1930

## The Parallel Development of the
## North American West

## Introduction

Chief Sitting Bull might well have been born in Canada. For years, his people, the Hunkpapa Sioux, had hunted on both sides of the border in present-day North Dakota, Manitoba, and Saskatchewan. Neither the Canadian nor the United States government seemed to mind. Then conflict erupted when the US government, in violation of a treaty, encouraged prospectors to look for gold on Sioux territory in the Black Hills, hoping that this would pressure the Sioux to sell their land or renegotiate the treaty. In 1876, the Sioux won the Battle of the Little Big Horn against General George Custer's Seventh Cavalry. Pursued by the US army, Sitting Bull and many of his people, perhaps 5,000 in all, fled to Canada. Once across the border there was no more violence, which to Canadians demonstrated their superiority in dealing with Aboriginal people. Yet Canada did not welcome Sitting Bull and his followers. The Sioux reminded Canadian officials that they had been allied with the British during the American Revolution and the War of 1812, but to no effect. Rather than offering the Sioux a reserve, the Canadian government starved them until they were forced to return to the United States, where they were held as prisoners of war for almost two years.

Both Canadians and Americans have mythologized their countries' westward expansion. Americans moved into a Wild West, where the strongest survived and where the settlers worked out their own rules and government. Canadians established law and order first, in the form of the North-West Mounted Police (NWMP)—the predecessor of the Royal Canadian Mounted Police (RCMP)—before large numbers of settlers arrived. The

American West was characterized by bloodshed, the Canadian West by sta-bility. For Canadians, the differing Western experiences are evidence of a superior Canadian character: Americans are violent, Canadians law-abiding. For Americans, the Wild West is emblematic of the rugged individualism that lies at the core of the American character. Or so the mythologies of the two nations tell us. As with most myths, these contain a hard kernel of truth. But as with most myths, the truth has been exaggerated and distorted.

# Aboriginal People in the Canadian and American Wests

Canadians frequently highlight the treatment of Aboriginal people as evi-dence of how Canada and the United States are different. The assumption is that Canadians lived in peace with the First Nations, while the Americans went to war against them. No one has expressed this point of view more succinctly than journalist Richard Gwyn: "The defining difference" in the Aboriginal policies of the two countries "was that Canadians did not kill Indians."[1] But Aboriginal people did die in conflicts with the Canadian gov-ernment, even if the death toll was much lower than in the United States.

There were differences on the two sides of the border, but they were largely a product of timing. American settlement crossed the Mississippi before 1840, and so Americans were moving into the Great Plains when the Aboriginal people were still economically and militarily strong. By the time large numbers of settlers arrived in the Canadian West, the bison were all but gone, meaning that a starving Aboriginal population was dependent on the government for survival and in no condition to mount an armed resist-ance to Canadian encroachment on traditional Aboriginal lands. One of the most resolute Aboriginal leaders, Big Bear, agreed to a treaty with Canada in 1882, after having held out for six years, rather than see his people starve to death.

Even after the 49th parallel was established as the western boundary between Canada and the United States, Aboriginal people continued to move back and forth across it as though the border did not exist. As one Oglala man said, referring to the piles of rocks that marked the border, "The Great Spirit makes no lines. The buffalo tastes the same on both sides of the stone heaps."[2] Yet over time, Aboriginal people discovered that the border could be useful. They understood that the American military and police would not follow them across the line, and used this knowledge to their advantage. Some signed treaties with both American and Canadian of-ficials. Realizing what was happening, the two governments began working to prevent the easy crossing of the border.

In the 1860s and 1870s, the Metis, a people of mixed Aboriginal and European (primarily French) ancestry, regularly traversed the 49th parallel in pursuit of the ever-dwindling bison, feeling at home on both sides of the border. In the 1860s, many Metis lived in Rupert's Land, a vast stretch of the Northwest owned by the Hudson's Bay Company, but they wintered in Montana and many of them claimed American citizenship. Louis Riel, who would later emerge as their leader, lived two years in Minnesota in the 1860s. "I have two hands, and I have two sides on my head, and I have two countries," he explained.[3]

When Canada arranged to purchase Rupert's Land in the late 1860s, the Metis of the Red River Colony (present-day Winnipeg) mounted a resistance. In 1869, they created a provisional government and insisted that their land could not become part of Canada without their consent. In response, the federal government agreed in 1870 to create the province of Manitoba, guaranteed the language and education rights of the Metis, and promised that they would have title to their land. Yet the government would not grant amnesty to those who had been involved in the execution of one of the provisional government's prisoners, Thomas Scott, who was shot by a firing squad after an ad hoc court found him guilty of insubordination.

When it came time to give the Metis their land, officials from Canada's Dominion Lands Commission, the government agency responsible for surveying and distributing the land in the Canadian prairies, had trouble distinguishing between those Metis who were Canadian, and thus eligible for land (or cash in exchange for abandoning title to the land), and those who were American. Some Metis never got their land. Others were swindled out of it. Still others sold it and left, often because they were being harassed by new settlers, many of whom were Ontario Protestants hostile to the Metis. Many fled Manitoba for the United States, while others settled in communities on the Saskatchewan River or near Fort Edmonton. Riel fled south when he heard rumours that Canadian troops planned to lynch him in retaliation for the execution of Thomas Scott. The Metis leader snuck across the border several times from 1870 to 1884, but spent most of his time in the United States. He worked as an organizer for the Republican Party, became an American citizen, and briefly served as a deputy US marshal. "I think I can help the Metis just as well in this country as another," he wrote to his brother.[4]

By 1884, the Metis on the banks of the Saskatchewan found that they were losing their new land to settlers and to the Canadian Pacific Railway (CPR). They forged alliances with other Aboriginal peoples, including the Plains Cree under Big Bear, who were starving because the government had cut off their rations in a dispute over the location of their reserve. Summoning Riel back from exile in Montana, where he was working as

a schoolteacher, the Metis tried to repeat their success of 1869 to 1870, when
they had forced the federal government
to recognize their land claims and their
education and language rights. In 1885,
the Metis once again took up arms and
elected a provisional government. This
time Canada responded with force, sending troops along the partially completed
CPR. The Metis and their allies were
defeated in a series of battles and skirmishes, in which Canadian forces were
aided by two Gatling guns (early machine
guns), one operated by a representative of
the weapon's American manufacturer, on
leave from his position in the Connecticut
National Guard. The death toll belied the
image of a peaceful Canadian West: an estimated 40 to 70 Aboriginal men (Metis,
Cree, and Assiniboine) and 30 Canadians
(soldiers, policemen, and volunteers).
Many Metis fled to North Dakota or

**Photo 4.1** ✦ Louis Riel

Louis Riel, an American citizen
who led the Metis resistance against
the Canadian government. (Source:
Library and Archives Canada, C-018082.)

Montana. Despite being an American citizen, Riel was found guilty of treason and was hanged, as were eight other Aboriginal men. "The executions
of the Indians," Prime Minister John A. Macdonald wrote to the lieutenant-governor of the North-West Territories, "ought to convince the Red Man
that the White Man governs."[5]

On both sides of the border, governments pursued a common goal,
the assimilation of Aboriginal people. Their approaches had the same three
steps. First, Aboriginal people were moved to lands set aside for them,
called reserves in Canada and reservations in the United States. Second,
they were taught to farm, so they could abandon hunting and other traditional means of feeding themselves. Third, the children were forced into
residential schools, where they were forbidden from speaking their native
languages and were taught about Western civilization. That children were
frequently abused and that these schools violated the terms of several treaties seemed to be of little consequence to either government. To speed up
assimilation, the two governments banned tribal ceremonies, including the
Sun Dance religious ceremony on the Canadian prairies, the large cultural
and trading events in British Columbia known as potlatches, and the Ghost
Dance spiritual movement in the United States. As a result of these policies,
Aboriginal people in both countries faced dispossession and destitution,

followed by dependence and despair. Canada's dealings with the Aboriginal people might have been more peaceful than the experience south of the border, but the outcome was much the same. As political scientist Martin Robin has said, "One cannot excuse a robbery by describing it as orderly."[6]

# Railways

The Canadian Pacific Railway (CPR) is often seen as one of the great accomplishments of Canadian history. Yet the project was truly a North American endeavour. The CPR was modelled on American railroads built with government subsidies. The 1856 Pacific Railroad Act authorized the United States government to finance railroad construction through bonds and land grants. Prime Minister Macdonald's approach was the same, as he acknowledged when he called his government's policy "a humble imitation of that pursued by the American government."[7] In fact, Macdonald's entire approach to national development mirrored a similar US program of protectionism and government support for the development of railways, a policy called "the American system" south of the 49th parallel.

The businessmen who built the railway were Canadian, American, and British, and had already completed another line from Minnesota to Manitoba. The general manager of the CPR was William C. Van Horne, responsible for the construction of most of the line between Callander, Ontario, and the BC interior; he later served 11 years as the company's president. Although he maintained his US citizenship until one year before his death in 1915, Van Horne was a proud Canadian. "To have built that road," one of his contemporaries later observed, "would have made a Canadian out of the German emperor."[8] In 2000, the Canadian Business Hall of Fame declared Van Horne its Laureate of the Century, though some Canadians criticized the choice, insisting that he was not a Canadian.

Many other Americans played prominent roles in the CPR's story. Andrew Onderdonk supervised construction from the West Coast to the BC interior. Thomas Shaughnessy acted as chief purchasing agent and was president of the company after Van Horne stepped down. Chief contractor David C. Shepard built more than 400 miles of the main line along the prairies. Engineer Albert Bowman Rogers found two important routes through the mountains: the Kicking Horse Pass through the Rockies and a pass through the Selkirks, named Rogers Pass in his honour. Before the CPR was complete, James J. Hill, a Canadian-born member of the company's board of directors, left the project to work on an American railroad, the Great Northern, which ran from St Paul, Minnesota, to Seattle, Washington. That meant that at the same time an American (Van Horne) was building a Canadian railway to the Pacific, a Canadian (Hill), was building a parallel line in the United States.

# Law and Order

The Mountie is one of the great symbols of Canada, but the power of the NWMP to establish law and order over the West has been greatly overstated. In 1873, 300 policemen had to cover almost 500,000 square miles of territory. Travel was slow, as Mounties carried not only their own provisions but also food for their horses. They did as well as could be expected under the circumstances, and as a result the Canadian West was never as lawless as the American West. But neither was the Canadian West as orderly as it appears in legend. Bootlegging, gambling, prostitution, and the theft of livestock were all common, as were clashes involving firearms. This should not be surprising. In the late nineteenth century both the American and Canadian Wests were populated by single, young men, often looking for work. They were frequently tempted to steal horses and cattle, to drink alcohol, and to sleep with prostitutes.

The NWMP was an institution created by the government in Ottawa to bring law and order to the West, but it was also very much shaped by the Western experience, right down to the force's uniform and equipment. Horses were originally outfitted with British military saddles, but the men quickly switched to the California saddle, better adapted for prairie riding because it was more durable and more comfortable for both rider and horse. The small standard-issue British pillbox hats provided little protection from the sun, so Mounties began wearing the Stetson, the large American cowboy hat, which became an official part of the uniform in 1901. The original English Snider–Enfield single-shot carbine, a gun similar to but shorter than a rifle, was difficult to reload, especially on horseback. It made way for the American-made Winchester lever-action repeating carbine in 1878.

A quick comparison of the NWMP and the Texas Rangers reveals much about the way the Western environment shaped law enforcement. Both police forces were created with the objective of imposing order on the frontier, and both became the stuff of legend. The two forces dealt with similar populations: Aboriginal people, individuals of mixed European and Aboriginal ancestry, homesteaders, and migrant workers. Both protected the property of wealthy ranchers and railway companies. Both implemented government policies that dispossessed the Aboriginal people. In Texas, the Rangers forcibly pushed the native population into present-day Oklahoma and New Mexico, while in Canada the Mounties confined the First Nations to reserves. If there was one significant difference, it was in the use of force. Although both the Mounties and the Rangers applied force when necessary, the NWMP usually did so with greater reluctance and as a last resort.

# Migration and Settlement

In Canada and the United States, governments pursued virtually identical land settlement policies. The Canadian West was surveyed the same way as the American West: townships of six square miles were created and divided into 36 sections of one square mile, each split into four quarters, making farms of 160 acres each. This contrasted with the situation in Ontario, where farms were 200 acres. The US Homestead Act of 1862 provided the 160-acre plots of land for a small fee to any homesteader living on the land and cultivating it for at least five years. Ten years later, the Canadian Parliament passed the Dominion Lands Act, which also gave 160-acre parcels of land to homesteaders for a nominal fee, requiring them to build a home on the land, live on it, and farm it for a minimum of three years.

The Wests were further shaped by frequent migration across the 49th parallel. Americans went to Canada, and Canadians went to the United States, usually for economic, not political, reasons. Many of Western Canada's original settlers were American, perhaps 750,000 arriving between 1896 and 1931.[9] The proportion of Americans varied from place to place in the Canadian West, being lowest in Manitoba and highest in Alberta. In Medicine Hat, Alberta, for instance, one-third of the population was American-born in 1911.[10] In addition to permanent settlers crossing the border, there were also migrant workers who moved back and forth to work in mining, logging, and fishing; to harvest grain; to build railroads and irrigation projects; and to work on ranches.

Work was largely the same on both sides of the border because the conditions were the same. Rainfall was scarce on the plains and prairies, so Ontario farming methods did not work in the West. Western Canadian farmers had no choice but to use dry-farming techniques from the United States. On both sides of the border, the main crop was wheat, which could be grown under semi-arid conditions. Canadian farmers quickly adopted American agricultural technology, including the grain elevator, the tractor, the mechanical binder, and the combine. Many of the emblems of the American West were ever-present on the Canadian prairies: the cowboy hat, the lariat (a rope with a noose to catch animals), the Western saddle with its deep seat and broad stirrups, the chuckwagon that fed cowboys, and the cattle guard (often called a Texas gate) that kept livestock from crossing roads and railways. The early cattle herds were American, though breeding cattle were later imported from Britain so the Canadian herds would be better suited for a colder climate. One of Canada's great annual events, the Calgary Stampede, was patterned after summer celebrations in the cattle-raising parts of the United States, and was initially developed, promoted, and managed by an American.

The Canadian government was not troubled by the presence of large numbers of Americans in Canada's West. The Liberal minister of the interior from 1896 to 1905, Clifford Sifton, was determined to encourage Americans to settle in Canada. Americans, he said, "were of the finest quality and the most desirable settlers."[11] One immigration official explained why: Americans "understand Canadian conditions . . . immediately on arrival they put large tracts under cultivation . . . they use the most recent machinery . . . and, lastly and most important of all, they employ upon their farms large numbers of immigrants."[12] Sifton established more than 20 immigration offices in the United States, particularly in the Western states. Some were opened in larger cities, such as Chicago and St Louis, but many were located in places where Canadian officials could encourage local farmers to migrate north, places like Crookston, Minnesota; Grafton, North Dakota; Reed City, Michigan; Sandusky, Ohio; Watertown, South Dakota; and Wausau, Wisconsin. The Canadian government placed advertisements in thousands of newspapers and magazines, distributed pamphlets at agricultural fairs, and sent immigration agents through rural areas looking for potential immigrants. The policy continued after Sifton left office, and even after the Conservatives replaced the Liberal government in 1911. That year's Conservative election platform had an anti-American tone, but the new Conservative minister of the interior, Robert Rogers, echoed Sifton when he announced that the government wanted "to get as many settlers from the United States as we can" because the Americans were "highly desirable settlers" with "a knowledge of the conditions prevailing here."[13]

For years, the most common route from Ontario to the prairies was through the US. No railway connected Ontario to Manitoba until 1885. The rocky Canadian Shield, which stretched across northern Ontario and Quebec, deterred farming north of Lake Superior, so settlement proceeded south of the lake through the United States, and then, slowly, back up into Canada. Many of Manitoba's settlers had followed the Red River through northern Minnesota and North Dakota, and then across the 49th parallel. For the same reason, there was no all-Canadian route for mail. In 1870, the US post office agreed that mail from western to eastern Canada could go from Winnipeg to Pembina, North Dakota, before heading through St Paul and Chicago, en route to Windsor, Ontario. Half the men who took part in the famous March West of the first units of the North-West Mounted Police followed this route in reverse. Instead of travelling across Canadian territory from east to west, they went by rail through the United States to Fargo, and then marched north, across the international border.

Because of the path of settlement and because of the commercial ties that developed between Minnesota and Manitoba, Minnesota business and political leaders became increasingly interested in taking over the Canadian

West. Confederation came about, at least in part, because Canadians wanted to ensure that they could grab the Northwest before Americans did. When in 1868 the British Parliament agreed to Canada's purchase of Rupert's Land, which included most of the territory between Ontario and British Columbia, the Minnesota legislature passed a resolution regretting that this was being done without a vote of the residents "who largely consist of emigrants from the United States." For the Minnesotans, this was an "unwarrantable interference with the principle of self-government."[14] The close ties between Manitoba and Minnesota continued after Canada annexed the territory. Winnipeg was connected by rail to St Paul in 1878, five years before the Canadian Pacific Railway linked Manitoba's capital to eastern Canada.

# Race

Canadians like to contrast their country's immigration policies with those of the United States, imagining that Canada is a mosaic that welcomes peoples from other lands, while the United States is a melting pot that forces conformity. Yet, in the late nineteenth and early twentieth centuries, the two countries had remarkably similar attitudes toward immigration, particularly when it came to immigrants from Asia. On both sides of the border, governments took steps to keep Asians out on the pretense that they drove down wages, carried disease, and undermined morals. The 1882 Chinese Exclusion Act imposed a ban on the entry of Chinese labourers to the United States. The same year, Prime Minister John A. Macdonald told the House of Commons that he shared the American feeling against Chinese immigrants: "I believe they would not be a wholesome element for this country. I believe it is an alien race in every sense, that would not and could not be expected to assimilate with our Arian population."[15] Still, because low-wage labour was needed to build the CPR, Macdonald resisted calls from trade unions and the government of British Columbia to stop Asian immigration. Immediately after the completion of the railway in 1885, the government imposed a head tax of $50 on each Chinese immigrant entering the country. The measure achieved its objective. The number of Chinese immigrants to Canada fell from 2,762 in 1884 to 212 in 1886. After taking office in 1896, Wilfrid Laurier's Liberals maintained the policy, even raising the head tax, first in 1900 to $100 and then in 1903 to $500, more than one year's wages for the average industrial worker.[16] The Chinese Immigration Act of 1923 (often known by the name of its American equivalent, the Chinese Exclusion Act) stopped virtually all immigration from China to Canada. Both Canada and the United States barred Chinese immigration until the 1940s.

In 1907, opposition leader Robert Borden spoke for many when he said, "We must not allow our shores to be over-run with Asiatics and become dominated by an alien race. British Columbia must remain a white man's country."[17] Anti-Asian riots broke out in Vancouver in 1907, with whites chanting racist slogans and breaking shop windows, causing thousands of dollars of damage to Asian-owned businesses. It took police four hours to quell the disturbance. The same year, the US and Japan negotiated a "gentlemen's agreement" on immigration. Japan would stop issuing passports to citizens wishing to immigrate to the US, except for certain businessmen and professionals. In exchange, the US government would work to end the segregation of Japanese students, often not allowed to attend the same schools as white children. In December 1907, Canada followed suit, negotiating its own "gentlemen's agreement" with Japan. In this case, Japan agreed to limit the number of immigrants to Canada to 400 per year. Many other discriminatory measures followed in both Canada and the United States.

One group of Americans also suffered from Canada's racist immigration policy. Blacks in Oklahoma had looked north for refuge after the state legislature began passing a series of discriminatory acts in 1907. The new laws forced African-Americans to attend segregated schools and ride in separate sections in streetcars and railway cars. No longer could blacks vote or marry non-blacks. These measures were punctuated by violence, including occasional lynchings. In 1908, blacks began moving from Oklahoma to the areas around Wildwood, Alberta, and Maidstone, Saskatchewan. By 1912, more than 1,000 had settled in the two provinces.

Blacks thought they would live in peace, away from the racism that had driven them from Oklahoma, but they encountered hostility in Canada as well. In Canada, the racial stereotypes were similar to those in the United States. *Strangers within Our Gates*, a book by a Methodist minister, J.S. Woodsworth, later a prominent politician celebrated for his high morals, was typical in its attitude toward blacks. Backing up his position with quotations from supposed experts, Woodsworth portrayed blacks as musical, amoral, unsanitary, unstable, impulsive, lazy, and highly sexualized.[18] In 1910, the Edmonton Board of Trade passed a resolution calling on the federal government to stop the immigration of blacks, described as "the most undesirable element."[19] Other boards of trade quickly endorsed the Edmonton position. In August 1911, the federal Cabinet responded by issuing an order-in-council that blocked blacks from immigrating, because their "race is deemed unsuitable to the climate and requirements of Canada."[20] The government quickly had second thoughts, rescinded the order in October, and embarked on a more subtle plan. Canadian agents were dispatched to Oklahoma to convince blacks not to migrate north by recounting exaggerated tales of a cold, desolate land, where schools, doctors, and churches were scarce, where food was expensive, where the drinking water made people sick, and where racism was rampant. The approach worked, and black immigration to Canada all but stopped.

In the 1920s, the Ku Klux Klan (KKK) spilled into Canada. Originally formed after the American Civil War by white supremacists, the KKK was revived in 1915 and began carrying out violent attacks against blacks. Local chapters (or klaverns, as they were called) sprung up across Canada. In British Columbia, the Klan used American membership forms, which required the applicant to declare allegiance to the constitution of the United States. The organization was active in anti-Asian campaigns in BC and in stirring up prejudice against Catholics, francophones, and East European immigrants in Alberta and Saskatchewan. In Manitoba, the Klan issued threats against the Catholic St Boniface College in 1922, which was torched later in the year, killing 10 students. The Canadian KKK was strongest in Saskatchewan, where 7,000 to 10,000 people attended the organization's 1927 Konclave in Moose Jaw. In 1929, the KKK played a role in defeating the Liberal government in that province's election. By then, it had more than 100 branches in Saskatchewan and an estimated 10,000 to 50,000 members.[21]

# Western Protest

Beginning in the late nineteenth century, Western farmers in both Canada and the United States increasingly felt that their country's wealth was not evenly distributed and that eastern interests were becoming rich at the farmers' expense. Railway companies charged unreasonably high rates to transport grain and equipment, banks were overly quick to foreclose on farms, and the price of grain was too low for farmers to survive. Canadian farmers also believed that the tariff was designed to enrich eastern manufacturers, by forcing consumers to buy domestic manufactured goods instead of less expensive items from across the border.

Farmers began to set up cooperative organizations to break the power of the eastern establishment. The 1890s saw the creation of the California State Raisin Growers Association, the Hood River Growers Union, and the Southern Californian Fruit Exchange. These organizations lobbied governments on behalf of farmers and worked to eliminate the middleman in the sale of their products. To increase prices, they pooled commodities and sold them through a central organization. In Canada, the Grain Growers' Grain Company (later the United Grain Growers) was created after a Saskatchewan farmer noted the success of the Minnesota Farmers' Exchange. In the 1920s, the idea of pooling grain spread throughout Western Canada with the help of Aaron Sapiro of Chicago, an activist who had helped develop the California Fruit Growers Exchange and the Oregon Growers Co-operative. Sapiro inspired the creation of the Alberta Cooperative Wheat Producers and other organizations for the cooperative selling of Western Canadian grain.

Farmers became active in party politics, too. In 1909, the United Farmers of Alberta (UFA), an organization with strong American ties, was founded to defend farmers' interests. It eventually evolved into a political party led by Henry Wise Wood. In 1918, eight of the nineteen members of the UFA's executive and board of directors, including Wood, were American-born.[22] In the US, the Nonpartisan League originated in 1915 in North Dakota and spread to surrounding states, advocating public ownership of grain elevators, flourmills, and other agricultural services. In 1916, the League's candidate, Lynn J. Frazier, became state governor, and by 1918, the League had control of both houses of the state legislature. An American-born farmer from Saskatchewan, S.E. Haight, worked for the league in North Dakota for a few months in 1916 and then established a Canadian branch on his return home. The organization was similar on both sides of the border, pushing for the same reforms and using the same slogans. The League's newsletters in Saskatchewan and Alberta regularly reprinted articles from their counterpart in North Dakota.

In the 1920s, economic conditions exacerbated Western discontent on both sides of the border. Although that decade was a period of overall economic growth in North America, farmers did not prosper. During the First World War, production of grain had dropped in Europe, as millions of men were fighting rather than farming and as large areas of arable land were turned into battlegrounds. This meant that demand for North American agricultural products increased, as did prices. But Europeans did not need as much North American grain after the end of the war in 1918, which in turn resulted in a dramatic drop in prices. In Canada, the wholesale price for a bushel of wheat, the predominant crop, plummeted from $2.24 in 1918 to $1.30 in 1921 and to $1.07 in 1923.[23] As farm incomes fell, banks foreclosed on farmers who could not pay their mortgages. The US response to these problems—raising tariffs—only made the situation worse.

Many in the American West began voting for farmers' parties, including several parties that had made alliances with organized labour. In the Southwest, the Oklahoma Farmer–Labor Reconstruction League worked within the Democratic Party and was successful in electing one of its own, Jack Walton, as governor in 1922. In Minnesota, the Nonpartisan League evolved into the Farmer–Labor Party, which managed to elect two candidates to the US Senate in the 1920s and four to the House of Representatives. In the 1930s, three successive governors of Minnesota were members of the Farmer–Labor Party. In Idaho, the Nonpartisan League became the

Idaho Progressive Party and elected a few members to the state legislature. Farmers' parties were less successful at the national level, though several senators and representatives formed the bipartisan Farm Bloc to regulate prices and make credit more easily available to farmers.

Farmers had more political success in Canada. With the help of the Nonpartisan League, the United Farmers of Alberta came to power in 1921 and remained the governing party in Alberta until 1935. In 1922, the United Farmers of Manitoba won the provincial election, changed names to the Progressive Party of Manitoba, and formed a government that held office until 1932. On the federal scene, Western farmers found voice through the Progressive Party of Canada, created in 1920. In the federal election of 1921, the Progressives placed second, winning more seats than the ruling Conservative Party. Like members of the Nonpartisan League, they pushed for an end to party discipline and for elected representatives to reflect the views of their constituents. Prime Minister William Lyon Mackenzie King was able to lure many Progressives into the Liberal fold by reducing both the tariff on farm equipment and the freight rate for grain. By the 1930s, the Progressive Party had collapsed, though Western discontent continued. In 1932, several former Nonpartisan League activists, including J.S. Woodsworth and Salem Bland, were instrumental in founding the Co-operative Commonwealth Federation, a socialist party that was forerunner to today's New Democratic Party.

# Summary

The Canadian and American Wests were different places, settled in different periods, but a similar environment meant that they had much in common. Settlers used the same farming techniques and had a similar reliance on railways, which required large government subsidies to be constructed. Both Wests were frontier societies that struggled in the nineteenth century to establish law and order. Both governments sought to deal with the presence of Aboriginal people by dispossessing and assimilating them, though American authorities were more likely to resort to violence. And both countries sought to limit non-white immigration. The parallel development of the American Great Plains and the Canadian prairies continued well into the 1920s, when farmers in the two countries felt a common distrust of the eastern establishment and sought comparable political solutions to their problems.

# Beyond the Book

1.  In what ways was the Canadian Pacific Railway a distinctly Canadian project and how was it more a North American enterprise?
2.  How did the Western experience shape the North-West Mounted Police?

3.  To what extent were protest movements in the US and Canadian West shaped by the Western environment as opposed to nationality?
4.  What light does the history of the Canadian and American Wests shed on the common assumption among Canadians that their country has not experienced the racism common in the United States?

# Further Reading

Borderlands histories of the West include Paul F. Sharp's classic *Whoop-Up Country: The Canadian–American West, 1865–1885* (Minneapolis: University of Minnesota Press, 1955); and Beth LaDow's superb *Medicine Line: Life and Death on a North American Borderland* (New York: Routledge, 2001). Sheila McManus's *The Line Which Separates: Race, Gender, and the Making of the Alberta–Montana Borderlands* (Edmonton: University of Alberta Press, 2005) sparkles on a range of topics, including the mapping of the border between the crest of the Rockies and the Lake of the Woods, homesteading policies, and government relations with the Blackfoot. For a sense of the historical West, one that scholars often have trouble capturing, read Wallace Stegner's brilliant *Wolf Willow* (New York: Viking, 1962), a book that is part history, part memoir, and part novel. Randy William Widdis's *With Scarcely a Ripple: Anglo–Canadian Migration into the United States and Western Canada, 1880–1920* (Montreal and Kingston: McGill–Queen's University Press, 1998) takes a balanced approach, neither ignoring nor overstating American influences on the Canadian West.

On the Canadian government's desire to expand westward to keep the prairies out of American hands, see Hugh G.J. Aitken, "Defensive Expansionism: The State and Economic Growth in Canada," in *The State and Economic Growth*, edited by Hugh G.J. Aitken (New York: Social Science Research Council, 1959), 79–114. Canadian efforts to encourage American immigration are the subject of Harold Martin Troper, *Only Farmers Need Apply: Official Canadian Government Encouragement of Immigration from the United States* (Toronto: Griffin House, 1972). Richard White takes a transnational approach to railways in *Railroaded: The Transcontinentals and the Making of Modern America* (New York: W.W. Norton, 2011). A.A. Den Otter presents the CPR as "primarily a co-operative business enterprise between Canadian and American capitalists" in "Nationalism and the Pacific Scandal," *Canadian Historical Review* 69, no. 3 (September 1988): 315–39.

Andrew R. Graybill explores the similarities and differences between two police forces in *Policing the Great Plains: Rangers, Mounties, and the North American Frontier, 1875–1910* (Lincoln: University of Nebraska Press, 2007). Charles Wilkins's *The Wild Ride: A History of the North West Mounted Police, 1873–1904* (Vancouver: Stanley Atkins and Dosil, 2010) is a glossy picture book with no footnotes and a limited bibliography, but do not be fooled: it is not only a pleasure to read but also a work of sound scholarship.

On Aboriginal people, see David G. McCrady, *Living with Strangers: The Nineteenth-Century Sioux and the Canadian–American Borderlands* (Lincoln: University of Nebraska Press, 2006), an inspired example of borderlands history.

Also excellent is Roger L. Nichols, *Indians in the United States and Canada: A Comparative History* (Lincoln: University of Nebraska Press, 1998). Jill St Germain argues that the main difference between US and Canadian Aboriginal policies relates to demographics and economics, not objectives; see her *Indian Treaty-Making Policy in the United States and Canada, 1867–1877* (Toronto: University of Toronto Press, 2001). In *Unsettling the Settler Within: Indian Residential Schools, Truth Telling, and Reconciliation in Canada* (Vancouver: UBC Press, 2010), Paulette Regan talks about the "settler myth" of Canadian virtue toward Aboriginal people. On Louis Riel, the best source remains George F.G. Stanley's *Louis Riel* (Toronto: Ryerson, 1963). There is still much of value in Stanley's *The Birth of Western Canada: A History of the Riel Rebellions* (1936; Toronto: University of Toronto Press, 1961).

On ranching, see Warren M. Elofson's *Cowboys, Gentlemen and Cattle Thieves: Ranching on the Western Frontier* (Montreal and Kingston: McGill–Queen's University Press, 2000) and his "Law and Disorder on the Ranching Frontiers of Montana and Alberta/Assiniboia, 1870–1914," *Journal of the West* 42, no. 1 (Winter 2003): 40–51.

W.L. Morton's *The Progressive Party of Canada* (Toronto: University of Toronto Press, 1950) provides a sophisticated analysis of the roots of Western discontent. A superb study of the power of the American model can be found in Ian MacPherson's "Selected Borrowings: The American Impact upon the Prairie Co-operative Movement, 1920–39," *Canadian Review of American Studies* 10, no. 2 (Fall 1979): 137–51.

On racism, readers should consult Julian Sher, *White Hoods: Canada's Ku Klux Klan* (Vancouver: New Star Books, 1983); and Martin Robin, *Shades of Right: Nativist and Fascist Politics in Canada, 1920–1940* (Toronto: University of Toronto Press, 1992). On the experience of Chinese immigrants to Canada, see Timothy J. Stanley's superb book, *Contesting White Supremacy: School Segregation, Anti-Racism, and the Making of Chinese Canadians* (Vancouver: UBC Press, 2011); and Lisa Rose Mar's *Brokering Belonging: Chinese Canadians in Canada's Exclusion Era, 1885–1945* (Toronto: University of Toronto Press, 2010). These should be read alongside Erika Lee's *At America's Gates: Chinese Immigration during the Exclusion Era, 1882–1943* (Chapel Hill: University of North Carolina Press, 2003). Sarah-Jane Mathieu deals with the treatment of black immigrants in *North of the Color Line: Migration and Black Resistance in Canada, 1870–1955* (Chapel Hill: University of North Carolina Press, 2010). R. Bruce Shepard looks at black immigration from Oklahoma in *Deemed Unsuitable* (Toronto: Umbrella, 1997).

# CHAPTER 5

# Destinies, 1871–1914

## Competing Visions of Canada's Future

## Introduction

"Gentlemen, Sir John Macdonald is dead," announced Joseph Pope, the prime minister's private secretary.[1] For 40 years the dominant figure in Canadian politics, Macdonald had died peacefully on a sunny June day in 1891. Two days later, there arrived at the house an elegant steel casket with a rosewood finish and with oxidized silver handles running its entire length and at each end. Macdonald's remains were taken to lay in state in the Senate chamber before a funeral at St Alban's Church in Ottawa's Sandy Hill neighbourhood. Then the casket travelled by train to Macdonald's home town of Kingston, where he lay at city hall before his burial beside his parents, his first wife, and his sisters at Cataraqui Cemetery.

Just three months earlier, Macdonald had scored a resounding victory—his sixth—in the federal election, which he had won in part by campaigning against a Liberal plan for free trade with the United States. But in death, Macdonald could not escape the Americans. His casket, manufactured in West Meriden, Connecticut, was a replica of the one used for US president James Garfield in 1881. We do not know why his survivors chose this casket, but for them it made sense to purchase a product manufactured in the United States. The casket was just one illustration of the difficulty of resisting the American influence. Canadians benefitted from being able to purchase American products, often cheaper or of higher quality than their Canadian equivalents. Still, most Canadians rejected freer trade with the United States because they did not want to be Americanized. Slowly, though, Canadians came to realize that they could be distinct within North America without having to appropriate the identity of the United States or Britain.

# Relations between Ottawa and Washington

Fisheries were a perennial issue in Canadian–American relations. The 1871 Treaty of Washington had allowed Americans to fish in Canadian coastal waters and had required the United States to pay for this right, the precise sum to be established later by an international commission. When the amount was set at $5.5 million in 1877, Americans were outraged, seeing the figure as absurdly high. At the first opportunity, they took advantage of a treaty provision that allowed them to reject the fisheries clauses, effective 1885. This meant that US vessels no longer had the right to fish in Canadian waters, which under international law extended three miles from the coast, often areas where fish were most abundant. Canadians vigorously enforced control over their waters, even preventing US vessels from entering Canadian harbours. In one extreme case, a US ship docked in Prince Edward Island, where the sailors purchased some potatoes. Wanting to completely nullify the transaction, local authorities not only insisted that the potatoes be returned to the seller, but also forced the seamen who had eaten some of the potatoes to take an emetic, a substance to induce vomiting.

In 1887, Britain and the US entered into negotiations to settle the issue, with one Canadian, Sir Charles Tupper, serving as a member of the British delegation. The result was the 1888 Chamberlain–Bayard Treaty, named after the chief negotiators, US Secretary of State Thomas F. Bayard and British member of Parliament Joseph Chamberlain. The US would remove its tariffs on Canadian fish, and American ships would be allowed to offload their catch, purchase bait and supplies, and hire seamen in Canadian ports. Anticipating that the US Senate might reject the treaty, the negotiators also agreed to a two-year *modus vivendi*, allowing US ships to conduct business in Canadian harbours upon payment of a licence fee. The negotiators had foresight: the Senate said no to the treaty, but the two countries honoured the *modus vivendi*, renewing it repeatedly until the issue was finally settled in 1910. In that year, an arbitration tribunal ruled that Canada could require American vessels to report to custom houses when entering a Canadian port but could neither compel them to pay harbour fees beyond those imposed on Canadian ships nor prevent them from employing Canadian sailors.

The hunting of seals for their furs proved to be another source of conflict. An American company leased the rights to hunt on the Pribilof Islands, an important breeding ground for seals in Alaska. British Columbians began sealing in the Bering Sea, beyond the American three-mile limit. Concerned that the seals were being overhunted, US Treasury Department ships started seizing Canadian vessels in 1886, a departure from the traditional American position in support of freedom of the seas. Both sides agreed to arbitration in 1892, with a tribunal ruling in 1893 that the US had no right to protect the seals beyond its three-mile limit and ordering that compensation be paid for the vessels that the US had seized. The American government offered $425,000, an amount the British accepted on Canada's behalf.

The Alaska Boundary Dispute was the most bitter of the disagreements between Canada and the United States in the late nineteenth and early twentieth centuries. The United States had purchased Alaska from Russia in 1867. The territory's boundaries were defined in an 1825 treaty between Russia and Britain, but, as was often the case in nineteenth-century treaties, the agreement's description of the border did not match the landscape, particularly when it came to the Alaska Panhandle, a narrow strip of land separating northern British Columbia and southern Yukon from the Pacific Ocean. The border was to follow either "the summit of the mountains situated parallel to the coast" or a line 56 kilometres from the coast, whichever was closer to the coast.[2] Yet it was not apparent which mountains the boundary should follow in the absence of a defined range. Nor was it clear how to delineate the coast, which was jagged, with countless bays, inlets, and fjords.

The unresolved boundary caused no significant problems until gold was discovered in the Yukon's Klondike region in 1896 and tens of thousands of prospectors hurried to the area. The easiest route to the gold was up the Lynn Canal through the Alaska Panhandle. Depending on how the border was drawn, Canadian prospectors going from Canadian waters to Canadian territory in the Yukon might have to set foot on US soil and clear US customs.

Canada was in a weak position in the Alaskan dispute because global power was slowly shifting away from Britain and toward the United States. In the late nineteenth century, Germany had launched a naval-building program, which the British feared might threaten their traditional supremacy at sea. With tensions mounting in Europe, the British came to believe that friendship with the US was crucial. In a series of disagreements between 1895 and 1905, Britain backed down in the face of American power. In the Venezuelan Boundary Dispute of 1895 to 1896, Britain gave up its claim over the border between Venezuela and British Guyana when confronted with American threats. In the Hay–Pauncefote Treaty of 1901, Britain allowed the United States to build a canal through Panama to link the Atlantic and Pacific Oceans, surrendering British rights in the area without compensation. The Panama Canal further strengthened the American strategic position by allowing the US Navy easy access to two oceans.

Canada was also vulnerable because the government did not have convincing legal arguments against the American claim in Alaska. Neither Britain nor Canada had ever protested the US exercise of sovereignty in the region, not objecting, for instance, when Americans founded the communities of Dyea and Skagway. The disputed area appeared as US territory on

Canadian maps, including a map that hung in the Parliament buildings in Ottawa. The Canadian position was so flimsy that not even the country's officials were convinced of its merits. O.J. Klotz, a surveyor working for the Department of the Interior, went to Alaska in 1889 to investigate, returning to say that the American claim was well founded. In 1898, the government sent Klotz to Britain and Russia to study the documents related to the Russian–British treaty that had defined Alaska's boundaries. When he came back without any evidence to support Canada's claim, Prime Minister Wilfrid Laurier refused to see him. For Klotz, the Canadian position was "utterly untenable and dishonest." Laurier and his advisers could ignore him, Klotz said, but they could not ignore the facts, "which they will be forced to face before the matter is settled."[3] Canadian officials knew they were in a poor position, but they also feared a public backlash should they give in to the Americans. They entered a fight they had virtually no chance of winning.

US President Theodore Roosevelt had no patience for Canadian stubbornness, which he described as "an outrage pure and simple." He rejected any compromise and refused to allow the matter to go to arbitration. He agreed that a joint British–American panel could settle the precise location of the border, but made it clear that he would instruct the American representatives "not to yield any territory whatsoever, but as a matter of course to insist upon our entire claim."[4] He dispatched 800 troops to the area and declared that he was prepared to use force if necessary, letting the British know that he was "going to be ugly."[5]

In January 1903, the United States and Britain agreed to each appoint three impartial legal experts to a commission charged with fixing the border. The British chose Lord Alverstone, chief justice of England; Louis Jetté, lieutenant-governor of Quebec and a former member of the Quebec Supreme Court; and George Armour of the Supreme Court of Canada. When Armour died before the tribunal began its work, he was replaced by Allen B. Aylesworth, a distinguished lawyer who had once declined an appointment to the Supreme Court. Canadians were incensed at Roosevelt's choices: Secretary of War Elihu Root; Senator Henry Cabot Lodge, who had publicly denounced Canada's claim and had once called for the American annexation of Canada; and Senator George Turner, who had also openly criticized Canada's position. The situation was worse than the Canadian public ever knew. Roosevelt had sent written instructions to the American commissioners, telling them that "in the principle involved, there will, of course, be no compromise."[6] He had also talked of using force, a threat that had made its way to Lord Alverstone.

Given Roosevelt's choice of commissioners and his bullying of the British, the outcome was a foregone conclusion, though Canada's case was so weak that the US would no doubt have won even had the matter gone before a truly impartial panel. The commission's October 1903 ruling, supported by the three Americans and by Lord Alverstone, upheld the American claim in all significant respects. In the disputed area, Canada received only one unimportant canal and two minor islands. The Canadian commissioners were incensed, refused to sign the ruling, and issued a public statement denouncing the process: "We have been compelled to witness the sacrifice of the interests of Canada. We were powerless to prevent it."[7] Alverstone responded haughtily: "If . . . they don't want a decision based on the law and the evidence, they must not put a British judge on the commission."[8]

The Canadian media was outraged, more at Britain than the United States. Canadian interests had been sacrificed, according to the Toronto *News*, "to the paramount desire of Great Britain to cultivate the good opinion of the United States." The *Ottawa Journal* suggested that Canada should take full control over its international relations. An independent Canada might well be robbed and bullied by the United States, but that was already happening. "The only difference now is that Englishmen inform us that it is justice and have the right to compel us to accept it as justice."[9]

After the Alaska boundary dispute, Canada became more determined to deal directly with the United States, rather than through Britain. The government created a tiny, unpretentious Department of External Affairs in 1909 and negotiated a series of treaties with the United States, though Britain still needed to countersign the final documents, as Canada did not have the power to enter into treaties on its own.

Many of the agreements related to a growing concern in both Canada and the United States over environmental conservation. The disappearance of the bison and the extinction of the passenger pigeon, both species once abundant in North America, raised concerns about the state of the natural world. The conservation movement gained a boost when Theodore Roosevelt became US president and began a passionate campaign to protect the environment, creating national parks, bird sanctuaries, and game preserves. Roosevelt understood that the United States could not act alone: "It is evident that natural resources are not limited by the boundary lines which separate nations, and that the need for conserving them upon this continent is as wide as the area upon which they exist."[10]

Over a period of eight years, Canada and the United States negotiated four agreements to protect the environment, three of them dealing with wildlife. Spurred on by declining fish stocks, the Inland Fisheries Treaty of 1908 created a commission to recommend common Canadian–American rules for fishing in the lakes, bays, and rivers that crossed the international boundary. The commission did its work, but the US House of Representatives refused to pass the necessary legislation to implement the regulations. The North Pacific Fur Seal Convention of 1911, which included Canada, the United States, Japan, and Russia, limited the hunting of seals, whose numbers were rapidly dwindling. The 1916 Migratory Birds Convention restricted or banned the hunting of various species of birds. The initiative for this agreement had come from the United States, where the conservation movement was pressing the federal government to protect wildlife. It proved to be a milestone in the history of environmental protection.

The fourth agreement was the 1909 Boundary Waters Treaty, which established the International Joint Commission (IJC) to deal with the use of water resources along the border and to prevent pollution of those waters. The IJC would be a permanent body composed of Canadians and Americans, with no representation from Britain. It was the first effort to institutionalize the relationship by creating permanent intergovernmental organizations to manage Canadian–American affairs.

## The Conservation Movement

The conservation movement had developed on both sides of the border, sparked in part by American politician, diplomat, and linguist George Perkins Marsh. Marsh had been born and raised in Woodstock, Vermont, about 200 kilometres south of Quebec, and had practised law in Burlington, Vermont, where Canadian lumber passed en route to New York along Lake Champlain. His 1864 book *Man and Nature* warned about the destruction of North American forests and led first to a campaign for forest conservation, and then to a broader movement to protect all renewable resources. Conservationists quickly understood that the Canadian and American ecosystems were one, and that conservation efforts had to operate in both countries.

In those early days, leadership came from Americans. Canadian conservationists were deeply influenced by the ideas of John Muir, founder of the Sierra Club, one of the world's first environmental organizations. Muir had lived for two years in Canada while avoiding the military draft during the American Civil War. Another giant of the movement was Gifford Pinchot, the US chief forester and a key speaker at a Canadian conference on forest conservation in January 1906. The American Forestry Association initially functioned as a North American organization, drawing Canadian members and holding its 1882 annual meeting in Montreal. Only in 1900 was the Canadian Forestry Association founded.

When it came to conservation, the Canadian government seemed content to follow the American lead. The American Congress passed the Forest Reserve Act in 1891, 17 years before the equivalent Canadian legislation. US President Theodore Roosevelt created the National Conservation Commission in 1908; Canada followed suit the next year with the Commission of Conservation. At Roosevelt's invitation, delegates from Canada, Newfoundland, the United States, and Mexico met in Washington, DC, in 1909 for the North American Conservation Conference.

# The National Policy

For decades after the Americans had withdrawn from the Reciprocity Treaty of 1854, both Liberals and Conservatives in Canada had wanted to re-establish some measure of free trade with the United States. John A. Macdonald's Conservative government had tried to talk the US out of abrogating the treaty and had sent emissaries to Washington in 1865 and 1869 in search of a new agreement. In 1871, as a member of the British delegation that negotiated the Treaty of Washington, Macdonald tried and failed to include a section on trade in the agreement. After Macdonald lost power in 1873, Prime Minister Alexander Mackenzie's Liberals took up the reciprocity cause. Canada and the US drafted a trade treaty in 1874, but the American Senate rejected it.

Realizing that the Americans would not soon agree to reciprocity, and always willing to exploit a political opportunity, Macdonald slid back into power in the 1878 election by promising higher tariffs. Implemented in stages beginning in 1879, Macdonald's National Policy was protectionist, consisting of tariffs high enough to discourage the import of manufactured products and in this way protect domestic industry from foreign competition. On most goods, tariffs rose from 17.5 per cent to between 20 and 35 per cent. The average duty increased from 21.4 per cent in 1878 to 26.1 per cent in 1880, to 31.9 per cent in 1888.[11]

Although Macdonald called his plan the National Policy, it was hardly nationalist at all. The tariff favoured Ontario and Quebec over the rest of the country, thus straining national unity. Animosity grew in the Maritimes, which initially benefitted from the National Policy, but then experienced a long, slow process of deindustrialization as companies consolidated their operations in Ontario and Quebec. Maritimers joked that the N.P., as the policy was often known, stood for National Poverty, not National Policy. Resentment was so powerful that in 1886 the Nova Scotia government of Premier W.S. Fielding was re-elected on a platform calling for his province to secede from Canada. In the West, people resented having to buy more expensive products from central Canada instead of cheaper American goods, often better suited to their needs. One example was the breaking plough. A Canadian-made 12-inch plough could be purchased in Winnipeg in 1882 for $22, but it was designed for the sandy and rocky soil of central and eastern Canada. Western farmers wanted John Deere's American-made Prairie Queen plough, which would

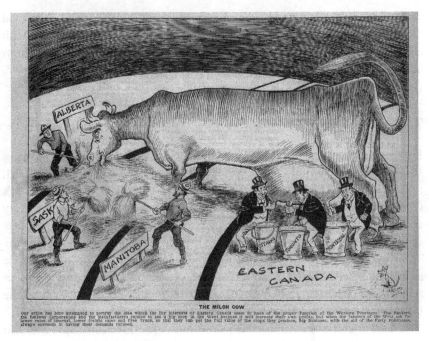

THE MILCH COW

Our artist has here attempted to portray the idea which the Big Interests of Eastern Canada seem to have of the proper function of the Western Provinces. The Bankers, the Railway Corporations and the Manufacturers rejoice to see a big crop in the West because it will increase their own profits, but when the farmers of the West ask for lower rates of interest, lower freight rates and Free Trade, so that they can get the full value of the crops they produce, Big Business, with the aid of the Party Politicians, always succeeds in having their demands refused.

**Photo 5.1 ✦ The Milch Cow**

Arch Dale's depiction of the National Policy, published in the Grain Growers' Guide in 1915. (Source: Glenbow Archives, NA-3055-24.)

have sold for less than the Canadian plough, but ended up costing $25, once the 35 per cent tariff was factored in.[12] Canada's pre-eminent political cartoonist, Arch Dale, summarized the western Canadian view of the tariff in an iconic drawing in which the National Policy is a cow, fed by Western Canadian grain and providing its milk to Central Canadian bankers and politicians. The Maritimes were not included in the cartoon, but it did not take much imagination to figure out what was left for them.

Economists have concluded that the National Policy lowered the Canadian standard of living, rather than raising it as its supporters claimed. The tariff increased the cost of manufactured goods, thus reducing the spending power of Canadians. It also created an inefficient economy, which produced small runs of virtually every product, rather than encouraging specialization in those items that Canada could manufacture most competitively. As a result of the policy, the average Canadian income was 1 to 5 per cent lower than it would otherwise have been, depending on which estimate one accepts.[13]

The National Policy also encouraged a large amount of American investment in Canada. Conservative MP John Charles Rykert explained the reason clearly: "The Americans, if debarred from our markets, would start manufacturing establishments here."[14] The high levels of foreign investment in Canada began to spark concern in the mid-twentieth century, but the roots of the phenomenon were much earlier. Geography, a common language, and a similar culture had long made Canada a logical place for American investors, but the Macdonald government provided a much greater incentive with the National Policy.

The most skilled Canadian politician of his age, Macdonald cleverly wrapped his high tariffs in a patriotic package. By using the term *National Policy*, by emphasizing that protectionism would lead to the development of industry in Canada, and by arguing that it would prevent American annexation, Macdonald turned the tariff into a national symbol and an emblem of Canadian loyalty to the British Empire in the face of the American presence. Macdonald portrayed the National Policy as a program to keep Canada British, but the policy discriminated against all imports, including those from the United Kingdom. Canadian trade with the United States grew at a much faster rate than Canadian trade with Britain during the National Policy era, which lasted until the 1930s.

Although in public Macdonald equated protectionism with patriotism, he never fully gave up on freer trade. The National Policy legislation contained provisions to allow the government to reduce or eliminate tariffs on some natural products if the US agreed to do the same. During the debate on the National Policy, Macdonald argued that his program would force the Americans to enter into a trade agreement with Canada: "It is only by closing our doors, and by cutting them out of our markets, that they will open theirs to us."[15]

In December 1890, with an election looming, Macdonald tried to undermine the Liberal platform, built around a policy of complete free trade, or unrestricted reciprocity in the language of the day. He proposed to the Americans that the two countries should negotiate a reciprocity agreement. Then, on the eve of the 1891 election, he asked if he could make these preliminary discussions public. US Secretary of State James G. Blaine refused, publicly denying rumours that negotiations were taking place. The election went ahead, with Macdonald going on the attack in a virtuoso performance of political deceit. Unrestricted reciprocity, he told the voters, would "inevitably result" in the American annexation of Canada. He accused the Liberals of "veiled treason" and promised to fight with his "utmost effort" any attempts "to lure our people from their allegiance."[16] Macdonald won the election of March 1891, his Conservatives winning 117 seats to 90 for the Liberals. It was the last of Macdonald's many political triumphs. He died three months later. For his part, Liberal leader Wilfrid Laurier abandoned the party's free trade policy, a move that helped him win office in 1896.

## Reciprocity and the 1911 Election

For 14 years, Wilfrid Laurier served as prime minister, never daring to challenge the National Policy. Then in 1910, he set off in a different direction. The United States, as always, was looking for access to Canadian raw materials and saw Canada as a market for American manufactured goods. In particular, American newspapers wanted to lower the costs of newsprint by removing the tariffs on paper and wood pulp. The newspapers began to campaign for a reciprocal trade agreement with Canada and received a sympathetic ear in Washington. The US was pursuing the Open Door policy, pushing for American companies to have open access to trade and investment opportunities around the world. Historians have often noted the US pursuit of an open door in China, but Canada was also a priority, particularly because the president felt a strong connection to the neighbour to the north. Until he entered the White House in 1909, William Howard Taft had vacationed every year in Murray Bay (now La Malbaie), Quebec, and developed an affection for Canada and its people.

In November 1910, the two countries launched negotiations, concluding with a deal in January 1911. Taft said it was "the most important measure of my administration."[17] The agreement provided for free trade in most natural products and in a small number of manufactured goods that farmers would use (e.g., cream separators, wire fencing), and it lowered tariffs on processed foods (e.g., canned meats, bacon, flour). On some products, the two countries would harmonize their rates at the lower existing rate, whether Canadian or American—so Canada would reduce its tariff on ploughs to the American rate, and the US would reduce its duty on iron ore to the Canadian rate.

In the United States, the response to the agreement was largely positive. Proponents emphasized that it would improve American access to Canadian resources and to the Canadian market. Without realizing the impact of his words, Champ Clark, speaker-elect of the House of Representatives, suggested that reciprocity was the first step to annexation: "I am for it, because I hope to see the day when the American flag will float over every square foot of the British–North American possessions clear to the North Pole. They are people of our blood. They speak our language. Their institutions are much like ours."[18] Opponents argued that the agreement favoured Canada and discriminated against American farmers. Their products were no longer protected, but most of the items they purchased were still subject to tariffs. Critics also pointed out that some Canadian products, such as lard, rough lumber, and paper, were cheaper, and Canadian wages were below American levels, meaning that free trade in these products would result in reduced incomes and fewer jobs. Similarly, lower Canadian wages in the fisheries industry gave Canada an unfair advantage that would hurt American fishers. Despite their objections to the agreement, the opponents were greatly outnumbered, and the measure easily passed both houses of Congress.

In Canada the agreement seemed certain to pass. Western farmers, who favoured free trade, would benefit from the opportunity to sell their products in the United States either duty-free or with a reduced tariff, and they could buy a small number of manufactured goods at a lower rate. At the same time, the agreement continued to protect central Canadian manufacturers by maintaining the tariff on most of the products they produced. Members of Parliament listened intently when W.S. Fielding, the minister of finance, announced the agreement in the Commons. "Triumph was written on the faces of the Liberals," reported the Montreal *Herald*, "and dismay painted on the visages of the opposition."[19] The Tory caucus met the next morning to decide how to respond to the agreement. The mood, in the words of party leader Robert Borden, was one of "deepest dejection."[20] An election was looming, and it seemed clear that the Laurier Liberals were about to win their fifth consecutive term.

Yet opponents were able to mobilize against the agreement, in part because their objections were not just about economics but also politics and identity. They capitalized on Champ Clark's words as proof that reciprocity would lead to Canada being swallowed by the United States. Business leaders formed the Anti-Reciprocity League in Montreal and the Canadian National League in Toronto to campaign against the agreement. The Canadian Manufacturers Association and several other business groups also came out against reciprocity. They feared that it was merely the first step toward total free trade and an end to the protection of the country's manufacturing industry, which would be unable to compete against American firms without the tariff. Critics argued that the presence of US investment was proof of the effectiveness of the National Policy. At a large public meeting shortly after the agreement was announced, Hamilton mayor George Harmon Lees declared that the 33 American factories in his city "were brought to Canada by tariff restrictions" and that reciprocity "is more than likely to change all this."[21]

The opposition further benefitted from the help of renegade Liberals. In Toronto, a group of Liberal lawyers and businessmen known as the Toronto Eighteen spoke out against the agreement, claiming that it would weaken Canada's British ties and make the country more susceptible to annexation by the United States. After Laurier, the best-known Liberal in Canada was Clifford Sifton, the former minister of the interior, who also came out against reciprocity, arguing that it would lead to annexation. The debate became so emotional that, as Governor General Lord Grey reported, "The feeling in Montreal and Toronto against the Agreement could hardly be stronger if the United States troops had already invaded our territory."[22]

On election day, the voters decisively rejected Laurier and his trade policy, ending 15 years of Liberal rule. The Conservatives won 121 seats, to 87 for the Liberals and 13 for the Nationalists from Quebec, who had run against Laurier's creation of a Canadian navy, which they feared would draw

Canada into Britain's wars. Support for Robert Borden's Conservatives was strongest in Southern Ontario, the area that benefitted most from Canada's branch-plant economy. "The moral is to make no appeal in good times for something better," the minister of labour, William Lyon Mackenzie King, wrote in his diary. "It is only when people are hard up that they see the advantage of change."[23] The words were prophetic. Only in the midst of the Great Depression, 25 years later, did Canada begin to undo the National Policy, steps taken by Prime Minister Mackenzie King.

## Annexationism, Imperialism, and Independence

The period from Confederation in 1867 until 1896 was one of deep pessimism for Canadians. In 1873, the Long Depression began, and the Canadian economy showed few signs of life for the next quarter century. In the 1880s alone, more than one million Canadians left their homeland, the majority of them settling in the United States. By 1900, Canadians made up more than 10 per cent of the American foreign-born population.[24] The fathers of Confederation had spoken of a "new nationality," but a distinct Canadian identity had not materialized and there was little common feeling across language groups or provincial boundaries. "We have come to a period in the history of this young country when premature dissolution seems to be at hand," opposition leader Wilfrid Laurier wrote to a colleague in 1891. "What will be the outcome? How long can the present fabric last? Can it last at all?"[25]

Some Canadians strove to forge a distinctive national outlook. Canada First, an organization created in 1871 by members of the Toronto establishment, aimed to generate a Canadian sentiment and put an end to colonial status, though members held differing views of Canada's destiny. Some favoured strong ties with the British Empire, while others wanted Canadian independence from Britain. Anti-Americanism united the members, who tended to be idealistic and politically naive. They created the Canadian National Party in 1874, but were unable to win significant support at election time. The group eventually faded away.

The failure of Canada First had a profound impact on Goldwin Smith. Born in England, Smith had been educated at Oxford before he became a history professor at that institution. After teaching for two years at Cornell University in upstate New York, he moved to Toronto, where he married a wealthy widow. Financially secure, he became a public intellectual, commentating regularly on a wide range of political questions. His views tinged with racism, Smith was convinced that Anglo-Saxon civilization was superior to all others. He regretted the "wretched quarrel" that had separated Britain and the US, and looked forward to the political union of the

Anglo-Saxon "race."[26] "Canadian nationality," he believed, was "a lost cause" because Canada made no sense in economic or geographical terms and English-speaking and French-speaking Canadians would never get along.[27] He came to support the American annexation of Canada, which would be a first step in bringing Britain and the United States back together and would help with the assimilation of French Canadians. He outlined these views in his 1891 book, *Canada and the Canadian Question*, which has been called "the most pessimistic book that has ever been written about Canada."[28]

Annexation had little support in the 1870s, when Canadians were still bitter over the Treaty of Washington, but the movement won some converts in the 1880s, when the US economy began to outperform Canada's. Most annexationists lived in larger cities, where people hoped that joining the US would lead to more trade, or in the borderlands (areas like Windsor, Ontario, and the Niagara peninsula), where Canadians had the opportunity to view American prosperity at close range. Annexationist ranks included some anglophone Quebeckers who felt politically dominated by franco-phones and a few francophone radicals who wished to join the United States to break the power of two conservative institutions: the British monarchy, to which they felt no allegiance, and the Catholic Church, which played a dominant role in Quebec society and politics.

The commercial union movement brought annexationists together with those Canadians who favoured closer economic ties with the United States but not political union. Commercial union meant not only free trade between Canada and the United States but also the harmonization of Canadian and American tariffs on items coming from third countries. Prominent Canadians, such as Liberal member of Parliament and former finance minister Richard Cartwright, favoured the policy. The Commercial Union League was formed in 1887, with Goldwin Smith as president, but it died after the election of 1891, when John A. Macdonald linked free trade with treason.

Annexationism horrified Canadian imperialists, many of whom were strongly anti-American. In the late nineteenth century, imperialism grew in power throughout the Western world. In Canada, imperialism won little support outside of southern Ontario or among farmers or workers. It was largely confined to members of the Ontario establishment who believed that Canada had a greater place in the world as part of the British Empire than it would as an independent country. As Canada grew in population, wealth, and power, it would end its subservient position and would play a leading role within the Empire. Imperialism would thus enhance Canada's status rather than detract from it. "I . . . am an Imperialist because I will not be a Colonial," writer Stephen Leacock said.[29] Like many—perhaps most—English-speaking Canadians, imperialists believed that race was a biological reality, that there was a hierarchy of races, and that Anglo-Saxons were at the top. Though Americans and English-speaking Canadians were part of this same race, Canadians were superior to Americans because the northern climate made them more rugged than their cousins to the south. Imperialists favoured Imperial Federation, but they never agreed on what this meant. For some, it was merely closer cooperation within the Empire on trade or defence issues. Others advocated the creation of an imperial Parliament to include representatives from the self-governing colonies and deal with matters of common concern.

In a highly influential book, historian Carl Berger argued that imperialism was a form of Canadian nationalism.[30] Canadian imperialists were deeply attached to Canada. They looked to the British Empire for economic and military support, but also for the opportunity for Canada to exercise power in the future. Imperialists did not want Canada to be dominated by the British, but rather looked forward to the day when Canada would play a leading role in the Empire and thus in the world. Yet Berger's interpretation is not entirely convincing. The imperialists saw their nation as composed of British people around the world. When they spoke of "national unity" they meant the unity of the Empire, not of Canada. Their pride in Canada was more a form of regionalism than nationalism. They were indeed nationalists—but they were pan-Britannic, not Canadian, nationalists.

For many Canadians the choice lay between close ties to either Britain or the United States, but there was a third option: Canadian independence.[31] Like the other two movements, independence never gained widespread support. Part of the problem was that the proponents of independence could not agree on their program. Some wanted a Canadian republic, others preferred to keep the British monarchy, and still others wanted a branch of the British royal family to move to Canada to create a distinctive Canadian monarchy. A few wanted a quick declaration of independence, but more favoured a gradual evolution in that direction. Another challenge was that the English-Canadian loyalist tradition had associated independence with treason: to separate Canada from Britain was akin to shattering the Canadian identity and preparing Canada for absorption by the United States. Few prominent Canadians dared touch the idea.

Yet support, though diffuse and disorganized, was there. Pro-independence organizations were created in Montreal, Toronto, Windsor, and other cities. Newspapers such as the London *Free Press* and the *Quebec Chronicle* supported independence, as did *L'Indépendance Canadienne*, a weekly newspaper in Trois Rivières founded by journalist and former MP Georges-Isidore Barthe, who favoured a Canadian republic. In 1889, the Toronto *Globe*, the most important paper in English Canada, argued

Canada's destiny lay in neither imperial federation nor annexation: "We have a third and better alternative, and we say that complete independence is perfectly consistent with the British connection."[32] Canada should keep the British monarchy, the *Globe* argued, but Ottawa should no longer be subordinate to the British government in London.

Despite the stigma, some politicians publicly supported independence. John Young, a member of the pre-Confederation Canadian legislature, came out publicly for independence in 1869. Lucius Huntington, a Liberal member of Parliament, campaigned for independence in 1869 and 1870, but found that his opponents branded him as a closet annexationist. He stopped promoting the idea, which had been embarrassing for his party, and later served in the federal Cabinet of Prime Minister Alexander Mackenzie.

By 1885, support for independence had grown to such an extent that the *Montreal Star* reported that one could no longer ridicule the movement or sneer at its supporters. August Tessier was elected to the Quebec legislature in 1889 on a platform that included a severing of Canada's ties with Britain. Former Quebec premier Honoré Mercier publicly endorsed the idea in Montreal in 1893. He later visited Washington, where he said that the dominant sentiment in his province was "for a separation from England and complete Canadian independence."[33] The next year, Joseph Royal, a former journalist and politician, who had served as a member of Parliament, Manitoba Cabinet minister, and lieutenant-governor of the North-West Territories, called for an independent Canada, with the consent of London.

American newspapers, hearing what they wanted to hear, exaggerated the strength of the independence movement, suggesting that Canadians were gripped with the desire to cut ties with Britain. In 1871, a *New York Times* reporter told John A. Macdonald of a prevalent belief in the United States that there was both a powerful annexationist movement in Canada and "an influential and numerous element in favour of separation from England and the establishment of complete Canadian independence."[34] In December 1889, the *Atlanta Constitution* reported that Canada was preparing to either "set up in business for herself" or to "knock at the doors" for admission to the United States.[35] In response to the large number of American media reports on the strength of the Canadian independence and annexationist movements, Liberal MP William Mulock introduced a resolution in the House of Commons in January 1890 to reaffirm Canada's loyalty to the monarch. The motion passed unanimously, but did not have the desired effect. The American press continued to report breathlessly on any support for Canadian independence. In February, the *Chicago Daily Tribune* reported that the movement had "received a very sudden and . . . healthy boom" in the two weeks since the passage of the Mulock resolution, and proceeded to inflate the importance of a pro-independence resolution passed by the Young Men's Liberal Club of Toronto.[36]

John S. Ewart, a well-known lawyer, laid the intellectual groundwork for Canada's eventual evolution toward independence. He believed Canada should remain within the Empire, but gradually move toward complete self-government. Beginning in 1904, he wrote countless letters to the editor, articles, pamphlets, and books in favour of a Kingdom of Canada, a country sharing a monarch with Great Britain but otherwise fully independent. Human beings had the right to self-government, Ewart argued, and in Canada's case, that meant ending the British Parliament's power to legislate for Canada and to handle Canada's foreign relations. Severing the imperial tie would have the added benefit of fostering national unity. French Canadians and non-British immigrants did not feel connected to the British identity that Loyalists had constructed for Canada. Only by becoming independent could Canada create its own distinctive image. Ewart's main reason for pursuing independence was to prevent Canada from being sucked into Britain's imperial conflicts. As a colony, Canada had no choice in the matter: when Britain was at war, Canada was also legally at war. Yet as Ewart noted, British and Canadian concerns were not the same. Canada's interests were in North America, and Canadians should be free to express those interests without being branded as annexationists.

Henri Bourassa, a prominent Quebec politician and journalist, shared many of Ewart's views. Bourassa wanted Canada to continue under the British Crown but to have independence from the British Parliament. He was particularly insistent that Canada have a distinct foreign and defence policy. British diplomats had not defended Canada's interests, and there was no reason for Canadians to give their lives fighting in the British Empire's wars. Independence, Bourassa believed, would bring together French- and English-speaking Canadians. His views differed from those of Ewart only in that Bourassa favoured a more gradual evolution toward independence.

## Culture and Society

In every generation, some Canadians have lamented the Americanization of their country as if it were a new phenomenon. Yet from the time of the Loyalists, there have been strong American influences in Canada. Canadians and Americans have shared many common values, spoken similar varieties of English, employed many of the same slang words, and lived similar lives. The same religions have existed on both sides of the border (though Canada always had a far greater proportion of Roman Catholics). Fashionable Canadians dressed as they did in New York. Service organizations, such as the Rotary Club, grew both in Canada and the United States. People in the two countries enjoyed the same distinctive North American sports.

Baseball was the most-played and most-watched sport in Canada and the United States in the late nineteenth century. Unlike other British colonies that took up cricket, Canadians embraced baseball, a sport played across the country and across class and language divides. It had more participants than any other game, leading one sport historian to say it was "truly Canada's national sport" in those early days.[37] By the 1860s, the Canadian variation of the game was abandoned in favour of New York rules, making it possible for Canadian teams to join American leagues. Players easily crossed the border, so much so that Toronto's team was composed entirely of Americans by 1887. Archibald MacMechan, an English professor at Dalhousie University in Halifax, wrung his hands at this state of affairs, as aging professors often do. "Canadian sport has become more and more American. Our one native game, lacrosse, is dead. Cricket, which flourishes in Australia, is here a sickly exotic. But baseball is everywhere. Our newspapers are filled with reports of various 'leagues.'"[38]

Hockey began to catch on in the late nineteenth century, both in Canada and the northern United States. Later generations of Canadians would grumble about the Americanization of their national sport, but in the early twentieth century, the Americans also had reason for concern. American hockey was a highly skilled gentleman's sport, played primarily by preparatory school and college students. They rejected the violence that characterized the Canadian game, which was dominated by the working class. Canadians playing in American leagues had a reputation for rough play.

The culture of the two countries was closely intertwined in many other ways. Canadian theatres produced American plays. Newsstands sold American magazines, more popular than British or even Canadian ones. In fact, all the Canadian magazines combined did not have the same circulation in Canada as the single most popular American magazine. Canadians followed the fashion advice and agreed with the moral judgments of *Ladies' Home Journal*. Canadian magazines and newspapers looked like their American counterparts and contained a considerable amount of American content. Canadians were more likely to read American novels than Canadian ones, and Canadian fiction was influenced more by American than by British writers. Before 1914, 60 per cent of movies shown in Canada were American; the vast majority of the rest were British or French, with virtually no Canadian films being screened.[39] From time to time, Canadians tried to push back. Film censors banned or edited films that contained too many images of the American flag, but in the day when governments played only a small role in society, there was not much Canada could do to limit the presence of American culture.

The American impact on Canadian higher education was marked. Some of the older Canadian universities were based on the British model, but many others followed the curriculum, organization, and administration of American colleges. The Ontario Agricultural College (now the University of Guelph) was distinctly American in its structure and approach, as were the country's first PhD programs at the University of Toronto and McGill University. Acadia College (Acadia University after 1891) was highly influenced by American institutions, offering the same curriculum, hiring mostly faculty members who had been educated in the United States, and producing many graduates—half of them—who would settle south of the border. The University of Saskatchewan was originally conceived as a smaller replica of the University of Wisconsin, with a similar structure and with roughly half of its faculty members from the United States. Across Canada, students followed American trends. Fraternities with Greek initials came to Canada directly from the United States, as did the practice of hazing first-year students.

## Social Movements

The late nineteenth and early twentieth centuries was a time of political and social activism. Reform movements popped up in the United States and Canada, with strong links across the border. The American and Canadian women's movements were closely intertwined. Canadian women were delegates to women's rights conventions in the United States as early as the 1850s. Canadians helped create the International Council of Women, established in Washington, DC, in 1888. Lady Aberdeen, the wife of Canada's governor general, was elected president of the organization at its 1893 meeting in Chicago and served 36 years in that role. She went on to found the National Council of Women of Canada, a federation of organizations devoted to improving the status of women. At international meetings, Canadian women felt far behind their American counterparts. "The American woman's mind is made up on lots of questions which we are just beginning to tackle," wrote Canadian journalist Grace Denison.[40] At the 1893 Chicago meeting, an American activist shook her umbrella at Denison, shouting, "You Canadians are indifferent. You must be aroused. You must canvass. You must *vote!*"[41] The American organizations were more successful than their Canadian counterparts. US states began giving the vote to women in the 1890s. By the time Manitoba became the first province to allow women to vote in 1916, 11 states had already done so. In 1922, Rebecca Latimer Felton became the first woman senator in the United States, eight years before Cairine Wilson earned this distinction in Canada. Frances Perkins became the first woman in the US Cabinet in 1933, 24 years before Ellen Fairclough entered Canada's federal Cabinet.

The first woman physician in Canada, Emily Howard Stowe, had to train in the United States because Canadian medical schools would not admit women. In 1877, she attended a meeting of the American Society for the Advancement of Women in Cleveland, Ohio. Inspired, she founded the Toronto Women's Literary Club, Canada's first organization dedicated to winning the vote for women. In 1889, she invited several American suffragists to Toronto for the founding of a national organization, the Dominion Women's Enfranchisement Association. A portrait of Susan B. Anthony, the most prominent suffragist in the United States, hung over the podium, and several other Americans were present, including Mary Seymour Howell, whom the association hired as an organizer.

Closely connected to the women's movement was the temperance movement, which began in the United States and spread into Canada. Most major American temperance associations had Canadian chapters, including the Sons of Temperance, the Daughters of Temperance, Dashaways, the Women's Christian Temperance Union, and the International Order of Good Templars. Canadians were receptive to the American message. When the temperance evangelist and former professional baseball player Billy Sunday spoke in favour of prohibition in Vancouver in 1916, 10,000 people went to hear him, at the time the largest audience assembled under one roof in Canada. In both countries, governments banned the sale of alcohol, though the approach often differed. In nineteenth-century Canada, the local option was popular, leaving the question of alcohol up to municipalities. The Canada Temperance Act of 1878 (often known as the Scott Act) allowed any city or county to prohibit the sale of alcohol after a majority accepted the measure in a referendum. In the United States, the more common practice was the statewide ban of alcohol, often called the Maine Law after the first state to adopt it. In the twentieth century, Canada increasingly came to follow the American lead. For instance, prohibition came into effect in Washington State in 1916 and in neighbouring British Columbia in 1917. During the First World War, both Canada and the United States enacted national prohibition. In the United States, the nationwide ban remained in force until 1933, while in Canada it ended in 1920.

The Canadian labour movement began independently of its American counterpart, but by the end of the nineteenth century, the two were tightly tied together. Printers, railway workers, ironworkers, shoemakers, and other Canadian workers joined locals of American unions. In 1902, Canada's Trades and Labour Congress affiliated with the American Federation of Labour. American unions were never powerful in Quebec, where they were impeded by the different language and culture, as well as the strong presence of the Catholic Church in the labour movement, but they were dominant in English Canada by the late nineteenth century. By 1911,

American unions represented 89.5 per cent of Canada's unionized work-force.[42] Canadian workers were drawn to American unions because they were larger and more powerful than their Canadian counterparts and were better able to offer strike support. The United Mine Workers of America, for example, spent $2 million on strike aid in Canada from 1904 to 1914.[43] Some Canadians grumbled that the growing number of strikes in Canada was a result of the influence of the American labour movement, and in 1903 Parliament debated, but did not pass, a bill to outlaw Americans from visiting Canada to assist striking workers. Canadian workers also followed the general approach of the labour movement in the United States. In Europe, the plight of the worker was improved at the ballot box, through the election of socialists to reform—or even overthrow—the capitalist system. In North America, the labour movement concentrated on collective bargaining to improve wages and working conditions for workers.

The close ties between American and Canadian labour could be seen in the creation of Labour Day, a distinctly North American holiday. In May 1882, Peter J. McGuire, a leader of the American Federation of Labor, visited Toronto's annual labour festival. Impressed, he organized a similar celebration in New York that September. It was so successful that it became an annual event and spread to other communities. Soon, American states began declaring it a holiday. In 1894, it became a national holiday in both Canada and the United States. While much of Europe and Latin America continue to celebrate the contribution of workers on the first of May, Canadians and Americans do so on the first Monday in September, a holiday they created together.

## Summary

After the Treaty of Washington of 1871, Canada increasingly found itself in an awkward triangular relationship. Lacking the status of an independent country, Canada had to work through British diplomats when dealing with the United States. Yet Britain's concerns were not Canada's, leading Canadian politicians to believe that they should talk with their American counterparts directly, without British intermediaries. This feeling was particularly strong after the Alaska Boundary Dispute, when Canadians believed their interests had been sacrificed for the sake of Anglo-American friendship.

A shared popular culture, as well as the closely intertwined social and labour movements, showed the degree to which history and geography had linked Canada and the United States at a level that politicians could not touch. Still, Canadians continued the debate: Are we British? Does our destiny lie with the Empire? For many in English Canada, the future was clear. Since the time of the Loyalists, Canada had been a British country, and British it would remain. Yet how could Canada ensure that British officials defended Canadian interests, when British concerns were often quite different from Canada's? And what to do about Aboriginal people, French Canadians, and the increasing number of immigrants from continental Europe who did not feel British at all? For other Canadians, Canada's destiny lay with the United States. The economic struggles of the late nineteenth century and the conflict between the language groups and among the regions proved that Canada could not survive. Canadians should acknowledge that Confederation was a failure and negotiate terms for Canada's annexation by the United States. Yet the majority of Canadians were equally determined that Canada not become part of the United States, as was clear in the clash over trade policy in the late nineteenth and early twentieth centuries, a debate that had little to do with economics and was instead bedevilled with questions of Canada's loyalty to Britain and the threat of American annexation. In the late nineteenth century, a third option emerged. A small group of Canadians insisted that their country could survive as an independent entity, friends with both Britain and the United States, but part of neither. Although few dared admit it, Canada's destiny lay in independence from both Britain and the United States.

## Beyond the Book

1. Was the National Policy truly nationalist? What makes a policy nationalist?
2. In the late nineteenth and early twentieth centuries, what did Canadian thinkers believe was Canada's destiny? What arguments did they raise in support of the various options?
3. What light do social movements cast on Canadian–American relations in the period from 1871 to 1914?

## Further Reading

On the relations between Ottawa and Washington, see Robert E. Hannigan, *The New World Power: American Foreign Policy, 1898–1917* (Philadelphia: University of Pennsylvania Press, 2002), which is particularly strong on the American side of the relationship. Much has been written on the Alaska Boundary Dispute, mostly one-sided work by Canadians determined to prove their country was wronged. The exceptions are two carefully balanced studies: Norman Penlington, *The Alaska Boundary Dispute: A Critical Reappraisal* (Toronto: McGraw–Hill Ryerson, 1972); and Tony McCulloch, "Theodore Roosevelt and Canada: Alaska, the 'Big Stick' and the North Atlantic Triangle, 1901–1909," chapter 17 in *A Companion to Theodore Roosevelt*, edited by Serge Ricard (Malden, Massachusetts: Wiley-Blackwell, 2011), 293–313.

Kurkpatrick Dorsey covers Canadian–American agreements to protect the environment in the early twentieth century in *The Dawn of Conservation Diplomacy: U.S.–Canadian Wildlife Protection Treaties in the Progressive Era* (Seattle: University of Washington Press, 1998). Two works that recognize the American influence on the Canadian conservation movement are Janet Foster, *Working for Wildlife: The Beginning of Preservation in Canada*, 2nd ed. (Toronto: University of Toronto Press, 1998); and Neil S. Forkey, *The Natural Environment to the Twenty-First Century* (Toronto: University of Toronto Press, 2012).

The mythology of Macdonald's National Policy is challenged in Michael Bliss, "Canadianizing American Business: The Roots of the Branch Plant," in *Close the 49th Parallel Etc: The Americanization of Canada*, edited by Ian Lumsden (Toronto: University of Toronto Press, 1970), 26–42; J.H. Dales, "'National Policy' Myths, Past and Present," *Journal of Canadian Studies* 14, no. 3 (Autumn 1979): 92–110; and Stephen Azzi, "Foreign Investment and the Paradox of Economic Nationalism," in *Canadas of the Mind*, edited by Norman Hillmer and Adam Chapnick (Montreal and Kingston: McGill–Queen's University Press, 2007), 63–88. Craig Brown provides a perceptive analysis of the politics of the policy in "The Nationalism of the National Policy," in *Nationalism in Canada*, edited by Peter Russell (Toronto: McGraw–Hill, 1966), 155–63.

Damien-Claude Bélanger's *Prejudice and Pride: Canadian Intellectuals Confront the United States, 1891–1945* (Toronto: University of Toronto Press, 2011) is a meticulous examination of English- and French-Canadian ideas about the United States. On John Ewart, see Douglas L. Cole, "John S. Ewart and Canadian Nationalism," *Historical Papers* [Canadian Historical Association] (1969): 62–73; David M.L. Farr, "John S. Ewart," in *Our Living Tradition*, 2nd and 3rd series, edited by Robert L. McDougall (Toronto: University of Toronto Press, 1959): 185–214; and Peter Price, "Fashioning a Constitutional Narrative: John S. Ewart and the Development of a 'Canadian Constitution'," *Canadian Historical Review* 93, no. 3 (September 2012): 359–81. After more than half a century, M.P. O'Connell's article on Henri Bourassa holds up well: "The Ideas of Henri Bourassa," *Canadian Journal of Economics and Political Science* 19, no. 3 (August 1953): 361–76. On Goldwin Smith, see Carl Berger's introduction to Smith's *Canada and the Canadian Question* (Toronto: University of Toronto Press, 1971); Elisabeth Wallace, *Goldwin Smith: Victorian Liberal* (Toronto: University of Toronto Press, 1957); and Frank H. Underhill, "Goldwin Smith," chapter 5 in *In Search of Canadian Liberalism* (Toronto: Macmillan, 1960), 85–103. On the imperialists, Carl Berger's work must be read alongside the penetrating but under-appreciated response from Douglas Cole. See Carl Berger, *The Sense of Power: Studies in the Ideas of Canadian Imperialism, 1867–1914* (Toronto: University of Toronto Press, 1970); Douglas L. Cole, "The Problem of 'Nationalism' and 'Imperialism' in British Settlement Colonies," *Journal of British Studies* 10, no. 2 (May 1971): 160–82; and Douglas L. Cole, "Canada's 'Nationalistic' Imperialists," *Journal of Canadian Studies* 5, no. 3 (August 1970): 44–9.

The crucial elections of 1891 and 1911 have each received thorough, book-length treatment: Christopher Pennington, *The Destiny of Canada: Macdonald, Laurier, and the Election of 1891* (Toronto: Allen Lane, 2011); and Patrice Dutil and David MacKenzie, *Canada 1911:The Decisive Election That Shaped the Country* (Toronto: Dundurn, 2011). On US trade policy in 1911, see R.E. Hannigan, "Reciprocity 1911: Continentalism and American Weltpolitik," *Diplomatic History* 4, no. 1 (Winter 1980): 1–18.

Much of the literature on the women's, prohibition, conservation, and labour movements tells only the American or Canadian side of the story, but a few authors see that people and ideas easily crossed the border. On the women's movement, see Catherine L. Cleverdon, *The Woman Suffrage Movement in Canada*, 2nd ed. (Toronto: University of Toronto Press, 1974); and N.E.S. Griffiths, *The Splendid Vision: Centennial History of the National Council of Women of Canada, 1893–1993* (Ottawa: Carleton University Press, 1993). Stephen T. Moore has written the best transnational work on prohibition: "Cross-Border Crusades: The Binational Temperance Movement in Washington and British Columbia," *Pacific Northwest Quarterly* 98, no. 3 (Summer 2007): 130–42; and "Defining the 'Undefended': Canadians, Americans, and the Multiple Meanings of Border during Prohibition," *American Review of Canadian Studies* 34, no. 1 (Spring 2004): 3–32. See also Cheryl Krasnick-Warsh, ed., *Drink in Canada: Historical Essays* (Montreal and Kingston: McGill-Queen's University Press, 1993); and Craig Heron, *Booze:A Distilled History* (Toronto: Between the Lines, 2003). On links between Canadian and American labour unions, see John Crispo, *International Unionism: A Study in Canadian–American Relations* (Toronto: McGraw–Hill, 1967); and Robert H. Babcock, *Gompers in Canada: A Study in American Continentalism before the First World War* (Toronto: University of Toronto Press, 1974).

Several works look at sports: Andrew C. Holman, "Playing in the Neutral Zone: Meanings and Uses of Ice Hockey in the Canada–U.S. Borderlands, 1895–1915," *American Review of Canadian Studies* 34, no. 1 (Spring 2004): 33–57; Don Morrow and Kevin B. Wamsley, *Sport in Canada: A History*, 3rd ed. (Toronto: Oxford University Press, 2013); William Humber, *Cheering for the Home Team: The Story of Baseball in Canada* (Erin, Ontario: Boston Mills Press, 1983); Bruce Kidd, *The Struggle for Canadian Sport* (Toronto: University of Toronto Press, 1996); and Colin D. Howell, *Blood, Sweat, and Cheers: Sport and the Making of Modern Canada* (Toronto: University of Toronto Press, 2001).

## CHAPTER 6

# Independence, 1914–1938

## Canadian Political Autonomy and North American Integration

## Introduction

"It was European policy, European statesmanship, European ambition that drenched this world in blood," the Canadian delegate told the League of Nations in 1920.[1] Newton Wesley Rowell, a former federal Cabinet minister, was in a belligerent mood. The Europeans seemed intent on running the world body with little input from anyone else. But, he told them, Canadians insisted on fair representation within the League and would not be content to have Britain speak for them. Rowell's speech—a "frightful attack on Europe and European statesmen,"[2] in the words of the French delegate—enunciated a distinctly North American point of view. In the 1920s and 1930s, Canadians and Americans came to believe that they understood peace and cooperation in a way that the Europeans did not. After all, the North American neighbours had lived beside each other in peace for 100 years, while the Europeans had gone to war time and again.

The First World War had reshaped the relations between Canada and the United States. The war revealed that Britain was declining as a great power and that the United States was emerging as a global economic and political force. The war reinvigorated a North American disillusionment with Europe, which helped foster a distinctive North American mindset. The United States had always been a primary factor in Canada's development, an influence that some Canadians tried to offset through strong ties with Britain. Yet after the First World War, Canadians found it increasingly difficult to use Britain to reduce the gravitational pull of the United States.

Instead, Canada now sought independence from both Britain and the United States.

# War and Peace

A flood of anti-American sentiment carried Robert Borden into the Prime Minister's Office in 1911, but he understood that Canadian interests lay in an amicable relationship with the United States. In December, he travelled to New York and Washington to reassure Americans that Canada was still friendly. He even joined in singing the American anthem at a dinner of the Canadian Society in New York City. Laurier's reciprocity agreement was now dead, but Borden worked to ensure that relations with the United States would continue on a cooperative basis, as they had since the settlement of the Alaska Boundary Dispute.

The First World War strained the relationship, at least at first. Canada still did not have control of its foreign policy when war erupted in Europe in the summer of 1914. In response to the German invasion of neutral Belgium, Britain declared war on Germany on 4 August 1914, a declaration that bound the entire British Empire, including Canada. The Americans followed a different path. President Woodrow Wilson declared American neutrality, asking his fellow citizens to be impartial toward the combatants, not just in deed, but also in thought. Many Canadians deeply resented the American position, particularly when it became clear that the war would be a long, brutal conflict with a catastrophically high death toll. Canadians believed that their boys were dying at the front in the cause of freedom, while the hypocritical Americans hid behind their neutrality, seeking to profit by trading with both sides.

Slowly, the United States was pulled into the war. German submarines repeatedly sank American vessels destined for British ports. After negotiations with the Germans failed, and after the Germans ignored American threats, President Wilson asked Congress for a declaration of war, passed on 6 April 1917. The relationship between the Canadian and American governments immediately became closer, more intense, and more complex. Two months after the US entered the war, Canada's finance minister, Thomas White, wrote to his American counterpart, hoping to win an exemption for Canada from an American ban on foreign lending. "We have in your time and mine always been good neighbors," White wrote. "Our people are very much alike and understand each other better I think than any other two peoples in the world today. The struggle in a common cause will I am sure greatly cement our friendship and respect for each other."[3] White had come a long way since 1911 when he was one of the Toronto Eighteen who had opposed reciprocity with the United States.

Freer trade now seemed essential to the war effort. Canada wished to sell munitions and airplanes to the American War Department and sought key materials from the United States, particularly coal, steel, and pig iron. The Americans wanted secure access to Canadian hydroelectric power for factories in upstate New York. These discussions were handled through the British Embassy in Washington, as Canada still did not send diplomats abroad, but increasingly the British found it difficult to keep up with Canada's business in the American capital. In February 1918, the Borden government created the Canadian War Mission in Washington, primarily to deal with munitions contracts. That same month, Borden visited Washington and was pleased to report later that American officials believed "the resources of the two countries should be pooled in the most effective co-operation and that the boundary line had little or no significance in considering or dealing with these vital questions."[4] Canada was eagerly embracing the American economy as the need to win the war overshadowed other concerns.

Borden also worked to foster close ties with Britain. He spent much time in London as a member of the Imperial War Conference and Imperial War Cabinet, bodies created to give the self-governing British dominions some say in imperial relations and in the conduct of the war. Upon his urging, in 1917 the Imperial War Conference passed Resolution IX, which called for Canada and other dominions to have "an adequate voice" in the empire's "foreign policy and in foreign relations" in the postwar years. The resolution did not spell out how this would be done, other than to call vaguely for "effective arrangements for continuous consultation in all important matters of common imperial concern" and "concerted action, founded on consultation."[5] That worked, to some extent, during the war, but would not succeed in peacetime.

When the war ended on 11 November 1918, Canada was in an ambiguous position. More than 60,000 Canadians had died in the conflict, and Canadians rightly expected to play a role in the Paris peace conference, which opened in January 1919. At first, American delegates were reluctant to consent to a Canadian seat at the table. American secretary of state Robert Lansing offended Canadian delegates by asking why Canada was concerned with European affairs, a question that seemed strange to Canadians after all they had done in Europe. Largely on the insistence of Britain, Canada was allowed representation at the conference, without having the country's international status clarified. In the plenary sessions, where all participant countries met, Canada would have two delegates, the same as Greece or Poland. But Canada would also have representation on the British delegation, which was a member of the Council of Four, the body where British, American, French, and Italian representatives made the key decisions. In the plenary, it was as if Canada were a small independent nation; in the Council of Four, it was a part of the British Empire. After some further struggle with the United States, Canada was permitted to join the new League of Nations, an organization composed of most of the world's countries and dedicated to world peace. Membership suggested that Canada was an independent country. Yet when it came time to sign the peace treaty, the lack of clarity remained. The major powers signed first, followed by the other countries in alphabetical order. Canada's representatives signed the treaty, but not with the lesser powers—after Brazil and before China—but with the great powers, right after the signatures of the British delegates.

The question of representation abroad highlighted Canada's confusing international status. At the end of the war, Borden wanted the Canadian War Mission in Washington to be replaced with a permanent diplomatic post. The British agreed that Canadian officials should be allowed to speak directly to American officials without working through a British intermediary, but they feared that a separate Canadian mission would break the unity of the empire. Eventually, the British decided that Canada could appoint a minister (a diplomat of lower rank than an ambassador) to represent Canada in Washington. The individual would work in the British embassy, would report to the British ambassador, and would act on the ambassador's behalf in his absence. Borden agreed to these terms shortly before he stepped down as prime minister in 1920, but never got around to appointing a Canadian minister. Borden's successor, Arthur Meighen, was opposed to separate Canadian diplomatic representation abroad. He closed the Canadian War Mission in 1921 and did not appoint the Canadian minister to Washington.

## The North American Mindset

Almost as soon as the troops returned home from Europe, a sense of disappointment developed in Canada and the United States. For people in both countries, the drawn-out, bloody war seemed to have accomplished nothing. Humanity was no better off in 1918 or 1919 than it had been in 1914. In fact, things seemed much worse. Europeans went back to their age-old squabbles, while the world suffered a severe recession. Canadians and Americans soured on international relations, particularly European disputes. The oceans seemed like an impenetrable fortress, giving North Americans the luxury of removing themselves from the affairs of Europe.

The war crystallized but did not create the North American mindset, the roots of which can be found in the period before the American Revolution, when Nova Scotians shared a similar outlook with the people of the other British North American colonies. By the 1920s, North America's era of war, or even the possibility of war, had long passed. Now the common interests of Canada and the United States were more obvious than their differences.

The North American mindset was characterized by an exaggerated sense of the superiority of North American values and institutions, particularly when compared to Europe. Europeans, it was often said, settled disputes through war, while North Americans preferred negotiation and compromise. Canadians and Americans believed they had something to teach Europe about peace, and they seldom missed an opportunity to lecture Europeans on how arbitration and disarmament had led to one hundred years of harmony between North American neighbours. In the new League of Nations, Europe's diplomats tired of hearing the standard Canadian speech, which was not much more than self-congratulation and a lecture about European failings. To the Europeans, Canadians were naive and had little understanding of the real problems facing the Old World.

Canadians and Americans were further linked by a distrust of arms manufacturers, a suspicion that swelled in the years between the two world wars. Countless books, pamphlets, magazine articles, and speeches dealt with the activities of the major munitions firms. Many Americans came to regret their country's participation in the First World War and searched for a scapegoat, rather than accepting that the United States had gone to war willingly. Following the widely accepted but illogical argument that those who benefit from a conflict must have caused it, Americans became convinced that arms companies somehow manipulated the United States into the war. Canadians knew that they had sent troops as part of the British Empire, but still wondered if arms merchants might have caused the tensions that led to the outbreak of hostilities in 1914. These concerns were widespread among the media and political elites of both countries. In 1928, Canadian prime minister Mackenzie King insisted that two new Canadian destroyers had to be built in Britain rather than Canada, because providing jobs for Canadians was less important than ensuring that the country did not have a "war industry."[6]

George Drew was one of the leading voices condemning the arms merchants. A Canadian artillery officer on leave from his unit during the First World War, Drew had been staying at London's Carlton Hotel when he stumbled into David Lloyd George. Curious about who was important enough to merit a visit from the British prime minister, Drew checked the hotel's register and discovered that Lloyd George had been meeting Basil Zaharoff, a corrupt businessman and part-owner of the Vickers arms manufacturing firm. This incident lingered in Drew's mind and continued to trouble him until 1931, when he published an article in *Maclean's* magazine, arguing that arms manufacturers had a vested interest in war. "Competition in armaments was very largely to blame" for the First World War, Drew argued. The only way to prevent the next war was to "attack the causes," the arms race being one of the most important.[7] Drew's piece was widely read, both in its original article form and then as a pamphlet that the Women's League of Nations Association circulated extensively in Canada and abroad.

Opinion makers in Canada and abroad picked up Drew's arguments. In a 1934 speech, Vincent Massey, president of the Liberal party and former Canadian minister to Washington, called for "an end to the manufacture for private gain of weapons for the destruction of human beings."[8] Companies that profited from war worked at cross-purposes to those groups and individuals trying to promote peace. As Massey told Drew, who helped with the research for the speech, arms manufacturers might not cause wars directly, but they did "stir up" the causes of war.[9]

No doubt inspired by Drew's work, American journalists H.C. Engelbrecht and F.C. Hanighen published the most successful of the many books on arms merchants that appeared in the 1930s. The book's title, *The Merchants of Death*, was strikingly similar to that of Drew's article, "Salesmen of Death." The two Americans made arguments often identical to those advanced by Drew, and devoted an entire chapter to Basil Zaharoff, the main villain in Drew's piece. *Merchants of Death* caused an outcry against arms manufacturers in the United States. Weeks after the book's publication, the US Senate appointed a special committee to investigate the munitions industry. The Nye Committee, named after its chair, Senator Gerald Nye, conducted hearings from 1934 to 1936, against a backdrop of growing anxieties about the deteriorating situation in Europe. To ensure that the US would not again be drawn into a European war, Congress passed a series of Neutrality Acts from 1935 to 1939, preventing Americans from selling arms or lending money to belligerents in wartime. In Canada, there was no similar political response. Because of the British tie, few thought that Canada could be neutral in the next European war.

North America's ambivalent view of Europe during the 1920s and 1930s has often been misleadingly labelled *isolationism*, though *independent internationalism* would be a better description. Both Canada and the United States were involved in European affairs. Canada joined the League of Nations, eager to advance its own international status. The United States refused to join the League, but was active in other ways. The Americans hosted the Washington Naval Conference of 1921–2, which resulted in a treaty to limit American, British, Japanese, French, and Italian naval armaments. American bankers sat on commissions that revised German obligations to pay reparations to Britain, France, and Belgium after the First World War. Together with French Foreign Minister Aristide Briand, US Secretary of State Frank Kellogg drafted the 1928 Pact of Paris (also known as the Kellogg–Briand Pact) that renounced war as a means to resolving international disputes. Virtually every country in the world eventually signed the treaty, including Canada. Yet neither Canada nor the United States

wanted to be tied to Europe. Americans were willing to play a role in international affairs, but not one that could lead to their being sucked into war.
Canadians wanted a role too, but their position on the next war was more
complex. Anglophones were generally willing for Canada to fight, but only
if Britain was threatened; most French Canadians would only go to war if
the threat was to Canada.

Canada and the United States had different approaches to the League
of Nations, but the divergences were not as deep as they appeared. The
Americans refused to join, largely because of article 10 of the League
Covenant, the organization's constitution, which said that all members
would protect the "territorial integrity and existing political independence"
of fellow members "against external aggression."[10] Critics feared that this
idea, known as *collective security*, would mean that the League could decide when the United States was at war, and that American troops would
be dispatched to settle disputes in places where the country had no interests. Although Canada had joined the League, the country's politicians
and diplomats shared the American uneasiness with article 10. At the Paris
peace conference, Prime Minister Borden worked unsuccessfully to have
the clause deleted or amended. When the peace treaty, which contained
the League Covenant, came before the Canadian Parliament, most of the
criticism related to the collective security provision. Liberal member of
Parliament Charles Gavin Power, later a Cabinet minister, declared that
Canada's destiny was "not in continental Europe but here on the free soil of
America." His views could not have been more distinctly North American:
"Our policy for the next hundred years should be that laid down by George
Washington in the United States for the guidance of his countrymen—
absolute renunciation of interference in European affairs—and that
laid down by the other great father of his country in Canada, Sir Wilfrid
Laurier—'freedom from the vortex of European militarism.'"[11] At League
meetings in 1920 and 1921, Canada campaigned unsuccessfully to have
article 10 struck from the League Covenant. Canadian delegates in 1922
pushed for an amendment to weaken the clause, but again failed. In 1923,
Canada tried to win support for a resolution that declared that each country
could determine how much military support it would provide when another
League member was attacked. The resolution failed to win the necessary
unanimous support to pass, but Canada had won a partial victory, as all
League members, except Persia, had voted in favour.

Wealthy American charities helped foster the North American mindset.
The Carnegie Corporation and the Rockefeller Foundation donated about
$20 million to Canadian universities, art galleries, libraries, and museums.[12]
Carnegie also sponsored a scholarly research program on the Canadian–
American relationship, developed by two Canadian-born historians at New

York's Columbia University: J.B. Brebner, an early practitioner of transnational history, and James T. Shotwell, who described himself as having a "North American nationality."[13] Four conferences grew out of the project, two at Queen's University in Kingston, Ontario, and two at St Lawrence University, in Canton, New York. In the late 1930s and early 1940s, Carnegie sponsored 25 book-length studies, each examining a specific aspect of the Canadian–American relationship. Most took a continental approach to understanding the development of the two countries, but there were exceptions. The series included groundbreaking research by Donald Creighton and Harold Innis, two Canadian scholars who were critical of American influence in Canada but who had to rely on backing from an American foundation in the days before the Canadian government provided funding for academic research.

Although many Canadians and Americans shared the North American mindset, Canadians still maintained a sense of their own superiority over Americans. The United States might be richer, but Canadians were more principled and honest. "You are big, but we are better," wrote one Canadian in 1932. "You are great, but we are good."[14] In a 1938 study of Canadian attitudes, a sociologist reported that Canadians believed their way of life was "simpler, more honest, more moral and more religious than life in the United States."[15] Canadians associated the United States with the materialism, secularism, and social conflict of the modern age. Canada, they believed, had managed to resist these corrupting influences more successfully than had the United States. That said, Canadian critiques of the United States were relatively mild and not as widespread as elsewhere. As historian C.P. Stacey noted, anti-Americanism was much less potent in Canada in the 1920s than it was in Britain.[16]

# Autonomy

In the 1920s and 1930s, Canada gained its independence, though the Canadian government never used the word, fearing it would conjure up images of the American Declaration of Independence. Instead, Canadian governments spoke of autonomy within the British Commonwealth, the self-governing parts of the empire. Independence was the political status that dare not speak its name.

The First World War had fundamentally changed the global balance of power. The United States emerged from the war much stronger relative to the other great powers, while Britain was exhausted—politically, economically, and militarily. The United States was now the richest country on earth. By the end of the 1920s, the country manufactured 46 per cent of the world's industrial goods and was the world's top exporter. As European capitalists liquidated their holdings, American investors bought businesses or established new firms around the world, making the US the world's largest foreign investor.[17] The financial capital of the Western world was now New York, not London.

In 1920, a new Canadian prime minister took office, and faced the challenge posed by this global power shift. Arthur Meighen wished to continue Robert Borden's policy of using membership in the British Empire to advance Canada's international position, but also wanted to be on good terms with the United States. In 1921, Britain's alliance with Japan was up for renewal, and Meighen pushed the British to let it lapse, arguing that it was not in Canada's interests. American officials viewed the treaty as a threat to their interests in the Pacific, and Meighen thought that renewing it would damage both Britain's and Canada's relations with the United States. Ultimately, the British decided to allow the treaty to lapse, though the decision reflected the British sense of their own priorities more than any particular concern over Canadian–American relations. Australia and New Zealand had wanted the alliance renewed, and were dissatisfied with the outcome of the conference. It was clear now that the empire could not create a common foreign policy by consensus.

Meighen's world view differed substantially from that of his successor, William Lyon Mackenzie King, who took office in late 1921. No Canadian prime minister, before or since, knew the United States better than King. He had studied at both the University of Chicago and Harvard University, where he received a master's degree and a doctorate. At Harvard, he made lifelong friendships with members of the American financial and political elite. During the First World War, he earned a great deal of money as director of industrial relations for the Rockefeller Foundation. King and John D. Rockefeller Jr, the family heir, became and remained friends. King also worked as a consultant for several large American companies, including General Electric and Standard Oil (now Exxon). After the war, King was offered, and turned down, a position as head of the Carnegie Corporation, one of the world's largest charities. Throughout his life, he visited the United States regularly, often choosing to vacation there. But this was only one part of King's outlook. Critics then and now have portrayed King as an American at heart, but he was thoroughly Canadian and dedicated to an independent Canada that was part of a cooperative British Commonwealth.

Between 1923 and 1926, King was responsible for the key advances in Canadian independence. In 1923, he insisted that Canada sign the Halibut Treaty with the United States without a British counter-signature. When the British balked at the suggestion, King threatened to open a Canadian legation in Washington, one that would be independent of the British embassy there. The British backed down and, for the first time, Canada signed a treaty as an independent entity, rather than as a component of the British Empire. In the fall of that year, King travelled to London, where he took part in an imperial conference. He insisted that each self-governing part of the empire had the right to pursue its own interests in international affairs.

King played a key role in the imperial conference of 1926, helping to find the language to define Canada's independence. A committee chaired by Lord Balfour, a member of the British Cabinet, issued a report that defined Britain, Canada, and the other dominions as "autonomous communities within the British Empire, equal in status, in no way subordinate one to another in any aspect of their domestic or external affairs, though united by a common allegiance to the Crown, and freely associated as members of the British Commonwealth of Nations."[18] The British reluctantly turned this sentiment into law with the Statute of Westminster of 1931. Canada was no longer a colony within an empire, but rather an independent country within a Commonwealth, though it would take many years before Canadians sorted out the essential elements of independence, including courts, citizenship, and constitution.

After the 1926 conference, King pursued a significant institutional change. He announced the creation of a Canadian legation in Washington, not connected to the British embassy. Vincent Massey, once briefly a Liberal Cabinet minister and the wealthy former head of farm equipment manufacturer Massey-Harris Co., would take the role of Canadian minister. Massey presented his credentials to the American president in 1927, and later that year the United States opened its own legation in Ottawa.

## Ottawa and Washington in the 1920s

The 1920s were a quiet time in the relations between the American and Canadian governments. The Alaska boundary, the subject of the final border dispute between the two countries, had been settled two decades earlier. Problems revolving around boundary waters and fisheries had been solved. When, in 1923, Warren Harding made the first official visit of a US president to Canada, his words captured the spirit of the times. "Let us go our own gaits along parallel roads, you helping us and we helping you," he told a Vancouver crowd of 250,000. "So long as each country maintains its independence, and we both recognize their interdependence, those paths cannot fail to be highways of progress and prosperity."[19]

It seems incongruous in this context that the Canadian military had plans for a war with the United States. Writers have mocked Canada's Defence Scheme Number 1, which called for Canada to defend against an American attack by taking offensive actions (such as seizing Fargo, North Dakota) and then holding on until the British Empire could send troops to drive out the Americans. In reality, military planners prepare for every eventuality, sometimes only as an intellectual exercise. For this reason, the US military also had plans for a war against Canada. But military plans are not political will. It is unlikely that the minister of national defence or prime minister even knew about Canada's plans. Certainly, neither imagined that Canada and the United States would go to war in this decade of North American peace and friendship.

As friendly as relations were in the 1920s, there were still minor sources of friction between Canada and the United States, the most prominent being prohibition. The 18th amendment to the US constitution banned the manufacture and sale of alcohol, beginning in 1920. One problem was that liquor, whether produced in Canada or elsewhere, could easily cross the Canadian–American border. The US government urged Canada to refuse to allow Canadian ships to leave port carrying alcohol intended for the American market. The US also wanted Canada to stop foreign vessels from docking in Canadian ports and offloading alcohol that would then make its way across the border. This put Mackenzie King in an awkward situation: he aspired to be on good terms with the United States but did not see it as Canada's role to enforce American law. Eventually, King backed down. In 1929, Canada stopped other countries from transporting alcohol to the US through Canada, and Parliament passed legislation in 1930 to stop Canadian ships from taking liquor to the United States. These measures, as with most efforts to stop American consumption of alcohol, did not have the desired effect. Canadians continued to sell liquor to Americans, but now Canadians shipped their cargo to the French islands of St Pierre and Miquelon, off the coast of Newfoundland, where others picked the cargo and took it to the US.

The struggle over the smuggling of alcohol into the United States provoked countless minor incidents, as well as one clash that came to preoccupy the two national governments. In the 1920s, the schooner *I'm Alone* was perhaps the most successful of several hundred rumrunners, ships that smuggled alcohol to the US. Registered in Canada and based in Lunenburg, Nova Scotia, *I'm Alone* was owned by a group composed primarily of Americans. A US Coast Guard ship came across *I'm Alone* off the coast of Louisiana in March 1929. The captains of the two ships later provided differing accounts of their exact distance from the US shore, a crucial issue because a 1924 treaty gave Americans the right to stop and search vessels within one hour's sailing time of the US coast. The captain of *I'm Alone* refused to stop to allow the Coast Guard to search his ship, insisting that he was on the high seas, outside of US jurisdiction. After a pursuit, Coast Guard vessels shot at and sank the ship, killing one man. The remaining sailors were placed in irons and taken to New Orleans, where they were jailed for a week, before being released on bail.

Unable to agree over responsibility for the confrontation and the crewman's death, the Canadian and American governments submitted the dispute to arbitration. In 1935, a panel ruled that the Coast Guard's actions were not justified under international law. The United States apologized to Canada and paid the nominal amount of $25,000. Another $25,000 went to the captain, the crew, and the widow of the deceased sailor. The US was not required to pay compensation to the owners, because they were Americans acting in contravention of US law.

The smelter in Trail, British Columbia, was another source of conflict. Built in 1896 to process lead-zinc ore, the smelter looked over the Columbia River, just 11 miles from the US border. "The great furnace upon the hill," wrote one observer in 1898, "looks like an outcrop of hell."[20] The great furnace also emitted tons of sulfur dioxide, scarring the local environment. To mitigate the problem, the smelter's owner, Consolidated Mining and Smelting, enlarged the facility's two smokestacks in the 1920s so that each was 125 metres tall. Yet the effect was merely to blow the pollution farther down the valley into Washington State, where it damaged crops, orchards, and grazing lands. US officials raised the issue with their Canadian counterparts, and the two governments agreed in 1928 to send the issue to the International Joint Commission. In 1931, the commission issued a report that called for $350,000 in compensation to affected Washington State farmers, but did not recommend any changes to the smelter, since Consolidated Mining and Smelting was already in the process of altering the facility to reduce emissions. The Canadian government accepted the recommendations, but the US rejected them.

In 1935, the two countries agreed that the company would pay $350,000 for all damage caused before 1 January 1932 and that subsequent damage would be dealt with by a tribunal composed of three members: one from each country and a neutral chair from Belgium. The tribunal's interim report of 1938 awarded farmers an additional $78,000 for damages since 1 January 1932, and the final report of 1941 required the company undertake a further $20 million in work to control the smelter's emissions. One of the most-cited rulings in international environmental law, the reports established the principle that no country had the right to use its territory, or to allow others to use its territory, in such a way that emissions could cause damage to the territory or property of another country.

## Culture and Ideas

Improvements in technology and the growth of a middle class with both disposable income and time for leisure activities led to a proliferation of mass media in the late nineteenth and early twentieth centuries. The popular culture of the United States, now the richest country in the world, easily crossed the porous border into Canada. Canadian newsstands, cinemas, and radio receivers all bore witness to the emergence of the United States as a cultural colossus.

Motion pictures were invented in the United States in the late nineteenth century. By 1920, they were enormously popular in the United States and in Canada, which was home to 830 commercial cinemas.[21] Yet Canada had no domestic movie industry after 1923. Motion pictures were a highly risky business, and the Canadian economy suffered from a shortage of investment capital. It was daunting for small Canadian companies to compete with Metro Goldwyn Mayer and other American production giants. European countries, faced with similar problems, imposed quotas on their cinemas. For instance, legislation required that 5 per cent of films shown in British theatres in 1928 had to be of British origin, with the quota gradually increasing each year until it reached 20 per cent. In Canada, provincial censorship boards edited out scenes from American films judged damaging to Canadian patriotism or loyalty to the monarch, but little was done to foster domestic film production.

The problem was similar for magazines, though the government response was different. By the mid-1920s, American magazines swamped the Canadian market. The top-selling magazine was *Ladies' Home Journal* with a Canadian circulation of 152,000, more than twice its chief domestic competitor, *Canadian Home Journal*. American periodicals like *Saturday Evening Post*, *Pictorial Review*, and *McCall's Magazine* all outsold the highest-circulating Canadian magazine, *Maclean's*. By the middle of the decade, Canadians were buying eight American magazines for every Canadian one.[22] Canadian publishers sought government protection from their American competitors, using lines of reasoning that have endured to this day. They maintained that the Canadian publishing industry provided an economic benefit to the country by supporting thousands of jobs. They argued that magazines were a source of ideas and values, and that American magazines were immoral and corrupting, threatening Canada's way of life. Critics responded that publishers were merely businesspeople selling a product, that they were motivated by self-interest, not by a desire to advance Canada's economy or culture.

The government's magazine policy changed over the course of the 1930s. Mackenzie King's Liberals were unmoved by the magazine industry's appeal. The government was in the process of gradually reducing tariffs and was not interested in a plea to raise import taxes on one sector. Besides, the Liberals believed that governments should not interfere with the free flow of ideas. The culture industries received a friendlier reception after R.B. Bennett's Conservatives won the election of 1930. The next year, the government introduced a tariff on foreign periodicals. The impact was profound. Circulation of American magazines in Canada dropped 62 per cent from 1931 to 1935, the years the tariff was in effect, while circulation of Canadian magazines increased 64 per cent.[23] But when the Liberals returned to office in 1935, the tariff was abolished. Sales of American magazines soared back to, and then beyond, their old levels.

Radio broadcasting also benefitted from the Bennett government's interventionist approach to popular culture. Radio took off in North America in the 1920s. By mid-decade most Canadians lived within range of American stations, which transmitted signals usually more powerful than those from Canadian broadcasters. Canadians could also hear American programming on Canadian stations affiliated with the NBC and CBS networks. Many Canadians worried that Americans would dominate the airwaves, just as they had dominated the movie industry. The only alternative, it seemed, was government intervention. As Graham Spry, chair of the Canadian Radio League, put it, the choices were "the state or the United States."[24] In 1928, Mackenzie King's government placed the issue in the hands of the Royal Commission on Radio Broadcasting, chaired by Canadian Bank of Commerce President John Aird. The Aird Commission reported in 1929, recommending that the government take over all broadcasting in Canada. There would be no more private stations, only ones owned by the government. King's Liberals had taken no action on the report by the time they were defeated in the 1930 election. The new Conservative government adopted Aird's recommendations in modified form, creating the Canadian Radio Broadcasting Commission (CRBC) in 1932 to regulate private radio stations and to establish a government-owned network. Yet the CRBC was poorly organized and had little money because of the fiscal constraints caused by the Great Depression. In 1936, the CRBC was replaced by the better-funded and better-organized Canadian Broadcasting Corporation (CBC).

The Americanization of Canadian culture included hockey, Canada's most popular sport. The American presence in professional hockey grew rapidly in the 1920s. The National Hockey Association had seven teams, all Canadian, in 1910, its inaugural season. When it was re-established as the National Hockey League in 1917, it still had only Canadian teams. The Boston Bruins became the league's first American team in 1924. Within two years, five other American squads joined: the New York Americans, the Pittsburgh Pirates, the Chicago Black Hawks, the Detroit Cougars (later named the Red Wings), and the New York Rangers. By 1926 there were ten teams, of which only four were Canadian. At the time, there was little handwringing over the entry of American teams, a necessary step to prevent the creation of a better-funded all-American league, against which the NHL would not have been able to compete for players.

Efforts to promote a distinct Canadian identity extended beyond sport and popular culture. English Canadians created social, political, religious, and intellectual organizations dedicated to the cause of helping Canadians know each other and to fostering a national will. In one way or another, each was dedicated to Canadian independence, though some sought autonomy from Britain and others sought to distance Canada from the United States.

In 1921, several writers, including Canada's best-known author, Stephen Leacock, formed the Canadian Authors' Association. They were driven by a concern over the low quality of American books, magazines, and newspapers in Canada, literature that they believed encouraged materialism and had an anti-British tone. The organization promoted Canadian books, campaigned for changes to Canadian copyright legislation to protect the country's writers, and inaugurated the Governor General's Literary Awards, long considered the most prestigious prizes for Canadian writers. Other Canadian organizations created in the 1920s included the Canadian Institute of International Affairs, the Association of Canadian Clubs, and the Canadian Historical Association. *Canadian Forum* began in 1920 as a nationalist magazine for debate about politics and culture.

In 1920, the Group of Seven formed with the goal of creating a Canadian style of painting—one that broke with European traditions—to communicate a common sense of the country. Political independence had to be matched with a cultural distinctiveness, including myths and symbols that could express Canada's identity. The painters' work focussed on the Canadian landscape, often depicting the rugged Canadian Shield in northern Ontario and Quebec, which bore little resemblance to the geography of the rest of the country. According to the best-known member of the group, Lawren Harris, the seven came "to realise how far this country of Canada was different in character, atmosphere, moods, and spirit from Europe and the old land. . . . It had to be seen, lived with, and painted with complete devotion to its own character, life, and spirit, before it yielded its secrets."[25]

The Native Sons of Canada was founded in Victoria in 1921, and had more than 100 chapters and 120,000 members by the end of the decade. In this context, *native* meant those born in Canada, not just those of Aboriginal descent. The organization was dedicated to keeping the Canadian-born from leaving for the United States, encouraging those who had left to return home, and fostering loyalty to Canada. The organization pushed for a Canadian flag and national anthem, a Canadian-born governor general, and an end of appeals from the Supreme Court of Canada to the Judicial Committee of the Privy Council, Britain's highest court. Members were concerned primarily with putting an end to symbols of Canada's colonial past, showing little concern over American influences.

In 1925, the United Church of Canada was formed as a merger of the Methodist, Presbyterian, and Congregationalist churches. It saw itself as a national church: a large, nation-wide, uniquely Canadian institution, bringing together people from across the country. The founders intended that the church create a national sentiment and a distinctly Canadian Christianity, one shaped for the Canadian context. For church leaders, Canada was an English-speaking and Protestant nation; they generally ignored French Canada and the Roman Catholic Church. They saw the United States as a corrupt and violent place, and believed that Canada had a divine mission for greatness; in particular, Canada would lead in the reunification of Christian churches around the world.

## Investment and Trade

In the wake of the First World War, British investors began selling off their assets abroad, often to American buyers. In 1922, for the first time, American investment in Canada exceeded British investment. Canadians expressed little unease as Americans continued to purchase Canadian companies and to set up Canadian branches of large American firms. As historian C.P. Stacey recalled, "Whenever a new American branch-plant opened in Canada we considered it a diplomatic victory; our government's policy, we told ourselves, was working well, and jobs were being created for Canadians."[26]

While Canada had easy access to American capital, selling Canadian products to the American market was considerably more difficult, particularly when a global recession hit after the First World War. In response to demands from farmers, the US government imposed an emergency tariff in 1921, replaced by the Fordney–McCumber Tariff in 1922. Canadian

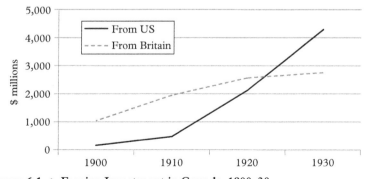

**Figure 6.1** ⊹ Foreign Investment in Canada, 1900–30

Source: Data provided by John Bartlet Brebner, *North Atlantic Triangle: The Interplay of Canada, the United States, and Great Britain* (Toronto: McClelland and Stewart, 1966), 244.

exports of grain and livestock to the United States fell dramatically and remained low throughout the 1920s.

The Great Depression of the 1930s had a devastating effect on both Canada and the United States. The October 1929 collapse of share values on the New York Stock Exchange was the beginning of an international economic downturn. Throughout the industrialized world, production fell and unemployment soared. From 1929 to 1933, consumer expenditures dropped 34.3 per cent in Canada and 41.2 per cent in the United States. Agricultural income fell 67.8 per cent in Canada and 61.4 per cent in the United States. Of the major Western countries, only Germany was hit as hard.[27] People in both Canada and the United States blamed their leaders. In the United States, automobiles that had to be pulled by horses because the owner could not afford gasoline became known as Hoover wagons, after the despised US president Herbert Hoover. In Canada, they were Bennett buggies, after the Canadian prime minister.

The two governments responded in much the same way, increasing tariffs to stop imports, a policy that only made matters worse. Canadian farmers, still suffering from the Fordney–McCumber Tariff of 1922, were now hit by the even more severe Smoot–Hawley Tariff of 1930. The impact was devastating, as the US was the Canadian farmer's greatest market. From 1920–1 to 1930–1, Canadian exports of fresh beef to the United States fell from $5.8 million to $460,000; wheat from $91.4 million to $7.7 million; flour from $12.0 million to $2,500; live cattle from $21.2 million to $1.4 million; and butter from $3.2 million to $17,000.[28] In the 1930 general election, R.B. Bennett capitalized on Canadian resentment of American trade policy, promising he would raise Canadian tariffs to force other countries to the negotiating table where all customs duties could be lowered. "I will use tariffs to blast a way into the markets that have been closed to you," he pledged.[29] When Bennett came to power, he quickly raised Canada's tariffs, the greatest increase since the implementation of the National Policy in 1879. Trade levels dropped, and unemployment continued to rise in both countries, though the impact of the trade war was greater on Canada, more dependent than the US on the Canadian–American trading relationship.

The US government's approach to the economic crisis changed dramatically when Franklin Roosevelt became president in March 1933. His New Deal program consisted of a wide range of measures that increased the role of government, both to provide immediate economic relief to Americans and to implement long-term reforms to prevent a future economic collapse. In June 1934, Roosevelt signed into law the Reciprocal Trade Agreements Act of 1934, giving the president the power, without the usually required approval of Congress, to negotiate trade agreements with other countries, reducing American tariffs by as much as half.

Few US presidents have had as strong an impact on Canada as Roosevelt. From the age of 2 until he was stricken with polio at 39, Roosevelt summered every year at the family home on Campobello Island in New Brunswick. Although he exhibited little interest in Canada after coming to office, he was popular throughout the country, where his radio addresses, known as fireside chats, could be heard. As a *New York Times* reporter noted, Roosevelt was "more widely known in Canada—even if only as a golden voice over the radio—than anyone who has ever held his position."[30] He was considerably more popular than either of his two Canadian counterparts, Bennett and Mackenzie King.

Bennett received frequent reports about Roosevelt's policies from the Canadian minister in Washington, William Duncan Herridge, who was both Bennett's friend and brother-in-law. According to the Washington correspondent of the *Winnipeg Free Press*, the Canadian legation in Washington became an "open house at all times to the New Deal crowd."[31] Herridge had befriended Secretary of Agriculture Henry A. Wallace, senior Roosevelt adviser Rex Tugwell, and high-ranking officials from the National Recovery Administration, a government agency that helped set minimum wages, maximum work hours, and minimum prices for products. Although skeptical about the economic impact of the New Deal, Herridge knew that it had enormous political value. He worked tirelessly to convince the Canadian prime minister to enact his own version of the program. "We need," wrote Herridge, "some means by which the people can be persuaded that they also have a New Deal, and that the New Deal will do everything for them *in fact* which the New Deal here has done *in fancy*."[32]

In the dying days of his government, with defeat imminent, Bennett pursued two initiatives inspired by Roosevelt's example. The first was a Canadian New Deal, announced in a Roosevelt-style series of radio broadcasts in January 1935. Bennett promised a maximum workweek, a minimum wage, and unemployment insurance, among a host of other measures. The second was an effort to reach a trade agreement with the United States. Roosevelt and Bennett had met in Washington in 1933 and had agreed to work toward lower tariffs, but negotiations only began in late August 1935. Expecting Bennett's defeat, Roosevelt might well have delayed the negotiations, hoping to deal with a more friendly Liberal government after the election.

Despite his reputation for caution and indecision, Mackenzie King often acted decisively when the time was right and the issue was right. His Liberals won the 1935 election, and King returned to office as prime minister on 23 October. The next day, he visited Norman Armour, US minister in Ottawa, and asked for a meeting with President Roosevelt. On 8 November, King was in the White House, conversing with the president. On the 9th,

King and the US secretary of state approved a draft trade agreement. The two men signed the final text six days later.

King was exaggerating when he called the agreement "the greatest political achievement of my life, and one of the greatest on this continent in a century or more," but it was still of great significance.[33] It was the first trade pact between Canada and the United States since the Reciprocity Treaty of 1854. The tariff reductions were slight, and Canada conceded more than the United States in the negotiations. Still, the 1935 agreement began a long, slow process of tariff reduction, marking the end of the end of the National Policy era, which had endured for more than half a century. The agreement was expanded with a more extensive trade accord signed in Washington in November 1938. After the signing, King gave a short statement, saying that relations between the two countries had "never been happier than in the three years" since 1935.[34] That time, he was not exaggerating.

King and Roosevelt had the warmest relations of any US president and Canadian prime minister. Both were graduates of Harvard. Although they attended the university in different periods (Roosevelt was seven years younger than King), they had met at Harvard in 1923, when the Canadian had received an honorary doctorate from their alma mater. Both were in the habit of doling out excessive praise to others. As C.P. Stacey has noted, King also had extensive experience in "cultivating good relations with wealthy Americans."[35] The terms in office for the two leaders overlapped for almost 10 years, the longest of any American president and Canadian prime minister. They served together through the momentous years of the Great Depression and the Second World War, and would come to forge an intimate relationship between their two governments.

## Summary

The First World War was a defining moment in Canada-US relations. It diminished British economic and political power and fostered closer ties between Canada and the United States. Prime Minister Borden abandoned his opposition to freer trade between the two countries, actively pursuing closer economic integration. Afterward, Canadians developed a North American mindset that distinguished them from the British—while still feeling superior to Americans. Canadians enjoyed American music, motion pictures, and magazines, though some Canadians remained troubled about the flood of cultural products across the Canada–US border. Few Canadians were concerned that American dollars were also flowing northward, buying up Canadian companies and establishing new factories.

Although the word was seldom used, the Canadian goal was independence—both from Britain and the United States. In the 1920s, the government of Mackenzie King won Canadian political autonomy from Britain. Canadians and Americans developed a similar outlook on international affairs, and their two governments pursued increasingly friendly relations, dealing directly with each other (rather than working through British intermediaries) and sending outstanding disputes to arbitration.

Yet independence did not mean poverty. The high tariffs of the early 1930s damaged both economies, particularly Canada's, clearly demonstrating the *inter*dependence of the two countries. To King, it seemed the only option was to begin dismantling the barriers to trade, putting an end to the National Policy era, which Macdonald had inaugurated more than 50 years earlier.

# Beyond the Book

1. Did the presence of American culture pose a threat to the Canadian identity?
2. Why did Canada seek independence from Britain?
3. Why did Canadians turn toward a North American mindset? Was there any alternative?

# Further Reading

C.P. Stacey, *Canada and the Age of Conflict: A History of Canadian External Policies*, 2 vols. (Toronto: Macmillan, 1977, 1981), is invaluable on a wide range of topics. Stacey's *Mackenzie King and the Atlantic Triangle* (Toronto: Macmillan, 1976) is highly perceptive and beautifully written.

On the North American mindset, see Norman Hillmer, "O.D. Skelton and the North American Mind," *International Journal* 60, no. 1 (Winter 2004–2005): 93–110. Donald M. Page looks at the Canadian tendency to lecture Europeans about the meaning of peace in "Canada as the Exponent of North American Idealism," *American Review of Canadian Studies* 3, no. 2 (Autumn 1973): 30–46. An insightful analysis of Canadian suspicions of Europe can be found in James Eayrs, "'A Low Dishonest Decade': Aspects of Canadian External Policy, 1931–1939," in *The Growth of Canadian Policy in External Affairs*, by Hugh L. Keenleyside et al. (Durham, North Carolina: Duke University Press, 1960), 59–80. James A. Macdonald, *The North American Idea* (Toronto: McClelland, Goodchild and Stewart, 1917) is full of bombast, but reflects North American sentiment in Canada. Carl Berger explores North Americanism in Canadian scholarship in chapter 6 of *The Writing of Canadian History: Aspects of English–Canadian Historical Writing since 1900*, 2nd ed. (Toronto: University of Toronto Press, 1986). On the role of wealthy American foundations in Canada, see Jeffrey D. Brison's thorough study, *Rockefeller, Carnegie, and Canada: American Philanthropy and the Arts and Letters in Canada* (Montreal and Kingston: McGill-Queen's University Press, 2005). A different perspective emerges in Damien-Claude Bélanger's *Prejudice and Pride: Canadian Intellectuals Confront the United States, 1891–1945* (Toronto: University of Toronto Press, 2011), which examines English- and French-Canadian critiques of the United States.

On Canadian autonomy from Britain, see John Hilliker, *Canada's Department of External Affairs*, vol. 1, *The Early Years, 1909–1946* (Montreal and Kingston: McGill–Queen's University Press, 1990); and H. Blair Neatby, *William Lyon Mackenzie King*, vol. 2, *1924–1932: The Lonely Heights* (Toronto: University of Toronto Press, 1963). John S. Galbraith examines Canadian diplomatic representation in *The Establishment of Canadian Diplomatic Status at Washington* (Berkeley and Los Angeles: University of California Press, 1951).

The best overview of the struggles over Canadian popular culture is Mary Vipond, *The Mass Media in Canada*, 4th ed. (Toronto: James Lorimer, 2011). Specific sectors are examined in Peter Morris, *Embattled Shadows: A History of Canadian Cinema, 1895–1939* (Montreal and Kingston: McGill–Queen's University Press, 1978); Mary Vipond, "Canadian Nationalism and the Plight of Canadian Magazines in the 1920s," *Canadian Historical Review* 58, no. 1 (March 1977): 43–63; and Mary Vipond, *Listening In: The First Decade of Canadian Broadcasting, 1922–1932* (Montreal and Kingston: McGill–Queen's University Press, 1992).

The pre-eminent work on Canadian–American trade relations in the interwar years is the superb book by Ian M. Drummond and Norman Hillmer, *Negotiating Freer Trade: The United Kingdom, the United States, Canada, and the Trade Agreements of 1938* (Waterloo, Ontario: Wilfrid Laurier University Press, 1989). Richard N. Kottman has contributed several valuable works, including "Herbert Hoover and the Smoot–Hawley Tariff: Canada, a Case Study," *Journal of American History* 62, no. 3 (December 1975): 609–35; and *Reciprocity and the North Atlantic Triangle, 1932–1938* (Ithaca, New York: Cornell University Press, 1968).

The most-cited work on Canadian defence policy in the 1920s is James Eayrs, *In Defence of Canada*, vol. 1, *From the Great War to the Great Depression* (Toronto: University of Toronto Press, 1964). The book is teeming with insights, but Eayrs has a tendency to mock when he should be trying to understand. Stephen J. Harris provides much-needed balance in *Canadian Brass: The Making of a Professional Army, 1860–1939* (Toronto: University of Toronto Press, 1988).

On the origins of R.B. Bennett's New Deal, see Larry A. Glassford, *Reaction and Reform: The Politics of the Conservative Party under R.B. Bennett, 1927–1938* (Toronto: University of Toronto Press, 1992); P.B. Waite, *In Search of R.B. Bennett* (Montreal and Kingston: McGill–Queen's University Press, 2012); and J.R.H. Wilbur, ed., *The Bennett New Deal: Fraud or Portent?* (Toronto: Copp Clark, [1968]).

# CHAPTER 7

---⌾---

# Allies, 1938–1945

## *The Second World War*

## Introduction

Franklin Roosevelt looked at the clouds over Kingston, Ontario. "Is it going to rain?" "No, Mr. President," responded William Lyon Mackenzie King, "it is going to be fine." The two leaders were in the small Ontario city, just 20 kilometres across the St Lawrence River from New York State, on 18 August 1938. Canada and the United States were still mired in an economic depression, and mounting tensions in Europe made war look increasingly likely, but Roosevelt was jovial, as he usually was. Thousands of spectators lined the streets to wave and cheer as the president's motorcade made its way to the stadium at Queen's University. Soon the clouds parted. Under a sunny sky, before a crowd of 10,000, the president received an honorary doctor of laws.

Then Roosevelt gave a 13-minute speech that defined the new reality of Canadian–American relations. He began by warning North Americans they could not isolate themselves from events in Europe. "We in the Americas are no longer a far away continent, to which the eddies of controversies beyond the seas could bring no interest or no harm." He developed this idea for a few more sentences before turning to the speech's key message. Officials in the State Department had written his text, but the crucial passage was added in the president's own hand. He spoke it loudly and clearly: "I give you assurance that the people of the United States will not stand idly by if domination of Canadian soil is threatened by any other Empire." The sentence electrified the crowd. Roosevelt's remarks were greeted by a standing ovation and, in the words of one reporter, a "thunder of applause that was sustained for several minutes." When members of the audience quieted

**Photo 7.1** ⊹ William Lyon Mackenzie King and Franklin Roosevelt

Mackenzie King and Roosevelt were all smiles on 18 August 1938, not long after the US president had pledged in his Queen's University convocation address that the United States would not allow Canada to be attacked. (Source: Library and Archives Canada, C-090217.)

and returned to their seats, Roosevelt continued with a line that defined the North American mindset as well as any other: "We as good neighbours are true friends because we maintain our own rights with frankness, because we refuse to accept the twists of secret diplomacy, because we settle our disputes by consultation, and because we discuss our common problems in the spirit of the common good."[1]

On the platform during Roosevelt's convocation address, Mackenzie King had not known what the president was about to say. Two days later, in a speech in Woodbridge, north of Toronto, King gave Canada's response. "We, too, have our obligations as a good friendly neighbour," King told his audience. One of those responsibilities was to ensure that enemy forces could not attack the United States from Canada "either by land, sea, or air."[2] King called this "reciprocity in defence," but it was not truly reciprocal.[3] The Americans had pledged to defend Canada if necessary, but with one-tenth the military strength of the United States, Canada was in no position to defend the United States. The best King could do was to promise that Canada would not be a security burden to the Americans. The two speeches, Roosevelt's and King's, laid the groundwork for a Canadian–American alliance, founded on a common world view and an understanding that each country had an interest in the security of the other.

# Jewish Refugees

Long before Adolf Hitler posed any threat to North America, he terrorized his own country's Jewish population. Shortly after he took power in January 1933, his Nazi party organized boycotts of Jewish businesses and public burnings of Jewish books. Jews were subjected to violence and their property was vandalized, often destroyed. Within months, the German legislature passed laws that prevented Jews from teaching in schools or universities, or working in the public service, the media, or the theatre. In 1935, the Nuremberg laws declared that Jews were no longer German citizens. Jews who married or had sex with Germans could be imprisoned or sentenced to hard labour. Subsequent laws prevented Jewish doctors from treating non-Jews and banned Jews from practising law. Jews sought refuge abroad, but there were few countries willing to accept them.

North Americans sympathized with Hitler's victims, but did not do enough to assist them. In the midst of the Great Depression, Canadians and Americans were hostile to any immigration, fearing that newcomers would either add to the large number of unemployed or would take jobs away from citizens. Some were motivated by anti-Semitism, a sentiment deeply rooted in North America. In both Canada and the United States, some private clubs had long refused to accept Jewish members, and major universities had quotas limiting the number of Jewish students.

In July 1938, the US government organized a meeting on Jewish refugees at Évian-les-Bains in France. Canada was one of 32 countries that took part in the conference, which accomplished little of substance. Beforehand, Hitler had taunted those countries that condemned his treatment of the Jews but were unwilling themselves to accept refugees: if they really were sympathetic to the Jews, they should "at least be generous enough to convert this sympathy into practical aid."[4] After the conference, Hitler again ridiculed the Western democracies: "They are not trying to solve the so-called problem. . . . Quite the contrary, they inform us very coolly that there is of course no room [for Jews] over there. . . . They offer no help, but, oh, the moralizing!"[5]

The gravity of the Jewish situation became clear on Kristallnacht, known in English as Crystal Night or the Night of Broken Glass. On 7 November 1938, a 17-year-old Jewish youth murdered a German diplomat in Paris. The Nazis used this crime as a pretense to organize mass riots against German Jews. Beginning on the night of 9 November, and continuing into the next day, mobs ransacked Jewish homes, businesses, synagogues, hospitals, and schools. Jews were beaten or shot, with more than 90 losing their lives. Firefighters were ordered to let Jewish buildings burn. Instead of stopping the violence, the police arrested tens of thousands of victims, without warrant, and placed them in concentration camps. Afterward, Jews were forbidden from claiming insurance money on their damaged property, and the Jewish community as a whole was fined one billion Reichsmarks, a massive sum in those days. (To put the figure in context, a new Opel automobile cost 2,100 Reichsmarks.[6])

The number of Jewish refugees increased dramatically in 1938 and 1939. Fearful for their security before Kristallnacht, German Jews were now terrified. Virtually all of them wanted to leave Germany. Adding to their numbers were hundreds of thousands of Austrian and Czech Jews who suddenly found themselves living under Nazi rule as Germany expanded its territory. They, too, desperately wanted out.

Kristallnacht had an emotional impact on both Mackenzie King and Franklin Roosevelt. "I myself could scarcely believe that such things could occur in a twentieth-century civilization," Roosevelt said in a public statement.[7] He was the only world leader to recall his country's ambassador in Berlin, one step short of breaking off diplomatic relations with Germany. Still, there was little else he could do without an increase in the country's immigration quotas, which Congress was unlikely to approve in the face of public opinion. Just two weeks after Kristallnacht, a public opinion survey showed that 77 per cent of Americans were opposed to allowing "a larger number of Jewish exiles from Germany to come to the United States to live."[8] The story was similar in Canada. "The sorrows which the Jews have to bear at this time are almost beyond comprehension," Mackenzie King wrote in his diary two days after Kristallnacht.[9] Although he resolved to do something to help the Jews, he did not increase the number of refugees Canada would accept. In late November 1938, a group of Jews met with King and his immigration minister to propose that Canada admit 10,000 Jewish refugees. King was courteous, but he warned the Jewish leaders that it would be difficult to take more immigrants during that time of high unemployment. The prime minister raised the issue in Cabinet, but none of his ministers supported taking in more refugees, believing that such an action might cost them political support.

The plight of Jewish refugees received further attention in the spring of 1939. In May, a German ship, the St Louis, departed Hamburg for Cuba with more than 900 Jewish refugees on board. The Cuban government allowed almost 30 passengers with visas to disembark, but rejected the rest, who held Cuban landing permits. With the ship anchored in Cuban waters, the refugees contacted other Latin American countries, but no government would accept them. Nor would Canada or the United States. After three weeks at sea and with nowhere else to go, the ship turned back to Europe, docking in Antwerp, Belgium. The refugees made their way to Britain, France, Belgium, and the Netherlands. During the Second World War, many of them again found themselves under Nazi rule, and 250 of them later perished in the Holocaust. In the late 1930s, though, no Canadian or American decision maker imagined that the Nazi regime would begin in 1941 the systematic extermination of Europe's Jewish population.

The American record is sad, the Canadian worse. From the time Hitler took office in 1933 until his regime collapsed in 1945, the US accepted 200,000 Jewish refugees, more than any other country in the world, but nowhere near enough to save all those seeking safe haven. Canada admitted fewer than 5,000—one-third the number of refugees welcomed in Australia, one-fifth of the number who settled in Brazil, and one-tenth the number admitted to Argentina.[10]

# To War Again

When Adolf Hitler took office in 1933, he resolved to undo the Treaty of Versailles, the agreement that had brought a formal end to the First World War. Because some of Hitler's complaints seemed legitimate, other countries took no action when he violated the treaty by sending troops into German territory on the French border or by annexing neighbouring Austria. Still, Hitler's continuing demands unsettled the international community. The British and French response was based on the belief that Germany had been unfairly treated in the aftermath of the First World War and that many Germans had channelled their anger into support for Hitler and his Nazi party. Once the problems with the treaty were solved, Naziism would lose its appeal—or so the British and French thought. Working from these premises, Britain and France launched a policy known as appeasement: the elimination, through negotiation, of the sources of German frustration. In case the policy failed, British prime minister Neville Chamberlain also prepared for war, beginning the process of rearming Britain.

Most Canadians and Americans supported appeasement, believing that it would help avoid another world war. They were disenchanted with the First World War, believing, in retrospect, that thousands of North Americans had died needlessly in a petty squabble. Historian Frank Underhill no doubt spoke for many Canadians when he said that his country should play no role in the next European conflict. The last war made clear that sending Canadian troops "is no contribution to European stability or prosperity." Underhill urged Canadians to "make it clear to the world, and especially to Great Britain, that the poppies blooming in Flanders fields have no further interest for us."[11]

Both the US and Canadian governments backed appeasement. In Washington and Ottawa, the consensus was that Germany had been harshly punished after the First World War and that Britain and France needed to compromise to avoid another global conflict. After Chamberlain and French prime minister Édouard Daladier agreed at Munich to allow Germany to annex the Sudetenland, a part of Czechoslovakia on the German border, Canadian prime minister William Lyon Mackenzie King sent a telegram to his British counterpart, expressing "unbounded admiration at the service you have rendered mankind."[12] US President Franklin Roosevelt's two-word message to Chamberlain was characteristically brisk: "Good man."[13] Historians have since made fun of King, but the prime minister's misreading of Hitler, which lasted only until the spring of 1938, was one shared by virtually all of the Western world's major statesmen, including Roosevelt.

But what if appeasement failed and Canada were threatened by an aggressive Germany or by Japan, which was at war to expand its territory in Asia? Roosevelt dealt with the subject in his August 1938 convocation address at Queen's University in Kingston, Ontario. Although replete with rhetoric about the friendship between the two countries, Roosevelt's speech was above all an expression of the national interest of the United States. Still hoping to keep the United States out of the coming war, Roosevelt had used the speech to warn Germany and Japan to stay out of North America.

Soon it became clear that British and French policy was built on a faulty premise. Not satisfied with the Sudetenland, Hitler seized the Czech territories of Bohemia and Moravia in March 1939, destroying any illusion that he was a reasonable man with limited demands. Britain and France abandoned appeasement and rejected Hitler's claim that Germany was entitled to a chunk of Poland. On 1 September 1939, Germany invaded Poland. Britain and France declared war on Germany two days later.

Was Canada bound by Britain's declaration of war? US officials were not so certain. Roosevelt was about to issue a neutrality proclamation that would prevent American companies from selling arms to belligerents, but he and his advisers could not agree on whether Canada should be included. The president and his secretary of state, Cordell Hull, called Mackenzie King on 5 September to ask if Canada was at war. The prime minister explained that Canada was not yet a belligerent—at least not until Parliament had a chance to decide the issue later in the week. "You see, I was right!" Roosevelt declared.[14] He scratched Canada's name from the neutrality proclamation he would issue later the same day. The US continued sending arms and military aircraft to Canada, a flow that stopped on 10 September, when Canada declared war on Germany.

Although Canada was at war and the United States was neutral, both governments pursued a similar policy of limited liability, supporting Britain without dispatching large numbers of ground troops. In the initial stages of the war, before Germany's May 1940 attack on its western neighbours, both Roosevelt and King imagined their countries would contribute more in arms than armies to Europe. Canadians and Americans would make a substantial contribution to the defeat of Hitler, but would lose few lives in the process, at least few relative to their losses in the First World War. "It is in the economic field that we can give aid that will be most effective to our allies and most consistent with Canadian interests," O.D. Skelton, undersecretary of state for external affairs, wrote in a memorandum to the prime minister.[15] Canada was immediately responsible for the British Commonwealth Air Training Plan, which trained pilots and other personnel for the air forces of Britain and other Commonwealth countries. King hoped then that the country's extensive role in air training would satisfy the British government and the Canadian public that Canada was pulling its weight. For his part, Roosevelt made it clear that the US sided with Britain morally and he convinced Congress to amend the Neutrality Act to allow the British to purchase arms in the United States.

North Americans took notice when the war in Europe became dire in the spring of 1940. German forces quickly overran the neutral countries of Denmark, Norway, Belgium, the Netherlands, and Luxembourg. France fell in less than seven weeks. Britain's only remaining allies were the members of the Commonwealth. The most important was Canada, which now undertook a much more extensive war effort, giving Britain billions of dollars of arms and cash, while sending thousands of soldiers overseas. In September 1940, Roosevelt traded fifty naval destroyers (six of which ended up in the Canadian navy) for land to build US bases or airfields on British territories around the world, including Newfoundland (which would become a Canadian province only in 1949) and several islands in the Caribbean. When Britain could no longer afford to purchase American arms, Roosevelt convinced Congress to pass the Lend-Lease Act of March 1941, which allowed the United States to give war *matériel* to the British under the pretense that these gifts were loans. Then in August, Roosevelt and British Prime Minister Winston Churchill met on an American warship in Placentia Bay, Newfoundland, and agreed to the Atlantic Charter, a lofty joint statement of war aims.

Eventually, both Canada and the United States would send large numbers of troops overseas. Canadians began preparing to deploy military personnel almost immediately after the outbreak of war. For the Americans, the turning point came on 7 December 1941, when the Japanese attacked American naval vessels at Pearl Harbor, Hawaii. The North American contribution to the war was massive. Both the US and Canadian navies helped convoy supply and troop ships across the Atlantic. Canadian and American aviators bombed German targets. Ground forces fought to push the Germans out of Italy and Western Europe, eventually taking the war to German soil. In Asia, Canadians were involved in the failed December 1941

effort to defend Hong Kong. US forces drove the Japanese out of their occupied territories and back to the home islands. In all, more than 1 million
Canadians and 16 million Americans served in the armed forces. More than
42,000 Canadians and 290,000 Americans were killed.

## The Canadian–American Alliance

On 16 August 1940, Roosevelt telephoned Mackenzie King. At the time,
the situation was bleak for all those wishing the defeat of Nazi Germany.
The Germans controlled most of Europe and days earlier had begun an
enormous air attack on Britain. The American president was heading off
to review US troops in Ogdensburg, New York, just 90 kilometres south
of Ottawa. Would King meet him there the next evening? Roosevelt had
made the call spontaneously, without seeking advice from his military advisers. King now acted likewise, leaving to meet the president without seeking advice from the military, his civilian aides, or his Cabinet colleagues.
The minister of national defence would have to learn about the trip from a
newspaper article.

At Ogdensburg, King and Roosevelt had a pleasant meeting in the
president's railway car. Roosevelt sketched out an agreement for the creation of a Canadian–American commission on defence, much to the surprise of the US secretary of war. He had not been consulted about the president's proposal, but at least he was present at the meeting. King had arrived
without any of his Cabinet ministers. The prime minister embraced the
plan, but suggested the organization be called the Permanent Joint Board
on Defence, a name that Roosevelt quickly accepted. The board would be
an advisory body to study and make recommendations for the common
defence of North America. The agreement was formalized not in a treaty
but in a press release, which neither the president nor the prime minister signed. The PJBD symbolized the beginning of a Canada–US military
alliance that continues to this day, though the board no longer performs
the same vital role that it did in the dark days immediately after Hitler's
conquest of Europe in 1940.

Having negotiated a defence agreement with the United States, King's
mind turned to economic issues. Canada had been manufacturing massive
amounts of war *matériel* for the British, with about one-third of the raw materials and components for these munitions coming from the United States.
For instance, Canada sent many trucks to Britain, each of which contained
several American engine parts. As a result, Canadian imports from south
of the border were increasing rapidly, but there was no corresponding rise
in Canadian exports to the United States, making it difficult for Canada
to pay for its purchases south of the border. When Congress passed the

Lend-Lease Act in March 1941, Canada's economic situation became more complex. Now that Britain could obtain war *matériel* in the United States without having to pay upfront, or perhaps ever, would the British stop their purchases in Canada?

In April 1941, Mackenzie King met with Roosevelt to rectify Canada's increasingly precarious economic position. The prime minister arrived at the president's estate in Hyde Park, New York, armed with a draft agreement to solve Canada's problems. Roosevelt made one insignificant change and then had the text retyped without the word "draft." When the revised version arrived, King asked if they should sign it. Roosevelt replied that signatures were not necessary, and wrote on the first page, "Done by Mackenzie and F.D.R. at Hyde Park on a grand Sunday, April 20, 1941."[16]

The president's casual acceptance of the Hyde Park agreement does not reflect its economic importance. Roosevelt had allowed Canada not to pay for American components used in producing equipment and munitions for Britain; instead, the cost would be charged to Britain's Lend-Lease account, to be settled after the war. The US further agreed to purchase between $200 million and $300 million of Canadian munitions and supplies in the coming year, money Canada could then use to pay for some of its purchases in the US. One short document had solved Canada's pressing balance of payments problem, a testament to the goodwill between Roosevelt and King and to their ability to work together, to say nothing of the self-interest that bound the two North American countries together tighter than ever.

# Defending the North

After the attack on Pearl Harbor, American military planners became anxious about a possible Japanese attack on the North American West Coast. Alaska was particularly vulnerable, because its remote location made it difficult to supply. Before the war, Canadians and Americans had considered building a highway to link Alaska to the Yukon and to northern British Columbia and Alberta. The road would have helped the economic development of the region, but Mackenzie King was reluctant to proceed. Now that it seemed a military necessity, King gave his approval.

In March 1942, Canada and the United States signed an agreement to construct a road from Alaska, through the Yukon, to Dawson Creek, BC, which was already connected by highway to all the major cities in North America. The US would pay the entire cost of building the highway and maintaining it during the war. Six months after the war, the portion on Canadian territory would be turned over to the government of Canada. In exchange, Canada would give the Americans the right of way for the road, would allow American labourers free access to Canada to work on the project, and would let them use gravel and timber from the surrounding area.

Work began in April 1942 under the supervision of the US Army Corps of Engineers. By October, crews had built a rough pioneer road from Big Delta, Alaska, to Dawson Creek, a distance of 2,200 kilometres. The next year, the road was improved and extended by more than 100 kilometres to Fairbanks, Alaska. A massive project, the construction of the Alaska Highway employed 11,000 American soldiers and 16,000 American and Canadian civilians.

Canadian officials were ambivalent about the highway. The Canadian government had little interest in owning it after the war, because it would be costly to maintain and would serve little peacetime use. Still, the government could not allow the United States to control a road on Canadian soil, so the federal government reluctantly accepted ownership in 1946. It did not help that the Americans never completed the road to civilian standards, as originally promised.

The Canadian government was similarly hesitant about the Canol Pipeline. Built from 1942 to 1944, the line took crude oil almost 1,000 kilometres from Imperial Oil fields at Norman Wells in the Northwest Territories to a Whitehorse refinery that produced fuel for US forces in the North. Canadian officials were annoyed that the United States negotiated the deal with Imperial Oil and informed them only on the day the deal was signed, before the Canadian Cabinet could discuss it. Some Canadian government departments had doubts about the project, misgivings that American officials ignored. While construction was underway, Americans were reluctant to share information about the project with their Canadian counterparts, acting as though the project was entirely on US soil. Mackenzie King became troubled by the American presence in the Canadian North and the possibility that it might continue in peacetime. "We ought to get the Americans out of the further development there, and keep complete control in our own hands," he wrote in his diary in February 1944.[17]

In the end, Canol was poorly built and massively over budget. It operated for 13 months, but only at about one-third of its planned capacity. In March 1945, with the Japanese no longer a threat to the North American Northwest, the military stopped using the pipeline. Oil companies were not interested in purchasing it, because the pipe diameter was too narrow for the line to be commercially viable. Having spent $134 million on the project, the US sold the pipe in 1947 to a company that dismantled it and shipped it south. The Americans left behind trucks and equipment, "a junkyard monument to military stupidity," in the words of journalist Leslie Roberts.[18]

# Between Britain and the United States

During the war, Mackenzie King imagined that Canada could be the linch-
pin between the United States and Britain, holding the two great powers
together. Briefly, from September 1939 to December 1941, King sometimes acted as intermediary between the two countries, interpreting one to
the other, but his position was based on an unusual and short-lived situation—Britain at war while the United States was a non-belligerent. All this
changed in late 1941. Now that the Americans were in the war, no intermediary was needed.

King understood and accepted his limited place in the direction of the
allied war effort. He was not included when Roosevelt and Churchill met
at Placentia Bay, Newfoundland, in August 1941. Nor was he present at
their conference in Casablanca in January 1943 or their subsequent meetings with Soviet leader Joseph Stalin. King was invited to Washington when
Winston Churchill visited the American capital in December 1941, June
1942, and May 1943, spending much time on all three occasions with the
president and the British prime minister, who provided him with updates
on the war but never consulted him on strategic questions. King acted as
host when the British and American leaders, and their military advisers, met
in Quebec City in August 1943. King had his picture taken with Churchill
and Roosevelt, but was not asked to join them—nor did he push for a place
at the table—when they met behind closed doors. The story was the same
at the second Quebec Conference, held in September 1944. Although allied
leaders were determining grand strategy on Canadian soil, the Canadian
leader was not consulted. He was satisfied with having the newspapers print
photographs of him with his popular American and British counterparts.

# The Forked Road

In the years after the war, some of Canada's leading historians attacked
King's record, arguing that he sold out Canada to the United States. By fostering the American connection at the expense of Canada's traditional ties
to Britain, King had essentially destroyed Canada, or so conservative scholars argued. The result of King's policies, historian W.L. Morton claimed in
1964, was that Canada was "so irradiated by the American presence that it
sickens and threatens to dissolve in cancerous slime."[19] Later in the 1960s,
political scientists on the left of the political spectrum adopted this argument as their own.

No one advanced this interpretation more passionately or in a more sustained fashion than Donald Creighton, the pre-eminent English-Canadian
historian in the 1940s and 1950s. In *The Forked Road: Canada, 1939–1957*

and in other books and articles, Creighton argued that Canada reached a crossroads during the Second World War: it could have either maintained the British connection or travelled the American route. According to Creighton, King chose the latter option. The British tie had distinguished Canada from the United States, but King destroyed that bond by pursuing Canadian autonomy in the 1920s, meaning that Canada would inevitably become American. King, the argument continued, closely linked the Canadian and American economies by signing trade agreements with the United States in the 1930s. Then, during the Second World War, King became a servant of the United States. "He behaved like a puppet which could be animated only by the President of the United States," in Creighton's words. In the Ogdensburg agreement, King "bound Canada to a continental system dominated by the United States."[20] At Hyde Park, he further tied the Canadian economy to that of the US.

Most historians accept that Canada became closely linked to the United States during the Second World War, though liberal historians insist that King never wanted Canada to become a satellite of the United States and that, indeed, Canada did not become a satellite. Canada's position between Britain and the US was shaped by forces beyond the control of the Canadian government. King had negotiated trade agreements with the US, much as Conservative prime minister R.B. Bennett had tried desperately to do. For both prime ministers, increased continental trade was a matter of economic necessity, not of selling out Canada to the United States. In the 1940s, King turned to the United States, as had the Conservative government of Robert Borden during the First World War. Larger forces pushed the two countries together, regardless of who was Canada's prime minister.

Another problem with the Forked Road interpretation is that Creighton and his like-minded colleagues largely misread King's attitudes toward Britain and the United States. King was not a closet American, as Creighton seemed to believe. The prime minister knew the United States well, but was also deeply suspicious of American motivations. "If the Americans felt security required it [they] would take peaceful possession of part of Canada," King wrote in his diary in October 1945.[21] Canada did not abandon Britain during the war, giving $1 billion to the mother country in 1942 and, over the course of the war, providing more than $2 billion in food and munitions.

The Ogdensburg and Hyde Park agreements were both designed to defend Canadian interests and promote the allied war effort. At the time of Ogdensburg, Britain was losing the war. It could barely defend itself, let alone Canada, leaving King no choice but to turn to the US. The agreement allowed Canada to concentrate its military efforts on Europe, knowing that the United States would see to the defence of North America. But King remained concerned about Canadian sovereignty, rejecting an American proposal that the United States take full control of strategic planning for the defence of North America and integrate the Canadian coasts into American defence command. A similar picture emerges when the Hyde Park agreement is assessed within its wartime context. Imports from the United States far exceeded Canada's exports to that country, creating a huge trade deficit that threatened Canada's economic stability. The agreement was a triumph of King's approach to Canadian–American relations, virtually solving Canada's economic problems at little cost to Canada.

Canadians, King included, did not want to be drawn into the American orbit, but this happened anyway. The war had bankrupted Britain and devastated the rest of Europe. Creighton wrote about a Forked Road, but never explained where the second path led. Historian J.L. Granatstein has asked the key question, one that Creighton never addressed: "What should Mackenzie King and his government have done that they did not do?"[22]

# Enemy Aliens and North Americans of Japanese Descent

After the outbreak of war in Europe, both Canada and the United States required the documenting of enemy aliens, residents who were citizens of enemy countries. In the United States, the Alien Registration Act of 1940 required them to register with the Justice Department and be fingerprinted. Every three months they had to confirm their place of residence. In Canada, the definition of *enemy alien* was broader: it included not just German, Japanese, and Italian citizens but also Canadians who had held German, Japanese, and Italian citizenship on 1 September 1929 (later changed to 1922). All enemy aliens and all individuals of Japanese ancestry over the age of 16 were required to register at the local office of the Registrar of Enemy Aliens, a process that included being fingerprinted and photographed. Afterward, they had to report regularly to the registrar's office. Their homes and businesses could be searched and they could be arrested without warrant.

In both countries, many foreigners were *interned*, a term that refers specifically to the confinement of enemy aliens during wartime. This was a common practice, recognized in international law, and undertaken by all, or virtually all, combatants in the Second World War. During the course of the war, Canada interned 800 Germans and 600 Italians, while the United States interned about 2,300 Germans and 200 Italians.[23] In addition, the Americans interned another 7,000 enemy aliens at the request of Latin American countries. Governments undertook these measures even though there were no reported cases of sabotage or espionage by German or Italian immigrants in North America.

The Japanese were treated differently. A longstanding racism toward Asians became more acute after the surprise attack on Pearl Harbor. On the West Coast of Canada and the United States, locals feared that Japanese immigrants would work for the enemy. In both countries, intelligence services had little information on the loyalties of the residents of Japanese descent, and in the absence of facts, longstanding rumours about spying and sabotage multiplied. The two governments decided to err on the side of security, not human rights.

Canada and the United States interned many Japanese citizens (perhaps 8,000 in the United States and 800 in Canada); in addition, thousands of individuals of Japanese descent were forcibly taken from their homes on the West Coast and transported to camps inland. In January 1942, the Canadian Cabinet authorized the mandatory relocation of all male Japanese citizens aged 18 to 45. President Roosevelt went a step further, on 19 February 1942 ordering that anyone of Japanese ancestry be removed from the coast. The Canadian Cabinet issued a similar order five days later. In all, 112,000 Japanese Americans and 21,000 Japanese Canadians were uprooted. Only a minority were Japanese citizens; most were Canadians or Americans. Included were individuals who had been born in North America and had never been to Japan, many of whom could not speak Japanese.

Men, women, and children of Japanese descent ended up in camps, the exception being some Japanese Canadians who worked as road labourers, others who chose to farm sugar beets in Alberta and Manitoba, and a small number—mostly those with means—who self-evacuated to the interior or beyond. The camps were desolate places where food, sanitation, and medical care were often inadequate. Most Japanese were not interned in the legal sense of the word, as the term applies only to enemy aliens who are incarcerated. Still, they were taken from their homes and their freedom was restricted, so their experience has often been called internment. In the US, the camps were surrounded by barbed-wire fences and guard towers, measures not necessary in Canada, where the camps were located in isolated areas often accessible by a single road. In the United States, only those judged loyal were allowed to leave, with about one-third of the residents departing in 1943 and 1944. By war's end in August 1945, half the camp residents remained. In Canada, individuals could leave the camps, with permission, provided they headed east of the Rockies. Most had nowhere to go, so by the end of the war only about one-third had left the camps. Although the two countries appeared to be operating in lockstep, there is no evidence that the governments coordinated their policies toward residents of Japanese ancestry. They acted in tandem because officials in both countries shared similar attitudes toward national security and toward racial minorities.

Canadian and American policy diverged after the war. Japanese Canadians were given a choice: go to Japan or settle east of the Rocky Mountains. Only in 1949 were the Japanese allowed to return to the British Columbian coast. Almost 4,000 left Canada—some willingly, but many under the threat of deportation. For their part, the Americans allowed the Japanese to return to the West Coast as early as January 1945. After the war, 4,000 Japanese Americans moved to Japan, about a third of whom were American-born.

In the 1980s, Canada and the United States made amends to their citizens of Japanese origin. The US Congress appointed a commission to examine whether the government should offer redress to those who had been forcibly removed from their homes. In 1983, the commission recommended that Congress apologize to the Japanese-American community and authorize payment of $20,000 in reparations to any surviving Japanese American who had been interned or taken to a relocation camp. Japanese Canadians also pushed their government to take similar steps. Weeks after President Ronald Reagan signed the American redress bill into law in August 1988, Prime Minister Brian Mulroney announced that his government would apologize to Japanese Canadians and pay $21,000 to all those who had their rights violated during the war. Forty years had passed, but the two countries were still following the same policies toward their Japanese residents.

# Summary

In the years leading up to the Second World War and during the conflict itself, Canada and the United States pursued a series of similar policies. They wanted European countries to stop their squabbles and to reach a compromise to prevent the outbreak of war. Canadians and Americans were sympathetic to Hitler's victims, but reluctant to admit large numbers of Jewish refugees. When war came, both governments wanted to keep the conflict from spreading to North America. They were willing to make a massive contribution in arms to defeat Germany, Japan, and Italy, but hoped victory could be accomplished with the minimal loss of Canadian and American lives. To defend North America and to help vanquish the aggressors, Roosevelt and King forged a close alliance between the North American neighbours. Though dissimilar in size and power, Canada and the United States had a common perception of their economic and security interests, making an alliance the logical choice in a time of global conflict. The common outlook also explains why the two governments moved from a war of limited liability to a broader campaign that included sending not only huge quantities of arms to Europe but also large numbers of military personnel.

Throughout, King worried about American domination of Canada, and sought to maintain some distance between the two countries.

## Beyond the Book

1. The close cooperation between Canada and the United States was made necessary by the demands of the Second World War. Are close relations between the two countries still a necessity?
2. King's friendship with Roosevelt helped Canada secure the Hyde Park agreement. What are the benefits of close relations between president and prime minister? Are there any drawbacks?
3. Did King sell out Canada to the United States during the Second World War?

## Further Reading

For overviews of the Canadian–American political and military relationship, see Robert Bothwell, Ian Drummond, and John English, *Canada, 1900–1945* (Toronto: University of Toronto Press, 1987); C.P. Stacey, *Arms, Men, and Governments: The War Policies of Canada, 1939–1945* (Ottawa: Department of National Defence, 1970); J.L. Granatstein, *Canada's War: The Politics of the Mackenzie King Government, 1939–1945* (Toronto: Oxford University Press, 1975); and Galen Roger Perras, *Franklin Roosevelt and the Origins of the Canadian–American Security Alliance, 1933–1945: Necessary, but Not Necessary Enough* (Westport, Connecticut: Praeger, 1998). A superb American source is Stanley W. Dziuban, *Military Relations between the United States and Canada, 1939–1945* (Washington: Department of the Army, 1959).

On the treatment of Jewish refugees before the war, the classic Canadian work is now in its second edition: Irving Abella and Harold Troper, *None Is Too Many: Canada and the Jews of Europe, 1933–1948* (Toronto: University of Toronto Press, 2012). For the American side, the most balanced account is Richard Breitman and Allan J. Lichtman, *FDR and the Jews* (Cambridge, Massachusetts: Belknap Press of Harvard University Press, 2013). Also see Sheldon Spear, "The United States and the Persecution of the Jews in Germany, 1933–1939," *Jewish Social Studies* 30, no. 4 (October 1968): 215–42. David S. Wyman is highly critical of Roosevelt in *Paper Walls: America and the Refugee Crisis, 1938–1941* ([Amherst]: University of Massachusetts Press, 1968). Sarah A. Ogilvie and Scott Miller describe the voyage of the *St Louis* clearly and concisely in *Refuge Denied: The St Louis Passengers and the Holocaust* (Madison: University of Wisconsin Press, 2006).

On the Alaska Highway, the leading works are K.S. Coates and W.R. Morrison, *The Alaska Highway in World War II: The US Army of Occupation in Canada's Northwest* (Norman: University of Oklahoma Press, 1992); P. Whitney Lackenbauer, "Right and Honourable: Mackenzie King, Canadian–American Bilateral Relations, and Canadian Sovereignty in the Northwest, 1943–1948," chapter 9 in *Mackenzie King: Citizenship and Community*, edited by John English,

Kenneth McLaughlin, and P. Whitney Lackenbauer (Toronto: Robin Brass Studio, 2002), 151–68; and Richard J. Diubaldo, "The Alaska Highway in Canada–United States Relations," chapter 9 in *The Alaska Highway: Papers of the 40th Anniversary Symposium*, edited by Kenneth Coates (Vancouver: University of British Columbia Press, 1985), 102–15. Diubaldo is also author of the best account of the Canol Pipeline: "The Canol Project in Canadian–American Relations," *Historical Papers* [Canadian Historical Association] (1977): 178–95.

Donald Creighton's most sustained attack on Mackenzie King appears in *The Forked Road: Canada, 1939–1957* (Toronto: McClelland and Stewart, 1976). J.L. Granatstein convincingly rebuts Creighton in *How Britain's Weakness Forced Canada into the Arms of the United States* (Toronto: University of Toronto Press, 1989). Galen Roger Perras adds valuable detail on the Canadian–American military alliance in "The Myth of 'Obsequious Rex': Mackenzie King, Franklin D. Roosevelt, and Canada–US Security, 1935–1940," in *Transnationalism: Canada–United States History into the Twenty-First Century*, edited by Michael D. Behiels and Reginald C. Stuart (Montreal and Kingston: McGill–Queen's University Press, 2010), 203–23.

Greg Robinson compares Canadian and American policies toward the Japanese in *A Tragedy of Democracy: Japanese Confinement in North America* (New York: Columbia University Press, 2009). For the Canadian side of the story, see Patricia E. Roy, *The Triumph of Citizenship: The Japanese and Chinese in Canada* (Vancouver: UBC Press, 2007); and Patricia E. Roy et al., *Mutual Hostages: Canadians and Japanese during the Second World War* (Toronto: University of Toronto Press, 1990). On the United States, see Roger Daniels, *Prisoners without Trial: Japanese Americans in World War II* (New York: Hill and Wang, 1993); Morton Grodzins, *Americans Betrayed: Politics and the Japanese Evacuation* (Chicago: University of Chicago Press, 1949); and Greg Robinson, *By Order of the President: FDR and the Internment of Japanese Americans* (Cambridge: Harvard University Press, 2001). On using the term *interment* for those relocated from the coast, see Roger Daniels, "Words Do Matter: A Note on Appropriate Terminology and the Incarceration of the Japanese Americans," chapter 9 in *Nikkei in the Pacific Northwest: Japanese Americans and Japanese Canadians in the Twentieth Century*, edited by Louis Fiset and Gail M. Nomura (Seattle: University of Washington Press, 2005), 190–214. In *Voices Raised in Protest: Defending North American Citizens of Japanese Ancestry, 1942–9* (Vancouver: UBC Press, 2008), Stephanie Bangarth examines those North Americans who opposed the wartime treatment of Canadians and Americans of Japanese descent.

# CHAPTER 8

---

# Consensus, 1945–1955

## *The Early Cold War*

## Introduction

"This could be . . . my last night on earth."[1] Igor Gouzenko left the Soviet Embassy in Ottawa just before 9:00 p.m. on a humid night in September 1945. The 26-year-old cipher clerk had been recalled to the Soviet Union, but had decided to defect to stay in Canada. He feared for his life because he knew that his country's secret police often murdered traitors. Carrying more than 100 top-secret documents, Gouzenko rode the streetcar to the headquarters of the *Ottawa Journal,* where he planned to reveal that Canada's wartime ally had been running a spy ring in Canada and the United States. Yet when he reached the newspaper offices, Gouzenko lost his nerve, turned around, and headed home. There, his wife talked him through his anxieties and convinced him to carry out his plan. He returned to the *Journal* and explained his story in barely comprehensible English. Not sure what to make of his tale, the night editor told Gouzenko to go to the RCMP or come back the next morning to talk to the senior editor. Gouzenko left the office and walked a few blocks to the Department of Justice building, where he requested a meeting with the minister, Louis St Laurent. It was just before midnight, and the minister had left hours ago. Gouzenko was told again to return in the morning.

After a fearful night at home, Gouzenko returned to the Justice Department, this time accompanied by his pregnant wife and their young son. Again, Gouzenko asked to speak to the minister, and again he was rebuffed. After failing to generate any interest at the Department of Justice or at the justice minister's Parliament Hill office, Gouzenko returned to the *Ottawa Journal,* where he spoke to the women's-page editor. "I am terribly sorry," she told him. "Your story just doesn't seem to register here." For years, allied propaganda had portrayed Soviet leader Joseph Stalin as a hero, to the point that no one in the media would say anything negative about him. The editor suggested Gouzenko go to the RCMP to apply for Canadian citizenship. Gouzenko went back to the Justice Department, now in search of citizenship, but was redirected to the Crown Attorney's office. There, he filled out the necessary forms to become a Canadian. How long would the process take? "Oh, I can't tell you for sure," the clerk responded. "A few months perhaps." When Gouzenko's wife began to cry, another clerk asked an *Ottawa Journal* reporter to hear the story. "It's too big for us to handle—much too big," the reporter said. "It is a matter for the police or the government. I suggest you take it to them." The clerk called *Le Droit,* but Ottawa's French-language newspaper was not interested. It was the fourth time a journalist had passed on the biggest Canadian news story of the decade.

Exhausted, the Gouzenkos returned to their apartment, where they noticed two men watching their building. After someone knocked on the door and began calling Gouzenko's name in a Russian accent, the family sought refuge in a neighbour's apartment, climbing from their balcony to the neighbour's. Around midnight, four Soviet secret police agents broke into the Gouzenko apartment. Someone called the Ottawa police, and officers confronted the men and forced them to leave. Gouzenko's nightmare ended only the next day. Ottawa police escorted him to the RCMP, where he was interviewed for five hours.

When Gouzenko's revelations became public, they rocked Canada and the rest of the Western world. Ostensibly allies of Canada and the United States, the Soviets were operating an espionage network in North America, with agents in the Canadian Department of External Affairs, the National Research Council, and the British High Commission in Ottawa. The news was too sensitive to be relayed through intermediaries, so Prime Minister Mackenzie King travelled to Washington to brief President Harry S. Truman in person. Then, in February 1946, the Canadian government created a secret royal commission to investigate Gouzenko's evidence. Suspected spies were arrested, held without charge, denied legal representation, and forced to testify before the commission. Reporting in June, the commission confirmed Gouzenko's allegations and recommended that the government act vigorously to combat espionage. These events and others that followed help forge a consensus in North America that the Soviets posed a lethal threat to Canada and the United States. The Cold War was underway.

**Photo 8.1** ÷ Igor Gouzenko

After defecting from the Soviet Union to Canada in 1945, Igor Gouzenko continued to fear for his life. He and his family lived under assumed names to protect them from Soviet retribution. In public appearances, Gouzenko always wore a hood, to protect his new identity. Here he is meeting with a reporter in 1954. (Source: The Canadian Press/AP Photo.)

# The Cold War at Home

The Cold War was a political, ideological, and economic struggle between two camps, one led by the United States, the other by the Soviet Union. Other than a few dissenters, Canadians and Americans tended to view the conflict through similar lenses. At home, the public was terrified about possible communist subversion, fears stoked by the revelations from Gouzenko and other defectors. Polls showed that most Canadians and Americans believed that communists should be stripped of their civil rights based on their political beliefs, blurring the line between dissent and subversion.

Headed by two justices of the Supreme Court of Canada, the Kellock–Taschereau Commission was appointed to investigate Gouzenko's claims. As a result of its June 1946 report, 21 Canadians were tried for espionage or conspiracy, of whom 11 were convicted, though one guilty verdict was later overturned on appeal. Among those sentenced were the national organizer of the Labour Progressive Party (the name the Communist Party used after it was outlawed in the early 1940s), a Labour Progressive member of Parliament (Fred Rose), scientists and engineers who had worked on defence projects, officials from the

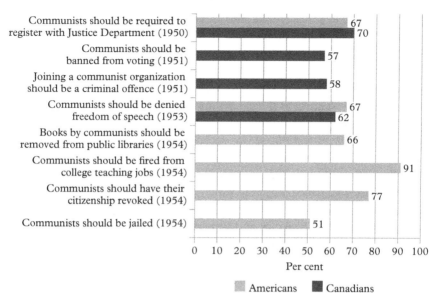

**Figure 8.1** ✣ **Canadian and American Opinion on Communism, 1950–4**

Sources: Data compiled from "Believe Registration of Communists Would Help if Crisis Came," *Toronto Star*, 11 March 1950, 1; George H. Gallup, *The Gallup Poll: Public Opinion, 1935–1971, vol. 2, 1949–1958* (New York: Random House, 1972), 910–1, 934, 1191; Canadian Institute of Public Opinion, *Gallup Poll of Canada*, 18 April 1951, 16 May 1953; Samuel A. Stouffer, *Communism, Conformity, and Civil Liberties: A Cross-Section of the Nation Speaks Its Mind* (Garden City, New York: Doubleday, 1955), 40–4.

Departments of External Affairs and of Munitions and Supply, an army officer, and the private secretary to the British high commissioner in Ottawa.

The Canadian government chose to handle security issues in a quiet manner, behind closed doors. In May 1946, Cabinet created the Security Panel, chaired by the clerk of the Privy Council, the country's highest-ranking public servant, and composed of representatives from the military, the RCMP, and the Department of External Affairs. The panel advised Cabinet on espionage and subversion, and created a screening program for public servants with access to classified material. Later, the program was extended to cover individuals working in defence industries, seamen working on the Great Lakes, and applicants for immigration, refugee status, or citizenship. Individuals were not told they had failed the security screening and had no right to appeal the decision; they were quietly dismissed or shuffled to positions that did not require security clearance.

In the United States, issues of internal security were handled in public view, in what became a political and media circus. Communists and alleged communists were socially ostracized, lost their jobs, and were blacklisted, making it next to impossible for them to work again in their chosen field. Originally, the targets were senior government officials, but slowly the net widened. Entertainers, professors, teachers, social workers, journalists, trade union officials, and lawyers were all subject to scrutiny. The best estimate is that 10,000 Americans lost their jobs during these communist purges.[2] It is true that most were communists; it is equally true that few posed any threat to US security.

Between 1950 and 1954, anti-communist hysteria tainted American political debate. Both the US Senate and House of Representatives held public hearings to uncover the communists in government. The House Un-American Activities Committee had existed since 1938 but became more vigorous in its investigations in the decade after the Second World War, going after Hollywood stars, atomic scientists, and labour leaders. Witnesses were first questioned behind closed doors. Those who admitted to being communists were asked to name other communists, who were then subpoenaed to appear before the committee. Uncooperative witnesses were questioned in public hearings and were assumed to be communists if they refused to answer questions. Using similar methods, the Senate Internal Security Subcommittee focussed on the question of who "lost" China, those American officials who could be blamed for the communist victory in the Chinese civil war and takeover of that vast land.

Although often associated with Republican Senator Joseph McCarthy, anti-communism existed before he came to national prominence and continued after he fell from grace. In a February 1950 speech, McCarthy claimed to have a list of 205 communist agents in the State Department. In subsequent statements, the number became 207, then 57, and then 81. Although the Wisconsin senator's often-wild allegations were based on no evidence, the news media covered them as if they were fact. McCarthy's committee, the Permanent Investigating Subcommittee of the Government Operations Committee, was particularly crude in its tactics. In later years, the term *McCarthyism* came to mean the persecution of the innocent by unproven allegations.

Canadian officials distrusted McCarthyism and the excesses of American congressional committees. In 1953, the Canadian government was reluctant to allow the US Senate Internal Security Subcommittee to meet with Gouzenko. The defector had told a *Chicago Tribune* reporter that the Soviets were still running a spy ring in North America, a claim likely designed to gain some media attention in advance of his forthcoming novel, *The Fall of a Titan*. When the US committee asked to interview Gouzenko in Washington, Canada refused on the basis that the US Senate had no jurisdiction over Canadian citizens. Canadians sought middle ground, eventually allowing committee members to meet secretly with Gouzenko on Canadian soil, in Montebello, Quebec, where they learned that Gouzenko had nothing new to offer.

Authorities in Canada and the United States worked to eliminate communist influences in the entertainment industry. The most renowned case

was that of the Hollywood Ten. In 1947, eight screenwriters and two directors refused to answer questions before the House Un-American Activities
Committee. After serving six months to one year in jail for contempt of
Congress, they were blacklisted, preventing them from working in the movie
business. In Canada, where there was no feature film industry to speak of,
the focus turned to the National Film Board (NFB), which produced docu-
mentaries and wartime propaganda films. In 1949, the RCMP reported that
36 employees were communists. When the NFB's head, Ross McLean, refused
to act, he was removed from his position. His replacement, Arthur Irwin, fired
three employees. Another 30 or so contract workers resigned before they could
be fired or were blacklisted so they could get no further NFB work.

In both countries, homosexuals were fired from important government
posts on the premise that they could become targets of blackmail should the
Soviets find out about their sexual activities. In 1950, a US Senate subcommittee issued a report entitled *Employment of Homosexuals and other Sex Perverts
in Government*, which concluded that gays were "unsuitable for employment
in the Federal Government," both because their behaviour was immoral and
because they were security risks.[3] In the US, the Immigration and Nationality
Act of 1952 (often called the McCarran–Walter Act) barred any immigrant
with a record of "sexual deviation," which included homosexuality. The same
year, Canada passed a new immigration act that explicitly banned gays. In
1955, the RCMP began a widespread investigation of homosexuality in the
public service. About six senior officials were forced out of the Canadian
Department of External Affairs, including John Holmes, the department's
second-highest-ranking official, and David Johnson, a former ambassador to
Moscow. Between 1956 and 1963, perhaps 100 public servants lost their jobs
because of perceived character weaknesses, including homosexuality.[4] The
Canadian government went so far as developing technology to detect homosexuality. A device, nicknamed the fruit machine, was created, but the project
was abandoned when the apparatus was unable to produce reliable results.

It was not always clear what motivated the search for homosexuals, but
one case sheds light on the claim that they were security risks. A clerk in the
Canadian embassy in Moscow told the ambassador that he had been photographed in a homosexual encounter with a Soviet citizen. By reporting this,
the clerk ensured that he could not be blackmailed—the Soviets could not
threaten to tell his boss, because his boss already knew. Yet the clerk was still
fired, suggesting that the pursuit of homosexuals was too often a product
of widespread homophobia in Canada and the United States, rather than
a concern over security. Certainly, there was never any evidence that a gay
public servant had handed information to the Soviets.

In a revealing 1955 letter to former US secretary of state Dean Acheson,
former Canadian defence minister Brooke Claxton explained the differences

between the Canadian and American approaches to internal security. In Claxton's view, Canadian officials were "quite reasonable." Often the suspect would "be watched or gradually shifted to a less sensitive position," a practice that was "not only more likely to ensure security but did less damage to the individual." Some public servants were fired. "They were given no publicity. Nothing was done to prevent the person from getting other employment which he could do without difficulty. . . . I never heard of an unjust result," Claxton concluded.[5] Eric Gaskell, secretary of the Security Panel, agreed. Canada had found a "happy medium between the dangers of unrestricted witch-hunting, on the one hand, and a too casual approach to the security problem on the other."[6] This self-congratulation was no doubt overstated. On several occasions, the RCMP tried to prevent former public servants from obtaining employment in the private sector if they were considered security risks. Canadians had pursued a less extreme approach to security, more moderate than that of the United States, but still directly at odds with the civil rights of the accused.

In the 1990s, historians gained new insights into the efforts to purge communists from government. The Soviet Union collapsed in 1991, and several scholars gained access to some documents in the old Soviet archives. Then in 1995, the US government released the records of the Venona project. During the Second World War, under the highest secrecy, the US Army's Signal Intelligence Service had begun intercepting cables to Moscow from Soviet operatives in the United States. Over the course of several years, American experts managed to decrypt several thousand messages. These newly available sources confirmed the Gouzenko revelations about espionage in Canada, showing that the Soviets had hundreds of informants in the US government and military, some at high levels. It turned out there was reason for Americans and Canadians to be concerned about espionage. Yet, at the same time, US congressional committees relied on crude methods that ensnared spies and innocent people in the same net, and both countries pursued homosexuals for no just reason.

## Postwar Economic Relations

After 1945, Canadian and American officials had to decide whether to continue the close economic ties they had built during the Second World War. To policy-makers on both sides of the border, the answer was clear. They wanted to ensure the maximum growth of the economy and to avoid a repeat of the Great Depression, when protectionism had made a bad situation worse. They believed that liberal economic policies— allowing the free flow of goods and capital—were essential to future prosperity. This was particularly important for Canadians, who wanted to benefit from living next to the United States, an economic dynamo in the postwar years.

Americans were interested in having access to Canada's abundant natural resources. The 1952 report of the President's Materials Policy Commission— usually known as the Paley report, after commission chair William S. Paley— predicted that the United States would become increasingly reliant on foreign countries for raw materials. Canada would be a primary source for a dozen strategic resources. For Canadian officials, this was good news, because it meant Canada had a guaranteed long-term buyer for its products. Ken Taylor, deputy minister of finance, kept the Paley Report in his desk. "Every time I get depressed about the future, I take it out and read it," he said.[7]

Tariffs fell substantially in the first decade after the Second World War. Both Canada and the United States were among the 23 original signatories of the 1947 General Agreement on Tariffs and Trade (GATT), which led to major tariff reductions in 1947 and 1951. In the late 1940s, the Canadian and American governments considered a bilateral free trade agreement that would remove all tariffs on products crossing the Canada–US border. After the prime minister approved exploratory talks, officials from the Canadian Department of Finance forged ahead, negotiating an agreement with their American counterparts. Mackenzie King recoiled when he heard the news and put an end to the idea of free trade between the two countries. He both distrusted American motives and feared that he would be accused, as his mentor Sir Wilfrid Laurier had been in 1911, of taking steps that would lead to an American takeover of Canada. "I felt sure that the long objective of the Americans was to control this continent," he wrote in his diary. "They would want to get Canada under their aegis."[8] Even with Mackenzie King's approval, the agreement would most certainly have died, as it was not likely to win Congressional support in the United States.

At the same time Canadian officials were removing trade barriers, they worked to promote foreign investment, believing that Canada had to compete for capital. Canada no longer enjoyed its privileged position as a home for American dollars, as other countries were becoming increasingly effective at luring US investors. To facilitate development, C.D. Howe, minister of trade and commerce from 1948 to 1957, believed that he could not discriminate against non-Canadians and would instead have to encourage all investment, a policy that included selling federal Crown corporations to foreign buyers. Howe helped sell Victory Aircraft to the British-owned A.V. Roe Company, Research Enterprises Limited to Corning Glass of the United States, and Canadair Limited to the American-owned Electric Boat Company (later General Dynamics).

In the 1950s, the economic activity in the Great Lakes region received a boost from the St Lawrence Seaway. Canada and the United States had long discussed the development of the St Lawrence River and the Great Lakes. New dams would allow the countries to generate more power, and locks and canals would allow the navigation of the St Lawrence from the Great Lakes to the Atlantic Ocean. In 1932, the two sides had signed a treaty to develop the seaway together, but the US Senate rejected the accord. After almost a decade of further discussions, Canada and the United States signed a similar agreement in March 1941, but Congress shelved the project after the United States entered the Second World War that December.

After the war, an urgent shortage of electric power in Ontario pushed the Canadian government to raise the issue once again with the United States. Prime Minister Louis St Laurent presented an ultimatum to President Harry Truman in September 1951. If the US would not take part in the project, Canada would go it alone, developing a Canadian seaway with all locks and canals on Canadian territory. In early 1952, Truman urged Congress to approve the 1941 agreement without further delay. "We should not be content to be merely a customer of Canada's for the use of the seaway after it is built," he argued. Railway interests and ports on the East Coast had lobbied against the seaway project, but for Truman it was "inconceivable" that the US would refuse to take part. "No great nation has ever deliberately abandoned its interest in any of the vital waterways of the world."[9] When Dwight Eisenhower became president in 1953, he too pressed Congress to act. Finally, in early 1954, Congress gave the necessary approval for construction to proceed. The seaway would be built as two coordinated national projects, one Canadian and one American, without a formal treaty or supervisory body. The shared objectives would be achieved through goodwill and collaboration.

The project began in 1954 and was completed in 1959, costing more than $1 billion. At the time, it was the largest transnational project ever undertaken by two countries. Once operational, grain was shipped eastward from Thunder Bay in the interior of the continent to ports along the seaway. Canada went from being a net importer to a net exporter of iron ore, transported cheaply from Labrador and Quebec to steel mills in Illinois, Ohio, and Pennsylvania. In turn, those three states provided coal to Canadian power plants and steel mills. The story of negotiating the seaway was one of struggle between Canada and the United States, but the construction and later use was primarily a record of cross-border cooperation.

## Canada's Place in the Postwar World

In the closing stages of the Second World War, Canadian and US policy-makers began planning for the postwar world. Deeply cautious about making commitments in the 1930s, they now embraced internationalism with a mixture of fear and hope—fear of the threat of Soviet communism and hope that they could create the institutions that would lead to world peace. Americans hosted the founding meeting of the United Nations, the international body created to replace the failed League of Nations, and donated land for the organization's headquarters in New York City. The framework for the new international economic system was established at Bretton Woods, New Hampshire, and Washington, DC, would be home to two key financial institutions, the World Bank and the International Monetary Fund. Canada was also determined to be active on the world stage. Canada was a founding member of the United Nations, the World Bank, and the International Monetary Fund. Canada's new stance reflected both an optimistic sense that Canada could contribute to creating a better world order and a belief that relations with many countries would help offset the powerful hold of the bilateral Canadian–American relationship. Canadian officials knew that they would need the United States, but were not prepared to surrender Canadian sovereignty.

Canada's greater role in international affairs raised a problem. How could a country of Canada's size expect to exert influence in international forums where it would be dwarfed by the United States and other great powers? The answer, according to Canadian diplomat Hume Wrong, was the functional principle. Those countries most willing and best able to deal with a particular international issue—whether because of resources, experience, or other qualities—should be given the greatest say in the relevant international body. Canada, which had large quantities of uranium, played a prominent role on the International Atomic Energy Commission. Because Canada's resources were necessary for rebuilding Europe, the country had a place on the executive committee of the United Nations Relief and Rehabilitation Administration (UNRRA). Although other countries did not endorse the functional idea, Canadians were crucial in creating the UN's many agencies, including the International Monetary Fund and the World Bank. A Canadian, Lester Pearson, chaired the founding meeting of the United Nations Food and Agriculture Organization in Quebec City. The new International Civil Aviation Organization was headquartered in Montreal.

# The Cold War Abroad

Canadians and Americans shared a similar outlook toward the postwar world. The primary threat to world peace was the Soviet Union, which North Americans saw as powerful and hostile, driven by a desire to dominate the world. Canada, the United States, and their friends in Western Europe represented liberty, while the Soviet Union became a symbol of repression. In 1946, former British prime minister Winston Churchill defined the world situation in a speech in Fulton, Missouri. Eastern and Central Europe were becoming a Soviet sphere, increasingly controlled by Moscow. To stop the spread of communism, Churchill said, the Western democracies had to unite and to stand up to the Soviets. Canada's ambassador to the United States, Lester Pearson, approved of the speech, as did Prime Minister Mackenzie King, who called Churchill to congratulate him.

Wartime propaganda convinced most Canadians and Americans that Russia would cooperate with Western powers, but Soviet aggression altered public opinion.[10] In the early postwar years, the Soviet Union established political domination over the countries of Eastern Europe, setting up totalitarian police states and crushing any hopes for democracy. Subsequent events reinforced Western fears. In 1949, the Soviets successfully tested an atomic bomb, and the communists took control in China, two events that shocked North Americans. Then in 1950, communist North Korea invaded the South.

Fear of communist aggression helped cement the Canadian–American alliance. Canada had "every interest in strengthening the US position as leader in the struggle against communism," Lester Pearson told Cabinet in 1950, a statement that reflected a consensus in Canadian government and in the country as a whole about the threat of the Soviet Union.[11] In 1950, the government announced in the House of Commons that Canada had reached an agreement with the United States that would integrate continental defence production. Brooke Claxton, the minister of national defence, received not a single question about it. Although Canadian policy-makers shared the world view of their American counterparts, they endeavoured to maintain some distance between Canadian and American policies. They engaged in a delicate balancing act, striving to be both a close ally to the United States and an independent player in the world.

Canada displayed its independence during the Berlin Blockade. After the Second World War, Germany had been divided into American, British, French, and Soviet occupation zones. The German capital of Berlin, in the middle of the Soviet zone, was further divided among the great powers. In June 1948, in the midst of a dispute over Germany's future, the Soviets cut off all road and rail entrances to the American, British, and French areas in West Berlin. More than two million Berliners lost their access to food and fuel. In response, the Americans organized the Berlin Airlift, a massive effort that delivered 13,000 tons of supplies to the city each day. Canada refused to provide planes for the operation, arguing that the country had no role in the crisis because it was not one of the four powers that signed the agreement on the occupation of Germany. Other countries, including Australia and New Zealand, willingly participated in the airlift.

# The Atlantic Alliance

By 1948, Canadians and Americans were more anxious than ever about the situation in Europe and the Middle East. The Soviets were putting pressure on Turkey to turn over former Russian territory and to allow Soviet naval bases on Turkish soil. In Greece, the communists were engaged in a civil war against the government. In Czechoslovakia, the Communist Party had seized the government, imprisoning political opponents or forcing them into exile.

Canadians were among the leading voices proposing the creation of an alliance of North American and Western European countries. In March 1948, Canadian, American, and British officials drafted the outline for the North Atlantic Treaty Organization (NATO), with Canada's Lester Pearson playing a key role. Twelve countries signed the resulting treaty in Washington in April 1949. In the 1920s and 1930s, both Canada and the United States had refused to make commitments to Europe. Now they were both tied to the Old World through a collective security alliance.

At the same time, Canadians wanted NATO to be more than just a military alliance. On the insistence of Canadian negotiators, and over the objections of their American counterparts, the treaty included a vague clause, article 2, in which the signatories pledged to "contribute toward the further development of peaceful and friendly international relations by strengthening their free institutions, by bringing about a better understanding of the principles upon which these institutions are founded, and by promoting conditions of stability and well-being." In addition, the member countries would "seek to eliminate conflict in their international economic policies and will encourage economic collaboration between any or all of them."[12] NATO never amounted to anything more than a military alliance, but article 2 demonstrated a Canadian realization that the fight against communism could not be waged by guns alone.

# The Korean War

Korea had been a Japanese colony from 1910 to 1945, at which point it had been divided at the 38th parallel into two temporary occupation zones, a northern zone occupied by the Soviet Union and a southern zone controlled by the United States. To help create a unified, independent Korea, the UN established in November 1947 the United Nations Temporary Commission on Korea (UNTCOK), with nine members, including Canada. At the time, the prime minister was in London, so Canada's secretary of state for external affairs, Louis St Laurent, authorized the country's participation. When Mackenzie King heard the news, he "blew a gasket," according to Defence

Minister Brooke Claxton.[13] To St Laurent and the other members of the Cabinet, Canadian membership on the commission was not a difficult issue. To King, it was. Canada had greater interests in Europe, he argued, and should avoid getting entangled in Asian affairs, which might draw the country into a conflict between the United States and the Soviet Union. UNTCOK was bound to fail, so Canada should avoid involvement.

Upon his return to Ottawa, King insisted on reversing the decision to accept a position on UNTCOK. St Laurent pointed out that Canada, as a member of the UN, would sometimes have to serve on such commissions in areas where it had no direct interest. The dispute dragged on for more than one month and became increasingly tense. US officials urged Canada to stay on the commission, but their plea had the opposite effect, as King became more determined to resist American pressure. King decided to lay the issue before Cabinet and to resign if ministers did not support him. Lester Pearson, the senior public servant in the Department of External Affairs, noted that he had never seen King "more worked up or impassioned." The prime minister "was very deeply stirred and very emphatic in his language."[14] King's priority was to make it clear that Canada would not routinely stand behind the US, just as he had refused to give Britain automatic support in the 1920s and 1930s.

There was a considerable backlash against King's stand. St Laurent and Justice Minister James Ilsley threatened to resign, and Defence Minister Brooke Claxton and a few others contemplated doing so. Confronted with this opposition, the prime minister backed down and found a face-saving compromise in January 1948. Canada would serve on the commission, but if the Soviets prevented the elections in the North, Canada would not help organize elections in the South only. In the end, Canada served one year on the commission. When the Soviets refused to cooperate, as King had predicted, UNTCOK proceeded with elections in South Korea, over Canadian objections. After the vote was held in May 1948, the United States recognized the new regime as the lawful government of Korea, but Canada refused to do so. UNTCOK was disbanded, replaced by the United Nations Commission on Korea, but Canada did not become a member of the new body. The Soviets responded by creating a government for the North, further solidifying the division of Korea.

The tense situation in Korea exploded in June 1950, when the North invaded the South. After US officials decided to send troops to support the South, Canada urged the Americans to seek UN approval, which they did. The Canadians feared that the UN would become as irrelevant as the League of Nations had been in the mid-1930s if members did not authorize the use of force when disputes could not be settled peaceably. With the Soviet Union boycotting the UN because of the organization's unwillingness to recognize communist China, the Security Council called on members to contribute troops to defend South Korea, and created the United Nations Command, under the leadership of US General Douglas MacArthur. The Canadian government, led by Prime Minister Louis St Laurent since November 1948, initially offered air and naval support, but American officials were unimpressed. In a Toronto speech, a defensive Lester Pearson, who had been promoted to the position of foreign minister, insisted that Canada's three destroyers were "no mere token." "Okay, let's call it three tokens," remarked a senior official at the US embassy.[15]

Mackenzie King's death on 22 July 1950 was a symbolic moment in the evolution of Canadian foreign policy. On 27 July, returning to Ottawa from King's funeral in Toronto, Cabinet members met on a train. St Laurent told his colleagues that he supported the sending of ground troops to Korea, an action that King likely would have vigorously opposed. Canada had urged the US to work through the UN, insisting on the importance of collective action, but this meant Canada had to supply ground troops or appear hypocritical. Collective security could not work if UN members were unwilling to dispatch troops to conflicts in other parts of the world. Also important to the decision was a desire to preserve the Western alliance and protect Canada's influence in Washington.

UN and South Korean forces were able to halt the advance of North Korean troops and push them out of the South before Canadians saw combat. As UN troops approached the old border between North and South, American officials debated what to do. Should the allies feel content at having saved the South? Or should they push on to defeat the North and reunite Korea? US President Harry Truman wanted a united Korea, but was concerned about widening the war. If UN troops moved through North Korea toward the Chinese border, would China feel threatened? Would it enter the war? Truman authorized MacArthur to cross the 38th parallel into North Korea, so long as there was no danger of the Chinese becoming involved.

Canadian officials were more cautious. A diplomat in the Canadian embassy in China, Chester Ronning, had warned that the Chinese might well intervene if UN troops came too close. Pearson urged the Americans to either not cross the 38th parallel, the border between North and South, without first offering the North Koreans the possibility of a ceasefire, or to advance only to the 39th parallel, still almost 200 kilometres from the Chinese border. The consensus in Washington was that North Korea had to be defeated, so American officials rejected Pearson's advice. MacArthur's forces drove north toward China, a decision that had an enormous cost. Chinese troops flooded across the border in late 1950, pushing UN forces toward the 38th parallel. After much deadly fighting, a costly stalemate set in by the summer of 1951. The two sides finally ended hostilities with an armistice, signed in July 1953.

In all, the Korean War saw the death of almost five million civilians and soldiers, including 500 Canadians and 37,000 Americans.

Because Canadian and American officials had a common view of the Cold War, they had similar goals in Korea, but they often differed over how to achieve them. Throughout the conflict, Canada pursued a "diplomacy of constraint," to use the phrase of political scientist Denis Stairs. Canada convinced the Americans to work within the UN to maintain the postwar international system, but Canadian officials were unsuccessful in preventing the US from drawing in the Chinese and unleashing a wider war. The difficulty of persuading the United States to act more cautiously left Lester Pearson pessimistic. "The days of relatively easy and automatic political relations with our neighbour are, I think, over," he told a Toronto audience in 1951.[16]

## Summary

Forged in the Second World War, the Canadian–American alliance continued in peacetime. It was nourished by a North American consensus about the world situation, particularly a fear of communist aggression abroad and subversion at home. That fear and a desire to avoid a return to the Depression of the prewar years forced Canadians to reconcile their differences with the United States. Canadians clung to the US, a like-minded country that was also the world's strongest military, economic, and political power. At the same time, Canadian leaders strove to keep some distance between the two countries to protect Canada's independence.

## Beyond the Book

1.  In the early Cold War, how could Canadian and American governments have balanced the need for security with the rights of the individual?
2.  Canadian officials sought to moderate American actions in international affairs, in part by maintaining a close relationship with the US. What are the strengths and weaknesses of such an approach?

## Further Reading

There are several superb overviews of Canadian foreign policy in the early Cold War years. See Robert Bothwell, *The Big Chill: Canada and the Cold War* (Toronto: Irwin, 1998); James Eayrs, *In Defence of Canada*, vol. 3, *Peacemaking and Deterrence* (Toronto: University of Toronto Press, 1972); and Denis Smith, *Diplomacy of Fear: Canada and the Cold War, 1941–1948* (Toronto: University of Toronto Press, 1988). Greg Donaghy, ed., *Canada and the Early Cold War, 1943–1957* (Ottawa: Department of Foreign Affairs and International Trade, 1998) contains several important essays, notably those by John English and Denis Stairs.

On the Cold War in Canada, see David MacKenzie, *Canada's Red Scare, 1945–1957* (Ottawa: Canadian Historical Association, 2001); Reg Whitaker and Steve Hewitt, *Canada and the Cold War* (Toronto: James Lorimer, 2003); Reg Whitaker and Gary Marcuse, *Cold War Canada: The Making of a National Insecurity State, 1945–1957* (Toronto: University of Toronto Press, 1994); Reg Whitaker, Gregory S. Kealey, and Andrew Parnaby, *Secret Service: Political Policing in Canada from the Fenians to Fortress America* (Toronto: University of Toronto Press, 2012); Reginald Whitaker, "Origins of the Canadian Government's Internal Security System, 1946–1952," *Canadian Historical Review* 65, no. 2 (1984): 154–83. For the United States, see the concise book by Ellen Schrecker, *The Age of McCarthyism: A Brief History with Documents*, 2nd ed. (Boston: Bedford/St Martins, 1994). The purge of homosexuals from the public service is examined in Daniel J. Robinson and David Kimmel, "The Queer Career of Homosexual Security Vetting in Cold War Canada," *Canadian Historical Review* 75, no. 3 (September 1994): 319–45; and Gary Kinsman and Patrizia Gentile, *The Canadian War on Queers: National Security as Sexual Regulation* (Vancouver: UBC Press, 2010). See also the judicious piece by Hector Mackenzie, "Purged . . . from Memory: The Department of External Affairs and John Holmes," *International Journal* 59, no. 2 (Spring 2004): 375–86.

On the founding of the UN and NATO, the best sources are Adam Chapnick, *The Middle Power Project: Canada and the Founding of the United Nations* (Vancouver: UBC Press, 2005); John C. Milloy, *The North Atlantic Treaty Organization, 1948–1957: Community or Alliance?* (Montreal and Kingston: McGill–Queen's University Press, 2006); Escott Reid, *Time of Fear and Hope: The Making of the North Atlantic Treaty, 1947–1949* (Toronto: McClelland and Stewart, 1977); Timothy P. Ireland, *Creating the Entangling Alliance: The Origins of the North Atlantic Treaty Organization* (Westport, Connecticut, 1981); and Lawrence S. Kaplan, *The United States and NATO: The Formative Years* (Lexington: University Press of Kentucky, 1984). Adam Chapnick explores functionalism in "Principle for Profit: The Functional Principle and the Development of Canadian Foreign Policy, 1943–1947," *Journal of Canadian Studies* 37, no. 2 (Summer 2002): 69–85.

Several authors examine Canadian–Soviet relations in David Davies, ed., *Canada and the Soviet Experiment: Essays on Canadian Encounters with Russia and the Soviet Union, 1900–1991* (Toronto: University of Toronto Centre for Russian and Eastern European Studies; Waterloo: University of Waterloo Centre on Foreign Policy and Federalism, [1993]); particularly valuable are the chapters by David Bercuson and John English.

Important biographies of key policy-makers include John English, *Shadow of Heaven: The Life of Lester Pearson*, vol. 1, *1897–1948* (Toronto: Lester and Orpen Dennys, 1989) and *The Worldly Years: The Life of Lester Pearson*, vol. 2, *1949–1972* (Toronto: Knopf, 1992); and Adam Chapnick, *Canada's Voice: The Public Life of John Wendell Holmes* (Vancouver: UBC Press, 2009). For Mackenzie King's views, see the edited version of his diaries: J.W. Pickersgill and D.F. Forster, *The Mackenzie King Record*, 4 vols. (Toronto: University of Toronto Press, 1960–1970). The complete diaries are available online through Library and Archives Canada at www.collectionscanada.gc.ca/databases/king/023011-1050.63-e.html.

For economic policy, see R.D. Cuff and J.L. Granatstein, *American Dollars, Canadian Prosperity: Canadian–American Economic Relations, 1945–1950* (Toronto: Samuel–Stevens, 1978). The best work on Canadian–American relations and the St Lawrence Seaway is Daniel Macfarlane, *Negotiating a River: Canada, the US, and the Creation of the St Lawrence Seaway* (Vancouver: UBC Press, 2014), though there is also useful detail in Ronald Stagg, *The Golden Dream: A History of the St Lawrence Seaway* (Toronto: Dundurn, 2010).

On Igor Gouzenko, start with his memoirs: *This Was My Choice: Gouzenko's Story* (Toronto: J.M. Dent and Sons, 1948). These should be supplemented with Robert Bothwell and J.L. Granatstein, eds., *The Gouzenko Transcripts: The Evidence Presented to the Kellock–Taschereau Royal Commission of 1946* (Ottawa: Deneau, [1982]); Hector Mackenzie, "Canada's International Relations in the Early Cold War: The Impact and Implications of the Gouzenko Affair," in *The Gouzenko Affair: Canada and the Beginnings of the Cold War,* edited by J.L. Black and Martin Rudner (Manotick, Ontario: Penumbra, 2006), 15–37; Amy Knight, *How the Cold War Began: The Gouzenko Affair and the Hunt for Soviet Spies* (Toronto: McClelland and Stewart, 2005); and John Sawatsky, *Gouzenko: The Untold Story* (Toronto: Macmillan, 1984).

The seminal work on Canada's role in the Korean War is Denis Stairs, *The Diplomacy of Constraint: Canada, the Korean War, and the United States* (Toronto: University of Toronto Press, 1974). Robert S. Prince adds nuance to Stairs's arguments in "The Limits of Constraint: Canadian–American Relations and the Korean War, 1950–51," *Journal of Canadian Studies* 27, no. 4 (Winter 1992–3): 129–52. Edelgard Mahant and Graeme S. Mount work almost entirely from American sources, providing valuable insights in *Invisible and Inaudible in Washington: American Policies toward Canada* (Vancouver: UBC Press, 1999). Finally, Lester Pearson's memoirs are particularly useful on Korea: *Mike: The Memoirs of the Right Honourable Lester B. Pearson,* vol. 2, *1948–1957* (Toronto: University of Toronto Press, 1973).

## CHAPTER 9

# Discord, 1955–1968

## *The Breakdown in the Consensus*

## Introduction

Frank Tinker was glad to be leaving Canada. Returning home in late 1954 after an unhappy two-year posting as US vice consul in Toronto, Tinker remembered encountering frequent animosities toward Americans in Canada. These were not legitimate differences of opinion, but "unthinking, overplayed and malicious" criticisms of his country. Canadians had traded "national pride" for "childish spite," making Americans in Canada "feel like unwelcome interlopers." Tinker vented his feelings in a *Maclean's* article that drew more mail than any other recent contribution.[1] Other Americans confirmed Tinker's experience. A student from the University of Rochester's Canadian Studies Program encountered anti-American sentiment on a visit to Toronto. "The chief parlor game seemed to be panning Americans," he observed. Another asked why "some Canadians seem to dislike us so much."[2] Anti-Americanism was not a new sentiment in Canada, though it had been largely dormant since the First World War. For a generation, Canadians had been satisfied with the security and affluence that Canada's close relationship with the United States provided. Now, in the mid-1950s, anti-Americanism was reawakening.

## Fissures in the Consensus

In the late 1940s and early 1950s, a consensus dominated public life in North America. For Canadians and Americans, the world was gripped with a struggle between good and evil. On the one side stood the United States, Canada, and their allies in Western Europe. On the other sat the forces of expansionist communism: the Soviet Union, China, and their collaborators in Eastern Europe and Southeast Asia. At home, Canadians and Americans worried about communist subversion; abroad, they were concerned with the global ambitions of the Soviet Union. In the mid-1950s, Canadians remained vehemently opposed to Soviet expansionism, but the North American consensus began to break down as Canadians became increasingly concerned about the conduct of the United States and about the high level of American political and economic influence in Canada.

McCarthyism stirred the first doubts. Canadians were troubled by the actions of US Senator Joseph McCarthy and the congressional committees investigating communism in the US government and the entertainment industry. Beginning in late 1953, Canadians across the political spectrum spoke out against McCarthy and his methods. M.J. Coldwell, leader of the Cooperative Commonwealth Federation (CCF), the predecessor of the New Democratic Party (NDP), condemned McCarthyism as a threat to "the welfare, peace and democracy of North America, perhaps of the world."[3] Liberal MP David Croll equated McCarthyism with fascism and communism, ideologies that aimed "to confuse, to divide, to conquer and ultimately to enslave."[4] A conservative newspaper, the *Ottawa Journal*, called McCarthy "irresponsible and vulgar."[5] Canadians and Americans valued the rule of law and the presumption of innocence, but Americans—or at least the members of Congressional committees—now seemed to be betraying common North American ideals. In November 1953, hundreds of University of Toronto students burned McCarthy in effigy, condemning his "terror tactics."[6]

# The Foreign Investment Debate

In 1955, the Liberal government of Louis St Laurent appointed the Royal Commission on Canada's Economic Prospects, chaired by Walter Gordon, a Toronto accountant and businessman. The commission's task was to investigate the Canadian economy, forecast its future, and recommend government policies to maximize the country's economic growth. Gordon was particularly concerned about American investment in Canada. Arnold Heeney, Gordon's friend and Canada's ambassador to the United States, feared that the commission's work would involve a "certain stirring up of anti-U.S. feeling."[7]

As the commission conducted hearings across Canada, interest in foreign investment grew. At the outset of the investigation, Gordon encouraged those submitting briefs or testifying before the commission to address the subject, and many witnesses responded to Gordon's prompting. Organized labour was the most vocal critic of foreign ownership, complaining that it meant fewer manufacturing jobs because foreign-owned companies were more likely to export Canadian natural resources to the United States for processing. In contrast, the government of British Columbia, the Canadian Manufacturers' Association, and a few large corporations insisted that outside capital was necessary for Canada's development.

The commission sparked the first widespread and critical consideration of foreign investment in Canada. The media caught on to the issue, with magazines and newspapers describing a flood of American investment that put Canada's destiny in the hands of foreigners. Opposition parties began to question Canada's close economic ties to the United States. "Canadians should declare their economic independence of the United States," announced Conservative leader George Drew.[8] CCF leader Coldwell agreed: "The domination of our economic life by these foreign corporations is threatening the independence of this country."[9]

The federal Cabinet worried about the growing opposition to foreign investment. External Affairs Minister Lester Pearson, one of Gordon's friends, spoke out in March 1956 in Montreal, saying that Canadian economic growth would not have been as robust "without outside participation, especially by investors from the United States." For Pearson, complaints that the United States was dominating Canada, either economically or politically, were uncalled for: "The times are too serious and the problems too real for irresponsible exaggeration."[10] C.D. Howe, the minister of trade and commerce, added his voice in defence of American investment. Foreign investors were "skilled and responsible," bringing "capital and often technical management which are not always available from domestic sources." "Why put unnecessary handicaps in the way of our future by adopting narrowly nationalistic and emotional attitudes towards foreign capital?"[11]

Objections to American investment became so common that US ambassador R. Douglas Stuart felt obliged to intervene in the debate, an unusual step for a diplomat. Without naming George Drew, the ambassador quoted and criticized the leader of the opposition's comments on Canada's economic independence. Stuart argued that foreign investment was a result of those Canadian policy choices, particularly the tariff, that encouraged American companies to set up plants in Canada.[12] The ambassador's words only made matters worse, provoking a backlash against his inference in domestic politics. Conservative MP John Diefenbaker, soon to be elected his party's leader, called Stuart's statement "an unwarranted intrusion by the ambassador." For CCF leader Coldwell, the speech was "not only unusual but a highly improper thing for an ambassador to do;" the Canadian government should object "to the entry of an ambassador into what is at the moment a very hot and controversial subject in Canada."[13]

Having stoked the debate over foreign investment, the Gordon Commission issued two widely circulated reports, a preliminary one in

December 1956 and a final report in November 1957. Both were over-
flowing with optimism about Canada's economic future, while raising
doubts about the value of foreign ownership. Canada benefitted from imported capital, and there was no evidence that foreign investors acted in
ways that damaged Canadian interests, but who knew what would happen
in the future? The reports suggested that foreign-owned firms might be less
likely to employ Canadians and to purchase their supplies and components
in Canada. More importantly, the commission hinted at a link between
economic and political dependence. "Many Canadians are worried about
such a large degree of economic decision-making being in the hands of
non-residents or in the hands of Canadian companies controlled by non-
residents," because it "might lead to economic domination by the United
States and eventually to the loss of our political independence."[14] The
commission proposed measures to encourage the sale of some shares of
foreign-owned companies to Canadians, helping ensure a Canadian point
of view in the management of those firms.

## The End of the Liberal Era

American influence was a central element of the pipeline debate of May and
June 1956. Parliament engaged in a heated battle over a government bill
to allow a largely American-financed company to build a pipeline to transport natural gas from Alberta to Ontario. The opposition denounced the
government, both for trying to curtail debate on the bill and for expanding
American economic power in Canada. Tempers erupted in the House of
Commons as MPs began yelling and singing, while the speaker struggled to
restore order. The ordeal was so stressful that three MPs were hospitalized
during the debate and one died of a heart attack in a House of Commons
washroom. The Liberals succeeded in having the bill passed, the pipeline
was built, and the project was highly successful—but the debate cracked the
image of a supremely confident and competent governing party.

Further doubts about the United States surfaced during the Suez
crisis. The Egyptian government had nationalized the Suez Canal in July
1956, taking the waterway from its British, French, and American owners
with a promise to reimburse them. The US government opposed the na-
tionalization of the canal but did not think that the situation called for the
use of force. The British and French disagreed, as did the Israelis, who
had a hostile relationship with Egypt. In October, Israel's troops invaded
Egypt in an effort to capture the canal. The UN Security Council began
discussing the matter, but before any decisions could be reached, France
and Britain dispatched troops to the region. The European powers were
secretly working with the Israelis, though they tried to portray themselves as

interested only in preventing the Israeli–Egyptian conflict from threatening canal traffic.

Canada warned the British that their actions could divide the Commonwealth, as India and other members opposed the invasion of Egypt. The British ignored Canadian concerns and lied to Canadian officials about their intentions. When the United States urged a ceasefire, Canada was curiously silent. Then, working with the Americans, foreign minister Pearson proposed a UN peacekeeping force to separate the belligerents, a plan that won widespread support and brought the crisis to a close. Pearson won the Nobel Prize for his work, but many older, English-speaking Canadians were unsettled by the crisis, believing Pearson had abandoned Britain to side with the United States.

During the Suez Crisis, Canada's ambassador to Egypt, Herbert Norman, had performed impeccably, but this did not stop American senators from doubting his loyalty. In 1950, the US Senate Subcommittee on Internal Security had pried into Norman's past. Norman had been a communist in his youth, but there was no indication that he had been anything but a faithful and trustworthy servant to Canada since becoming a diplomat. Concerned about the allegations, the Department of External Affairs investigated in the Canadian style, behind closed doors and away from the glare of camera lights. Norman was exonerated, but his ordeal had not ended. A few weeks after Suez, the US Senate subcommittee once more questioned Norman's integrity. Rather than again suffer innuendos and interrogations, Norman chose to end his own life, jumping from a seventh-floor apartment in Cairo.

Norman's suicide generated a wave of anti-American sentiment in Canada as politicians and media commentators blamed the US Senate subcommittee for the diplomat's death. "I believe Mr. Norman was murdered by slander," CCF MP Alistair Stewart declared in the House of Commons. "I believe he was killed as if someone had put a knife in his back."[15] A Canadian diplomat reported that he had never seen such Canadian hostility toward the United States. "There have been fights, squabbles, and bickering between us before, but never has there been a time when the whole country was raging mad at the United States."[16]

Not realizing that the Liberal party was suffering from growing anti-American sentiment, Prime Minister Louis St Laurent called an election eight days after Norman's death. The fiery new Conservative leader, John Diefenbaker, exploited the developing skepticism about American economic and political power, attacking the Liberals for deserting Britain over Suez, encouraging foreign investment, and allowing the development of the country's resources by Americans. Voters rewarded the Conservatives with more seats than the Liberals, making Diefenbaker prime minister at the head of a minority government. He continued the assault in the 1958 election, in which his party won the largest majority in Canadian history. "There is a very definite feel of nationalism in Canada—anti-Americanism if you will," Walter Gordon wrote to Lester Pearson, the new Liberal leader, in 1958, "and the Tories capitalized on this."[17]

## The Diefenbaker Government

Few Canadian politicians were more enigmatic that John Diefenbaker. On Canadian–American relations, his public statements were a series of contradictions. On the one hand, he often rushed to defend the United States when he suspected that others were being anti-American. He denounced Donald Creighton in 1954 after the historian said that the United States was "engaged in what can only be described as the greatest sales campaign in its history, the campaign to sell the Cold War, in an exclusive American package, to the rest of the Western world."[18] In 1955, Diefenbaker suggested that some people attacked the Americans because "the United States represents the greatest example of free enterprise which exists anywhere in the world."[19] Yet, on the other hand, he could also be alarmist about the United States, particularly at times when he perceived that anti-Americanism could help him politically. In 1956, Diefenbaker condemned the high levels of US capital in Canada and declared, "If the St Laurent government is re-elected, Canada will become a virtual forty-ninth economic state in the American union."[20] The next year, he denounced the government for being "too timid, too fearful, and too timorous" in dealing with the United States after the Senate subcommittee questioned Herbert Norman's loyalty.[21] In the late 1950s, Diefenbaker delivered countless speeches about the threat of American control over the Canadian economy.

Once in power, Diefenbaker did little to carry out the promise of his campaign rhetoric or even to clarify his position on Canada's relationship with the United States. He frequently peppered his remarks with critical comments about the US and may well have considered himself an economic nationalist, but he had little ability to turn speeches into policy and legislation, and his Cabinet opposed measures that might upset the Conservative Party's business supporters in Toronto and Montreal. The government introduced some nationalist legislation, including acts to restrict foreign control of insurance companies, broadcast outlets, and firms applying for oil and gas leases in the North and offshore. The government also imposed a 15 per cent withholding tax on interest and dividend payments to non-residents, but this measure was designed less to reduce foreign control than to address unemployment and foreign exchange problems.

These initiatives did not affect ownership in any but a few narrow areas, and Diefenbaker shunned policies that would have a broader effect. Concerned about Canada's economic dependence on the United States, the prime minister announced in 1957 that he would divert 15 per cent of the country's trade to Britain. He appeared to have pulled the figure out of nowhere in the middle of a media interview and he backed away from the proposal almost immediately. He buried the final report of the Gordon Commission, distrusting the Liberal ties of the commission's chair. When the governor of the Bank of Canada, James Coyne, pursued a tight monetary policy to reduce foreign ownership, the Conservative government, worried about the impact on unemployment, publicly denigrated him and forced him from office.

Despite the nationalist rhetoric, Diefenbaker forged close connections to the US in his first few years in office. He developed a solid personal relationship with President Dwight Eisenhower, one based on mutual respect. This harmonious period culminated when the two leaders signed the Columbia River Treaty in January 1961, just three days before Eisenhower stepped down as president. The river flows from the Rocky Mountains in British Columbia through Washington State, and then along the Washington–Oregon border to the Pacific. Under the agreement, Canada would build three dams north of the border, both to prevent the river from flooding on the US side and to produce power, half of which would be shared with the United States. In exchange, the US paid Canada $64.4 million.

# The Defence Crisis

The early Diefenbaker years were characterized by close military relations between Canada and the United States. In 1957 Canada joined NORAD, the North American Air Defence Command, an agreement negotiated by the St Laurent government, but finalized by Diefenbaker. NORAD integrated the home defence squadrons of the Canadian and American air forces under an American commander and a Canadian deputy, with headquarters at Colorado Springs. Essentially, NORAD turned North America into a single country for the defence of the continent against the Soviet threat. In July 1958, Diefenbaker and Eisenhower agreed to the Development and Production Sharing Programme. It was similar to the 1941 Hyde Park agreement, except it came at a less urgent time because the world was not at war. Under the agreement, Canadian firms were able to share in orders from American military procurement, producing a sharp increase in American purchases of Canadian arms and contributing to the further integration of the North American economy, a process Diefenbaker had long condemned.

When the Conservatives came to office, A.V. Roe Canada was building the AVRO Arrow, a supersonic fighter plane designed for Canadian conditions. Everyone agreed the aircraft was superb, but other countries would not buy it. For their part, the Americans preferred a less-expensive, American-made aircraft, one designed for US needs. The Liberals had planned to cancel the Arrow project after the 1957 election, because it was not cost-effective to build the plane for just the Canadian air force. After taking office, Diefenbaker delayed a decision until 1959 when he finally abandoned the Arrow, forcing AVRO to lay off 14,000 workers. Then and now, commentators have attacked this decision, but it is hard to see that Diefenbaker had any other realistic option.

For continental air defence, Diefenbaker turned to the American-made Bomarc missile, designed to intercept Soviet planes at a much lower cost than the Arrow. Canada and the United States agreed that Canada would build two Bomarc sites, the US would supply the weapons, and NORAD headquarters would control them. Around the same time, the Diefenbaker government also decided to purchase the CF-104 Starfighter fighter/bomber and the Honest John rocket for Canada's NATO units in Europe, as well as the CF-101 Voodoo interceptor aircraft for the country's NORAD forces. All four systems were designed to be equipped with nuclear arms, but not long after agreeing to take on the weapons, the prime minister began to worry that the decision would cost him public support. He paid close attention to correspondence from Canadians opposed to nuclear arms, dismissing public opinion polls that showed majority support for the weapons. When the first Bomarcs were installed in Canada, they had sandbags in the place of warheads, while Canada and the United States worked out the details of the joint custody of the nuclear arms. Negotiations dragged on as Canadian officials contributed little to settling the issue and Americans became increasingly concerned. The Canadian Bomarc sites were an integral part of the NORAD system, and unarmed missiles meant there was a gap in North America's air defences.

By 1960, the Cabinet was deeply split on the question. The minister of external affairs, Howard Green, was playing a leading role in disarmament discussions at the United Nations and felt it hypocritical for Canada to take on nuclear weapons while working to end their proliferation. The minister of national defence, Douglas Harkness, wanted to accept nuclear arms, arguing that they were necessary for the defence of North America and Western Europe. Besides, he said, Canada had agreed to take them. Diefenbaker delayed, as he did when facing any difficult decision.

The situation became more complicated after John Kennedy became president of the United States in January 1961. Diefenbaker and Kennedy had incompatible personalities, with Kennedy insensitive to the prime minister, and Diefenbaker overly sensitive to perceived slights. Before the new president even took office, Diefenbaker's senior foreign policy adviser noted that the prime minister had "formed an irrational prejudice against Kennedy."[22] A few days after Kennedy's inauguration, the president told the press that he had invited Prime Minister "Diefenbawker" to Washington. The prime minister was furious at the mispronunciation of his name, even suggesting to his Cabinet that Canada should lodge a formal protest.

Diefenbaker and Kennedy had a friendly first meeting in Washington in February 1961, but one minor annoyance stuck with the prime minister. Kennedy showed the prime minister a stuffed sailfish that he had caught in Acapulco. "Have you ever caught anything better?" he asked. As a matter of fact, Diefenbaker had. He told the president that he had recently reeled in a 140-pound marlin in Jamaica. "You didn't catch it," Kennedy scoffed.[23] It might have been a joke, but Diefenbaker was wounded. The president had thrown sand in his eyes; the prime minister became determined to throw some back.

The president's visit to Ottawa in May 1961 got off to a bad start. Diefenbaker welcomed Kennedy in a speech that included two sentences in tortuous French. Kennedy gently teased the prime minister, saying that after hearing Diefenbaker, he was tempted to speak French himself. The crowd laughed, and so did Diefenbaker, but inside the prime minister seethed. Diefenbaker had made sure his marlin was stuffed and mounted for the president's visit, but Kennedy seemed unimpressed. At a dinner at the American ambassador's residence, Kennedy talked at length with Lester Pearson, showing that he preferred the Liberal leader's company to that of the prime minister. For Diefenbaker the bigger offence came with a memorandum the Kennedy people left behind, in which an aide advised the president to "push" Canada on various issues. The document ended up with Diefenbaker, who refused to return it, as diplomatic protocol required. He found the tone insulting and fumed about it for years. Prone to paranoia, Diefenbaker eventually convinced himself and others that the president had referred to him as an "SOB" in a marginal note. One week after the visit, Diefenbaker told reporters that Americans took Canada for granted and should not expect him automatically to accept US foreign policy. In private, Diefenbaker described Kennedy as "a hothead" and a "fool"—"too young, too brash, too inexperienced, and a boastful son of a bitch!" In Kennedy's view, the Canadian prime minister was "a sanctimonious, platitudinous, old bore."[24] It was unlikely that the two men would cooperate in the future.

The Canadian election of June 1962 put further strain on the relationship between Canada and the United States. With the Conservative Party on the

**Photo 9.1** ✦ John F. Kennedy and John Diefenbaker

Kennedy and Diefenbaker had a friendly first meeting in the White House in February 1961, but they would eventually come to despise each other. (Source: University of Saskatchewan, University Archives & Special Collections, Diefenbaker fonds MG 411, JGD1377.)

verge of defeat, Diefenbaker became increasingly unpredictable. He was incensed that President Kennedy's wife, Jacqueline, had invited Lester Pearson to dinner at the White House during the campaign. It made no difference to Diefenbaker that the invitation had been issued before the election call or that Pearson was just one of 49 Nobel Prize winners at the event. Already hostile to the Kennedy White House, the prime minister decided to run an anti-American campaign and release the memorandum that the president's people had accidentally left in Ottawa in 1961. After the US ambassador warned that making the document public would have catastrophic consequences for Canadian–American relations, Diefenbaker backed down, but held onto the memo for future use. Upon hearing of Diefenbaker's threat, the president shouted a series of foul insults about the prime minister and vowed never to talk to him again.

In mid-campaign, Diefenbaker was confronted with an economic crisis. The value of the Canadian currency was fixed, but economic uncertainty led many investors to sell their Canadian dollars. The Bank of Canada sold off exchange reserves to maintain the value of the dollar, but could not do so forever. Cabinet decided to lower the value of the Canadian dollar from 95 to 92.5 cents

US, a move that damaged Conservative election prospects. The International Monetary Fund and the US government helped Canada through the crisis with $300 million in loans and credits, but Diefenbaker remained suspicious of American motivations, convincing himself that somehow Kennedy had caused the exchange crisis. On election day, the Conservative government was reduced to a minority of the seats in the House of Commons. With the prime minister's position increasingly precarious, Diefenbaker became more erratic and more obsessed with Kennedy.

In the Cuban Missile Crisis, relations between the two leaders deteriorated further still. In October 1962, the Americans discovered Soviet missiles in Cuba, within striking distance of major American cities. Kennedy blockaded the island to prevent Soviet ships from getting to Cuba. Diefenbaker hesitated. In international affairs, he had backed Eisenhower automatically, but now, fuelled by his hatred of Kennedy, Diefenbaker refused to let the United States fly nuclear fighters to Arctic bases or to arm the Bomarcs, which still held sandbags instead of nuclear warheads. The prime minister would not place Canada's NORAD forces on alert, not realizing that his approval was unnecessary and that the minister of national defence would soon issue the alert order without Diefenbaker's knowledge. As the world moved terrifyingly close to nuclear war, the prime minister asked Kennedy for more proof that the Soviets had placed weapons in Cuba. Eventually, Kennedy made a deal to end the crisis: the Soviets would remove the missiles from Cuba, and the US would withdraw American missiles from Turkey. Afterward, Kennedy remained outraged at Diefenbaker's actions, seeing him as an unreliable ally. "Kennedy gave up on Diefenbaker," recalled the president's national security adviser, McGeorge Bundy. "He never gave up on anybody else. . . . But he did on Diefenbaker."[25]

The tragedy of the Diefenbaker government entered its final act in January 1963. US general Lauris Norstad, NATO's supreme allied commander in Europe, visited Ottawa and told a press conference that Canada had committed to taking nuclear weapons, a comment at odds with Diefenbaker's public statements. A few days later, Liberal leader Lester Pearson reversed his party's opposition to nuclear arms. The Liberals might disagree with Diefenbaker's earlier decision to take the weapons, but the larger issue was whether Canada would keep its word. Pearson's position—that Canada should take nuclear weapons and then negotiate to get rid of them—no doubt won the Liberals much public support at a time when polls showed that a majority of Canadians favoured their country's acquisition of nuclear arms.[26]

In a confusing two-hour speech, Diefenbaker seemed to tell the House of Commons both that Canada had not agreed to take nuclear weapons and that negotiations to obtain them were going well. Not so, responded the US government. In a highly unusual move, the US State Department issued a press release contradicting the prime minister: "The Canadian government has not as yet proposed any arrangement sufficiently practical to contribute effectively to North American defence."[27] Diefenbaker read the statement with a glow in his eyes. "We've got our issue now," he told Justice Minister Donald Fleming. "We can call our general election now."[28] The prime minister recalled Canada's ambassador from Washington, the only time Canada has used this form of diplomatic protest against the United States. Shaking with anger, Diefenbaker announced to the House of Commons that Canada would "not be pushed around or accept external domination or interference in the making of its decisions."[29] In response, Social Credit leader Robert Thompson uttered a line that best describes Canada's always close but frequently uneasy attitude toward the United States: "The United States is our friend, whether we like it or not."[30]

On Sunday, 3 February 1963, Diefenbaker chaired the most chaotic Cabinet meeting in Canadian history. The ministers calmly began discussing the prime minister's desire to call an election, but before long they were engaged in heated debate, with several of them talking at once. Defence Minister Harkness said that Diefenbaker had lost public confidence and should resign. Diefenbaker slammed his fist on the table and demanded that everyone who supported him stand up. About half the Cabinet remained seated, some because they had lost confidence in the prime minister, but others because they thought he had asked them to stand if they backed an election call. Stunned at the response, Diefenbaker announced he would step down in favour of Fleming and he left the room as several ministers began yelling at each other. "You treacherous bastards!" "Nest of traitors!" "You son of a bitch!"[31] After calm was restored, the Cabinet passed a resolution reaffirming its support for the prime minister, and Harkness announced he would resign.

On 5 February, the opposition parties combined to defeat the minority Diefenbaker government, leaving the prime minister no choice but to call an election. The Conservative government continued to disintegrate during the campaign, with two more ministers resigning and several others refusing to seek re-election. A brilliant campaigner, Diefenbaker railed against the Liberals and the Americans in speech after speech, even arguing that the Liberal party and the United States wanted Bomarcs in Canada as decoys, to draw Soviet fire away from the United States. It was not sufficient to win, but was enough to deprive Pearson of a House of Commons majority. In the end, the Liberals won 129 seats to 95 for the Conservatives, 24 for the Social Credit, and 17 for the New Democrats. Lester Pearson would form a minority government, needing support from at least one of the opposition parties.

The circumstances that led to Diefenbaker's fall incensed Canadian philosopher George Grant. In 1965, his fury appeared in book form as

*Lament for a Nation: The Defeat of Canadian Nationalism.* Grant endorsed Donald Creighton's view of the Liberal governments of the King and St Laurent epochs: "For twenty years before its defeat in 1957, the Liberal party had been pursuing policies that led inexorably to the disappearance of Canada. Its policies led to the impossibility of an alternative to the American republic being built on the northern half of this continent." During the 1963 defence crisis, Diefenbaker had taken "the strongest stand against satellite status that any Canadian government ever attempted." Yet against the "full power of the Canadian ruling class, the American government, and the military," he was doomed to fail. For Grant, Diefenbaker's defeat proved that an independent Canada was impossible.[32] The message had a powerful effect, particularly on young Canadians. "It's the most important book I ever read in my life," remembered James Laxer, a student leader in the 1960s. Grant "woke up half our generation. He was saying Canada is dead, and by saying it he was creating the country."[33]

Later historians have been inclined to blame Diefenbaker for his own downfall, rather than believing in a conspiracy involving Americans, Canadian Liberals, and the military of the two countries. Diefenbaker, the historians say, fell from office because of his own incompetence. He pledged to take nuclear weapons and then tried to break his promise. He was unable to make a decision and did not have the necessary leadership skills to keep his Cabinet united.

# The Pearson Government

When Lester Pearson became prime minister in 1963, it seemed that order would return to the Canadian–American relationship. Pearson was Canada's most accomplished diplomat and the only Canadian to have won the Nobel Peace Prize. He was well known—and well liked—in Washington. A few months after taking office, he met with Kennedy at the president's summer home in Hyannis Port, Massachusetts. The two men got on well, exchanging baseball trivia and joking about Diefenbaker. "The meeting . . . was tinged with euphoria," the Canadian ambassador, Charles Ritchie, recorded in his diary.[34] Yet there was no chance of a return to the easy relationship of the late 1940s and early 1950s, when Pearson had been Canada's senior diplomat.

The mastermind of Pearson's election victory was Walter Gordon, the same man who had chaired the mid-1950s royal commission that had warned about the dangers of American economic influence in Canada. So important was Gordon's role in rebuilding the Liberal party and bringing it back to office that Pearson allowed Gordon to select his own reward. He chose to be finance minister, a position that he thought would allow him to reduce American control of the Canadian economy. In his first budget, released in June 1963, Gordon introduced both a 30 per cent tax on foreign takeovers of Canadian firms and tax incentives to encourage foreign companies to sell shares to Canadians. Gordon immediately faced vehement opposition from the business community and discovered that his Cabinet colleagues—whom he had never tried to persuade about the dangers of foreign investment—did not share his nationalist views. Gordon was forced to withdraw the takeover tax, but the damage had been done. His budget had destroyed what Canadian ambassador Ritchie had called the Hyannis Port honeymoon.

Days after Walter Gordon had abandoned key elements of his first budget, Canadian officials had to confront the country's dependence on American capital. President Kennedy announced that the US would impose a 15 per cent tax on the purchase of shares in foreign companies and another tax, ranging from 2.75 to 15 per cent, on the acquisition of foreign bonds. The purpose was to restore the country's balance of payments by discouraging the outflow of US dollars.

The interest equalization tax would have had a devastating effect on Canada. It would have lessened the return to Americans investing in Canada, meaning that Canadian interest rates would have to rise to prevent a significant loss of capital. If, for instance, Ontario Hydro wished to issue bonds to raise capital, the company would need to offer an additional one percentage point in interest to make up for the tax. Higher interest rates would have slowed, perhaps stalled, the growth of the Canadian economy. News of the tax was greeted with heavy selling on Canadian stock exchanges, with the Toronto industrial average falling 21 points in two days, a 3 per cent drop and one of the largest in the market's history.[35]

The tax would help accomplish Gordon's goal of reducing the amount of foreign investment in Canada, but the finance minister still hoped Canada would be exempted from it. For Gordon, the tax would have too broad an impact. It would deal not only with direct investment, the controlling ownership of companies operating in Canada, but also with portfolio investment, the purchase of stock or debt securities, including federal, provincial, and municipal bonds. Still, there was something to the judgment of Dean Rusk, Kennedy's secretary of state: "I came to the conclusion that Canadians wanted American investments but, at the same time, wanted to complain about them, too."[36] Another US official was more scathing: "What Canadians need in financial questions is a psychoanalyst's couch."[37]

Bank of Canada governor Louis Rasminsky led a delegation to Washington to convince American officials to exempt Canada from the tax. He pointed out that the United States exported more goods and services to Canada than capital. Canadians paid for American goods and services with all the investment dollars they received from the United States plus money earned in other countries. Restricting the flow of American dollars to Canada would thus limit the American imports Canadians could purchase, meaning that neither country would benefit from the interest equalization tax. After two days of discussion and negotiation, US officials accepted Rasminsky's arguments and agreed to a partial exemption for Canada.

Yet problems remained with the balance of payments between the two countries. Imports from the United States far exceeded Canada's exports to that country. This created a troubling trade imbalance, two-thirds of which was in automobiles and auto parts. In 1964, Canada imported $723 million in cars and parts from the US, but only exported $105 million back across the border. American officials recognized the unfairness of the situation and feared that Canadians might act unilaterally to solve it. The solution was a 1965 trade agreement on automotive products, usually known as the Auto Pact. An auto manufacturer would be allowed to move cars and parts across the border duty-free so long as the company produced in Canada the same proportion of vehicles as it sold in Canada. As a result of this incentive, manufacturers produced more cars and parts north of the border, and the Canadian automotive industry thrived. By 1970, Canada's automotive imports were $3.1 billion and its exports were $3.3 billion.[38]

The actual signing of the Auto Pact highlighted the sharp contrast between Pearson and Lyndon Johnson, who had become US president after Kennedy's assassination in November 1963. Coarse, overbearing, and politically brilliant, Johnson could hardly have been more different from the urbane and modest Pearson. Johnson chose to finalize the trade agreement not in an imposing building in Washington but at his Texas ranch. Pearson arrived in diplomatic garb: a black three-piece suit, with a flower in the lapel, a bowtie, and a homburg hat. Johnson showed up dressed like a ranch hand. In front of the television cameras, Johnson called Pearson "Mr Wilson," mixing up the Canadian prime minister with the British leader, Harold Wilson.[39] Always talking, never listening, the president offered his guest a tour of the ranch, drinking bourbon as the entourage flew over the Texas countryside in a helicopter and later drove around in a jeep. At one stop, Johnson asked Pearson to take "a leak" with him.[40] Pearson was troubled by the trip, both because of the president's style and his failure to discuss any substantive issues in Canadian–American relations. The prime minister did not know that the worst was yet to come.

**Photo 9.2** ✣ Lyndon Johnson and Lester Pearson

President Lyndon Johnson (right) prepares to give Prime Minister Lester Pearson a tour of the LBJ ranch near Stonewall, Texas, January 1965. Pearson had prepared for a state occasion, but Johnson was dressed in cowboy garb. The contrasting clothing was only a small indication of the major differences between the men. (Source: United Press International / Library and Archives Canada, PA-117604.)

## Cultural Policy

Canadians had long worried that their identity could be drowned in a deluge of American popular culture. In the 1950s and 1960s these fears became more pronounced. "For years we Canadians have been flooded with American moving pictures, American radio programs, American magazines, American books," read a 1951 Canadian Authors Association brief. "Something should be done before the Canadian viewpoint is lost entirely."[41]

In 1949, the St Laurent government had appointed the Royal Commission on National Development in the Arts, Letters, and Sciences, chaired by Vincent Massey. The commission's report, published in 1951, encouraged the government to increase funding for the CBC and the National Film Board, while establishing an agency to provide financial support for the arts, a recommendation that the government implemented when it created the Canada Council in 1957. These measures would help offset the alien influence of American mass culture, which the commissioners saw as mindless, coarse, and materialistic. Yet there was another way to look at the presence of American culture in Canada. "We cannot escape the fact that we live on the same continent as the Americans," historian Frank Underhill argued, "and that the longer we live here the more we are going to be affected by the same continental influences which affect them." These influences were not "alien;" they were "just the natural forces that operate in the conditions of twentieth-century civilization."[42] Yes, American films were shallow and vulgar, but that was because the public demanded such fare. Canadian films, if produced for a mass audience, would be no different.

The Massey Commission had recommended that the CBC continue to have a dominant role in Canadian broadcasting, but the Diefenbaker government wished a larger place for the private sector. The CBC had functioned both as a broadcast network and as the regulatory body for the Canadian broadcast industry. In 1958, the government stripped the CBC of its regulatory role, leaving the corporation solely in charge of its own radio and television networks. The Board of Broadcast Governors (BBG) would now oversee the broadcast sector and would be charged with ensuring a minimum level of Canadian content. In 1959, the BBG created the first content regulations for television, requiring that 45 per cent of programming be Canadian after 1 April 1961, and at least 55 per cent after 1 April 1962.

Throughout the 1950s and 1960s, Canadian magazines struggled for survival against their American competitors. Canadian publishers had to deal with imports of foreign (mostly American) magazines, but there were other forms of competition. Split-run magazines were American publications that kept all the original editorial content (stories, articles, photographs, etc.) but contained advertising targeted at the Canadian market. Canadian editions of American magazines were the same as the split-runs, but included a few pages of Canadian content. The Canadian edition of *Time* magazine, for instance, was identical to the American version, except for four pages of stories about Canada and some different advertisements. Canadian publishers found it difficult to compete against these American publications, which had lower editorial costs, often charged lower advertising rates, and reached a broader audience than their Canadian counterparts. By 1954, 80 per cent of the magazines purchased in Canada were of American origin.[43]

For the St Laurent government, the solution was to tax the foreign periodicals. In March 1956, Finance Minister Walter Harris introduced a 20 per cent levy on the advertising revenues of split-run editions, a holding operation until the government could provide more support to Canadian magazines. The United States protested that the measure was discriminatory and would harm *Time* and *Reader's Digest*, two publications that had long been established in Canada. The tax also came under attack in the House of Commons, where members of the Conservative opposition argued that Canadian publishers simply needed to produce a better product if they wanted to attract a broader readership.

Shortly after the Conservatives came to office in 1957, they repealed the Harris tax. Within months, four American magazines launched Canadian editions, and one began a Canadian split-run. Representatives of the Periodical Press Association warned that the major Canadian magazines would cease to exist in two or three years if the government did not take immediate action. Cabinet ministers now doubted the wisdom of their decision to rescind the Harris tax, but were caught in a bind. For political reasons, they could neither admit their mistake and re-impose the tax nor allow major Canadian magazines to fail. Unable to decide, Diefenbaker referred the matter in 1960 to the Royal Commission on Publications, chaired by Grattan O'Leary, president, publisher, and primary owner of the *Ottawa Journal*.

The O'Leary Report, issued in June 1961, asserted that "communications are the thread which binds together the fibers of a nation. . . . The communications of a nation are as vital to its life as its defences, and should receive at least as great a measure of national protection."[44] O'Leary recommended that the government discontinue the tax deduction for advertising in foreign periodicals and stop the import into Canada of split-runs, which could continue to circulate in Canada, so long as they were printed in Canada. *Time* was outraged, complaining that the commission was trying to destroy its Canadian edition. But even with the commission's report in hand, Cabinet could not decide what to do. After much dithering, Diefenbaker promised to implement a revised version of the O'Leary proposals, but his government had taken no action by the time it was defeated in April 1963.

After the Liberals took office, Finance Minister Walter Gordon suggested that the government do nothing to help Canadian magazines, concerned as he was with American economic control, not with American culture. The prime minister's senior policy adviser disagreed. Tom Kent, who had been a newspaper editor before going to work for Pearson, convinced the prime minister that the government had to act. In 1965, Gordon reluctantly introduced legislation to stop the import of split-runs and end the tax deduction for advertising in foreign magazines, except for *Time* and *Reader's Digest*. These measures gave Canadian periodicals some reprieve but did not solve the problem. Canadian publishers continued to struggle, while their American competitors flourished.

Motion pictures presented a greater challenge. "Hollywood refashions us in its own image," the Massey Report had warned.[45] The problem for the Canadian government was that there was no significant Canadian feature film industry. Imposing quotas on cinemas would not solve the problem, because there were hardly any Canadian films to screen. Subsidies were not an option because the movie business was extraordinarily expensive.

In 1948, the Canadian government had entered into the Canadian Co-operation Project with the Motion Picture Association of America. Some feature films would be shot in Canada and scripts would include favourable references to the country. The goal was to create jobs and promote tourism, not to foster Canadian culture or express a distinctly Canadian point of view through film. In this sense, the government saw the movie business as just another industry. The agreement quietly died in 1958, with no one lamenting its demise.

A more productive government initiative came in 1967, when Parliament created the Canadian Film Development Corporation (CFDC), now known as Telefilm Canada. With a five-year, $10 million fund, the company began operating in 1968, lending money to Canadian filmmakers. In those early days, the average budget for a CFDC-financed film was $250,000—this in an era where a major Hollywood film cost 10 times that amount.[46] The result was predictable: the CFDC helped make some duds and some Canadian masterpieces, such as *Goin' Down the Road*, films that won critical acclaim but were seen by few Canadians, other than students who enrolled in Canadian Studies courses in the decades that followed. Some of the films were good—some superb—but they seldom had the production qualities necessary to go head-to-head against Hollywood productions.

Even had they been good enough to compete against their Hollywood rivals, Canadian films rarely had the opportunity to do so. The major distribution companies, all American-owned, had little interest in Canadian films. The CFDC might help create a Canadian film, but then the producers found that they could not get it screened in cinemas, whether in Canada or the United States. Years later, the president of Odeon Theatres, Christopher Salmon, gave his explanation for the reluctance of distributors to handle Canadian films. The problem was not that the movies were Canadian, but that they were "no fucking good."[47] But even those films that went on to win international awards could not find a place in a large number of cinemas, suggesting that the American companies already had their minds made up about Canadian movies.

# The American War in Vietnam

The relationship between Lester Pearson and Lyndon Johnson, never close, all but came apart over the American war in Vietnam. Formerly part of French Indochina, Vietnam had been occupied by the Japanese during the Second World War. Afterward, the French tried to re-establish imperial control, while a disparate group of Vietnamese created the League for the Independence of Vietnam (Vietminh), led by a communist, Ho Chi Minh. War broke out between the Vietminh, which controlled the northern part of the country, and the French, whose forces were concentrated in the South and were almost entirely funded by the United States. When the French withdrew in 1954, Canada became part of the International Control Commission (ICC) established to unify Vietnam under a single national government. At the same time, the US began providing financial and military support directly to the anti-communist dictatorship that ruled South Vietnam.

When Johnson became president, he found himself in a hopeless political situation. He could not withdraw from Vietnam, an American admission of defeat that would have destroyed his public standing and made it all but impossible to carry out his extensive domestic agenda. Nor could he beat the communists merely by continuing to support South Vietnam, an approach his predecessors, Eisenhower and Kennedy, had tried. In 1965, Johnson intensified the war, launching a massive bombing campaign against the North and dispatching large numbers of ground troops, 400,000 by the end of 1966.

Canadian officials engaged in a delicate balancing act over Vietnam. On the one hand, Canada was a close ally of the United States and supported American efforts to prevent the spread of communism. Canadian officials shared with their American counterparts confidential information Canada received as a member of the ICC. Under trade agreements that encouraged American purchases of Canadian military goods, Canadian manufacturers sold more than $2 billion of arms, including chemical weapons, to the United States during the Vietnam years.[48] On the other hand, Canadian officials knew that the United States had got it wrong in Vietnam. Pearson had warned Johnson that escalation would cause problems. Canada declined the American request to send troops to Vietnam, arguing that Canada's membership on the ICC required that Canada stay out of the war. On the ICC, Canada aimed to be fair-minded, but was under pressure to support the US position to offset the Polish delegate who was overly sympathetic to communist North Vietnam. Then and since, leftist critics have charged that Canada consistently defended US interests on the ICC, but American officials saw it differently. Both Dean Rusk, secretary of state for most of the 1960s, and Walton Butterworth, US ambassador in Ottawa from 1962 to 1968, grumbled that Canada did not do enough to defend Western interests.[49] The ICC votes show that Canada managed to find a middle position. Canadian delegates supported South Vietnam 53 per cent of the time, a much more balanced record than the Poles, on side with North Vietnam on 84 per cent of the votes.[50] In the end, the Canadians pleased neither the American government nor the Canadian left.

Canada wanted the Americans to pull out, but Pearson thought that quiet diplomacy, friendly advice offered in private, would be more effective than public confrontation. Pearson believed that Canada had a special influence behind the scenes in Washington and could shape decisions before they were made. Speaking out publicly against the United States would cost Canada this status and much of the country's influence over the American government.

The benefits of quiet diplomacy were outlined in a report commissioned by the two governments and co-authored by a former Canadian ambassador to Washington, Arnold Heeney, and a former US ambassador to Ottawa, Livingston Merchant. Entitled *Canada and the United States: Principles for Partnership*, the July 1965 document argued that both countries would benefit when they resolved their disputes privately. Diplomats on both sides of the border accepted the wisdom of the report, but the public response was quite different. In the United States, the report was largely ignored, while in Canada journalists and opposition MPs condemned it. For critics, it appeared that Heeney and Merchant wanted to place Canada in a submissive position toward the United States by preventing Canada from criticizing its more powerful neighbour.

By the time the Heeney–Merchant Report appeared, it was already clear that quiet diplomacy was not working, at least when it came to Vietnam. When Pearson received an award in April 1965 from Temple University in Philadelphia, he used his acceptance speech to encourage the United States to suspend the bombing in the hopes that the North Vietnamese could be lured to the negotiating table. This infuriated Johnson, who invited the prime minister to meet with him afterward. At the presidential retreat at Camp David, Johnson was ill-mannered, talking on the phone throughout lunch. Afterward, when Pearson asked what Johnson thought of the speech, the president responded with one word: "Awful." He led the prime minister outside to the terrace and launched into a loud denunciation of the speech. Canadian ambassador Charles Ritchie witnessed the scene from a distance: The president "strode the terrace, he sawed the air with his arms, with upraised fist he drove home the verbal hammer blows. He talked and talked . . . expostulating, upbraiding, reasoning, persuading." The prime minister would start a sentence, "only to have it swept away on the tide."[51] At the climax of the tirade, Johnson grabbed Pearson by his coat lapel and yelled, "You pissed on my rug!"[52] Upon his return to Ottawa, Pearson wrote to Johnson to explain his speech: Canada supported the United States and meant to be helpful by proposing a ceasefire. Pearson ended the letter diplomatically: "I am grateful to you . . . for your consideration in speaking to me so frankly last Saturday."[53]

In one sense, Johnson's treatment of Pearson spoke to the familiarity between the two countries. The president had frequently said that Pearson was the foreign leader he "felt closest to."[54] And, as the president's brother often remarked, "If he doesn't bawl you out now and then, you ain't part of the family."[55] Still, the president's outrageous behaviour damaged his relationship with the prime minister, who was worried about the implications of being part of the president's "family."

Despite this rupture between the two leaders over Vietnam, Canadian and US officials continued to reconcile their differences on a myriad of other issues. As historian Greg Donaghy has shown, the relationship in the Pearson years was characterized not just by conflict but also by cooperation, as the two sides negotiated the Auto Pact, worked together to lower tariffs, and struggled to resolve difficult disputes over magazines and banking.

## The Watkins Report

Walter Gordon's political career was largely an unhappy one. He remained in the finance portfolio after his disastrous budget of 1963, but his influence had been greatly diminished and he was unable to implement measures to reduce foreign investment in Canada. In 1965, he advised Pearson to call an election, hoping that the Liberal party would win a majority, but then resigned from Cabinet when the government returned to office with another minority. He remained a backbench member of Parliament, trying to convince the Liberal party to adopt his ideas at a policy conference, but the delegates soundly rejected his proposals.

Gordon returned to Cabinet in 1967, determined to tackle the problem of foreign ownership. Entrusted with drafting a report on the issue, he recruited eight university economists. The resulting study took a moderate approach to the issue. The Watkins Report, named after the task force's chair, Mel Watkins, rejected the idea that the government force "any wholesale substitution of domestic for foreign capital over any short period of time."[56] Canadians had to accept a high level of foreign investment, but could work to maximize its benefits and reduce its costs. One of the costs was extraterritoriality, the application of foreign laws to foreign-owned companies in Canada. The US Trading with the Enemy Act, for example, banned American-owned companies, including those in Canada, from doing business with countries designated as enemies of the United States. This led to one of the most publicized cases of extraterritoriality: Ford Motors' 1958 decision to prevent its Canadian subsidiary from selling trucks to China. The task force was also concerned about a lack of competition in the Canadian economy, the result of the dominance of a few large, foreign firms. In response, it urged the government to strengthen anti-combines legislation and to reduce the tariff. These recommendations were far from radical, but the Pearson government refused to endorse the report. Gordon again resigned from Cabinet, having never convinced his colleagues of the need to reduce American economic influence in Canada.

# Americanism and Anti-Americanism

The 1960s are frequently identified as a period of anti-Americanism in Canada, though the term is often misused. *Anti-Americanism* does not apply to just any criticism of the United States—after all, most people have had occasion to find fault with some element of American politics, culture, or society. Instead, *anti-Americanism* refers to reflexive or visceral reactions to the US. Anti-Americanism is a prejudice, expressed in one-sided, sweeping generalizations about the United States. This would include a tendency to see the United States as a monolith—rather than as a complex society composed of differing impulses—and to associate all Americans with their government. The problem with describing the 1960s as an anti-American decade in Canada is that Canadian critiques of the United States developed out of the complex and intense relationship between the two countries. Ideas described as anti-American were often not anti-American at all, but were the product of distinctly American influences.

In the 1960s and early 1970s, Canadians and Americans both reacted to the increasing turmoil and violence in American society. Police and white civilians assaulted peaceful black civil rights protesters in Birmingham, Selma, and other Southern communities. As racial tensions grew, violence became common in major cities, both in the American North and the South. The biggest explosion came after the assassination of civil rights leader Martin Luther King in 1968, when more than 100 riots broke out. Unrest became a regular feature on college campuses, as many students protested against the American war in Vietnam, and some challenged every aspect of the status quo. The most shocking campus conflict was at Kent State University in Kent, Ohio, where members of the National Guard shot four unarmed students during a demonstration in May 1970.

The key issue was the American war in Vietnam, which played a seminal role in spurring nationalism in English Canada. Vietnam was, in the words of writer Michael J. Arlen, "the Living-Room War," the first armed conflict to be covered extensively on television.[57] Canadians and Americans could turn their television sets to the evening news and see graphic scenes from a war half a globe away. Because of Vietnam, thousands of Americans flooded across the border, seeking refuge in Canada. Some had deserted the American armed forces, others were avoiding the military draft, and still others were political refugees disgusted by what the United States had become. They had a strong influence in Canada, particularly on university campuses.

Prosecuting the war in Vietnam was the official policy of the United States government, but the United States had anti-Vietnam protesters, too, and they were an important part of the American experience. Many

Canadians who reacted against American foreign and domestic policies were reflecting ideas increasingly widespread in American public debate. Much of the Canadian critique of the US was not of American values, but of American hypocrisy: the failure of the United States to live up to its democratic ideals in its foreign policy and in its treatment of its racial minorities.

In the late 1960s and early 1970s, many Canadians, particularly in the media, called the United States a "sick society." The term has been labelled anti-American, but it originated in 1967 with US Senator William Fulbright. The phrase and the opinion it captured—that the US had taken a wrong turn and was now betraying its own principles—were commonplace in American political debate by mid-1968. Indeed, the sentiment was as widespread in the US as it was in Canada. When the Gallup organization asked Canadians and Americans in October 1968 whether the US was a "sick society," the results were remarkably similar: 36 per cent of Americans agreed that the US was a sick society, compared to 37 per cent of Canadians.[58]

The same American influences were visible in the academic world. One of the best-known nationalist books of this period was *Close the 49th Parallel Etc: The Americanization of Canada*, a collection of essays edited by political scientist Ian Lumsden and published by the University of Toronto Press. Then and now, many of the essays in this book have been described as anti-American. Certainly, there was much in the book critical of the United States, but there were also many distinctly American elements. Several of the contributors relied on the work of American sociologists, historians, and philosophers. Lumsden's chapter on the impact of the United States on Canadian intellectuals was based almost entirely on the work of American Marxists. The chapter by Ellen and Neal Wood, which deplored the American approach to political science, rested heavily on arguments made a decade earlier by American scholars who deplored the trend away from qualitative and toward quantitative research.[59] The book's contributors might have been criticizing the United States, but they were using ideas and analysis that had their origins in that same country.

American ideas were equally apparent in the political realm. In May 1967, Walter Gordon became the first prominent Liberal to break party ranks on the issue of Vietnam. In a Toronto speech, Gordon said that the US had become "enmeshed in a bloody civil war in Vietnam which cannot be justified on either moral or strategic grounds." He called on the American government to stop the bombing of North Vietnam as the first step toward a negotiated settlement of the war.[60] For this, Gordon was widely dismissed in the Canadian media as anti-American. Yet there was nothing particularly anti-American about Gordon's sentiments. His argument relied heavily on the analysis of American politicians and journalists. He did not quote Canadian philosopher George Grant, British philosopher Bertrand Russell,

Vietnamese leader Ho Chi Minh, or other prominent non-American critics of the war. Instead, he turned to American arguments, including those
of senators George McGovern and Robert Kennedy. Gordon's ideas on
Vietnam were reflective not of anti-Americanism, but rather of the ideas of
the American left.

## The New Nationalism

A growing suspicion of the US government and American corporations
found its outlet in the New Nationalism, a movement with intellectual roots
in the foreign investment debate of the mid-1950s. Nationalists were more
likely to be young, well educated, and from southern Ontario. They were
concerned about trade, culture, defence, and foreign policy, but above all
they worried about the impact of American branch plants on both Canada's
economy and the country's sovereignty. They pushed for measures to limit
new American investment in Canada or even to encourage foreign owners
to sell their assets to Canadians.

Canada's economic and demographic situation in the late 1960s and
early 1970s created a greenhouse where the New Nationalism could bloom.
Canadian politics became radicalized as the first baby boomers came of age
and an increasing number of young people became engaged in public debate. Equally important was an unprecedented growth in personal income
in Canada. Foreign investment might have been necessary in an earlier age,
but now many Canadians thought their country was prosperous enough
that it could afford to turn away American dollars. A 1967 poll showed that
60 per cent of Canadians believed that Canada now had "enough U.S. capital," compared with 46 per cent just three years earlier.[61]

Much of the growth in Canadian nationalist sentiment can be attributed to events south of the border. In the late 1960s and early 1970s an
ugly side of the United States emerged with that country's war in Vietnam,
the struggle over civil rights, and riots in American cities and on college
campuses. The result, in the words of historian Frank Underhill, was that
Canadians could not "discuss our relations with the United States in a cool,
rational frame of mind."[62] The two countries appeared to have profoundly
different values, as Canada's neighbour now came to symbolize violence
both at home and abroad.

American corporations looked no better. Economist John Kenneth
Galbraith, born and educated in Canada before pursuing an academic
career in the United States, published two influential books, *The Affluent
Society* and *The New Industrial State*, that portrayed an unhealthy marketplace controlled not by individuals but by large corporations that moulded
consumer behaviour. Although often dismissed by mainstream economists,

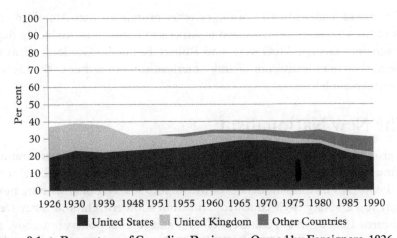

Figure 9.1 ✣ Percentage of Canadian Businesses Owned by Foreigners, 1926–90

Source: Data provided by *Canada's International Investment Position: Historical Statistics, 1926 to 1992* (Ottawa: Statistics Canada, 1993), 232.

Galbraith's work was widely read in Canada and the United States. American lawyer and consumer advocate Ralph Nader also received much attention in both countries after publishing *Unsafe at Any Speed*, a book that exposed the automotive industry's lack of concern for public safety. Dependent on advertising from auto manufacturers, the American networks initially ignored Nader, so he made his North American television debut in November 1965 on the CBC program *This Hour Has Seven Days*. His book helped to inspire the consumer protection movement in both the United States and Canada, which in turn led to many more disturbing revelations about the activities of large multinational corporations.

Nationalists had three fundamental concerns about the large American economic presence in Canada. First, they charged that foreign ownership of Canadian industry had long been increasing at a rapid pace, often suggesting that it would not be long before Americans owned all Canadian industry. They usually advanced this claim either without evidence or with the support of figures demonstrating a rise in the dollar value of American investments. In fact, the percentage of the Canadian economy owned by foreigners was increasing only marginally, if at all, as the entire economy was growing at roughly the same rate as foreign investment. Second, nationalists criticized the performance of American branch plants in Canada, repeating the Gordon Commission's suspicions that foreign-owned companies were unwilling to conduct research in Canada or to seek export markets, and that they preferred to import parts and hire non-Canadian executives and professional firms. Subsequent research suggested that foreign firms were indeed less likely to hire Canadian professionals, but the other concerns were unfounded. Third, nationalists expressed distress over the impact of foreign investment on Canadian sovereignty. They asserted vaguely and without much explanation that foreign control of Canadian business would eventually lead to the loss of the country's independence. More specifically, and more convincingly, they objected to extraterritoriality, the intrusion of foreign laws into Canada.

Nationalists pushed for measures to reduce the flow of foreign investment into Canada or even to force foreigners to sell their Canadian assets to Canadians. These proposals were at the centre of Canadian political debate but were not put into law in the 1960s. The story would be different in the early 1970s, as the nationalist movement hit its peak.

## Summary

The postwar North American consensus broke down in the 1950s. The first fissures appeared when Canadians became distressed about the excesses of the US congressional committees determined to purge communists from American government and society. Concern over the levels of American investment in Canada led to further doubts over the close relationship between the two countries. Canada and the United States continued their alliance, determined to resist communist expansion abroad, but Canadians became more convinced of the need to assert their independence of their neighbour to the south.

Personality conflicts bedevilled the relationship at an official level. John Kennedy's lack of respect for John Diefenbaker and, more significantly, the prime minister's obsession with setting the president straight brought the relationship between the two governments to a historic low. Friendly interaction was restored when Pearson became prime minister, but Canada never again had the influence in Washington that the country had enjoyed in the late 1940s and early 1950s. By 1965, Lyndon Johnson's escalation of the war in Vietnam and his angry refusal to listen to any advice from Canada suggested that tensions between the two countries had become the new norm.

Vietnam had an enormous impact on public opinion in Canada and the United States, as did the struggle over civil rights and the assassination of American leaders. In both countries, young people became disillusioned with the US government. In Canada, this disenchantment was at the core of the New Nationalism, a movement that would have its moment in the 1970s.

## Beyond the Book

1. What were the strengths and weaknesses of Canada's quiet approach to the American war in Vietnam?

2.   Did foreign culture pose a threat to the Canadian identity? Does it now?
3.   What are the benefits and costs of having a large proportion of a coun-
     try's economy owned by foreigners?
4.   What do the Diefenbaker/Kennedy and Pearson/Johnson relationships
     suggest about the relevance of individuals to relations between countries?

# Further Reading

For overviews of the late 1950s and early 1960s, see Robert Bothwell, Ian
Drummond, and John English, *Canada since 1945: Power, Politics and Provincialism*,
2nd ed. (Toronto: University of Toronto Press, 1989); and J.L. Granatstein, *Canada,
1957–1967: The Years of Uncertainty and Innovation* (Toronto: McClelland and
Stewart, 1986). A valuable but underappreciated journalist's account of the period
is Blair Fraser, *The Search for Identity: Canada, 1945–1967* (Toronto: Doubleday,
1967). There is much on Canadian–American relations in Jamie Glazov, *Canadian
Policy toward Khrushchev's Soviet Union* (Montreal and Kingston: McGill–Queen's
University Press, 2002). On economic issues, there is Bruce Muirhead, *Dancing
Around the Elephant: Creating a Prosperous Canada in an Era of American Dominance,
1957–1973* (Toronto: University of Toronto Press, 2007).

Joseph Barber looks at the growing anti-Americanism of the mid-1950s
in *Good Fences Make Good Neighbors: Why the United States Provokes Canadians*
(Toronto: McClelland and Stewart, 1958). On Herbert Norman, see Roger Bowen,
*Innocence is Not Enough: The Life and Death of Herbert Norman* (Vancouver: Douglas
and McIntyre, 1986); and Greg Donaghy, ed., *Herbert Norman: A Documentary
Perspective* (Ottawa: Department of Foreign Affairs and International Trade, 1995).
In late 1989, the Department of External Affairs commissioned political scientist
and former diplomat Peyton V. Lyon to review the Norman case. The resulting re-
port concluded that Norman was neither a spy nor a Soviet agent of influence: "The
Loyalties of E. Herbert Norman," *Labour/Le Travail* 28 (Fall 1991): 219–59. James
Barros's *No Sense of Evil: Espionage, the Case of Herbert Norman* (Toronto: Deneau,
1986) is unreliable and should be handled with care. On the pipeline debate, the
best sources are Robert Bothwell, *C.D. Howe: A Biography* (Toronto: McClelland
and Stewart, 1979); and William Kilbourn, *Pipeline: Transcanada and the Great
Debate, a History of Business and Politics* (Toronto: Clarke Irwin, 1970).

Denis Smith has written an elegant and powerful biography of John Diefenbaker:
*Rogue Tory: The Life and Legend of John G. Diefenbaker* (Toronto: McFarlane, Walter
and Ross, 1995). Diefenbaker's own three-volume memoir, *One Canada: Memoirs of
the Right Honourable John G. Diefenbaker* (Toronto: Macmillan, 1975–7), often gets
the facts wrong but is useful for what it reveals about the prime minister's petty and
paranoid mindset. More factually reliable is Donald Fleming's *So Very Near: The
Political Memoirs of the Honourable Donald M. Fleming*, 2 vols. (Toronto: McClelland
and Stewart, 1985). Several Cabinet ministers spoke off the record to journalist
Patrick Nicholson, who details the collapse of the Diefenbaker government in *Vision
and Indecision* (Don Mills, Ontario: Longmans, 1968). Another journalist, Peter
Stursberg, compiled interviews in *Diefenbaker: Leadership Lost, 1962–67* (Toronto:

University of Toronto Press, 1976). Asa McKercher looks at the prime minister's early relations with Eisenhower's Washington in "Dealing with Diefenbaker: Canada–US relations in 1958," *International Journal* 66, no. 4 (Autumn 2011): 1043–60. The best source on NORAD is Joseph T. Jockel, *Canada in NORAD, 1957–2007: A History* (Montreal and Kingston: McGill–Queen's University Press, 2007).

On the Kennedy–Diefenbaker relationship, start with the book by Knowlton Nash, a journalist in Washington in the early 1960s: *Kennedy and Diefenbaker: Fear and Loathing across the Undefended Border* (Toronto: McClelland and Stewart, 1990). Diefenbaker's senior foreign policy adviser, H. Basil Robinson, has contributed a valuable work that is part memoir, part history: *Diefenbaker's World: A Populist in Foreign Affairs* (Toronto: University of Toronto Press, 1989). In a thorough and convincing study, Patricia I. McMahon emphasizes the role of political considerations in Diefenbaker's actions during the defence crisis: *Essence of Indecision: Diefenbaker's Nuclear Policy, 1957–1963* (Montreal and Kingston: McGill–Queen's University Press, 2009). On the Cuban Missile Crisis, see Asa McKercher, "A 'Half-Hearted Response'? Canada and the Cuban Missile Crisis, 1962," *International History Review* 33, no. 2 (June 2011): 335–52.

The best work on the Pearson government is the second volume of John English's magisterial biography of the prime minister, *The Worldly Years*, vol. 2 of *The Life of Lester Pearson, 1949–1972* (Toronto: Alfred A. Knopf, 1992). Greg Donaghy focuses on Canadian–American relations in his superb *Tolerant Allies: Canada and the United States, 1963–1968* (Montreal and Kingston: McGill–Queen's University Press, 2002). The published diary of Canada's ambassador in Washington contains many valuable insights: Charles Ritchie, *Storm Signals: More Undiplomatic Diaries, 1962–1971* (Toronto: Macmillan, 1983). On the Auto Pact, see two works by Dimitry Anastakis: *Auto Pact: Creating a Borderless North American Auto Industry, 1960–1971* (Toronto: University of Toronto Press, 2005); and "Multilateralism, Nationalism, and Bilateral Free Trade: Competing Visions of Canadian Economic and Trade Policy, 1945–70," in *Creating Postwar Canada: Community, Diversity, and Dissent, 1945–75*, edited by Magda Fahrni and Robert Rutherdale (Vancouver: UBC Press, 2008), 137–61. Asa McKercher looks at the Heeney–Merchant Report in "Principles and Partnership: Merchant, Heeney, and the Craft of Canada–US Relations," *American Review of Canadian Studies* 42, no. 1 (March 2012): 67–83.

Many members of the Pearson Cabinet wrote memoirs. On the interactions between the Canadian and US governments, the most valuable are Lester B. Pearson, *Mike: The Memoirs of the Right Honourable Lester B. Pearson*, vol. 3, *1957–1968* (Toronto: University of Toronto Press, 1975); Paul Martin, *A Very Public Life*, vol. 2, *So Many Words* (Ottawa: Deneau, 1985); Walter Gordon, *A Political Memoir* (Toronto: McClelland and Stewart, 1977); Mitchell Sharp, *Which Reminds Me . . . A Memoir* (Toronto: University of Toronto Press, 1994); and Paul Hellyer, *Damn the Torpedoes: My Fight to Unify Canada's Armed Forces* (Toronto: McClelland and Stewart, 1990).

On Canada's Vietnam policy, the best place to start is Robert Bothwell, *Alliance and Illusion: Canada and the World, 1945–1984* (Vancouver: UBC Press, 2007). Scholarly narratives can be found in Douglas A. Ross, *In the Interests of Peace: Canada and Vietnam, 1954–1973* (Toronto: University of Toronto Press,

1984), which largely defends Canadian policy; and in the highly critical account by James Eayrs: *In Defence of Canada*, vol. 5, *Indochina: Roots of Complicity* (Toronto: University of Toronto Press, 1983). Further detail and valuable nuance appear in John English, "Speaking Out on Vietnam, 1965," chapter 9 in *Canadian Foreign Policy: Selected Cases*, edited by Don Munton and John Kirton (Scarborough, Ontario: Prentice–Hall, 1992), 135–49; and Greg Donaghy, "Minding the Minister: Pearson, Martin, and American Policy in Asia, 1963–1967," in *Pearson: The Unlikely Gladiator*, edited by Norman Hillmer (Montreal and Kingston: McGill–Queen's University Press, 1999), 131–49. More tendentious versions include Charles Taylor, *Snow Job: Canada, the United States and Vietnam (1954 to 1973)* (Toronto: House of Anansi Press, 1974); and Victor Levant, *Quiet Complicity: Canadian Involvement in the Vietnam War* (Toronto: Between the Lines, 1986).

On the New Nationalism, see Stephen Azzi, *Walter Gordon and the Rise of Canadian Nationalism* (Montreal and Kingston: McGill–Queen's University Press, 1999); "The Nationalist Moment in English Canada," chapter 11 in *Debating Dissent: Canada and the Sixties*, edited by Lara Campbell, Dominique Clément, and Gregory S. Kealey (Toronto: University of Toronto Press, 2012), 213–28; "Foreign Investment and the Paradox of Economic Nationalism," in *Canadas of the Mind: The Making and Unmaking of Canadian Nationalisms in the Twentieth Century*, edited by Norman Hillmer and Adam Chapnick (Montreal and Kingston: McGill–Queen's University Press, 2007), 63–88; "'It Was Walter's View': Lester Pearson, the Liberal Party and Economic Nationalism," in *Pearson: The Unlikely Gladiator*, edited by Norman Hillmer (Montreal and Kingston: McGill–Queen's University Press, 1999), 104–16.

The best overview of cultural policy is Mary Vipond, *The Mass Media in Canada*, 4th ed. (Toronto: James Lorimer, 2011). Paul Litt has an important book on the Massey Commission: *The Muses, the Masses, and the Massey Commission* (Toronto: University of Toronto Press, 1992). He provides more detail on the Canadian–American dimensions of the commission's report in "The Massey Commission, Americanization, and Canadian Cultural Nationalism," *Queen's Quarterly* 98, no. 2 (Summer 1991): 375–87. On magazines, see Stephen Azzi, "Magazines and the Canadian Dream: The Struggle to Protect Canadian Periodicals 1955–1965," *International Journal* 54, no. 3 (Summer 1999): 502–23; and Isaiah Litvak and Christopher Maule, *Cultural Sovereignty: The Time and Reader's Digest Case in Canada* (New York: Praeger, 1974). For the screen, big and small, see Michael Dorland, *So Close to the State/s: The Emergence of Canadian Film Policy* (Toronto: University of Toronto Press, 1998); and Paul Rutherford, *When Television Was Young: Primetime Canada, 1952–1967* (Toronto: University of Toronto Press, 1990). Pierre Berton's *Hollywood's Canada: The Americanization of Our National Image* (Toronto: McClelland and Stewart, 1975) includes a section on the Canadian Co-operation Project.

## CHAPTER 10

# Resilience, 1968–1984

## *The Rise and Fall of Canadian Nationalism*

## Introduction

Pierre Thomas de Gaspé was a Canadian hero of the early 1970s. Born to a wealthy, bilingual Quebec family, de Gaspé studied engineering at the Royal Military College before obtaining an MA in economics from Queen's University, where he wrote a thesis excerpted in the *Globe and Mail*. He went on to Harvard where he completed a PhD thesis, later published in the Sunday *New York Times*. De Gaspé joined the world's largest oil company, Exxon, as an economist, but after a series of rapid promotions, he left to pursue a law degree at McGill University, where he won the gold medal for academic achievement. Upon graduating, he returned to the energy sector, eventually becoming the first president of Petro Canada, the government-owned oil company. At the same time, he served as Toronto district commander for the Canadian militia. These positions allowed him to play a key role both in masterminding the Canadian purchase of Exxon and in foiling an American invasion.

De Gaspé was the main character in *Ultimatum*, the bestselling Canadian novel of 1973. It was not written by one of the giants of 1970s Canadian literature—Margaret Atwood, Robertson Davies, Mordecai Richler, or Margaret Laurence. Instead, the book came from Richard Rohmer, part-time author, part-time air force reserve officer, and full-time attorney with a specialty in land development. *Ultimatum* was the first of two Rohmer novels—the other being *Exxoneration*—that described the origins, nature, and outcome of a US invasion of Canada.[1] Each novel sold more than 100,000 copies, despite tedious plots and prosaic dialogue. For several months, *Ultimatum* managed to outsell works by Graham Greene, Gore Vidal, and Agatha Christie—at least in Canadian bookstores. Yet, as one critic remarked, *Exxoneration* "is a book because it has printed pages between hard covers and there is some semblance of a story, but any similarity between it and what we have come to know as the novel form is purely accidental."[2] The sales figures for *Ultimatum* and *Exxoneration* say little about their stylistic merits, and much about the way they tapped into anxieties about Canada's future and about the motives and military might of the United States.

## Protests

The late 1960s and early 1970s were a time of protest in both Canada and the United States. Frequent demonstrations had begun in the mid-1950s with the campaign for black civil rights in the Southern US. In the mid-1960s, young people took to the streets, rallying against the American war in Vietnam. In both Canada and the United States, these protests grew in size and frequency throughout the late 1960s and early 1970s.

There were striking similarities between the Canadian and American protestors. They tended to be young, middle class, and university-educated. In their view, American society was shallow and materialistic, the US had no right to intervene in other countries, and it was responsible for poverty in the developing world. In Canada and the United States, protestors abhorred American hypocrisy—the gap between the ideals and the reality of American society—particularly on the issues of civil rights and the war in Vietnam.

Demonstrators on both sides of the border used many of the same slogans. Americans often focussed on President Lyndon Baines Johnson's prosecution of the war in Vietnam, chanting, "Hey, hey, LBJ, how many kids did you kill today?" The same words could be heard on Canadian campuses and outside US consulates in major Canadian cities. When Johnson visited Montreal for the world's fair, Expo 67, Canadians greeted him with the same chant.[3] In both countries, protesters organized teach-ins, campus events that were part protest, part educational experience. The first, held at the University of Michigan in March 1965, consisted of seminars, speeches, and a rally. By the end of the year, similar events had taken place on more than 100 campuses in the United States and Canada. North of the border, the largest teach-in, held in October 1965 at the University of Toronto, drew a crowd of 6,000.

Many of Canada's most prominent critics of the United States had strong connections to that country. Walter Gordon, who devoted much of his life to trying to reduce American investment in Canada, had long done business with American entrepreneurs, even selling Canadian companies to American buyers. Among Canadian intellectuals, almost all the detractors of the United States seemed to be educated there, including economist

**Photo 10.1** ⊹ **Vietnam war protest**

Canadian students demonstrate against the American war in Vietnam outside the US consulate in Toronto, 14 April 1966. There were striking similarities between the protests and protestors in Canada and the United States. In Canada, the war did much to undermine faith in the United States and to foster Canadian nationalism. (Source: Dick Darrell/GetStock.)

and politician Cy Gonick (University of California, Berkeley), economist Mel Watkins (Massachusetts Institute of Technology), novelist and poet Margaret Atwood (Radcliffe College), and poet and English professor Robin Mathews (Ohio State University).

Americans who rejected their country often found a home on Canadian campuses. The University of Saskatchewan's John W. Warnock, an oft-quoted critic of Canada's military alliance with the United States, had begun his career as a US foreign service officer. Eugene Genovese taught at Montreal's Sir George Williams University after being dismissed from Rutgers University for saying that he would welcome an American defeat in Vietnam. Another opponent of US foreign policy, Gabriel Kolko, taught at York University in Toronto from 1970 until his retirement in 1992. Economist Andre Gunder Frank, who convinced countless scholars that the United States had become wealthy by exploiting the underdeveloped world, taught for two years at Sir George Williams.

American protest leaders also appeared in Canada. Members of the radical civil rights organization the Black Panther Party visited many Canadian cities. When one of them, Fred Hampton, spoke at the Regina campus of the University of Saskatchewan in 1969, he declared that the only difference between Canada and his hometown of Chicago was that

Canada was "further north." He made such an impact that when he died later that year, killed in his sleep by Chicago police, more than 100 people gathered in Regina for a torchlight parade in his honour. Metis leader Harry Daniels, who had met with Hampton, said that the struggle of the Black Panthers was the same as that of the "exploited" people in Canada.[4] Stokely Carmichael, chair of the Student Nonviolent Coordinating Committee (SNCC), visited several Canadian universities, drawing crowds of 2,000 at the University of Toronto and at McGill University in Montreal. A student reported that Carmichael "electrified" the McGill crowd and was "interrupted countless times by wild applause."[5] Jerry Rubin, a leader of the Yippies protest group, spoke to students at the University of British Columbia in 1968, sparking a 20-hour occupation of the faculty club. The next year, he addressed 2,000 at the University of Toronto, making him "the person who stirred us up the most in those years," according to writer J.A. Wainwright, then a student at the university.[6] Former prime minister John Diefenbaker was distressed by the rabble-rousing of Rubin and Carmichael, urging the government "to keep out of Canada well recognized revolutionaries who are coming here and disturbing the peace in various universities and colleges."[7]

Canadians had a wide range of attitudes toward their southern neighbour. Some celebrated the United States as the beacon of freedom and democracy in the world. In 1973, Toronto radio personality Gordon Sinclair broadcast an editorial in defence of Americans, describing them as "the most generous and possibly the least-appreciated people on all the earth." "I'm one Canadian who is damned tired of hearing them kicked around."[8] He praised the United States for providing money to foreign countries for a variety of causes: disaster relief, postwar reconstruction, and propping up weak currencies. Listeners in Buffalo, New York, liked what they heard and called the station to ask if they could purchase a recording of the talk. After a record company released it as a single, it sold almost 800,000 copies and was played regularly on radio, making it to number 24 on the Billboard chart in the US and number 30 on the RPM chart in Canada. At the same time, a cover version by Byron MacGregor, a radio news announcer in Windsor, Ontario, sold even more, making it to number 4 in the US.[9] Other Canadians expressed measured opposition to the violence in the US and the country's failed policies in Vietnam—critiques very similar to those voiced by American liberals. Further along the spectrum, still other Canadians felt visceral hatred toward the United States, often expressed in violent tones. In 1968, writer Ray Smith suggested that Canadians send President Johnson a gift, "an American tourist's ear in a matchbox."[10] Journalist Heather Robertson confessed her "desire to toss a hand grenade into every American camper I pass on the highway."[11]

# Movements for Social Reform

As in earlier generations, Canadian and American movements for social reform were closely linked, particularly among Aboriginal people, who organized protests on both sides of the Canadian–American border. The boundary was "an imaginary line," in the words of Aboriginal leader Vern Harper. "We saw ourselves as Native people, not as Canadians or Americans."[12]

In December 1968, about 100 Mohawks blocked the Seaway International Bridge linking Cornwall, Ontario, and Massena, New York. They came from the nearby Akwesasne community, which spanned the Canada–US border, and were objecting to the Canadian government's practice of charging them duty on products purchased in the US, in violation of the clause in Jay's Treaty of 1794 that guaranteed free commerce across the border. The blockade ended after two hours, when Canadian police arrested more than 40 Mohawks. After a second blockade in February 1969, the Canadian government backed down and agreed not to charge the duty to any Mohawks who carried newly issued passes.

The most important periodical for North American Aboriginal people, *Akwesasne Notes*, was a product of these protests. Founded in 1969 by Rarihokwats of the Bear Clan (who, as Gerald T. Gambill, had immigrated to Canada from the United States in 1960), the publication was originally a mimeograph of newspaper stories about the bridge confrontation. Rarihokwats discovered that the events at Akwesasne had a larger significance, as Aboriginal people across North America were captivated by what had happened at the Seaway International Bridge. Quickly, *Akwesasne Notes* transformed into a 48-page tabloid newspaper with original stories about Aboriginal activities across the continent. By 1977, it had a circulation of 85,000 copies.[13] Because subscriptions were free, the periodical subsisted on donations and revenues from the sale of posters and books. Aboriginal groups had been cut off from one another, but now there was a way for them to share the news about their common struggles.

In November 1969, Aboriginal people from both countries began an occupation of Alcatraz Island in San Francisco Bay, an event often seen as a spark that helped ignite the Aboriginal movement in North America. The Alcatraz penitentiary had closed in 1963, and the US government intended to transfer ownership of the island to the city of San Francisco. Protestors said that abandoned or unused federal lands should revert to Aboriginal ownership as stipulated in a 100-year-old treaty with the Sioux. When the federal government rejected the claim, Aboriginal activists began the occupation, led by Richard Oakes, a Mohawk from the New York side of the Akwesasne community. The protest lasted until June 1971, when the number of occupiers had dwindled to 15. Federal marshals easily removed them.

Canadians were active in the most militant Aboriginal group in the United States, the American Indian Movement (AIM), founded in Minneapolis in 1969. "Remember Wounded Knee," the organization reminded its followers, a reference to the US Army's 1890 massacre of more than 200 Sioux near Wounded Knee Creek on the Pine Ridge Indian Reservation in South Dakota. By 1973, AIM had 79 chapters, including eight in Canada.[14] Its most prominent female leader was Anna Mae Aquash, a Mi'kmaq born and raised in Nova Scotia. She travelled across Canada and the United States organizing protests until 1975, when she was murdered by AIM members, including one Canadian, who suspected she was a police informant.

AIM members moved back and forth over the Canadian–American border. Aquash and others from Canada took part in the organization's 1972 Trail of Broken Treaties convoy, which crossed the United States protesting government policies toward Aboriginal people, culminating with the occupation of the Bureau of Indian Affairs headquarters in Washington. Aquash was present too for the 1973 armed standoff between the police and AIM members at Wounded Knee, after the Aboriginal peoples had declared the area an independent nation. Similar protests took place in Canada. Aboriginal youth organized a sit-in at the Department of Indian Affairs offices in Ottawa in 1973, an event much like the previous year's occupation of the US Bureau of Indian Affairs. AIM members provided most of the leadership for the 1974 Native Peoples' Caravan, patterned after the Trail of Broken Treaties. The caravan travelled from Vancouver to Ottawa, where violence broke out between protestors and police in front of Parliament Hill.

In 1974, Dennis Banks, one of AIM's founders, spoke at an Ojibwa conference in Anicinabe Park in Kenora, Ontario. After his talk, several of those present, including other AIM organizers, began an occupation of the park. Banks could not stay; he had to return to the United States, where he was on trial for his role in the Wounded Knee occupation, but one month later the judge called a recess so Banks could go back to Kenora to act as mediator in the dispute. Eventually, Banks convinced both the police to pull back from the park and the local Aboriginal people to lay down their arms and enter into negotiations with authorities, ending the standoff.

The growing Aboriginal movement had a similar influence on government policies in both countries. In the United States, the administration of President Lyndon Johnson repudiated the longstanding termination policy, which had aimed to end special rights and privileges for Aboriginal people and assimilate them into the mainstream of American society. In its place, the US government slowly began pursuing a policy of self-determination. In 1975, Congress passed the Indian Self-Determination and Education

Assistance Act, giving Aboriginal peoples more control over their reservations and schools. The story was similar in Canada, though the Canadian government was slower to react. The Indian Act of 1876 encouraged individuals to abandon their Indian status as a step toward assimilation. In 1969, the government of Pierre Trudeau announced it would go one step further. The *Statement of the Government of Canada on Indian Policy* (usually known as the White Paper, a generic Canadian term for any government policy statement) proposed that the government abolish the Department of Indian Affairs and rescind the Indian Act. Reserve lands would be given to the Aboriginal peoples and treaties would be "equitably ended."[15] The provinces would take responsibility for the health and welfare of Aboriginal people, treating them as other Canadians. Aboriginal people would lose all their special rights. In the face of widespread protests, the government backed down. Within a few years, the government was working to satisfy unfilled treaty obligations and to deal with unresolved Aboriginal land claims.

There were similar close ties between feminists in the two countries. In both Canada and the United States, middle-class women were moved by American writer Betty Friedan's 1963 book, *The Feminine Mystique*, which argued that many women were bored and frustrated with gender roles that confined them to childrearing and housework. The house had become a "comfortable concentration camp" for middle-class women.[16] Women's magazines had been dealing with the same issues for years, but they did not have the same impact as Friedan, whose book influenced countless women on both sides of the border. "Somewhere in those days," said one young Canadian mother, "many of us read Betty Friedan and were refreshed to learn we didn't have to feel guilty if we still felt unsatisfied after being both wife and mother and finding we still needed something more."[17]

The women's liberation movement grew out of a conviction that the victories of earlier feminists were not enough. Activists in both Canada and the United States pushed for a range of political and legal reforms, including equal pay for work of equal value, the provision of maternity benefits, improved access to child care and birth control, and the legalization of abortion. The Canadian movement had the same diversity as its American sister, with liberal, socialist, and radical strands.

## Pierre Trudeau and the Americans

Canada and the United States might have travelled similar paths in the 1960s, but as the decade closed, the two countries set off in different political directions. In 1968, Americans elected as president, by a slim margin, Richard Nixon, a cynical old-style politician who would do virtually anything for a vote. Nixon was the quintessential Washington insider, serving four years in the House of Representatives, two years in the Senate, and eight years as Dwight Eisenhower's vice-president. By contrast, in 1968 Canadians chose a political neophyte as prime minister. Pierre Trudeau, an idealistic intellectual, had first been elected to Parliament three years earlier and had only one year's experience in Cabinet. In his first few years as prime minister, he often seemed more interested in winning academic debates than votes.

When it came to the Cold War, Trudeau's and Nixon's views were starkly different. In the 1950s, Nixon had been a fervent communist hunter of the McCarthy school, an outspoken member of the House Un-American Activities Committee who later promised to "drive the crooks and the Communists and those that defend them out of Washington."[18] Trudeau, who liked to provoke others, occasionally claimed to be a communist. He was not, but he was more understanding of communist nations than most Canadian or American politicians of his generation. As a young man, Trudeau had visited China twice and the Soviet Union once, coming away with some sympathy for those countries. As a result of his trip to Moscow, he was denied entry to the United States in 1954, a decision later over-turned on appeal. Trudeau had been against Canadian participation in the Korean War and was in favour of a reconciliation between the West and the Soviet Bloc. By the early 1960s, he was deeply troubled about nuclear arms and the threat they posed to humanity. He was about to run for Parliament under the Liberal banner in 1963, but backed away when Lester Pearson came out in support of Canada's acquisition of nuclear weapons, a decision Trudeau bitterly denounced.

Trudeau did not know the United States well and had an ambivalent at-titude toward the country, neither particularly pro- nor anti-American. In the 1940s, he had attended Harvard University for one year, but did not enjoy it, spending much of his time in his room, not participating in extracurricular activities or making friends. "I hate Americans, their jazz, their cigarettes, their elevators," he wrote to a friend.[19] Like so many Canadians and Americans, he was put off by McCarthyism, but at the same time he felt drawn to the American intellectual community. He was deeply influenced, for example, by John Kenneth Galbraith, the Canadian-born American economist.

Nixon knew and cared little about Canada. As president, his focus was on those countries and regions that had the greatest implications for American global strategy: the Soviet Union, China, the Middle East, Japan, and Vietnam. At a 1969 event in Massena, New York, he referred to the "prime minister and his lovely wife," showing that he did not even know that Trudeau was unmarried.[20] In 1971, Nixon claimed that "Japan is our biggest customer in the world," at a time when the US trade relationship with Canada far eclipsed any other.[21]

Nixon's ignorance reflected Canada's diminished place in Washington. American leaders had less and less time for their neighbour to the north. Nixon and Henry Kissinger, who served as national security adviser and then secretary of state, were interested in large geopolitical issues, not the mundane details of Canadian–American relations, such as the frequent disputes over fisheries. "I hope you haven't come to talk to me about the sex life of the salmon," Kissinger said to the Canadian ambassador at the outset of one meeting. On another occasion, the State Department's Canadian experts arrived to brief Kissinger, only to be shooed out of his office. "These are small things. Solve them."[22]

In background, personality, and temperament, Trudeau and Nixon could hardly have been more different. "I wasn't Nixon's kind of guy," Trudeau later commented. "Nor was he mine."[23] Nixon resented Trudeau's wealthy background and saw the prime minister as a "pompous egghead" who was soft on communism.[24] In private, Nixon seemed incapable of uttering Trudeau's name without prefacing it with "that asshole" or "that son of a bitch."[25] But the two leaders managed to maintain stable relations between their two governments during some difficult years. For his part, Trudeau practised quiet diplomacy toward the United States: he was always polite and respectful when meeting Nixon and did not publicly condemn US actions in Vietnam. Trudeau and his advisers understood the difficult equilibrium they had to find: maintaining a close enough relationship with the Americans to serve Canadian economic and security interests, while keeping a measured distance to preserve Canadian sovereignty. Kissinger later admired the way the Canadians struck that balance: "Convinced of the necessity of cooperation, impelled by domestic imperatives toward confrontation, Canadian leaders had a narrow margin for maneuver that they utilized with extraordinary skill."[26] In one of his most frequently quoted lines, Trudeau pilfered a simile long employed in Mexican politics to explain the difficulty of managing his country's relationship with the United States: "Living next to you is in some ways like sleeping with an elephant: No matter how friendly and even-tempered is the beast, one is affected by every twitch and grunt."[27]

Trudeau got along well with Nixon's two immediate successors. He had little in common with Gerald Ford, but the two still worked well together. Ford came from Michigan, a border state, and had some understanding of Canada. What set him apart, according to the prime minister, "was that he did nothing I can remember that rubbed Canada the wrong way."[28] Trudeau was particularly grateful when the president pushed successfully for Canada to be admitted, along with Italy, to the G5 group of major industrial nations, which became the G7. The two men developed a warm friendship and continued to go skiing together long after both retired from politics. Jimmy Carter was from Georgia, far from Canada, but his politics were more in line with Trudeau's and the two also became friends. They were both concerned about the environment and human rights, and both interested in defusing Cold War tensions. It helped the Canada–US relationship that Carter assigned Vice-President Walter Mondale, who was from the border state of Minnesota and was friendly to Canada, to deal with several of the issues related to the US's northern neighbour.

## Control of the Arctic

In the late 1960s, Canada and the United States came into conflict over the Northwest Passage, the route from the Atlantic to the Pacific Oceans that ran between Canada's Arctic islands. Years earlier, Canadian officials had talked with their American counterparts about whether the passage constituted Canadian internal waters. The Americans insisted that the passage was an international strait, not wanting to set any legal precedents that would affect the US military's access to strategically important straits and archipelagos around the globe.

The problem was largely an academic one until 1968, when large quantities of oil and natural gas were discovered at Prudhoe Bay in Alaska. The question was how best to transport the resources to the 48 American states south of Canada. Humble Oil, a subsidiary of Standard Oil (later Exxon), announced it would send a ship through the Northwest Passage to test the feasibility of transporting oil across the Arctic by tanker. The *Manhattan* would travel from the Atlantic coast to northern Alaska in August–September 1969. Humble's plans raised Canadian concerns over the Arctic waters and the possibility of an oil spill that would ravage the fragile northern ecosystem. The growing environmental movement gained strength after a tanker ran aground off the coast of Nova Scotia in February 1970, spilling 10,000 tons of oil and devastating the coastline. The Trudeau government found itself in a tricky position. As the prime minister's senior foreign policy adviser, Ivan Head, later remembered, the issue aroused "an unprecedented volume of public outcry," placing the Canadian and US governments "on a most uncomfortable adversarial footing."[29]

The Canadian government announced its response in April 1970, shortly after the *Manhattan* began a second voyage. Previously, Canada had claimed a three-mile territorial zone off its coasts and a nine-mile exclusive fishing zone. Now it followed more than 40 other countries in asserting a 12-mile territorial limit, meaning that ships travelling through the Northwest Passage would pass through Canadian territorial waters. Arguing that a country had as much right to protect its natural environment as its sovereignty, the government also declared a 100-mile pollution prevention zone off Canada's Arctic shores. Ottawa strictly limited waste disposal from ships passing through or near Canada's Arctic waters, specified safe shipping zones that vessels could use, and created regulations to ban from the area any ships that presented a risk to the environment. Canada was willing to allow its new 12-mile limit to go to the International Court of Justice, which only heard cases where both sides agreed to accept its jurisdiction, but refused to allow the court to consider the 100-mile pollution prevention zone, suggesting that the government was less than confident of Canada's legal position. The Nixon administration rejected Canada's claim and responded by cutting the quota for imports of Canadian oil.

Standard Oil eventually decided that transporting oil by tanker through the Northwest Passage was not worth the cost. Instead, the company would send oil by pipeline from Prudhoe Bay to the port at Valdez, Alaska, where it would be transported by ship down the Pacific coast to Seattle and Los Angeles. The Canadian government was troubled by this proposal, fearing an oil spill off the coast of British Columbia. Instead, Canada proposed a double pipeline to transport both oil and natural gas from Prudhoe to the Mackenzie River Delta in the Northwest Territories. From there, the pipeline would pass through the Mackenzie Valley to Alberta, where it would connect to existing lines. Aside from removing the threat of an oil spill on the West Coast, this plan offered several advantages for Canada: American investors would help pay for the line, it could also be used to transport Canadian resources to the American market, and Canadians would benefit from the economic activity generated by the pipeline's construction, maintenance, and operation. The Canadian government would need time to conduct some research on the feasibility of the plan, while the Americans, concerned about shortages of oil, were eager to move quickly.

The New Democratic Party (NDP), which held the balance of power in the House of Commons, opposed the Mackenzie Valley Pipeline. In March 1974, the federal government launched the Mackenzie Valley Pipeline Inquiry, chaired by Judge Thomas Berger, former NDP leader in British Columbia. Berger's report, released in 1977, recommended a 10-year delay to settle northern Aboriginal land claims. No pipeline should be built from Alaska, across the environmentally fragile Northern Yukon, to the Northwest Territories, although a line through the Mackenzie Valley to Alberta was feasible. By this time, large American oil companies had already begun construction of the Trans-Alaska Pipeline System, with the first oil arriving in Valdez just weeks after the release of the Berger report. The Mackenzie Valley pipeline was never built, and Alaskan oil continues to flow to Valdez, where it is transported down the West Coast by tanker. In 1985, one of those ships, the *Exxon Valdez*, ran into a reef off the Alaskan shore, spilling hundreds of thousands of barrels of oil.

# Aboriginal Peoples in the North

The discovery of energy resources in the North highlighted the conflicting interests of governments, oil companies, and Aboriginal peoples. The American approach was to sort out these conflicts before developing the resources. Aboriginal leaders in Alaska were better organized than their counterparts in Northern Canada, and US officials were more eager than those in Canada to get the oil and gas to market. In 1966, the US government imposed a land freeze in Alaska, so that no resource development could take place and no pipelines could be built until Aboriginal land claims had been settled. Five years later, the Alaska Native Claims Settlement Act recognized Aboriginal title to about 11 per cent of Alaska and provided financial compensation for territory the Aboriginal peoples had ceded.

The story was different in Canada. In Quebec, the provincial government launched the James Bay hydroelectric project in 1971 without first consulting with the people of Northern Quebec. Only after the Cree and Inuit took the issue to court did the province agree to negotiate. Under the James Bay and Northern Quebec Agreement of 1975, the Aboriginal peoples ceded land in exchange for financial compensation, recognition of their hunting and fishing rights, and a greater Aboriginal input into the governance of northern Quebec.

Similarly, in the early 1970s, the federal government pushed ahead with the Mackenzie Valley Pipeline without conferring first with the Aboriginal peoples. By the time the Berger Commission halted the project, the northern Aboriginal peoples were vigorously pushing for their rights. Both the Dene (who inhabited the Canadian Northwest) and the Inuit (who lived to the north and east of the Dene) pushed for self-government and a recognition of their land claims. Slowly, power devolved from Ottawa to the Aboriginal groups. By 1975, the federal government had agreed that all members of the Northwest Territories council could be elected locally (instead of having some appointed by Ottawa). Negotiations between the Dene and the federal government dragged on for years, with some Dene groups signing agreements in the 1990s. Talks with the Inuit were similarly slow, but culminated with the 1999 creation of Nunavut (meaning *our land*), a distinct territory carved out of the eastern portion of the Northwest Territories. Under the agreement, the Inuit received 350,000 square kilometres of land and compensation of more than $1 billion over 10 years.

# Reviewing Canadian International Policies

Pierre Trudeau came to office in 1968 vaguely promising change. Responding to growing public disenchantment with Canadian politics and policies, he pledged to challenge old truisms and to rethink long-held Canadian positions. Trudeau was particularly concerned that Canadian foreign and defence policies did not reflect Canadian interests and were seen as too closely aligned to the United States. In part, he was responding to the views of an increasing number of Canadians who saw quiet diplomacy and Canada's membership in NATO and NORAD as subservience to the Americans. Trudeau shook up the Ottawa establishment by posing fundamental questions about the way Canadian officials perceived and responded to the world. "Is there a Russian threat?" he asked—to the alarm of officials in the Departments of External Affairs and National Defence.[30]

The defence policy review came first. Cabinet considered withdrawing Canadian forces from NATO, but eventually decided merely to reduce the size of Canada's commitment. In 1969, the government announced that Canada would cut its NATO troops in Europe by half, to 5,000. The high ranks of the military and the diplomatic corps were troubled by this move, as were American officials, but the decision seems not to have damaged Canada's relationship with the United States.

The foreign policy review was released in 1970. Entitled *Foreign Policy for Canadians*, the document consisted of six small booklets, several with pastel-coloured covers, tints as soft as the review's content. Five booklets covered specific topics, such as Latin America and Europe. The overview booklet set out a self-interested foreign policy, one with more emphasis on fostering economic growth and protecting Canadian sovereignty, and less on promoting international peace and security. There was no booklet devoted to the United States. The government denied overlooking Canada's neighbour, arguing that the Canadian–American relationship affected all aspects of Canadian foreign policy and was covered in the overview. Some officials claimed, more convincingly, that the US was too large a subject and would have to be dealt with separately at a later date. The review's jargon and vague analysis provided little basis for a foreign policy; the booklets were quickly forgotten, in and out of government.

## Recognizing Communist China

A more substantive change in Canadian foreign policy came later in 1970, when the Trudeau government recognized communist China. In 1949, the communists under Mao Zedong had won the Chinese Civil War, driving Chiang Kai-shek's nationalist government from the mainland to the Chinese island of Taiwan. From its headquarters in the city of Taipei, Chiang's regime claimed to be the legitimate government for all of China, while Mao made the same claim from Beijing. Canada had considered establishing diplomatic relations with mainland China as early as November 1949, but had backed way. At a time when Canada had few interests in China, there was little benefit in extending a hand to the new regime, but there was a significant drawback to annoying the Americans, who were committed to supporting the nationalists in Taipei.

In May 1968, just one month after taking office, Trudeau announced that Canada would seek to establish diplomatic ties with Red China. Two years later, after negotiations with Mao's regime, Canada recognized the government in Beijing as the sole legal government of China and "noted" Beijing's position that Taiwan was part of Chinese territory. At the same time, Canada withdrew recognition of the government in Taipei. American officials were angry at Canada, one of them claiming that Canada had "crawled on its belly" before the Chinese government.[31] But the Americans were moving in Canada's direction. Before long, State Department officials learned that the Nixon administration had been holding secret discussions with mainland China since 1969 and would soon begin limited contacts between the two countries. Six months after Canada recognized the communist regime, the US sent a table tennis team to China—*Ping-Pong diplomacy*, it was called. Kissinger made a covert visit three months after that.

Tensions between Canada and the United States over Canada's recognition of communist China bubbled up in 1976, when Montreal hosted the Olympic Games. Despite the Nixon administration's limited contacts with Beijing, the United States continued to recognize Taipei as the government of China. For its part, the International Olympic Committee (IOC) had struggled since the Chinese revolution to keep politics out of the games and to allow athletes from both the mainland and Taiwan to compete. But neither Beijing nor Taipei would participate in the games if athletes from the other regime were competing. The issue was crucial: a truly international competition had to include China, the most populous country on the globe and home to almost one-quarter of the world's people.

The IOC recognized a Taiwanese body as the National Olympic Committee for China, but Canada refused to issue visas to Taiwanese athletes for the Montreal Olympics. When the IOC threatened to cancel the games, Canadian officials sought a compromise: Taiwanese athletes were welcome in Canada, so long as they did not compete under the names *Republic of China* or *China*, and did not use the flag and anthem of the Taipei regime. Ronald Reagan, who was challenging Gerald Ford for the Republican nomination for president, condemned Canada, saying that the American team should refuse to participate in the Montreal games and the IOC should consider moving the event to the United States. Forced to take a stand, President Ford criticized Canada's compromise and hinted at a possible US boycott of the games. Only days before the opening ceremonies, the IOC backed down, ruling that Taiwan should compete as Taiwan. The Taiwanese withdrew in protest, but the American team took part in the games.

The conflict was an important first step to the Chinese mainland's return to the Olympics, though that would not happen for several more years. The United States recognized mainland China in 1979 and refused to allow the Taiwanese to compete as the Republic of China at the 1980 Winter Olympics in Lake Placid, New York, using the same arguments the Canadians had employed four years earlier. Again, the Taiwanese withdrew in protest. In 1981, the issue was finally settled. Henceforth, mainland China would compete in the Olympic Games as the People's Republic of China and the Taiwanese would compete as Chinese Taipei.

# The American War in Vietnam

By 1968, the United States had half a million men under arms in Vietnam, most of them conscripts. Faced with the prospect of being forced to serve, and perhaps die, for a cause they did not believe in, many young American men fled for Canada.

Canadian immigration law did not exclude those who were avoiding the draft or deserting the US armed forces. Yet, in practice, each immigration officer handled the matter differently, some turning away Americans fleeing military service, others admitting them. The government clarified the policy in 1969: military status would not be a factor when deciding whether or not to accept an immigrant to Canada. That was a matter between an American and his government, not an issue for Canadian concern.

There were already thousands of Americans entering Canada to flee the war. Now the flow increased. Their numbers included deserters, draft dodgers, and political refugees—individuals who left the United States in protest against American policies, usually the war in Vietnam. The draft dodgers were generally white, middle class, and college educated. Deserters, who were fewer in number, were more likely to be working class with less education. Since Canada did not ask immigrants about their military status, there are no official figures on the number of draft dodgers and deserters who entered the country. Estimates range from 30,000 to 125,000, though the lower figure is more likely closer to the mark.[32]

Nixon won the presidential election of 1968 with an ambiguous promise to end the war. It was not clear if he would do so by defeating the enemy on the battlefield or by negotiating peace. The answer was a bit of both: he stepped up the attacks on North Vietnam, in the hopes of winning concessions at the bargaining table. Although he promised to end the war, large numbers of young Americans continued to die in Vietnam for years. All along, the Nixon administration promised that peace was at hand.

For 11 days in December 1972, the US heavily bombed the Hanoi–Haiphong area of North Vietnam, shocking Canadians and Americans. The Christmas Bombing created a problem for the Trudeau Liberals, who had been reduced to a minority in the House of Commons in the October election and were dependent on support from the NDP, a party highly critical of US policies. When Parliament began sitting in early January 1973, one of the first orders of business was a resolution deploring US action, a motion that passed unanimously. Canadian diplomats tried to explain to the Nixon administration that Trudeau's Liberals had only supported the motion for domestic political reasons, as part of an effort to woo the NDP and public opinion, but to no avail. The Americans expressed their displeasure subtly but unmistakably, turning down invitations to events at the Canadian embassy and declining to meet with their Canadian counterparts when they were in the American capital. An angry Nixon refused to send condolences after Trudeau's mother passed away in mid-January 1973, a petty display of pique all too typical of the little man who was president of the United States.[33]

Yet the dispute did not last long. The war in Vietnam ended with the Paris Peace Accords of late January 1973, and suddenly the US needed Canada. Canada agreed to an American request to serve for 60 days (later extended to six months) on the International Commission of Control and Supervision, which oversaw the repatriation of prisoners of war. Almost immediately after the war ended, Canadian opinions of the United States began to improve.

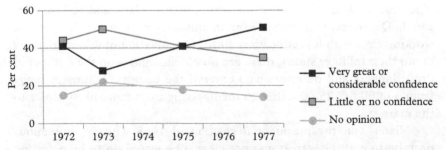

**Figure 10.1** ⊹ Canadian Confidence in the Ability of the US to Deal Wisely with World Problems, 1972–7

Source: Data provided by "Majority Believe US Can Handle World Problems," *Toronto Star*, 27 August 1977, B3.

# The Nixon Shock and the End of the Special Relationship

The United States had long suffered from problems with its balance of payments. The American share of global manufacturing was dropping, and demand for the US dollar was falling as consumers chose to purchase products made in Japan or Germany or elsewhere. Many investors took the US Treasury up on its longstanding promise to exchange US dollars for their fixed value in gold, reducing the US gold supply to a dangerously low level. The Nixon administration's solution to the problem was brutal, as Treasury Secretary John Connally illustrated in a casual comment to a group of economists: "My basic approach is that the foreigners are out to screw us. Our job is to screw them first."[34]

On 15 August 1971, the US announced that it would screw the foreigners with a package of measures that became known as the Nixon Shock. The US would impose a 10 per cent surtax on almost all imports and would allow the value of the American dollar to float, no longer linking it to the price of gold. At the same time, Congress was in the process of approving tax breaks to encourage multinational companies to export from their American factories, not their branch plants abroad. The American media focussed on the impact of these measures on Japan, even referring to them by their Japanese name, Nixon *Shokku*, but the country hardest hit was Canada, which sent two-thirds of its exports to the United States.[35] By one estimate, the measure would have cost 40,000 to 100,000 Canadian jobs had it remained in effect for more than a few months.[36]

Canada could have been hit much harder. Not until much later did Canadians learn that Connally had intended to cancel the Auto Pact. Two US State Department officials—a senior bureaucrat who had been one of the fathers of the agreement and the commercial counsellor at the US embassy in Ottawa, who happened to be in Washington at the time—discovered the plans at the last minute. They intervened with Secretary of State William P. Rogers, who in turn convinced Connally not to terminate the Auto Pact.

Canada had often been spared from US measures to deal with the country's international economic problems, but this was no longer automatic. With the 1963 Interest Equalization Tax, Canadians had to make a case for an exemption, an argument the Canadians won. After the announcement of the Nixon Shock, Canada quickly sent a delegation to Washington to appeal for special treatment, but the discussions did not go well. Connally began by speaking from notes intended for a meeting with Japanese officials. The confusion was quickly cleared up, but it demonstrated how little the Treasury secretary knew or cared about Canada. In any case, he was intractable; there would be no exemption. In December, Trudeau led another Canadian delegation to Washington to talk about a range of issues, including Nixon's economic measures. While Trudeau met politely with Nixon in one room, Canadian and American officials clashed over the surtax in another room down the hall. "The blood in there was knee-deep," according to Trudeau's chief foreign policy adviser, Ivan Head.[37]

For Canada, the significance of the surtax was less in its economic impact than its long-term implications for Canadian–American relations. In December 1971, the US withdrew the measure, after Canadian and other major industrialized nations met in Washington and agreed to realign their currency values. In place for only four months, the Nixon surtax did no lasting damage to the Canadian economy, but it did mark a turning point in the relations between Canada and the United States. No longer could Canada expect to hold a privileged place in American policies based on common economic interests, as had been the case since the Hyde Park agreement of 1941.

Nixon spelled out the end of the special relationship during a visit to Ottawa in April 1972. Canadians and Americans had "to move beyond the sentimental rhetoric of the past," he told the Canadian Parliament. "It is time for us to recognize: that we have very separate identities; that we have significant differences; and that nobody's interests are furthered when these realities are obscured." Each country needed "autonomous independent policies" and had to "define the nature of its own interests."[38] To a large extent, Nixon had missed the point. The special relationship between Canada and the United States had been forged on national interests, not in spite of them. Both countries benefitted from giving each other a preferred place in their economic policies. Still, the Nixon Shock and the president's speech marked a turning point in Canadian–American relations. The immediate and unintended consequence of Nixon's announcement was to liberate the Trudeau government to implement measures to reduce American influence over the Canadian economy, to the detriment of American interests.

## The New Nationalist Victory

The New Nationalism had its roots in the Canadian political mainstream. In the 1950s, many Conservatives believed that Louis St Laurent's government was selling Canada out to the Americans. In the late 1950s and early 1960s, Walter Gordon, a Liberal, tried to convince the St Laurent and Pearson governments to reduce the flow of American capital into Canada. By the late 1960s the far left was seeking to make the nationalist issue its own.

In 1969, radicals within the NDP created the Waffle Movement with the goal of marrying Canadian socialism and nationalism. The group's 1969 Manifesto for an Independent Socialist Canada suggested that American and Canadian owners were essentially the same, both primarily motivated by the pursuit of profit. The solution to the problem of American control was for the government to seize control of industry in Canada, regardless of the owner's citizenship. The Waffle Movement's unappealing name came from a glib comment that one of the members made at an early meeting—"If we're going to waffle, I'd rather waffle to the left than waffle to the right"—and illustrated the group's failure to understand the basics of political marketing, just one of the reasons for its inability to win widespread popular support. The organization was composed of members of the middle class, often university professors or students, with about half of the members under the age of 35.[39] Most came from southern Ontario, though a few supporters lived in Western Canada. There were virtually no Waffle members in the Maritimes or Quebec. From the outset, the organization had little support from organized labour, whose ranks viewed the Waffle as "posturing academics," to quote Murray Cotterill of the United Steelworkers.[40] Waffle members believed they were the vanguard of change in Canada, but all too often they engaged in sterile debates that had little connection to the experience of Canadians.

Concerned that the left might gain control of the nationalist movement, a group of Canadians created a non-partisan organization to advance the cause of Canadian independence from the United States. In September 1970, Walter Gordon, University of Toronto economist Abraham Rotstein, and *Toronto Star* editor Peter C. Newman launched the Committee for an Independent Canada (CIC). The organization's vague "Statement of Purpose" called for the government to reduce foreign control through a variety of measures, including the creation of an agency to screen new investment and to oversee the operations of non-Canadian firms. The organization's membership included individuals from the three main political parties, but like the Waffle, they came primarily from the middle class in southern Ontario. In the early 1970s, the media paid considerable attention to the CIC and the organization seemed to be winning widespread public support for its policies. "Canadians have become a lot more nationalist economically than they were before," Trudeau observed.[41]

Pierre Trudeau was no nationalist. He had built much of his career on his opposition to nationalism in principle and to Quebec nationalism in practice. Still, he was concerned about American domination and did, in the words of his Cabinet minister Alastair Gillespie, "come to recognize the political and economic significance of the issue in vote-rich Ontario," particularly in the period from 1972 to 1974, when the Liberals were in a minority position and dependent on support from other parties in the

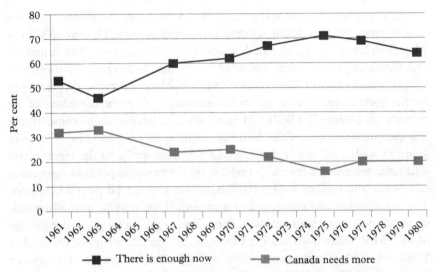

**Figure 10.2** ✛ Canadian Attitudes on American Investment, 1961–80

Sources: Data compiled from F.J. Fletcher and R.J. Drummond, *Canadian Attitude Trends, 1960–1978* (Montreal: Institute for Research on Public Policy, 1979), 38; Sylvia B. Bashevkin, *True Patriot Love: The Politics of Canadian Nationalism* (Toronto: Oxford University Press, 1991), 96.

House of Commons.[42] Reluctantly, Trudeau agreed that his government could undertake several moderately nationalist measures.

In 1971, the government created the Canada Development Corporation (CDC), designed to increase the proportion of domestic industry owned by Canadians. Shares in the firm were held by the federal government and by individual Canadians. The CDC took ownership of some former Crown corporations, purchased a few foreign-owned firms, and helped start new Canadian companies. It was highly popular among Canadians, with 83 per cent of respondents telling pollsters that it was a very important measure and only 7 per cent saying it was not very important.[43]

Just two weeks before the October 1972 federal election, which Trudeau feared he might lose, the government declared its desire to distance Canada from the United States. In a document entitled *Canada–US Relations: Options for the Future*, External Affairs Minister Mitchell Sharp laid out three choices for Canada's relations with its powerful neighbour: (1) Canada could maintain the status quo; (2) Canada could seek closer integration with the Americans; or (3) Canada could "develop and strengthen the Canadian economy and other aspects of its national life and in the process reduce the present Canadian vulnerability."[44]

The government chose the Third Option and began working to create stronger economic ties with Japan and Europe. "Lots of luck, Canada," quipped an American diplomat familiar with Canada–US trade.[45] Canada did succeed in creating a "contractual link" with Europe in 1975 and with

Japan in 1976, largely meaningless agreements that contained no tariff reductions, just empty promises that the two sides would cooperate on economic issues. Certainly, it made sense to promote Canadian economic ties with Europe and Japan, but the government was wildly unrealistic if it expected these agreements would significantly offset Canada's trade with the US. Geography made Canada and the United States natural trading partners, a reality that "contractual links" could not overcome. "Theatrical, mystical, idealistic" were the words Canadian trade expert Simon Reisman used to describe the Third Option. "You know, we're a North American country."[46]

A more meaningful step in the nationalist direction came after the Trudeau government lost its House of Commons majority in the 1972 election. In November 1973, the House of Commons unanimously passed the government's bill to create the Foreign Investment Review Agency (FIRA), responsible for screening foreign investment in Canada. The agency began reviewing the foreign takeover of Canadian firms in 1974 and the establishment of foreign-owned businesses in 1975. The agency was unpopular in Western and Atlantic Canada, areas eager for new investment, and among nationalist leaders upset that it approved most of the applications it received. The administration of President Gerald Ford disliked FIRA, but did not put pressure on Canada to abandon it. Secretary of State Kissinger did not like to confront Canada, for fear of generating a backlash against the United States. "We are so powerful," he commented in 1974, "whatever identity they have, they get in opposition to us."[47]

# Culture and Education

Although the focus of the nationalist movement was on the economy, the Canadian government also responded to pressure to protect Canadian culture. In 1968, the new Broadcasting Act replaced the Board of Broadcast Governors with the Canadian Radio and Television Commission (CRTC), a more muscular agency to regulate the Canadian broadcast industry. In 1969, the government directed the CRTC not to issue broadcast licences to companies that were less than 80 per cent Canadian-owned. In 1970, the CRTC implemented the first Canadian content regulations for radio stations. Henceforth, 30 per cent of music on AM stations had to be Canadian. For FM stations, the quota was more complex and depended on the station's format. To qualify as Canadian, a song needed either a Canadian composer, lyricist, or performer, or it had to be performed and recorded in Canada. Beginning in 1971, a song had to be Canadian in two of these four elements.

In 1972, the CRTC began a long, complicated struggle over advertising on American television stations near the Canadian border. In that year, the agency began requiring cable companies to delete commercials randomly on US stations and replace them with public service announcements. When the same program was broadcast simultaneously on a Canadian station, cable providers had to broadcast the Canadian signal on the American channel, so that viewers would see the advertisements intended for the Canadian market. This would encourage companies to advertise on Canadian stations, increasing their revenue. The stations in Buffalo, New York, responded by suing the CRTC and Rogers Cable in Toronto, a case the Americans lost before the Supreme Court of Canada in 1977. In the meantime, the government had also ended the tax deduction for companies that advertised on foreign stations or in foreign periodicals, a measure that roughly doubled the cost for a Canadian company advertising on an American station.

There was a similar struggle over magazines. In the mid-1960s, the Pearson government had changed the tax laws to prevent foreign magazines from publishing Canadian editions, though *Time* and *Reader's Digest*, established in Canada since the 1940s, were exempted. In the 1970s, nationalists went after these two periodicals, convincing the government to rescind the exemptions in 1976. *Time* immediately stopped publishing a Canadian edition, but *Reader's Digest* responded by Canadianizing its operations north of the border. Three-quarters of the shares in Reader's Digest Magazines (Canada) Ltd were given to a new charitable foundation led by Canadian directors, so that the publication would qualify as Canadian.

The battle for Canadian content extended to university campuses. Two professors at Carleton University in Ottawa, Robin Mathews and James Steele, objected to both the shortage of Canadian professors on the country's campuses and the lack of courses on Canadian issues, igniting a debate that quickly spread to other universities. Mathews and Steele preferred to talk about Canadianizing the country's universities, rather than restricting American influence, but anti-American sentiments were certainly present. For Mathews, the United States was a "racist, imperialistic, militaristic, two-party, chauvinistic, culturally-aggressive community."[48]

# The Energy Crisis

An energy crisis struck the world while the Trudeau government was in its precarious minority situation. The problem originated in the 1973 Arab–Israeli War between Israel and its Arab neighbours. The United States had supplied Israel with arms; in retaliation the Arab states cut off oil exports to the US. At the same time, the Organization of Petroleum Exporting Countries (OPEC), composed of several Arab states and Venezuela, announced that it would raise the price of oil for other countries. The cost soared from an average of US$2.48 a barrel in 1972 to US$11.45 in 1974.[49]

To shelter Canadian consumers from fluctuations in energy prices, the federal government announced the creation of a two-price system. Canadian oil, most of which came from Alberta, would sell abroad at the international price, but at a lower price at home. To maintain the system, Ottawa imposed an export tax on oil, the amount being the difference between $3.80 per barrel (the domestic price) and the higher international price. In other words, oil exporters would receive $3.80 per barrel, whether they sold at home or abroad, with the federal treasury pocketing the difference between the two prices on any oil sold abroad. Albertans were outraged that the province's primary resource would be sold at below the international price, with Premier Peter Lougheed calling the new system "the most discriminatory action taken by a federal government against a particular province in the entire history of Confederation."[50] Many Albertans resented Ontarians and Quebeckers for being able to buy Alberta resources at below their market price. "Let the eastern bastards freeze in the dark," appeared on bumper stickers in Alberta.

In December 1973, the government announced one more element of its oil policy: it would create a national oil company. Petro Canada came into being in 1975, and represented another victory for the nationalist movement. The company provided a Canadian presence in all aspects of the oil industry, from oil exploration and extraction, to retail sale at the pump.

# Crises in Central and Western Asia

Late 1979 was a period of political turmoil in Canada. Joe Clark had become Canada's prime minister after his party won the May election of that year, but his Conservatives only held a minority of seats in the House of Commons and were dependent on smaller parties for support. In December 1979, the government lost a crucial budget vote, forcing another election. The Trudeau Liberals won the February 1980 vote, returning to office with a majority. In the midst of this domestic political commotion, two international crises exploded.

In November 1979, militants stormed the US embassy in the Iranian capital of Tehran and took more than 50 American hostages. Six Americans managed to evade capture and were offered safe haven in the homes of Canadian embassy officials. Working with the CIA, Canadian Ambassador Ken Taylor arranged for the Americans to receive Canadian passports and to leave the country, which they did in January 1980, an event later overdramatized in the Oscar-winning film *Argo*. American gratitude was overwhelming. "Thank you, Canada, from the bottom of our hearts," read a full-page ad from Citicorp in the *New York Times*. "In our time of need, you were there, keeping alive the principles of decency and freedom that we share as human beings and as neighbors." Greyhound ran a full-page ad in major Canadian newspapers, thanking Canadians for their "heroic act of friendship" and offering Canadians a 30-day pass for travel in the US at one-third the normal price.[51]

Just one month after the hostage taking in Iran, the Soviet Union invaded Afghanistan to prop up a faltering pro-Soviet regime. The US government, which had decried Canada's politicization of the 1976 Olympics over the status of Taiwan and China, decided that the country would boycott the 1980 Olympics in Moscow unless Soviet troops withdrew from Afghanistan. Clark announced in January 1980 that Canada would join the Olympic boycott, a decision Trudeau accepted when he returned to office, joining more than 60 countries that refused to send athletes to Moscow.

## Quebec

Quebec had always been a distinct part of Canada, with a French-speaking majority and a culture different from that of the rest of the country. While many English Canadians were preoccupied with asserting Canada's independence from the United States, Quebeckers were more likely to push for Quebec's separation from Canada. The separatist movement scored a triumph in the 1976 provincial election with the election of the Parti Québécois, which promised to hold a referendum on Quebec's independence. Suddenly there appeared the possibility of political, economic, and social upheaval on the Americans' traditionally quiet northern border.

US officials quickly concluded that their country's interests lay with a united Canada, but they did not want to interfere with what was a domestic Canadian issue. Eager to win US support, or at least neutrality, the Parti Québécois adapted its policies. Originally, the party had promised that an independent Quebec would be neutral, not allied to the United States. In 1979, the party changed positions, promising that the new country would seek membership in both NATO and NORAD. Yet, for Americans, a sovereign Quebec remained an uncertain quantity. As the 1980 referendum approached, the United States delicately but clearly indicated a preference for a united Canada. While recognizing that the issue was for Canadians to decide, both President Carter and Vice-President Walter Mondale said publicly that they would prefer that the country remain united. It is not clear if these statements had any impact on the vote, in which Quebeckers rejected independence by a vote of 60 to 40 per cent.

# The National Energy Program

In 1979 and 1980, oil prices again rose, leading the Trudeau government to react as it had to the energy crisis of the early 1970s. In October 1980, the government announced the National Energy Program (NEP) with the goals of making Canada self-sufficient in energy, keeping prices low for consumers, promoting a greater degree of Canadian ownership in the oil and gas industry, and ensuring that the federal government received a higher proportion of resource revenues. Ottawa would now have a 25 per cent interest in all oil and gas development in those areas where the federal government controlled natural resources: offshore and in the Yukon and Northwest Territories. This included past discoveries, leading investors and the US government to complain that Canada was retroactively expropriating American property. The old tax incentives for exploration were replaced with subsidies for resource companies based on their level of Canadian ownership. To encourage development, the government would pay up to 25 per cent of exploration costs for foreign-owned firms and up to 80 per cent for Canadian-owned companies. In the future, only companies with at least 50 per cent Canadian ownership could take part in oil and gas production offshore and in the northern territories.

The government announced the NEP just days before the US election, which saw Ronald Reagan defeat Jimmy Carter. During the transition from Carter to Reagan, US officials objected to the policy. The Trudeau government responded to complaints about the retroactive feature of the NEP by providing compensation for its expropriation of a 25 per cent interest in oil and gas development, but remained firm on the rest of the policy. The Reagan administration, which took office in January 1981, was hostile to the NEP and pressed for its withdrawal but never retaliated against Canada. The Americans likely understood that the measure was highly popular in central and eastern Canada, and any countermeasures might well backfire by fostering anti-American sentiment.[52]

# Trudeau and Reagan

In intellect, personality, and politics, Ronald Reagan had little in common with Trudeau. The prime minister was an intellectual who enjoyed a good debate; the president was a conflict-avoider who sought to be on good terms with everyone, using humorous stories to defuse difficult situations. Trudeau was a liberal, who favoured a rapprochement with communist countries, and believed that government had a role in the economy. Reagan was a free-enterprise and anti-government conservative who saw the world in an uncomplicated way, showing little interest in subtleties or details. For him, the Soviet Union was "an evil empire," and the Cold War was a "struggle between right and wrong," between "good and evil."[53] Trudeau thought the president had "an obsession with communism."[54] Still, the prime minister maintained a working relationship with Reagan and occasionally defended him publicly. Demonstrators greeted Reagan when he visited Ottawa in March 1981, protesting against both the American failure to act on acid rain and US policies in El Salvador, where the US was providing large amounts of armaments to a brutal military dictatorship in the midst of a civil war. Trudeau chastised the protestors: "Hey, guys, when I go to the United States, I'm not met with these kinds of signs. You know, the Americans have some beefs against us, too, but they receive us politely. So how about a great cheer for President Reagan?"[55] Deep down, despite the many differences between the two men, Trudeau liked the president. "Whatever else he may be, he's a good man," the prime minister said in his final days in office.[56]

Reagan's rhetoric and massive arms spending increased global tensions, but Trudeau sought to ease them in his final months in office. In the fall of 1983, he naively set off on a mission to lessen Cold War hostilities and promote nuclear disarmament. Visiting major world capitals, Trudeau urged his fellow leaders to support a ban on testing and deploying high-altitude weapons, an arms-control conference of the world's five major nuclear powers, and measures to strengthen the nuclear Non-Proliferation Treaty. Already seeing Trudeau as soft on defence, the Reagan administration was hostile to the peace mission. "Oh, God," a US Defense Department official declared, "Trudeau's at it again."[57] Laurence Eagleburger, the third-ranking member of the State Department, compared Trudeau's trek to the "pot-induced behavior" of "an erratic leftist."[58] Reagan met with Trudeau and listened politely to the proposals, later writing in his diary that Trudeau's mission was not "a sound idea."[59] In the end, it accomplished little.

Although Trudeau seemed to be diverging from the United States, he remained committed to the Canadian–American alliance. In June 1983, the United States asked Canada to permit the testing of the cruise missile over Canadian territory. Trudeau allowed a lengthy debate in Cabinet, but ultimately decided that Canada had to honour its alliance commitments and agree to the tests, a decision that outraged the Canadian left.

# Decline of the Nationalists

In the early 1970s, Canadian nationalists seemed triumphant. The government implemented measures to reduce foreign control of Canadian industry, to increase the Canadian presence in the resource industries, and to offset the power of American popular culture. But the victories were short-lived. As early as the mid-1970s, the influence of the nationalist movement was waning as the public image of the US improved. Although there was still some real distance to go before blacks achieved equality, the civil rights struggle in the United States had died down. The United States withdrew its troops from Vietnam in 1973, putting an end to a major cause of an-ti-Americanism in Canada. The next year, Richard Nixon, never popular in Canada, resigned from office in the midst of the Watergate scandal, in which he had covered up a break-in at Democratic Party headquarters by some of his Republican operatives. Equally important was an economic recession sparked by the oil embargo of 1973. Facing unemployment and inflation, most Canadians were less interested in restricting foreign investment than in encouraging it. To most Canadians it appeared that the foreign investment issue had been dealt with. Nationalist leaders were never satisfied with FIRA, which they believed accepted too much foreign capital, but many Canadians believed that the government had taken care of the problem.

When the Liberal majority was restored in the 1974 election, Trudeau was no longer dependent on the NDP for support. Slowly, the government began backing away from the nationalist measures it had implemented. Herb Gray, one of the fathers of FIRA, was pushed out of Cabinet in 1974. In a 1976 Cabinet shuffle, the external affairs portfolio went to Don Jamieson, who a few months earlier had declared to an audience of American busi-nessmen, "All my life I have had a love affair with the United States."[60] At the same time, Jean Chrétien, who valued foreign investment, was made the minister responsible for FIRA. He dismissed nationalists as people often "using the flag for their own interests." There were "a lot of places in Canada where people don't give a damn who owns what," Chrétien said. "They want a job."[61]

By the early 1980s, the Canadian economy had been performing so poorly for so long that the Trudeau government began casting about for new approaches. In 1982, the government appointed the Royal Commission on the Economic Union and Development Prospects for Canada, chaired by Donald Macdonald, a former finance minister. Charged with investigating Canada's economic future and the country's economic policy options, the commission worked away while the Trudeau government began to explore limited free trade with the United States on a sector-by-sector basis. The Auto Pact would form the model for a series of free trade agreements covering specific industries. The United States responded positively, but little progress had been made by the time Trudeau left office in 1984.

# Summary

The late 1960s and early 1970s were characterized by Canadian anxieties about the values of the United States and about American intentions toward Canada. The New Nationalism grew in popularity, and the Trudeau government found that it had to respond, particularly from 1972 to 1974 when it was in a minority position. With the Canada Development Corporation, the Third Option, FIRA, and Petro Canada, the government pledged to lessen Canada's dependence on the United States. Yet the similarities between the two countries persisted. Young Canadians and Americans took part in similar demonstrations in favour of civil rights for black Americans and against the American war in Vietnam. Aboriginal and women's liberation movements grew on both sides of the border, using similar techniques in pursuit of similar goals.

The relations between the two governments were marked by tensions—over Vietnam, Arctic sovereignty, energy, and economic policy. But the friendship continued, with the two sides struggling to maintain the connection. The major difficulties always passed. The Americans pulled out of Vietnam, the unpopular Richard Nixon resigned, and the Trudeau Liberals won back their majority, meaning that they were no longer beholden to the nationalists. The government began backing away from its earlier policies and was soon exploring the idea of limited free trade with the United States. The Canadian–American friendship was more resilient than the nationalists had thought.

# Beyond the Book

1. To what extent did nationalists raise legitimate concerns about American influence in Canada?
2. Are Canadian cultural policies a reasonable effort to ensure a distinct Canadian culture or an infringement on the rights of individuals to choose which magazines they will read, television programs they will watch, and music they will listen to?
3. What are the costs and benefits of national policies to shelter consumers from high oil prices?

# Further Reading

For relations between the two governments, the best source is J.L. Granatstein and Robert Bothwell, *Pirouette: Pierre Trudeau and Canadian Foreign Policy* (Toronto: University of Toronto Press, 1990). Bothwell is particularly good at explaining US policy in "Thanks for the Fish: Nixon, Kissinger, and Canada," chapter 15 in *Nixon in the World: American Foreign Relations, 1969–1977*, edited by Fredrik Logevall and Andrew Preston (Oxford: Oxford University Press, 2008), 309–28. Henry Kissinger provides a few insightful comments on Canada in *The White House Years* (Boston: Little, Brown, 1979). On the Nixon Shock, see Bruce Muirhead, "From Special Relationship to Third Option: Canada, the US, and the Nixon Shock," *American Review of Canadian Studies* 34, no. 3 (Autumn 2004): 439–62.

Understanding Trudeau is difficult. The best source is the biography by John English, *Just Watch Me*, vol. 2 of *The Life of Pierre Elliott Trudeau, 1968–2000* (Toronto: Alfred A. Knopf, 2009). Pierre Elliott Trudeau, *Memoirs* (Toronto: McClelland and Stewart, 1993) conceals more than it reveals, making it perhaps the least satisfying and most disappointing prime ministerial memoir. Trudeau's senior foreign policy adviser, Ivan Head, has written an odd book on the prime minister's policies, which misleadingly claims the former prime minister as a co-author: Ivan L. Head and Pierre Elliott Trudeau, *The Canadian Way: Shaping Canada's Foreign Policy, 1968–1984* (Toronto: McClelland and Stewart, 1995). On the economic nationalism of the Trudeau government, the essential work is Alastair W. Gillespie with Irene Sage, *Made in Canada: A Businessman's Adventures in Politics* ([Montreal]: Robin Brass Studio, 2009). Several other Trudeau Cabinet ministers wrote memoirs, most of which have nothing to say on Canada–US relations. The exceptions are Mark MacGuigan, *An Inside Look at External Affairs during the Trudeau Years: The Memoirs of Mark MacGuigan* (Calgary: University of Calgary Press, 2002); Mitchell Sharp, *Which Reminds Me . . . A Memoir* (Toronto: University of Toronto Press, 1994); and the fine introductory section to Don Jamieson, *No Place for Fools*, vol. 1 of *The Political Memoirs of Don Jamieson*, edited by Carmelita McGrath (St. John's: Breakwater, 1989).

For Canadian policies on Vietnam, see Bothwell's *Alliance and Illusion: Canada and the World, 1945–1984* (Vancouver: UBC Press, 2007), which is also strong on a host of other issues. The best sources on draft dodgers are John Hagan, *Northern Passage: American Vietnam War Resisters in Canada* (Cambridge, Massachusetts: Harvard University Press, 2001); Renée G. Kasinsky, *Refugees from Militarism: Draft-Age Americans in Canada* (New Brunswick, New Jersey: Transaction Books, 1976); and Lara Campbell, "'Women United Against the War': Gender Politics, Feminism, and Vietnam Draft Resistance in Canada," chapter 34 in *New World Coming: The Sixties and the Shaping of Global Consciousness*, edited by Karen Dubinsky et al. (Toronto: Between the Lines, 2009), 339–46.

Canada's recognition of mainland China is examined in Paul M. Evans and B. Michael Frolic, eds., *Reluctant Adversaries: Canada and the People's Republic of China, 1949–1970* (Toronto: University of Toronto Press, 1991), particularly in the chapters by Frolic and Stephen Beecroft. On the struggle over Chinese representation at the 1976 Olympics, see Donald Macintosh et al., *Sport and Canadian Diplomacy* (Montreal and Kingston: McGill–Queen's University Press, 1994); and Xu Guoqi, *Olympic Dreams: China and Sports, 1895–2008* (Cambridge, Massachusetts: Harvard University Press, 2008).

There is still much to be done on energy issues. The best book remains G. Bruce Doern and Glen Toner, *The Politics of Energy: The Development and Implementation of the NEP* (Toronto: Methuen, 1985). Edward Wonder examines the American side of the story in "The US Government Response to the Canadian National Energy Program," *Canadian Public Policy* 8, supplement (October 1982): 480–93. Christopher Kirkey provides a clear analysis in "Moving Alaskan Oil to Market: Canadian National Interests and the Trans-Alaska Pipeline, 1968–73," *American Review of Canadian Studies* 27, no. 4 (Winter 1997): 495–522. On Arctic waters, see John Kirton and Don Munton, "The *Manhattan* Voyages and Their Aftermath," chapter 4 in *Politics of the Northwest Passage*, edited by Franklyn Griffiths (Montreal and Kingston: McGill–Queen's University Press, 1987), 67–97.

On the origins of Aboriginal protest in the 1960s and 1970s, see Roger L. Nichols, *Indians in the United States and Canada: A Comparative History* (Lincoln: University of Nebraska Press, 1998); Laurence M. Hauptman, *The Iroquois Struggle for Survival: World War II to Red Power* (Syracuse: Syracuse University Press, 1986); and Bryan D. Palmer, "'Indians of All Tribes': The Birth of Red Power," chapter 10 in *Debating Dissent: Canada and the Sixties*, edited by Lara Campbell, Dominique Clément, and Gregory S. Kealey (Toronto: University of Toronto Press, 2012), 193–210. Peter Matthiessen, *In the Spirit of Crazy Horse* (New York: Viking, 1983) tells the story of AIM and Anna Mae Aquash. On Canadian government policy, see J.R. Miller's outstanding work, *Skyscrapers Hide the Heavens: A History of Indian-White Relations in Canada*, 3rd ed. (Toronto: University of Toronto Press, 2000). John David Hamilton looks at the impact of energy development on northern Aboriginal people in *Arctic Revolution: Social Change in the Northwest Territories, 1935–1994* (Toronto: Dundurn, 1994).

There are several sources on the New Nationalism, all listed at the end of chapter 9.

On cultural policy, see Barry Berlin, *The American Trojan Horse: US Television Confronts Canadian Economic and Cultural Nationalism* (New York: Greenwood, 1990); and Richard Collins, *Culture, Communication, and National Identity: The Case of Canadian Television* (Toronto: University of Toronto Press, 1990). Jeffrey Cormier examines the efforts to increase Canadian content and the number of Canadian professors at universities in his important book, *The Canadianization Movement: Emergence, Survival, and Success* (Toronto: University of Toronto Press, 2004).

## CHAPTER 11

# Reconciliation, 1984–1993

## The Political and Economic Partnership of the Mulroney Years

## Introduction

The high point of the Shamrock Summit was a nationally televised gala. Prime Minister Brian Mulroney was hosting President Ronald Reagan in Quebec City on St Patrick's Day 1985 and was making the most of their common Irish heritage. As the singers wrapped up the evening event with a rendition of "When Irish Eyes Are Smiling," Mulroney led the president and their wives, both clad in green dresses, onto the stage. Reagan sang along in good humour, but had earlier ordered that no microphone was to come anywhere near him. The prime minister was not so shy. When the performers got to the last line, they stopped and put a microphone in front of Mulroney, who finished the song himself. Many Canadians were embarrassed that Mulroney seemed to be trying so hard to impress Reagan. "I wanted to take a shotgun to the TV," recalled novelist Mordecai Richler. For historian J.L. Granatstein, it was "a public display of sucking up" that might well "have been the single most demeaning moment in the entire political history of Canada's relations with the United States."[1]

Mulroney undertook a systematic effort to improve the Canada–US relationship. Mulroney and Reagan held annual summits to discuss issues of common concern, and the Canadian external affairs minister met quarterly with the US secretary of state. Canadian officials constantly reassured the United States of Canada's friendship, while forcefully pushing Canada's interests, an approach that led to the closest relations between the two governments since the Second World War. The two countries reached significant agreements on free trade and acid rain, and a limited accord on the Northwest Passage. Although perceived as fawning over Reagan, Mulroney held firm against American pressure for Canada to take part in ballistic missile defence. Later generations can debate the value of the free trade pact, but there can be little doubt that the agreement happened largely because of Mulroney and his close relationship with Reagan.

## Brian Mulroney and the Americans

American money played a decisive role in Brian Mulroney's life from the beginning. The future prime minister was born in Baie-Comeau, Quebec, a town founded on the North Shore of the St Lawrence River by Robert R. McCormick, owner of the *Chicago Tribune* and *New York Daily News*. Mulroney's father moved the family there to take a job as an electrician in the mill that McCormick had built to provide his papers with newsprint. In his memoirs, Mulroney remembered the town's founder fondly: "Colonel McCormick was in fact a larger-than-life figure who dreamed the great dreams necessary to carve a thriving community out of bedrock and forest on the North Shore, while building a newspaper empire in the United States."[2]

Mulroney himself became an imposing figure with his own great dreams. After completing law school and earning respect for his skills as a labour lawyer, he was appointed executive vice-president and then president of Iron Ore Canada, a firm controlled by the M.A. Hanna Company of Cleveland. Soon after, Mulroney purchased a beautiful home in Westmount, a wealthy part of greater Montreal where the houses become more opulent the higher one travels up the mountain. When a journalist asked about the location of Mulroney's new house, the future prime minister could not hide his pride: "You know the mountain? Right at the top! Right at the fucking top!"[3]

Mulroney became Conservative Party leader in 1983 in his second run for the job. During the leadership race, he had been cautious, avoiding positions that could cost him support from party traditionalists. When the *Globe and Mail* asked about free trade with the United States, Mulroney mocked the idea, even borrowing an analogy from his political rival, Pierre Trudeau: "Now there's a real beauty for you. There's a real honey. Free trade with the United States is like sleeping with an elephant. It's terrific until the elephant twitches, and if the elephant rolls over, you are a dead man."[4] As he later admitted, "it was a less than honest position for me to take."[5]

After winning a landslide in the 1984 election, Mulroney formed a government with a promise to restore the Canadian–American friendship that had suffered in the Trudeau years. "Good relations, super relations, with the US will be the cornerstone of our foreign policy," he gushed in an interview with the *Wall Street Journal*.[6] To the Economic Club in New York, he delivered a clear

**Photo 11.1** ✦ Brian Mulroney and Ronald Reagan

Prime Minister Brian Mulroney, Mila Mulroney, President Ronald Reagan, and Nancy Reagan join the performers on stage at the conclusion of the Shamrock Summit gala in Quebec City, 17 March 1985. The two couples sang along as the chorus performed "When Irish Eyes Are Smiling." (Source: The Canadian Press/Bill Grimshaw.)

message: "Canada is open for business."[7] Then came the Shamrock Summit, the first of Mulroney's annual summits with the American president. Mulroney reassured Reagan that he would not neglect the Canadian–American relationship as Trudeau had done: "It's my baby, and I watch it like a hawk."[8]

Mulroney established close friendships with Reagan and his successor, President George H.W. Bush. Both presidents spoke in their memoirs of their warm relationship with Mulroney, which other witnesses confirmed.[9] "Reagan liked Mulroney immensely," remembered Frank Carlucci, the president's national security adviser.[10] Colin Powell, chairman of the Joint Chiefs of Staff, said that he always feared calls to Reagan from Mulroney and British prime minister Margaret Thatcher, because they "could get the president to do anything they wanted."[11] Subsequent events suggested that the friendships extended beyond politics and continued into retirement. Mulroney fished with Bush at his summer home in Kennebunkport, Maine, and the former president attended the Montreal wedding of Mulroney's daughter, Caroline, in 2000. Mulroney was the only foreigner to speak at Reagan's 2004 funeral.

## Dismantling the Nationalist Legacy

Even before Mulroney came to power, nationalist policies were under attack in Canada. In the early 1980s, the Canada Development Corporation (CDC) and Foreign Investment Review Agency (FIRA) continued, but the Trudeau government's commitment to these institutions was fragile. In 1982, the government announced that an abbreviated foreign review process, previously available for investments of up to $2 million, would now apply to any investment under $5 million. The change was not enough to placate the Reagan administration, which remained hostile to FIRA and challenged it under the General Agreement on Tariffs and Trade (GATT), the international trade agreement to which both Canada and the United States were signatories. In July 1983, a GATT panel ruled that Canada could not require foreigners to promise to purchase goods and services in Canada as a condition of FIRA's approval for their investments in the country. The Trudeau government revised the legislation and talked of changing FIRA's name to Investment Canada, all while denying that the government was watering down the screening process. The record tells a different story. In the three months before the GATT ruling, FIRA approved 99 per cent of the applications it received.[12] The Trudeau government further signaled that it was changing its international economic policies in 1982 when it appointed a royal commission to recommend a new economic strategy and in 1983 when it began flirting with the idea of sectoral free trade with the United States.

When Mulroney came to office, he buried the nationalist policies of the early 1970s. The Conservatives completed the declawing of FIRA that the Trudeau Liberals had begun. Now named Investment Canada, the agency's mandate included encouraging foreign investment. It would no longer review investments in new firms and would only screen the takeover of existing companies worth more than $5 million, up from the previous threshold of $250,000. The Mulroney government eliminated most provisions of the National Energy Program, taking advantage of falling world oil prices. The government broke up the Canada Development Corporation and sold its assets to private buyers. In 1991, the government began the privatization of Petro Canada.

## Free Trade

Mulroney believed in free trade, but he did not imagine that it would be politically possible until events in the mid-1980s changed his mind. A recession had hurt Canadian manufacturers, as had increasingly protectionist US trade policies. Under US law, the country could unilaterally impose countervailing duties whenever it believed a trading partner was subsidizing an industry and could apply anti-dumping duties if a country was selling a product at a lower cost in the United States than at home. Faced with these challenges, the Canadian Manufacturers Association, long a resolute defender of the tariff, slowly reversed its position. Other voices of corporate Canada—the Business Council on National Issues, the Canadian Export Association, the Canadian Federation of Independent Business—joined in the call for free trade. Public opinion was changing as well. A poll in June 1985 showed that 51 per cent of Canadians supported free trade, while only 32 per cent were opposed.[13]

Important, too, was the work of the Royal Commission on the Economic Union and Development Prospects for Canada, often called the Macdonald Commission after its chair, former Liberal finance minister Donald Macdonald. In a November 1984 interview, Macdonald said that Canada should make a "leap of faith" and embrace free trade with the United States, a position developed in more depth in the commission's September 1985 report.[14] Macdonald's views could not be dismissed as those of a pro-American conservative. The Trudeau government appointed the commission, and Macdonald himself had been both a protégé of the nationalist finance minister Walter Gordon and the energy minister in the early 1970s responsible for Canada's nationalist oil policies and for the creation of Petro Canada.

The Macdonald Commission provided Mulroney an opportunity. After reading an advance copy of the report, the prime minister, who was down in the polls, told his senior officials that he would use it to defeat the Liberals in the next election. Three weeks after the report's release, Mulroney was on the phone with Reagan, who shared his faith in free trade. The same day, Mulroney made a statement to the House of Commons announcing that the two countries were exploring the feasibility of a trade agreement.

Negotiations began in April 1986. The American negotiator was the shy Peter Murphy, whose superiors had given him little authority to make concessions. In contrast, Mulroney appointed Simon Reisman, a blunt and outspoken official with an explosive personality. Reisman expected the work would be the crowning achievement of his many years in Ottawa, a distinguished career that included the negotiation of the Auto Pact. With Reisman as negotiator, Mulroney believed, there could be no doubt that Canada was standing up to the Americans. But over time, Reisman became increasingly irritated with the lack of progress in the negotiations. Murphy would refuse to make concessions or, worse yet, would make a concession but then go back on it the next day.

As negotiations dragged on, Reisman found himself under increasing pressure. The US Congress had given the Reagan administration fast-track authority to reach a deal with Canada, meaning that negotiators had until midnight on the night of 3 October 1987 to conclude an agreement that could be put to a yes-or-no vote before Congress. If negotiators missed the deadline, the agreement would most certainly die, because members of the Senate or House of Representatives would be allowed to amend it to meet their political needs, needs that would conflict with those of the Canadian government. Just two weeks before the deadline, a CBC camera caught Reisman exploding in frustration at a reporter from the *Toronto Star*, Canada's largest-circulation newspaper and an opponent of free trade. Reisman called the journalist "a hack" and the *Star* a "rag" and "a very poor excuse for a newspaper."[15] The next day, Reisman reluctantly suspended negotiations, announcing that the US was refusing to respond to Canadian proposals on key issues.

Mulroney dispatched a high-level team, including two Cabinet ministers, to Washington. Desperate, last-minute negotiations were now in the hands of US Treasury secretary James Baker and Mulroney's chief of staff, Derek Burney. Ten minutes before the US deadline, the two sides reached an agreement. The messenger carrying the news arrived at Congress just one minute before midnight. It would take two more months to draft the final legal text, which Mulroney and Reagan signed in separate ceremonies on 2 January 1988.

Long and complicated, the Free Trade Agreement is difficult to assess. Most importantly, the agreement gradually removed all tariffs on goods produced in Canada or the United States over a 10-year period, beginning on 1 January 1989. In individual sectors, each side had a roughly equal number of gains and losses. The Americans agreed to an exemption for Canada's agricultural supply management system, which effectively blocked most imports of eggs, poultry, and dairy products to Canada. Canada agreed to remove many of the impediments to imports of American wine, though the agreement preserved measures that protected the powerful Canadian beer industry. The agreement enshrined the Auto Pact, meaning that Canada could continue to guarantee that a significant proportion of North American automotive manufacturing would take place north of the border. Both sides agreed to free trade in services (pretty much anything other than physical goods), but exempted transportation, as well as health, education, and social services. The exemption for the cultural sector cut both ways: Canada could continue to discriminate against foreign cultural products, but the United States could respond with "measures of equivalent commercial effect." In essence, nothing had changed on the culture front: Canada could retain its cultural policies, but the United States could retaliate.

The Americans scored significant victories on foreign investment and energy. Canada agreed not to screen the establishment of new businesses by American investors and, after 1992, to screen only the takeover of existing firms worth more than $150 million. This would stop Canada from ever again reviewing foreign investment the way FIRA had in the 1970s. Both countries pledged not to impose taxes on energy exports, beyond those applied to energy consumed domestically. In times of shortage, either country could reduce its energy exports, so long as it did so at the same rate that it reduced domestic consumption. These clauses would prevent future Canadian governments from imposing measures similar to Trudeau's National Energy Program. American negotiator Peter Murphy later acknowledged the significance of these clauses: "We didn't enter the agreement over tariffs. The Canadian agreement is a political one—to make sure you don't go back to those policies like the National Energy Policy."[16] Mulroney had already abandoned Trudeau's policies on energy and investment; the Free Trade Agreement guaranteed that they could never be restored.

Canada had yearned for guaranteed access to the American market, but had largely failed to achieve this. The United States kept its laws that allowed Congress to impose countervailing or anti-dumping duties when it believed another county was competing unfairly. This was a clear defeat for Canada, which had entered into negotiations, in part, because it wanted an end to these American practices. The best Canada could achieve was a concession that these duties could be reviewed by a binational panel to ensure that Canadian and American laws were being applied correctly. On the one hand, this was not what Canada wanted, but on the other hand, the Americans were unyielding and there was no way Canada could have achieved more. The deal contained no definition of *subsidy* and no rules for when governments could impose countervailing or anti-dumping duties, but the two countries committed to settle these issues over the next five to seven years. Negotiations took place, but the two sides could not find common ground on these vital matters.

The Free Trade Agreement set off a debate in Canada that went to the very heart of the country's identity. For the supporters of free trade, the deal was a triumph. Canada now had access to the largest market in the world, allowing Canadian manufacturers to have larger production runs, which in turn would mean that Canadian industry would be more efficient. For Canadian consumers, the agreement would lead to lower prices, as American products could enter the country duty-free. Opponents, mostly on the Canadian left, argued that the agreement spelled the death of Canada. The integration of the Canadian and American markets meant the dominance of American firms, which in turn would undermine Canadian sovereignty. Canada could only compete with the US by cutting costs, including the significant amounts Canada spent on social programs, a major symbol of Canada's distinctiveness from the United States.

The agreement was approved by the US Congress, but ran into problems in the Canadian Parliament, where it faced opposition from both the Liberals and the New Democrats. The House of Commons, where the Conservatives had a large majority, accepted the deal in August 1988, but the Liberals announced that they would block it in the Senate, where they held well over half the seats. His trade agreement in jeopardy, Mulroney decided to call an election, which he was confident he would win.

A poll released less than a week before the election call showed the Conservatives well ahead of the two other parties. The Liberals were in third place, partly because of leadership problems. In his four years as Liberal chief, John Turner appeared weak and indecisive, unable to manage his own caucus. Some pundits were predicting that his party would permanently drop to third-party status, as had the British Liberals years earlier. The Liberal image deteriorated further after the election call on 1 October. Despite piercing back pain, Turner performed well before crowds, but the media gave the impression of a failing campaign. CBC Television reported that some senior Liberal Party officials had begun discussing whether to replace Turner as party leader in the middle of the campaign.[17]

The leaders' debates would be critical. Mulroney had crushed Turner in the 1984 debate, and all signs pointed to a repeat in 1988. Turner performed poorly in the rehearsals that his aides had staged for him, and they worried about what would happen when the cameras were turned on. But Turner surprised even his own followers. In the French-language debate on 24 October, he was controlled and self-assured, forcefully attacking the Tories on their record of giving jobs to every friend in sight. The turning point came the next day in the English debate, when the discussion moved to free trade.

Two hours into the debate, Turner touched off a dramatic confrontation by accusing Mulroney of abandoning Canada's independence: "I happen to believe that you have sold us out. I happen to believe that once you . . ."

"Mr Turner, just one second," Mulroney interjected. While Turner struggled to continue, Mulroney appeared to lose his temper: "You do not have a monopoly on patriotism and I resent . . . your implication that only you are a Canadian."

Ignoring Mulroney's reprimand and repeated interruptions, Turner found the words to tap into English Canada's perennial fear of falling into Uncle Sam's grasp. "We built a country east and west and north. We built it on an infrastructure that deliberately resisted the continental pressure of the United States. For 120 years we've done it. With one signature of a pen, you've reversed that, thrown us into the north-south influence of the United States and will reduce us, I am sure, to a colony of the United States, because when the economic levers go the political independence is sure to follow."

**Photo 11.2** ✣ John Turner and Brian Mulroney

In one of the most dramatic events in Canadian political history, Liberal leader John Turner (left) accused Prime Minister Brian Mulroney of selling out Canada by signing a free trade agreement with the United States. The two were taking part in a nationally televised debate during the 1988 election campaign. (Source: The Canadian Press/Fred Chartrand.)

Mulroney was dismissive, referring to the agreement as "a commercial document that is cancellable on six months' notice."

"Commercial document?" Turner was incredulous. "That document relates to . . . every facet of our life!"

"Please be serious," Mulroney snorted.

"Well, I am serious," Turner countered, "and I've never been more serious in my life."[18]

That moment transformed the campaign. Mulroney had appeared defensive and arrogant, while Turner had established free trade as the election's sole issue. The country's future was at stake, Turner had argued, and he would save it. For a week after the debate, the Liberals rose in the polls. By 1 November, they were six points ahead of the Tories.[19]

Senior Conservatives decided that they had to smash Turner's credibility, capitalizing on the low level of public confidence in the Liberal leader. Mulroney took on the role of street fighter, aggressively attacking Turner as shameful and dishonest. "He wraps himself in the flag," Mulroney scoffed, "in the hope you won't notice he's naked underneath."[20] In response to Turner's assertion that free trade would cost many Canadians their jobs, Mulroney quipped, "It's pretty clear that the only job John Turner is interested in protecting is his own."[21] Tory advertising reinforced the message. Ten days after the debate, the party responded to criticisms of free trade with a pamphlet entitled "Ten Big Lies." One Conservative television spot claimed that Turner "lied to us on free trade and is unable to lead his own party."[22] Aimed at those most likely to respond to the negative message, Conservative ads were broadcast during daytime soap operas. Conservative Party pollster Allan Gregg explained the tactic: "I say this without a hint of condescension or of attempting to be patronizing, but there's no other way to say it—we're trying to get the real dumb ones."[23]

The Canadian business community, under an umbrella group called the Canadian Alliance for Free Trade and Job Opportunities, provided support to the Conservatives. More than $1 million was poured into an advertising campaign in support of free trade, including a four-page supplement that appeared in more than six million Canadian newspapers. At the same time, several large corporations urged their employees to support the agreement.

The Conservative assault convinced many Canadians that Turner opposed free trade because of political opportunism, not personal conviction. "Our numbers are starting to come back," Gregg told Mulroney on 6 November.[24] Five days later, he reported that Mulroney was about to win a majority. On election day, 21 November, the Conservatives won 169 seats, compared to 83 for the Liberals and 43 for the NDP.

The result fundamentally altered Canadian politics. The free trade deal went ahead, coming into effect on the first day of 1989. In the words of historian Norman Hillmer, it marked "a final recognition of Canada's inevitable destiny as a North American nation."[25] In Ottawa, Mulroney reigned supreme, the first prime minister in 30 years to win two consecutive majorities. Within a few months, Turner had announced his resignation. He had rescued the Liberals from oblivion, but could no longer fend off the critics in his own party. He was replaced by Jean Chrétien, who would accept free trade with the United States as a fact of Canada's economic life.

Shortly after the Free Trade Agreement came into effect, the United States and Mexico announced that they would begin negotiating a bilateral trade pact. Canada asked to join them to create a trilateral agreement, with the Canada–US Free Trade Agreement providing a template for a new North American Free Trade Agreement (NAFTA). Virtually all the key provisions of the earlier agreement were carried over to this new accord, signed in December 1992 by Mulroney, George H.W. Bush, and Mexican president Carlos Salinas. NAFTA had yet to be passed by the US Congress and the Canadian Parliament by the time Bush and Mulroney left office in 1993, leaving an important issue for their successors to handle.

The economic impacts of the Canada–US Free Trade Agreement and NAFTA have generated considerable discussion among scholars. The

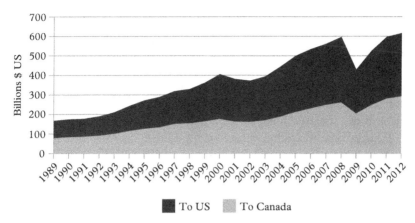

**Figure 11.1** ❖ Merchandise Trade between Canada and the US, 1989–2012

Source: Data provided by United States International Trade Commission, Interactive Tariff and Trade DataWeb, http://dataweb.usitc.gov/.

consensus has been that the agreements had a positive impact on the countries involved. Factories moved and people lost jobs, but these were only short-term adjustments. Although there was a recession in the early 1990s, it had little to do with trade agreements; it was primarily the product of government spending cuts and the efforts of central banks to prevent inflation. Over the long term, the trade agreements increased productivity, exports, investment, and employment.[26]

# Acid Rain

Cross-border pollution had long been a challenge for Canada and the United States. Canadians imagined the problem was that pollution drifted up from the United States, but often it flowed the other way, as was the case with the dispute over the smelter in Trail, BC, during the 1920s and 1930s. By the 1980s, emissions from industry and automobiles were causing acid rain, which in turn was damaging the environment, killing freshwater fish and preventing trees from growing. Residents of Sudbury, Ontario, knew acid rain all too well. Until the early 1970s, when mining giant INCO built the Superstack, then the world's tallest chimney, the company's smelter pumped millions of tons of pollution into the Sudbury environment every year. The city's lakes were polluted, trees could not grow, and the pinkish-grey rock in the landscape turned black. The city looked like the surface of the moon.

For the Reagan administration, the environment was a low priority. Reagan once suggested that trees and vegetation were a serious cause of pollution.[27] His secretary of the interior, James Watt, was a fundamentalist Christian who made an odd statement about the environment before a committee of the House of Representatives, suggesting that it was not necessary to protect the environment because the Second Coming of Christ was at hand. He believed that the environment should be preserved for future generations. But then he added, "I do not know how many future generations we can count on before the Lord returns."[28] On another occasion, Watt said that environmentalists wanted "centralized planning and control of the society," ideas he equated with Naziism and communism.[29] The Reagan administration relaxed pollution regulations and slashed the budget of the Environmental Protection Agency. As scientists were developing a consensus that industrial emissions caused acid rain, the Reagan administration insisted that more research was needed. When a panel of scientists, appointed by the White House, recommended immediate action on acid rain in 1983, the administration dismissed the report. The Trudeau government could find few sympathetic ears when it raised the acid rain issue in Washington in the early 1980s.

Yet over time, Mulroney did achieve success on acid rain. He and Reagan agreed to appoint two high-level envoys—former US transportation secretary Drew Lewis and former Ontario premier Bill Davis—to prepare a report on the issue. Submitted in January 1986, the report recommended that the US government and American industry spend $5 billion over five years on pollution control, though Lewis and Davis did not propose any targets for emission reductions. Under pressure from Mulroney, Reagan endorsed the report in March, the first time the president acknowledged that pollution caused acid rain. Yet the US government put no money into implementing the recommendations, and Reagan's energy secretary, John Herrington, described the problem as "small," insisting that there was no urgency in dealing with it.[30] The administration agreed to provide funding only after Mulroney intervened directly with Vice-President Bush and after Canadian officials warned their American counterparts that Reagan's failure to act was undermining Mulroney at home. In 1987, Reagan overruled his advisers and agreed that the United States could negotiate an acid rain agreement with Canada. But the president did not keep a close watch on the negotiations, and they went nowhere.

Significant progress on acid rain was only possible after Reagan left the White House and was replaced by Bush, who was genuinely concerned about the environment. In 1991, Bush and Mulroney signed the Canada–US Air Quality Agreement, in which both countries agreed to reduce the emissions of sulfur dioxide and nitrogen oxides, the compounds that cause acid rain. Over 20 years, American emissions of sulfur dioxide fell by 67 per cent and Canada's by 57 per cent. From 2000 to 2010, the US had a 42 per cent drop in emissions of nitrogen oxides, while Canada had a 40 per cent reduction.[31] Without Mulroney's constant pressure and close connection to two American presidents, the agreement would not have happened.

# The *Polar Sea* and the Arctic

The United States reignited the debate over Arctic waters when it sent a Coast Guard icebreaker, the *Polar Sea*, through the Northwest Passage in August 1985. This dispute was not over Canadian sovereignty, as it has often been portrayed. In fact, the US recognized Canadian sovereignty in the area while also asserting that Canada had no right to prevent peaceful foreign vessels from navigating the Northwest Passage, a position that is not contradictory in international law. For the Americans, there was an international strait that passed through Canadian *territorial* waters, allowing US ships the right of innocent passage through the area.

The Mulroney government announced its position in September. Canada now formally claimed the Northwest Passage as Canadian *internal* waters, meaning that there could be no international strait and that no other country had the right to navigate the area. Canada would allow commercial shipping through the Northwest Passage, so long as other countries sought permission, but would also begin building the world's largest and most powerful icebreaker to assert Canada's claim over the waterway. To settle the legal dispute, Canada would seek bilateral discussions with the US and allow the issue to go to the International Court of Justice.

Negotiations with the United States were unsuccessful. Mulroney discussed the issue directly with Reagan during the president's April 1987 visit to Ottawa, but made little progress at first. Reagan insisted that accepting Canada's claim over the Northwest Passage would have a negative effect on the US military's right to use other strategic waterways around the world. But then Reagan had a private word with his national security adviser, Frank Carlucci: "I think we ought to do something for Brian."[32] With Mulroney elsewhere in the house, Reagan and his key officials met in the prime minister's living room for two hours, trying to draft a new US position on the Northwest Passage. "It was the only time I saw Ronald Reagan lose his temper," Carlucci later recalled. Carlucci was reluctant to abandon his country's traditional stand, but Reagan turned and snapped, "You do it."[33] Reagan announced in his address to the House of Commons later the same day, "The prime minister and I also had a full discussion of the Arctic waters issue, and he and I agreed to inject new impetus to the discussions already underway. We are determined to find a solution based on mutual respect for sovereignty and our common security and other issues."

Mulroney had convinced Reagan to restart the stalled discussions and, finally, in January 1988, the two countries signed the Arctic Cooperation

Agreement. Each country held fast to its position on the Northwest Passage, but the US agreed to seek Canadian permission before US ships sailed in what Canada claimed were internal waters, and Canada agreed that it would grant that permission. In 1990, just before construction was about to begin, Canada abandoned the project to build a large icebreaker. No longer viewed as necessary, the project now became a victim of budget cuts.

## The Strategic Defense Initiative

In 1983, President Reagan proposed the Strategic Defense Initiative (SDI), a research program to develop a system that would defend the United States from a nuclear attack. The initiative was quickly nicknamed Star Wars, because it called for laser battle stations on earth and in space to intercept intercontinental ballistic missiles. Any missiles that made it through this first layer of protection would be shot down by land- and air-based missiles. The US Congress approved initial funding despite arguments from critics who claimed the program would launch a new arms race with the Soviets and objections from technical experts who insisted it was not feasible.

The US government invited Canada to participate in SDI, promising that Canadian companies would receive about $30 million a year in research contracts, but Mulroney feared the project's domestic political implications.[34] The Reagan administration was unpopular in Canada, with many Canadians seeing the president as a dangerous hawk; Mulroney did not want to risk cooperating with Reagan on a high-profile defence project. The timing was particularly important: Mulroney made his decisions on free trade and SDI at the same time, linking the two issues in his mind. He feared that he could not both sign a free trade agreement with the US and take part in SDI without looking like Ronald Reagan's puppet. The prime minister decided that the Canadian government would take no part in the project, but that Canadian companies and universities were welcome to contribute to the research. Meanwhile, by defending SDI in public, Mulroney helped prevent tensions developing between Canada and the United States over the issue.

## The Gulf War

The Cold War came to a sudden end while Mulroney was prime minister. In 1989, the Soviet Union withdrew its troops from Eastern Europe and allowed democratic elections in the communist countries in the region. The East German government announced that it would allow its citizens to leave and began dismantling the Berlin Wall, the barrier separating the eastern and western sectors of the city that had become a symbol of the Cold War. The Soviet republics (provinces or states divided on ethnic lines) began proclaiming their independence. On Christmas Day 1991 Soviet President Mikhail Gorbachev resigned, declaring that the Soviet Union had ceased to exist.

Reagan's supporters maintained that the US president had won the Cold War by starting a new arms race that forced the Soviets to spend until they destroyed their economy. Others insisted that Reagan was not as far-sighted as his supporters claimed and that it was primarily longstanding internal problems, including low productivity and a demoralized workforce, that brought down the Soviet Union.

Many hoped that the end of the Cold War would lead to a long era of global peace, but instead the world faced a series of regional conflicts, the first of which began when Iraq invaded and annexed Kuwait in August 1990. There was little justification for Iraq's actions, motivated above all by desires to seize Kuwait's large oil reserves and to cancel a large debt that Iraq owed to Kuwait. The UN condemned the invasion and gave a deadline of 15 January 1991 for Iraq to withdraw from Kuwait.

Throughout the crisis, Canada was firmly onside with the Americans. In public, Mulroney fully supported the United States and rejected efforts to have Iraq withdraw peacefully in exchange for the initiation of a large international process to settle the outstanding disputes in the Middle East. Behind closed doors, Canada urged the Americans to ensure that the UN approved any military response and to operate within a broad coalition, and the Americans did just that.

For the first time since the Korean War, Canada dispatched troops into combat. Canada's contribution was modest, consisting of a squadron of fighter aircraft, two destroyers, a supply ship, and an army field hospital. US-led coalition forces began an aerial bombardment of Iraq on 16 January. Beginning on 24 February, the coalition launched a ground campaign, which was over in four days, after Iraqi forces were battered and driven from Kuwait. In the peace settlement, Iraq agreed to recognize Kuwait's independence and to abandon all weapons of mass destruction. Afraid of getting bogged down in Iraq as it had in Vietnam, the United States did not insist on the removal of Iraqi dictator Saddam Hussein, who would continue in power for years as a source of exasperation to the Americans, some of whom wondered why the Bush-led coalition had not finished the job by driving to the Iraqi capital of Baghdad and eliminating the dictator.

# Summary

No Canadian prime minister worked harder to get along with the United States than Brian Mulroney. He built strong personal relationships with Ronald Reagan and George H.W. Bush. Without Mulroney and without his connections in the White House, it was unlikely that Canada would have entered into a comprehensive free trade agreement with the United States or that the US would have signed on to the acid rain agreement. At the same time, there were limits to Mulroney's approach. The best he could achieve on the Northwest Passage was a document declaring that the two sides would agree to disagree. The Canadian and US positions on the Arctic were incompatible, and there was nothing Mulroney could do in the face of entrenched American interests. The domestic political situation provided further constraints on the Mulroney method. The prime minister understood that he would be seen as too close to the Americans should he choose to negotiate a free trade agreement and join the Strategic Defense Initiative at the same time. Personality mattered, but only so much.

## Beyond the Book

1. What are the costs and benefits of a close personal relationship between a Canadian prime minister and an American president?
2. How would you assess the Free Trade Agreement?
3. Is free trade now a way of life for North America or are there reasons for Canada and the United States to rethink their agreement?

## Further Reading

There is still much research to be done on Canadian–American relations in the Mulroney years. Some initial work can be found in Nelson Michaud and Kim Richard Nossal, eds., *Diplomatic Departures: The Conservative Era in Canadian Foreign Policy, 1984–93* (Vancouver: UBC Press, 2001). Particularly useful are the chapters by Tammy L. Nemeth on energy policy, Heather A. Smith on the environment, and Rob Huebert on Arctic sovereignty. More on the Arctic can be found in Christopher Kirkey, "Smoothing Troubled Waters: The 1988 Canada–United States Arctic Co-operation Agreement," *International Journal* 50, no. 2 (Spring 1995): 401–26. For a critical view of Mulroney's approach from a senior journalist, see Lawrence Martin's lively and provocative book, *Pledge of Allegiance: The Americanization of Canada in the Mulroney Years* (Toronto: McClelland and Stewart, 1993).

On the views of the leaders, see Brian Mulroney, *Memoirs, 1939–1993* (Toronto: McClelland and Stewart, 2007); Ronald Reagan, *An American Life* (New York: Simon and Schuster, 1990); Ronald Reagan, *The Reagan Diaries*, edited by Douglas Brinkley (New York: HarperCollins, 2007); and George Bush and Brent Scowcroft, *A World Transformed* (New York: Alfred A. Knopf, 1998). Peter C. Newman's *The Secret Mulroney Tapes: Unguarded Confessions of a Prime Minister* ([Toronto]: Random House, 2005) contains little of substance on Canadian–American relations, but does offer glimpses into Mulroney's expansive personality.

There is no shortage of literature on the negotiation of the Free Trade Agreement. No source is better than G. Bruce Doern and Brian Tomlin, *Faith and*

*Fear: The Free Trade Story* (Toronto: Stoddart, 1991). Several participants cover the agreement in their memoirs: Derek H. Burney, *Getting it Done: A Memoir* (Montreal and Kingston: McGill–Queen's University Press, 2005); Michael Hart with Bill Dymond and Colin Robertson, *Decision at Midnight: Inside the Canada–US Free-Trade Negotiations* (Vancouver: UBC Press, 1994); and Gordon Ritchie, *Wrestling with the Elephant: The Inside Story of Canada–US Trade Wars* (Toronto: Macfarlane Walter and Ross, 1997).

The best work on the pivotal 1988 Canadian election is Graham Fraser, *Playing for Keeps: The Making of the Prime Minister, 1988* (Toronto: McClelland and Stewart, 1989). Also valuable are Alan Frizzell, Jon H. Pammett, and Anthony Westell, *The Canadian General Election of 1988* (Ottawa: Carleton University Press, 1989); Robert Mason Lee, *One Hundred Monkeys: The Triumph of Popular Wisdom in Canadian Politics* (Toronto: Macfarlane Walter and Ross, 1989); Gerald Caplan, Michael Kirby, and Hugh Segal, *Election: The Issues, the Strategies, the Aftermath* (Scarborough, Ontario: Prentice–Hall, 1989); and Rick Salutin, *Waiting for Democracy: A Citizen's Journal* (Markham, Ontario: Viking, 1989).

Allan Gotlieb, Canada's ambassador to Washington through most of the Mulroney years, has published two important books. The first deals with the process of Canadian–American relations, specifically how an ambassador works in Washington, told through examples from Gotlieb's career: *"I'll Be with You in a Minute, Mr Ambassador": The Education of a Canadian Diplomat in Washington* (Toronto: University of Toronto Press, 1991). Gotlieb's second volume provides a day-to-day account of his work in the American capital: *The Washington Diaries, 1981–1989* (Toronto: McClelland and Stewart, 2006).

# CHAPTER 12

⁓

# Unipolarity, since 1993

## The United States and
## Canada after the Cold War

## Introduction

In February 2002, almost 1,000 members of the Canadian Forces went off to war in Afghanistan, where they would be integrated into a US Army task force. Canadian planners had never imagined that so many soldiers would end up fighting in an arid climate and had not stocked the appropriate uniforms for the troops. While soldiers from allied nations were wearing tan-coloured uniforms that camouflaged them in the desert, the Canadians had only heavy, dark-green outfits, suitable for combat in cooler, wooded areas. Domestic suppliers reported that they could not provide the necessary uniforms until mid-July.

US officials proposed a solution. The Pentagon, headquarters of the Department of Defense, offered to sell desert camouflage uniforms to Canada, guaranteeing delivery in 10 days. But Canadian officials declined, worried about the negative publicity if the nation knew that members of the Canadian Forces were wearing American uniforms, even with the Canadian flag attached. Officials also feared that morale would suffer if the soldiers learned the origin of their clothing.

So Canadian troops went off to fight in the desert wearing dark green, with the government insisting that they were in no additional danger. After all, the darker uniforms were safer for nighttime combat, and Canadian soldiers could always drape themselves in sand-coloured capes if they wished. Long accustomed to government neglect, the troops were annoyed, but responded in good humour. Referring to the speckled green uniforms, Lieutenant Colonel Pat Stogran called his men "the relish jars from hell."[1]

The incident said much about Canadian attitudes toward the United States. Canadian troops were fighting side by side with the Americans in a US-led mission. Yet Canadian officials were preoccupied by what the public would think should it be discovered that the country's soldiers were outfitted in uniforms supplied by the United States. The reality of Canada's close military relationship with the United States mattered less than the public image of Canadian independence. In a unipolar world, a world where the United States was the only superpower and had greater strength relative to its rivals than ever before, it was crucial that Canada have good relations with its neighbour. But Canadians were also anxious—sometimes irrationally so—to assert their autonomy.

# Jean Chrétien and the Americans

Jean Chrétien's background contained some striking similarities to that of Brian Mulroney. Both came from small Quebec towns where many families depended on American money for their livelihood. In Chrétien's case, the place was Shawinigan Falls, now simply called Shawinigan. Chrétien's father was a machinist at a paper mill owned by a Canadian company, Consolidated Paper, but many of the other workers relied on American firms for their jobs. Shawinigan's major employers included Canadian Industries Limited (a subsidiary of the American-owned DuPont chemical company), Canadian Resins and Chemicals (more than half owned by Union Carbide of New York), the Aluminum Company of Canada (controlled by the same investors who owned the Aluminum Company of America), St Maurice Chemicals (half owned by Heyden Chemical Corporation of New York), and Shawinigan Resins (half owned by the Monsanto Chemical Company of St Louis). When Mackenzie King negotiated a trade agreement with the United States in 1935, the year after Chrétien was born, the chief beneficiaries included several companies in Shawinigan Falls, because the agreement lowered US duties on chemicals, one of the town's main exports.[2] American trade and investment were essential to local prosperity.

Chrétien was first elected to Parliament in 1963, and quickly became a protégé of Mitchell Sharp, the Cabinet minister who had consistently opposed Walter Gordon's efforts to limit American investment in Canada. Later, as Pierre Trudeau's minister responsible for the Foreign Investment Review Agency (FIRA), Chrétien made it clear he believed that continued infusions of foreign capital were essential for Canadian prosperity. But Chrétien was never particularly pro-American. Unlike Mulroney, Chrétien never knew the United States very well and had few American friends.

Chrétien's first task upon taking over the leadership of the Liberal Party in 1990 was to shake off the party's anti–free trade position. The key moment was a 1991 conference in Aylmer, Quebec, when liberal-minded thinkers came together to discuss the politics and policies of the future. "Protectionism is not left-wing or right-wing," Chrétien said in his closing address. "It is simply passé."[3]

At the same time, Chrétien wanted to be sure that he was never seen as too chummy with the Americans. When he was leader of the opposition, Chrétien frequently criticized Mulroney for his close relationship with US president George H.W. Bush. Chrétien promised not to let personal relationships interfere with his pursuit of Canadian interests, as he charged Mulroney had done. "Business is business and friendship is friendship," he told a *Washington Post* reporter. "You cannot mix the two."[4] But this position was primarily about domestic political tactics, not international diplomacy. "I like to stand up to the Americans," he told fellow NATO leaders at a 1997 meeting in Madrid, four years into his term as prime minister. "It's popular . . . people like it, but you have to be very careful because they're our friends."[5]

Despite his desire to maintain his distance, Chrétien developed a friendship with Bill Clinton, becoming one of thousands to fall under the

**Photo 12.1** ✧ Bill Clinton and John Chrétien

Prime Minister Jean Chrétien (right) promised he would not become too close to the US president, criticizing Brian Mulroney for going fishing with George H.W. Bush. Still, Chrétien enjoyed Bill Clinton's company. (Source: The Canadian Press/Andrew Vaughan.)

president's mysterious charm. "I wanted our relationship to be friendly yet professional," Chrétien later recalled. "But Clinton proved a very hard guy not to get close to. We both came from modest circumstances, small towns, and rural areas. We frequently talked on the phone or exchanged letters."[6] After having criticized Mulroney for fishing with George H.W. Bush, Chrétien was careful never to go fishing with Clinton, but did golf with the president a dozen times.

# The Trade Agenda

Immediately upon becoming prime minister in November 1993, Chrétien was caught in a dilemma. During the election campaign, his party had attacked the North American Free Trade Agreement (NAFTA), which the Mulroney government had negotiated with the United States and Mexico but had yet to ratify. The Liberal Party promised to renegotiate the deal to include "a subsidies code; an anti-dumping code; a more effective dispute resolution mechanism; and the same energy protection as Mexico." The Liberals also threatened that Canada would refuse to ratify NAFTA and would cancel Mulroney's Free Trade Agreement with the United States as "a last resort if satisfactory changes cannot be negotiated."[7] But Chrétien did not really mean it. He was not about to reopen negotiations on NAFTA, which would have effectively scuttled the deal. Nor did he have any intention of cancelling the Canada–US Free Trade Agreement. Instead, the new prime minister engaged in a bit of political trickery. The NAFTA partners agreed to create working groups to come up with definitions of *subsidy* and *dumping*, a largely meaningless pledge after the failure of similar panels created under the earlier Free Trade Agreement. The Americans might agree to talk about definitions but, as Canadian trade consultant Peter Clark pointed out, "they never agreed to agree."[8] Sure enough, the three sides never saw eye to eye on what constituted subsidies and dumping. Another empty gesture was a statement from the three governments that no country had a right to another's water resources, an announcement that merely restated the terms of the NAFTA agreement. Finally, unable to convince the United States to make even a hollow gesture on energy, the Chrétien government issued a unilateral declaration, saying that Canada would "interpret and apply the NAFTA in a way which maximizes energy security for Canadians," a statement that in no way overrode Canada's commitments under the agreement, as American officials were quick to point out.[9]

Having accepted NAFTA, Chrétien proceeded to make trade one of his government's priorities. In 1994, he led the first Team Canada trade mission, with nine premiers and hundreds of businesspeople accompanying him to China, where Chinese and Canadian firms signed $9 billion in agreements. Subsequent Team Canada trips went to South Asia (1996); South Korea, the Philippines, and Thailand (1997); Latin America (1998); Japan (1999); and back to China (2001). After the first trip, Chrétien said that the goal was to diversify Canadian trade to avoid an overreliance on the American market, but a 2001 Team Canada trip to Dallas and Los Angeles showed that the real objective was to increase all Canadian trade, even with the United States. Under Chrétien, the Canadian government was also an enthusiastic supporter of the new World Trade Organization (WTO), which began operating in 1995. The organization had a more effective dispute resolution system than the GATT secretariat, the WTO's predecessor as the governing body for international trade agreements. Countries would now have the opportunity to pursue binding and relatively quick solutions to trade disputes.

Still, there were problems with the trade agenda during the Chrétien years, the most prominent over softwood lumber, essential for the construction of homes. The issue was a recurring nightmare for Canadian trade negotiators, haunting governments from the early 1980s. In the US, logging is conducted on private land, which companies either purchase or lease, or on public land, with the logging rights auctioned off to the highest bidder. In Canada, most logging is on land owned by provincial governments, which charge companies a stumpage fee, a small charge for each tree they harvest. In general, Canadian companies pay less than their American counterparts for the right to cut trees, which in the minds of US trade officials constituted an unfair subsidy. In 1986, the US imposed a 15 per cent duty on Canadian softwood lumber. The two sides then quickly agreed that the US would lift its duty, and that Canada would impose its own 15 per cent tax, to be phased out as the provinces increased their stumpage fees. The Americans were pleased that the agreement increased the cost of Canadian lumber on the American market, and the Canadians were satisfied in knowing that the tax revenues would be going to the government of Canada, not the US. During the drafting of the Canada–US Free Trade Agreement, the two sides agreed to continue the 1986 softwood lumber agreement.

Canada exercised its right to cancel the softwood lumber agreement in 1991, arguing that the problem had been solved by increases in stumpage fees, which rendered the Canadian duty unnecessary. The US quickly imposed retaliatory duties. With the two countries in the midst of NAFTA negotiations, Mulroney was furious. "If you had told me that some tinpot dictator in some tiny little country somewhere was engaging in this kind of harassment, I'd say, 'So what else is new?' But for the United States, this is most unworthy."[10] Several panels established under the Free Trade Agreement and the GATT agreement reviewed the case and sided with

Canada. The US finally backed down in 1994, rescinding the duty and agreeing to refund $800 million to Canadian companies if Canada would enter into discussions about trade in softwood lumber. Despite the favourable decisions of numerous trade panels, Canadian officials concluded that the US would continue to discriminate against Canadian softwood lumber until the two sides negotiated a settlement.

In 1996, the two countries signed a five-year agreement. Canada pledged that only 14.7 billion board feet of lumber would enter the United States duty-free per year and that there would be an export tax on any additional lumber going to the United States. In the meantime, the two sides continued to look for a permanent settlement. When the five-year pact expired in 2001, they had not yet solved the problem, and the US Congress again imposed duties on Canadian lumber. Canada immediately complained to the WTO. Although Canada again won, the US would not back down. The two sides returned to the bargaining table, but all they could do was draft another temporary agreement, signed in 2006, more than 30 years after the dispute first erupted. Under the seven-year deal, the United States agreed to return most of the duties it had charged (giving back about $4 billion of the $5 billion the US had collected), and Canada agreed to limit lumber exports and to impose export taxes. In 2013, the agreement was extended for another two years. In essence, the Canadian government had accepted that it could not litigate forever and would have to seek a compromise, despite having a winning hand under international trade law. Having a strong case did not mean that Canada would prevail—so the two sides had to continually return to the negotiating table to reconcile their differences.

## Canadian Unity

Unity has been the most persistent domestic problem for Canadian governments, one that has often bled into the country's foreign relations. In the early Chrétien years, the challenge to Canada came from a resurgent separatist movement in Quebec. After the 1993 federal election, the second-largest party in the House of Commons was the Bloc Québécois, a separatist party that became the official opposition after winning 54 of Quebec's 75 seats. In 1994, the Parti Québécois returned to power in Quebec with a promise of holding a vote on the province's independence. When the referendum campaign began in September 1995, Chrétien was confident the federalist forces would win, but he had not realized the extent to which a vaguely worded, misleading referendum question could undermine the federalist position. Nor could he have known what would happen when Premier Jacques Parizeau surrendered the leadership of the *yes* side.

Down in the polls three weeks before the vote, Parizeau handed the campaign to Lucien Bouchard, the mercurial and magnetic leader of the Bloc Québécois in Ottawa. Separatist fortunes quickly rose, and soon the *yes* and *no* sides were tied. Then suddenly the separatists were ahead. The future of the country was at stake, and the Chrétien government was left scrambling.

The US government was deeply troubled. Since at least the 1970s, the US had judged that its interests lay with a united, stable Canada on the northern border. Less than two weeks before voting day, with the separatists ahead in the polls, Secretary of State Warren Christopher told a press conference that he did not wish to intervene in Canadian domestic politics, but that he did "want to emphasize the very, very important value that we place—the high value that we place on the relationships that we have with a strong and united Canada."[11] But officials in both Washington and Ottawa believed that a statement had to come from the president himself. Clinton was enormously popular in Quebec, with a 74 per cent approval rating, higher than that of any other politician—even Bouchard.[12] Five days before the referendum, Clinton carefully waded in, telling a press conference that the issue was "for the Canadian people to decide," but that "a strong and united Canada has been a wonderful partner for the United States and an incredibly important and constructive citizen throughout the entire world." Canada had been "a strong and powerful ally of ours," and he hoped that would continue.[13] On referendum night, the early returns showed the *yes* side in the lead. It looked like the country was lost. Finally, after two hours of counting, the *no* side edged ahead and held on for the rest of the night. It is impossible to know how many votes, if any, Clinton swayed, but given the close result of the vote—the federalists won with 50.6 per cent of the vote to 49.4 for the separatists—it is likely that Clinton's statement was one of several factors that made a difference.

## Human Security and the Environment

In the mid-1990s, the Chrétien government adopted a new policy in foreign affairs, one that occasionally put Canada on a different path from that of the United States. The key figure was Lloyd Axworthy, Canada's activist foreign minister from 1996 to 2000. The United States had been a crucial part of Axworthy's intellectual formation. In the 1960s and early 1970s, he had pursued his graduate studies at Princeton University, where he came to admire the optimistic rhetoric of President John Kennedy and the idealism of the civil rights activists. "I came away from the U.S. with respect for both its power and its capacity to use that power positively in the international arena," Axworthy wrote in his memoirs. "I remain an admirer of the incredible creativity and enormous resources of American universities, think tanks, research centres and foundations for innovation and public problem solving. And I became fascinated with the open and dynamic quality of American politics." But as with many Canadians, Axworthy's experience with the United States brought his Canadian identity to the fore. "It was while living and studying in the U.S. that I came to appreciate that although we share a continent, are closely tied economically, watch U.S. television and movies and rely on Washington's goodwill to manage our border, we are not Americans."[14]

Axworthy came to believe that, with the end of the Cold War, Canada's foreign policy should concentrate more on human security—the safety and well-being of individuals—and less on state security. Military force would still be necessary, but Canada could achieve many of its goals with soft power, a concept Axworthy had borrowed from Harvard political scientist Joseph Nye. According to Nye, hard power consisted of "tangible resources like military and economic strength," while soft power was the use of intangible resources to get "others to want what you want."[15] Under Axworthy, Canadian diplomats would work to convince other countries to sign on to international treaties to deal with child soldiers, the small arms trade, drug trafficking, transnational organized crime, and other global problems. Axworthy believed that soft power played to Canadian strengths in "negotiating, building coalitions and presenting diplomatic initiatives; in other words, for influencing the behaviour of other nations not through military intimidation, but through a variety of diplomatic tools."[16] For Nye, Axworthy's approach made a lot of sense, though he warned that it should not be allowed to degenerate into an exercise in US-bashing: "Sticking a finger in the American eye might make you feel self-righteous, but you won't have changed the world."[17]

Axworthy's signature cause was the elimination of anti-personnel landmines, which killed 10,000 people a year—90 per cent of them civilians—and injured another 16,000.[18] He worked closely with American political activist Jody Williams, head of the International Campaign to Ban Landmines, a coalition of non-governmental organizations. In 1996, Axworthy launched what became known as the Ottawa Process by organizing a meeting in Canada's capital of 50 countries, including the United States. At the end of the event, Axworthy called for the signing in Ottawa of an international agreement prohibiting the use of landmines, before the end of the next year. In 1997, the representatives of 122 countries signed the Ottawa Convention (also known as the Mine Ban Treaty), with Canada being the first country both to sign and to ratify the agreement. Eventually, more than 160 countries signed and ratified, but there were several conspicuous exceptions, including Russia, China, and, most importantly, the United States. President Bill Clinton had helped spark the anti-landmine movement when he endorsed a ban in a 1994 speech to the United Nations General Assembly, but the US armed forces saw mines as a military necessity, particularly in the demilitarized zone between North and South Korea. Still, the Clinton administration supported the cause, putting forward a considerable amount of money to decommission landmines in the developing world, spending 10 times as much as Canada on the campaign.[19]

The International Criminal Court (ICC) was another Canadian initiative that received a mixed response from the United States. After the Second World War, the allies put senior German and Japanese officials on trial for war crimes, crimes against peace, and crimes against humanity. In the Nuremberg and Tokyo trials, several were found guilty and were sentenced either to prison or to death. But the international community did not establish a permanent court to deal with war crimes, and, as a result, the verdicts were often dismissed as nothing more than victor's justice. In 1948, the UN General Assembly proposed the establishment of a permanent court, but the idea was lost in the politics of the Cold War. Only in the 1990s, after atrocities in Rwanda and the former Yugoslavia, was there again strong impetus to create a permanent criminal court, with the United Nations General Assembly organizing a conference in Rome in 1998 to deal with the issue.

Canada played a leading role in the discussions that led to the Rome Statute, which established the ICC as a court of last resort in those cases where domestic courts refused to deal with genocide, war crimes, and crimes against humanity. A Canadian diplomat, Philippe Kirsch, chaired the commission that produced the final text of the statute and became the court's first president. The statute passed by a vote of 120 to 7, with the US in the minority alongside human rights abusers like Libya and Iraq. President Clinton was sympathetic, but faced opposition from the US military and from Republicans in Congress. Concerned about politically motivated prosecutions of American officials, the United States pushed for the ICC to hear only cases referred from the UN Security Council, meaning the US government would have a veto over court prosecutions. Canada and like-minded states rejected this argument. In his last month in office, Clinton signed the treaty, but did nothing to win Congressional approval for it. His successor, President George W. Bush, son of the first president Bush, repudiated the US commitment in 2002.

A similarly ambiguous US position emerged on the environment. In 1997, almost 40 industrialized nations signed the Kyoto Protocol, an agreement to reduce greenhouse gas emissions in an effort to halt climate change. Canada pledged to reduce its emissions by six per cent of 1990 levels by 2012, while the US promised a seven per cent reduction over the same period. By 2001, it was clear that the US Senate would not ratify the treaty, which was also opposed by President George W. Bush. Canada ratified the protocol in December 2002, but without a plan for achieving the required emission reductions. After coming to office in 2006, the Conservative government of Prime Minister Stephen Harper made it clear that it would not implement the terms of the Kyoto Protocol, formally pulling Canada out of the agreement in 2011. Instead, Canada would follow the American lead and implement less stringent goals to reduce greenhouse gases.

The Chrétien government's foreign policies were generally popular in Canada, though they were often attacked by the country's international relations scholars. Some saw Canada as engaged in "pulpit diplomacy," moralizing and grandstanding instead of using traditional diplomatic methods to pursue real change.[20] Others saw the human security agenda as "pinchpenny diplomacy," an effort to conduct foreign policy on the cheap. For political scientist Kim Nossal, soft power, at least as employed by the Chrétien government, was "little more than an elaborate justification for not spending more on so-called 'hard' power resources, such as well-equipped military forces, well-endowed intelligence services, and a diplomatic service that is not constantly being downsized and reorganized."[21]

Certainly, the Chrétien government's ambitious foreign policy came at the same time Canada was slashing spending on diplomacy, defence, and international development. The Department of Foreign Affairs found its budget cut by about one-third in the 1990s, resulting in a poorly paid and demoralized foreign service.[22] Canada's foreign aid budget was reduced from 0.44 per cent of the country's gross domestic product (GDP) in 1993–4 to 0.25 per cent in 2001–2.[23] Funding for the Department of National Defence shrank 23 per cent from 1993 to 1998.[24] Long the most important contributor to peacekeeping around the world, Canada was 34th on the 2002 list of countries ranked by the number of troops that they dedicated to UN peacekeeping missions.[25]

The human security agenda often created tensions between the Canadian and US governments. Axworthy's goal was to strengthen and expand international law, for which the Bush administration had little time. On landmines and the International Criminal Court, the two countries found themselves on different sides. Canada's military weaknesses also came in for criticism from the United States. US Ambassador Paul Cellucci repeatedly complained that Canada was not spending enough on defence. John Hamre, deputy secretary of defense, noted the irony in the US position: "We look to Canada, frankly, with a bit of alarm. . . . We are the only country in the world that wants a stronger military power on its border."[26]

Despite the complaints about the state of the Canadian military, Canada did maintain a combat-capable military throughout the Chrétien years and begin increasing funding for the armed forces in 2000. When Yugoslavia broke into warring provinces at the end of the Cold War, Canadian troops were part of the 1992–5 UN force sent to establish peace in Croatia and in Bosnia and Herzegovina. Canada supported the 1995 NATO bombing of Bosnian Serb targets, though the Canadian air force did not take part. Canada contributed to the NATO force that implemented the Dayton Accords, which the belligerents had negotiated, under US pressure, in 1995. Then in 1999, the Canadian air force took part in the NATO bombing of Serb targets in Kosovo, and Canadian troops were part of the subsequent mission to establish peace there. For Axworthy, these uses of hard power were in the cause of human security. Canada, along with its NATO allies, had fostered the security of individuals by putting an end to the massacres in the former Yugoslavia.

## The Culture/Trade Quandary

The Canadian and US governments had long differed in how they approached popular culture. For Canadian officials, a distinctive culture was essential to the maintenance of a Canadian identity in the face of an overwhelming American presence. But US officials spoke not of culture, but of entertainment, which was merely another product in the marketplace. A television, for instance, was "just another appliance—it's a toaster with pictures," to quote one senior American official.[27] And what of Canada's claim that it needed to protect its culture? US trade representative Charlene Barshefsky responded that Canada and other countries often used the word *culture* "as an excuse to take commercial advantage of the United States."[28]

For decades, the US had opposed the cultural policies of the Canadian government. American officials argued in 1956 that Canada's magazine tax violated the GATT agreement. They complained in 1961 about television quotas imposed by Canada and several other countries, but the GATT secretariat was unable to settle the dispute. In 1965, Americans similarly claimed that Canadian magazine policies contravened the country's international obligations. Yet the US never retaliated, despite being convinced that Canada's cultural policies violated the country's international trade agreements.

The dynamic began to change in the 1990s. Trade was becoming more important to the US economy, and entertainment was, by 1999, the country's largest export. American media companies were merging, becoming larger and more powerful, better able to advance their interests in Washington. The US was increasingly inclined to challenge the cultural policies of foreign countries, particularly after the birth of the WTO, which had a much more effective dispute resolution system than that of the old GATT secretariat.

In 1994, the Canadian and American governments came into direct conflict over, of all things, country music. In that year, the Canadian Radio-television and Telecommunications Commission (CRTC) ruled that Country Music Television, an American station that had been on the air in Canada for almost a decade, should be replaced on Canadian cable systems by a new Canadian station, New Country Network, effective the beginning of 1995. With the cultural exemption in NAFTA, Canada was free to discriminate against an American network, but the United States was also free to square the account by imposing measures of equal economic impact against Canada. The US government immediately warned that it would retaliate—the first time it had threatened to use that right under the cultural exemption. The issue was settled in June, one month before the US would have imposed sanctions. The Canadian company sold 20 per cent of its shares to its American competitor and changed the name of the channel to Country Music Television Canada, a variation on the American network's name. The CRTC announced that it would abandon its delisting policy, under which it took American cable networks off the air when a Canadian alternative appeared.

A more serious, bitter, and long-lasting conflict erupted over magazines in January 1993, when *Sports Illustrated* announced that it would begin publishing a Canadian split-run edition, prepared in the United States and then sent electronically to a printing plant in Canada. The Mulroney government appointed a task force to investigate the matter. Its report, submitted to the Chrétien government in 1994, recommended an 80 per cent tax on the advertising revenues of split-run magazines. The government adopted the proposal, arguing that it did not violate the GATT agreement because advertising was a service, not a good, and GATT dealt only with goods. The US decided to pursue the issue as a test case. "We want to say to the world," declared Mickey Kantor, the United States trade representative, "this will not to be tolerated."[29]

The US took the issue to the WTO, which ruled against Canada in 1997. Advertising was indeed a service, but was tied to a good (the magazine), so it was subject to GATT rules. Not only did the WTO strike down the new 80 per cent tax on the advertising revenues of split-runs, but it also voided the 1965 measure that banned the import of split-runs printed abroad. Despite this clear defeat, the Canadian government refused to give up the fight. Canadian heritage minister Sheila Copps proposed a law to ban split-run magazines from accepting any advertising in Canada. Her reasoning was that advertising was a service, not a good, an argument the WTO had already rejected. The United States threatened to retaliate by strategically applying tariffs against several Canadian products, such as steel, an important export from Copps's city of Hamilton, Ontario.

Finally, in May 1999, the two sides reached an extraordinarily complex agreement. Canada would allow foreigners to establish new magazines in Canada or buy up to a 49 per cent interest in existing Canadian magazines (an increase from the previous limit of 25 per cent). Split-runs would now be permitted in Canada, so long as they carried no more than 12 per cent Canadian advertising (increased to 15 per cent after one year and to 18 per cent after two). Canadian companies could claim a full tax deduction for advertising in magazines with at least 80 per cent original content (i.e., content not taken from an American magazine) or they could claim a 50 per cent deduction for advertising in other magazines. The Canadian government continued to hope that these measures would encourage companies to advertise in Canadian magazines, rather than split-runs.

Canadian cultural policy had been dealt a near-fatal blow, leaving policy-makers staggering, desperate for a new approach. Copps decided that the solution was to enlist the support of like-minded countries to mount an offensive against the United States. In 1998, she hosted a meeting of culture ministers in Ottawa, where they created the International Network on Cultural Policy (INCP). Without a Cabinet minister responsible for culture, the US had no seat at the table—which, no doubt, is what Copps had intended. The Americans asked to send a trade official to the meeting, but the Canadians said no. In 2001, the INCP agreed to the Canadian idea of an international agreement on cultural diversity, allowing countries to pursue their own cultural policies without worrying about retaliation from trading partners. To ensure that culture trumped trade, and not the other way around, the agreement would be administered by the United Nations Educational, Scientific, and Cultural Organization (UNESCO), not by the WTO. In 2003, UNESCO passed a resolution calling for the negotiation of an agreement on cultural diversity within two years.

In 2005, UNESCO approved the Cultural Diversity Convention by a vote of 148 to 2, with only the United States and Israel voting against. Canada had won—but what had it won? Canada was still obliged to honour its commitments under the GATT agreement. The United States had rejected the Cultural Diversity Convention and therefore would not be bound by its terms. At best, the Canadians had scored a symbolic victory, one that did nothing to achieve their goal of protecting the country's cultural policy from future US challenges. The Cultural Diversity Convention would only have meaning if it included the United States. UNESCO's director general, Kōichirō Matsuura, posed the key question, one that Canadian negotiators should have asked themselves at the beginning of this process: "What is a consensus without the United States?"[30]

# The Terrorist Attacks of 11 September 2001

On 11 September 2001, members of the al Qaeda terrorist group hijacked four American commercial airliners. Two planes smashed into the World Trade Center in New York City, igniting the twin towers and collapsing them, killing almost 3,000 in the process, including two dozen Canadians. A third plane flew into the Pentagon, the US military headquarters in Washington, taking the lives of almost 200 people. The terrorists intended to crash another plane into either the White House or the US Capitol building, but it went down in a field in Pennsylvania, killing all 44 on board, after passengers stormed the cockpit and tried to wrestle control of the plane from the hijackers. "The world just changed," Prime Minister Chrétien observed to staff members.[31] The terrorist attacks shone a bright light on the relations between Canada and the United States: the common values were now more visible than ever, but before long the differences would also be brought into sharp focus.

On the day of the terrorist attacks, Canadians quickly came to the aid of the United States. A Canadian, Major-General Rick Findley, was in charge of NORAD and responsible for scrambling hundreds of fighter jets to protect North American air space. Commercial air traffic was quickly shut down, meaning that more than 250 planes approaching the United States were diverted to Canada, where 44,000 passengers were given food and shelter.[32] Gander, Newfoundland, population 10,000, took in 6,500 passengers and crew members.[33] Prime Minister Chrétien called President Bush and pledged Canada's complete support. Canadians sent thousands of letters of condolence to the White House and the US embassy in Ottawa, and placed flowers outside the embassy and US consulates in major Canadian cities.

In their grief, Canadians and Americans frequently acknowledged their close ties. Three days after the attacks, Canada held a memorial service on Parliament Hill to coincide with the National Day of Mourning in the United States. The US ambassador, Paul Cellucci, had expected a gathering of 10,000 to 15,000 and was astonished to see 100,000 in attendance.[34] The crowd, Americans and Canadians, sang the national anthems of both countries. "We will be with the United States every step of the way," pledged Prime Minister Chrétien. "As friends, as neighbours, as family." "You are truly our closest friend," Cellucci responded. When Chrétien visited Dallas in November, he told an audience that Americans should be proud "of the leadership of a great Texan, President George Bush."[35] A *Dallas News* editorial told readers that if they saw Chrétien, they should shake his hand and thank him. After all, "Canada didn't just condemn the atrocious attacks on the United States. It unhesitatingly enlisted to defeat the people and countries that perpetrated them."[36]

**Photo 12.2** ✣ National Day of Mourning, Parliament Hill

On the National Day of Mourning, 100,000 showed up at Parliament Hill for a service in memory of the victims of the 11 September terrorist attacks. (Source: © Reuters/CORBIS.)

There were also tensions—and from the very beginning. On 12 September, ABC News reported incorrectly that most of the terrorists had entered the United States through Canada, a story later repeated in several major US newspapers. Long after the rumour had been disproven, Senator Hillary Clinton claimed the hijackers had passed through Canada en route to the United States. When pressed for proof, she responded, "Well, everybody knows they came through Canada."[37] This myth continued for years. In 2005, both US senator Conrad Burns and Newt Gingrich, former speaker of the House of Representatives, claimed that some of the 11 September terrorists had come from Canada.

As Americans became jittery about their security, Canadians were hypersensitive about their country's relationship with the US. In a 20 September speech to Congress, Bush thanked several countries but not Canada, an omission that Chrétien's critics saw as evidence of inadequate Canadian support for the United States. When Chrétien visited the White House two weeks after the attack, Bush went out of his way to explain that no snub was intended. "There should be no doubt in anybody's mind about how honored we are to have the support of the Canadians," declared the president "and how strong the Canadian prime minister has been."[38] Opposition politicians and media commentators thought Chrétien was cold in his reaction to the terrorist attacks and denounced him for waiting two and a half weeks before visiting Ground Zero, the site of the World Trade

Center. Hardly anyone noticed that Chrétien was the first world leader called by Bush after 11 September.

Chrétien's critics became ferocious when the prime minister seemed to blame the United States itself in an interview for a CBC-TV documentary marking the first anniversary of the attacks. "You know, you cannot exercise your powers to the point of humiliation for the others," the prime minister said, arguing that hostility toward the United States came, at least in part, from the growing divide between the world's rich and poor countries. "This is a uniquely disgraceful statement, even by Mr. Chrétien's worrisome standards," said former prime minister Brian Mulroney, who described the prime minister's remarks as "false, shocking and morally specious." For opposition leader Stephen Harper, Chrétien's words were simply "shameful."[39]

# International Campaign against Terrorism

The war in Afghanistan began shortly after the terrorist attacks. The members of NATO, for the first time in its history, invoked article 5 of the alliance's founding treaty, declaring that the assault on the United States was an attack on the entire alliance. The United States demanded that Afghanistan shut down al Qaeda's training camps and turn over the group's leaders, who had been operating under the protection of that country's ultraconservative, theocratic Taliban regime. The Afghans refused. In October, the United States began military operations with the bombing of Afghan targets. The Canadian government immediately announced that it would take part in a US-led, multinational campaign to capture members of al Qaeda, dismantle their camps, and overthrow the Taliban government.

Canada's contribution to the campaign was multifaceted. In late 2001, as US and other NATO forces were toppling the Afghan regime, Canadian ships in the Persian Gulf conducted interdiction operations to prevent the escape of al Qaeda and Taliban members. In February 2002, Canada sent an infantry battle group to the southern Afghan province of Kandahar to operate as part of a US Army task force. Canadian troops were involved in combat against al Qaeda and Taliban forces and provided protection for humanitarian relief operations and for Afghanistan's new interim government. Canada also provided special forces, as well as airlift and long-range air patrol detachments.

The Canadian–American relationship was strong in the first few months of the war. At the end of 2001, 84 per cent of Canadians approved of the US military response to the terrorist attacks and 79 per cent supported Canada's involvement in the war. Despite the criticism of Chrétien's actions after 11 September, 68 per cent of Canadians were satisfied with the federal government's response. At the same time, Canadians were clear about the differences between the two countries. Only 25 per cent would seize the opportunity to become a citizen of the US and live there. When asked to describe the Canadian–American relationship, most respondents rejected the official descriptions: "like family" or "best friends." Almost half of those surveyed thought that Canada and the United States were "friends, but not especially close." The terrorist attacks had pushed the two countries together, but Canadians were still acutely aware of the differences.[40]

# Border Management

Long before the al Qaeda attacks, Canadian and American officials had been preoccupied with border security. The challenge was to ease the passage of goods and legitimate travellers across the border, while closing it to criminals and terrorists. In 1995, Canada and the US had signed the Shared Border Accord, which sought to use advanced technology to modernize border crossings. The two countries then agreed in the 1997 Border Vision agreement to coordinate policies and share intelligence to deal with illegal immigration. The Canada–US Partnership Forum (CUSP) began working in 1999, consulting with business leaders on how to improve the border. There was much talk, but progress was slow. Only in late 2000 did the countries begin NEXUS, then a pilot project at the Blue Water Bridge linking Sarnia, Ontario, and Port Huron, Michigan. Under the program, frequent travellers could receive, after a background check, a NEXUS card allowing them to bypass regular customs and immigration checks. Each country already had its own similar project in effect at some border crossings, but those passes only worked in one direction. The NEXUS card was a common Canada–US initiative and could be used either way when crossing the border.

The terrorist attacks of 11 September added urgency to discussions about improving the border. For Canadian officials, the key was to keep the border open to trade and to avoid a repeat of the long lines at crossings in the days after 11 September. For Americans, the priority was to close the border to terrorists, a position Canadians generally understood. A poll taken shortly after the terrorist attacks showed that 53 per cent of Canadians would accept a common Canada–US security perimeter, "even if it means we must effectively accept American security and immigration policies."[41] The Canadian government had the challenge of balancing the country's sovereignty with American concerns about border security.

In December 2001, Canada and the United States signed to the Smart Border Accord. The two countries would improve information sharing over issues like terrorism and criminal activities. They also agreed to increase personnel at border crossings and to improve infrastructure to allow pre-authorized clearance in more places. Some border crossings already had fast lanes for frequent travellers who carried a NEXUS card. Now, it could be used at more crossings, and would be expanded to cover air travel. Beginning in 2002, the Free and Secure Trade Program (FAST) would register manufacturers, importers, trucking companies, and drivers, so that cargo trucks could travel through fast lanes at the border, bypassing long lines.

# The Relationship Deteriorates

Although Canadian and US troops worked together successfully in Afghanistan, relations between the two countries began to deteriorate in 2002. Canadians were troubled by the US practice of incarcerating Taliban and al Qaeda members at the US naval base in Guantánamo Bay, Cuba, while refusing to recognize their rights as prisoners of war under the Geneva Conventions. Detainees were hooded and forcibly sedated, both violations of international law, as was the US practice of shaving the beards of Muslim fundamentalists. In January, a debate erupted in Canada over whether the Canadian military should turn prisoners over to American authorities, with legal experts and some Liberal members of Parliament arguing that Canada would itself be breaching the Geneva Conventions and betraying the country's values if it continued to do so.

Many Canadians were further troubled at the death of four Canadian paratroopers in April 2002 after a US pilot dropped a 500-pound bomb on them. The airman, nicknamed Psycho, thought the Canadians were hostile forces and acted before confirming their identity. The Canadian media censured President Bush for remaining publicly silent about the incident. The US military charged the pilot with manslaughter, but the charges were dismissed and the pilot was simply fined and reprimanded, a decision that sparked outrage in Canada.

It was the Bush foreign policy that caused the deepest problems between Canada and the United States. Before he came to office in January 2001, Bush had promised a more humble America, one that would not use its power to dominate others. But with the terrorist attacks the president quickly developed what others called the Bush Doctrine, a new US policy toward the world. Through the Cold War, the United States had defended itself by threatening a massive nuclear strike against any country that might attack American soil. As this approach did not work against terrorist groups, Bush claimed the right to use force against others long before they could attack the United States. International law always recognized the right to pre-emption, attacking others before they attacked, but Bush claimed that right even when a strike was not imminent. His policy was to eliminate threats before they emerged. In the past, the United States had consulted its allies when determining whether to deploy military force, and it suffered when it ignored their advice—in Vietnam, for example. Now the United States would define its missions on its own and would proceed with coalitions of the willing—those countries wishing to cooperate with the US. At the same time, the United States would not recognize neutrality in its war against terrorism. "Either you are with us, or you are with the terrorists," Bush told the world.[42] The United States was the world's pre-eminent military power and, Bush declared, would maintain that status. Its strategic objective would be to eliminate the nexus of terrorism, weapons of mass destruction, and rogue states. For Bush, all this was justified by the traditional mission of the United States, to bring peace and liberty to the world.

The Bush Doctrine squeezed Canada. Multilateralism had been a keystone of Canadian policy, the field on which Canadian diplomacy operated, but the Bush administration cared little about consulting allies. Canada had traditionally tried to restrain Americans when they were in danger of acting rashly, but now the United States demanded that everyone take sides, allowing no middle ground and doubting the loyalty of anyone who questioned American policy. "The United States has a totally different perspective than we do on the world," noted Canada's foreign minister, Bill Graham, in January 2002. "They feel that they can have their will."[43] Canadians agreed: in late 2002, a poll showed that 67 per cent of Canadians thought the US was "starting to act like a bully with the rest of the world."[44] It did not help when US secretary of state Colin Powell told Graham that Canadians would do better in Washington if they behaved more like Brian Mulroney had. After all, President Reagan had given Canada "whatever Brian wanted."[45]

# The American War in Iraq

In the George W. Bush years, nothing did more damage to the Canadian–American relationship than the US decision to go to war in Iraq. The conflict had deep roots. In the 1990–1 Gulf War, a US-led coalition had defeated Iraq but left Saddam Hussein in power. The Iraqi dictator agreed to a UN resolution calling on his regime to surrender all chemical, biological, and nuclear weapons and to cooperate with UN weapons inspections. Yet the Iraqis obstructed the work of the inspectors. The UN passed several resolutions condemning Iraq, but to no avail. On several occasions in the 1990s, the US launched missiles at Iraqi targets, and the Iraqi government quickly agreed to cooperate with weapons inspections. But cooperation would only last a few months or weeks—if that. The issue took on a new urgency shortly after the 11 September terrorist attacks, when Bush began linking al Qaeda to Saddam Hussein and pushing for war against Iraq.

The Canadian government was torn. In September 2002, Chrétien said Canada would only go to war in Iraq if there was proof that Saddam Hussein had weapons of mass destruction. When a reporter asked what would constitute proof, Chrétien responded with his own form of haiku: "I don't know. A proof is a proof. What kind of a proof? It's a proof. A proof is a proof, and when you have a good proof, it's because it's proven."[46] Days later, Bush laid out his case to Chrétien in a meeting in Detroit. The prime minister was not impressed. "I started my career as a small-town lawyer," he told one of his aides, "and I heard nothing today from the president that would convince any judge in a rural courthouse."[47] Canada began preparing for war, tentatively offering the US a battle group of 600 to 800 soldiers for a conflict in Iraq. Canadian officials hoped that the UN might resolve the crisis and were frustrated when Bush suggested that he did not need UN approval and might go to war without it. "What a moron!" exclaimed Francie Ducros, Chrétien's communications director, after Bush pushed for war at a NATO meeting in Prague.[48] At first, the prime minister rejected Ducros's resignation, but after a week of controversy in the Canadian and US media, she was gone.

The Canadian position became no clearer over the subsequent months. If the UN Security Council decided that military action was necessary, Canada would take part. But if the Security Council voted against war? Chrétien refused to answer, saying that he would not speculate. After consulting with officials in the Departments of Foreign Affairs and National Defence, US ambassador Paul Cellucci concluded that Canada would take part regardless of the UN's position, even if the prime minister "would prefer to avoid having to make that politically tough decision."[49] But Chrétien's position was not so clear to the Canadian media. On the same day in late January, the lead story in both the *Globe and Mail* and the *Toronto Star* was a Chrétien statement on Iraq, but the newspapers had come to utterly different understandings of the prime minister's remarks. "PM to Bush: Hold Off on War," read the *Globe*'s headline, while the *Star*'s proclaimed, "Chrétien Supports U.S. Push for War."

Public opinion made the difference. In early February 2003, a poll showed that 60 per cent of Canadians favoured their country's participation if the action had UN sanction. If not, only 28 per cent were in support, while 67 per cent were against.[50] The opposition to war was strongest in Quebec, an important consideration for a government preoccupied with national unity. The same month, the Canadian government announced a 12-month commitment to provide troops to the International Stabilization Assistance Force (ISAF) in Kabul. At any given time from the summer of 2003 to the summer of 2004, Canada would have almost 2,000 troops in Afghanistan, making it impossible to send a significant number of ground forces elsewhere. American officials believed that Canada would offer public support for the mission in Iraq, even if no troops were available. When war came, Canadian officials would "say good things about the president and bad things about Saddam Hussein," or so the US ambassador expected.[51]

Tensions slowly mounted as war approached. Canadian diplomats were working desperately at the UN to find a way to avoid war, at times making American officials feel that Canada was working at cross-purposes with the US. In late February 2003, Liberal MP Carolyn Parrish was caught on microphone saying, "Damn Americans, I hate those bastards!"[52] Parrish's remark was picked up by scores of American media outlets, many of which rarely reported on Canadian events, triggering a brief but heated controversy. In March, protests against a possible war began in major world cities; in Montreal 200,000 marched, with much smaller demonstrations in other Canadian cities.

Chrétien announced Canada's position on 17 March, three days before the war began, a statement broadcast live on CNN. Unless the UN authorized an attack on Iraq, Canada would not take part. The prime minister came under attack—often in near-hysterical tones—from the media, the business community, international relations scholars, and opposition politicians for a decision that they were sure would damage Canada's relationship with the United States. They were correct that the Canadian–American friendship was strained, but on the road to Iraq the US had injured its relations with many other countries—including France, Russia, and Germany. If there was blame for the deterioration of Canadian–American relations, a large portion of it must go to George W. Bush and his unilateral approach to international affairs. Yet the Liberal Party had a knack for making bad situations worse. Two days after Chrétien's announcement, Natural Resources Minister Herb Dhaliwal said that Bush had let the world down "by not being a statesman," a comment that upset American officials, including Ambassador Paul Cellucci.[53]

US officials sought to send clear signals that Canada had harmed its friendship with its closest ally. In a 25 March speech in Toronto, Cellucci rebuked the Chrétien government for its decision on Iraq. The ambassador described Iraq as a "direct security threat to the people of the United States." The speech's key passage was a stern reprimand, delivered from the perspective of a wounded relative:

> There is no security threat to Canada that the United States would not be ready, willing and able to help with. There would be no debate. There would be no hesitation. We would be there for Canada, part of our family. That is why so many in the United States are disappointed and upset that Canada is not fully supporting us now.[54]

Somehow, Cellucci missed the key point: the dispute was not over whether Canada would help the United States deal with a security threat, but whether the threat existed at all. The next month, the US announced that Bush would not visit Ottawa in May as originally planned. The cancellation was, Cellucci wrote privately, "a harsh but necessary reality check for Canada" after the Chrétien government had refused to go to war in Iraq and after senior officials had criticized Bush.[55]

Chrétien's decision proved popular at home, particularly after the Iraq war began going badly for the United States. Although Bush declared the end of hostilities in May 2003, US troops found themselves battling a fierce insurgency, one that kept the Americans in Iraq for years while the country descended into civil war. It became clear that Iraq did not have nuclear, biological, or chemical weapons, as American officials had claimed as the justification for the invasion. The image of the US further suffered when it emerged that prisoners in American custody were being tortured, particularly in 2004 when the media published vivid photographs showing US troops abusing detainees at the Abu Ghraib prison near Baghdad.

Canadians were pleased not to be part of the conflict. At a convention in November 2003, just weeks before Chrétien stepped down as prime minister, the Liberal Party paid tribute to his accomplishments, with the crowd cheering loudest for his decision to stay out of Iraq. By March 2004, polls showed that 74 per cent of Canadians believed the government had made the right decision on Iraq, while 67 per cent thought Bush had "knowingly lied to the world to justify his war."[56] The popularity of the US continued to drop, though most Canadians continued to view the country favourably.

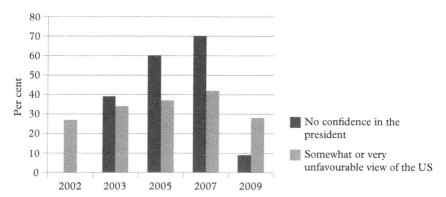

**Figure 12.1** ✦ Canadian Attitudes toward the US and the American President, 2002–9

Note: George W. Bush was president during the 2002–7 surveys. Barack Obama was president during the 2009 survey.

Source: Adapted from Pew Research Center, Global Attitudes Project, www.pewglobal.org.

# Fire and Ice

While many Canadians were becoming doubtful of the US, they feared they were becoming more like Americans. Comfort came in the form of a book by pollster Michael Adams. *Fire and Ice: The United States, Canada and the Myth of Converging Values* appeared in bookstores two months after the invasion of Iraq and spent 18 weeks on the *Maclean's* bestseller list.[57] Adams accepted Seymour Martin Lipset's interpretation that Canada and the United States were founded on different values (see pp. 17–18), but not the common view that mass culture and economic integration were bringing the two counties together. Polling showed that 58 per cent of Canadians believed their country was becoming more American.[58] Not so, Adams replied.

Adams based his conclusions on surveys conducted in Canada and the US. He had polled more than 8,000 Canadians every year from 1983 to 2001, and more than 6,000 Americans in 1992, 1996, and 2000. His questions were not those usually associated with public opinion research, but rather ones that probed values, motivations, and mindsets.

"At the most basic level—the level of our values, the feelings and beliefs that inform our understanding of and interaction with the world around us—Canadians and Americans are markedly different, and are becoming more so," Adams argued. He found that Americans were becoming increasingly religious, more accepting of authority, more sexist and racist, and more willing to take risks. Less idealistic and more accepting of violence, Americans were "increasingly resigned to living in a competitive jungle" ruled by "consumption and personal thrills," with little concern for the environment or the less fortunate.[59] Canadians were moving in the opposite direction, becoming less religious, less accepting of authority, and less sexist.

As seductive as some Canadians might have found Adams's message, the argument was not always convincing. His conclusions came from the answers to a small number of questions, and he ignored, rather than confronted, evidence that contradicted him. Often the differences between Canada and the United States were minor—10 percentage points or less. At other times, Adams simply interpreted data to fit his argument. For instance, Americans were more likely to own SUVs than minivans by a ratio of 2 to 1, while Canadians had the opposite tendency. For Adams, this proved that Americans were less caring about the environment. After all, SUVs consume more gasoline and produce more pollution. Yet Adams had failed to consider that average incomes were considerably higher in the US than in Canada, meaning Americans were more likely to have the means to purchase the more expensive SUVs. A more significant failing was that Adams had studied a short 10-year period, not long enough to determine if he was witnessing a long-term trend or merely a blip in his polling data.

The most sustained and intelligent response to Adams came from two Canadian sociologists, Edward Grabb and James Curtis. They argued that upper North America was composed not of two societies, Canada and the United States, but of four: Quebec, the rest of Canada, the American South, and the rest of the United States. If one excluded "permissive" Quebec and the conservative Deep South, Canadian and American values were largely the same.[60] Indeed, the values of Canadians and Americans were closer than those of the people of any two other countries.

# Paul Martin and the Defence of North America

Paul Martin lost to Jean Chrétien at the 1990 Liberal leadership convention and spent the next 13 years impatient for his chance to be prime minster. The two men were remarkably close in their political views, making it difficult for Martin to differentiate himself from his rival. After leaving the Chrétien Cabinet in 2002, Martin began presenting himself as the man to restore Canada's tarnished relations with its powerful neighbour, promising that dealings between the two countries would be conducted "on a far more sophisticated basis" than before.[61]

When Martin became prime minister in December 2003, he created a Cabinet committee on Canadian–American relations, chaired by the prime minister, as well as a House of Commons committee dedicated to the relationship. A secretariat on US affairs was added to the Privy Council Office, the prime minister's government department, and Martin appointed a parliamentary secretary on Canada–US affairs, reporting directly to the prime minister. In 2004, he created a secretariat in Washington, independent of the Canadian embassy, to help the federal and provincial governments lobby Congress. Finally, Martin launched a review of Canada's foreign, defence, trade, and international development policies. The resulting International Policy Statement of 2005 repeated Martin's pledge to strengthen Canada's most important bilateral relationship.

One pressing problem was the future of NORAD. After 11 September, homeland security became paramount for the United States. The chiefs of staff recommended that the air, sea, and land defence of the continent be coordinated by a single command: either NORAD or a new US-only command. The Americans wanted to move quickly, but the Canadians were reluctant to commit to expanding NORAD's role. In April 2002, the Americans announced they would create the US Northern Command

(USNORTHCOM), led by the commander of NORAD and responsible for continental defence. The danger for Canada was that the defence of North America was becoming increasingly an American venture. The Americans appeared willing to defend North America as they saw fit with far less input from Canada. There was even the possibility that USNORTHCOM would push NORAD to the sidelines, reducing Canada's role in continental air defence. The International Policy Statement suggested one partial solution: the creation of a Canadian equivalent of USNORTHCOM that could work directly with the American command for the defence of Canada. This was done in 2006 with the formation of Canada Command (later called the Canadian Joint Operations Command).

Canadian officials continued to ponder the possibility of enlarging NORAD. In December 2002, Canada and the US created the Bi-National Planning Group (BPG), located at NORAD headquarters, to examine the idea. In its 2004 interim report, the BPG recommended a unified command for North America, including air, land, and maritime defence. Yet by 2006, the mood had changed. USNORTHCOM had been running for several years, while NORAD had become less of a priority for the US military. The Martin government was gasping for breath and had little time for long-term defence planning. The BPG's bland final report laid out several options for improving North American defence, one of which involved expanding NORAD's scope, while another called for NORAD to be placed under USNORTHCOM, subordinating a binational Canada–US command to a US-only command, an idea that never would have been acceptable to the Canadian government. The idea of expanding NORAD slowly withered away.

An equally difficult challenge was the Bush administration's Ballistic Missile Defense (BMD) program. Ronald Reagan had begun the Strategic Defense Initiative, but it had come nowhere near accomplishing its goal of creating a system to defend the United States from missile attacks. Reagan's successors, George H.W. Bush and Bill Clinton, had allowed work to continue. Researchers made slow but steady progress toward developing a much more modest system than Reagan had envisaged. When the younger Bush, George W., came to office, he made missile defence a much higher priority for the US, a priority that enjoyed support from both major political parties in the US.

The US had asked for Canadian participation in the BMD program, but the Chrétien government was wary. In a sense, it should have been an easy decision. The US was asking for nothing from Canada, other than political support: BMD required neither Canadian money nor territory. Canadian participation would ensure the continued relevance of NORAD, which had been responsible since the 1960s for missile warning. If Canada opted out of missile defence, the system could not be run in the same binational way from NORAD, and a US command would likely need to take on the BMD component of North American aerospace defence. By taking part in the BMD system, Canada would have retained some role in decision making, especially important if missiles were going to be shot down over Canada. Yet having clashed with the Bush administration over Iraq, Chrétien was not inclined to provide support for BMD and he remained worried that the system might lead to an arms race and the weaponization of space. Under no pressure from the United States to make a quick decision, he simply left the matter to his successor.

In the months before Paul Martin assumed office, when he was promising to restore Canada's friendship with the United States, he gave every indication that his government would sign on to the BMD program. "If somebody is going to be sending missiles over Canadian airspace, we want to be at the table."[62] For Martin, it was a question of Canadian sovereignty: "My sovereignty says you don't send missiles up over my airspace unless I'm there."[63] After he became prime minister in December 2003, polls showed that a majority of Canadians shared his views. The Liberal Party's pollster discovered in February 2004 that 64 per cent of Canadians favoured participation in the BMD program.[64] Officials from the two countries agreed to the terms for Canadian participation in the program, but public opinion began to change as Bush's standing in Canada collapsed. In March, public servants responsible for BMD were ordered to stop working on the file and not to speak publicly about the issue. References to BMD were scrapped from Martin's first major speech on defence. The subject was also dropped from the agenda for his April visit to Washington. But what about Martin's goal of friendlier relations with the United States? A public opinion poll showed that only 39 per cent of Canadians supported it.[65]

In the election of 28 June 2004, the Liberals clung to power but lost their majority in the House of Commons, mostly because of a domestic political scandal held over from the Chrétien years and mismanaged by Martin's team, though the NDP was able to steal some votes by calling on the prime minister to say no to missile defence. In August 2004, Canada and the US amended the NORAD agreement to allow the binational command to handle the missile warning and assessment function for BMD. The step was necessary to ensure the continuation of NORAD, but it was as far as the Canadian government would go. By November, 52 per cent of Canadians were against participation, while only 46 per cent were in favour. In Quebec, where the Martin government desperately hoped to gain some seats to restore its majority, 65 per cent were opposed.[66]

In February 2005, the prime minister announced that Canada would not participate in Ballistic Missile Defense. In his memoirs, Martin explained that he opted out because the Americans would not answer two key questions: would Canada be asked to provide money in the future and would Canadian interests be taken into account when deciding to shoot down missiles? "I did not want to have a situation, to put it starkly, in which the Americans sacrificed Edmonton to save Denver," Martin explained.[67] Yet the prime minister offered a different reason when he called the US ambassador the day before making the BMD announcement. Martin "was driven by concern that the debate in the Commons and at the Liberal convention would be extremely divisive and would serve as a platform for loud anti-Americanism," Cellucci reported to Washington. "The Prime Minister and his political advisors see everything through the prism of regaining a Liberal majority in the next elections," was the ambassador's shrewd assessment of the decision.[68] American officials were exasperated at Canada's handling of the issue, but secretly some were pleased, never having wanted to involve Canada in ballistic missile defence. As a result, Martin's decision did little damage to the political relationship, but it did reduce Canada's role in the defence of North America, as it meant that NORAD would be limited to missile warning, while Americans would run the rest of the BMD system with no input from Canada.

## Anti-Americanism and the End of the Martin Government

Anti-American sentiment emanated from Ottawa as the Martin government desperately clung to power. The prime minister subtly tried to capitalize on this emotion in the days leading to the June 2004 election. "I love the United States," he declared on the opening day of the campaign, "but I love much far greater that we are different. I love that we are Canada, and we're going to stay that way."[69] He tried to link Conservative policies to the US, saying that Opposition Leader Stephen Harper favoured "US-style tax cuts" and "American-style health care."[70]

After the Liberals were reduced to a minority, Carolyn Parrish re-emerged to do more damage. When she called BMD supporters the "coalition of the idiots," Martin chastised her, but allowed her to stay in the Liberal caucus.[71] After Bush was re-elected in November, Parrish said that the president was a warmonger and American voters were "completely out of step with most of the free world," again earning a rebuke from the prime minister.[72] Fancying herself an entertainer, Parrish then went on the television comedy show *This Hour Has 22 Minutes,* where she stomped gleefully on a George Bush doll before sticking a pin in its head, "where it will do the least damage." Asked later what would happen if the prime minister wanted her to stop criticizing Bush, Parrish responded that Martin and his team could "go to hell."[73] With that last remark, Parrish had gone too far. She was expelled from the Liberal ranks.

Martin tried again in the 2006 federal election to harness anti-American feelings. Liberal attack ads did their best to link Harper and the Conservatives to the United States. Quoting the *Washington Times*, one ad said that, if elected, Harper might be "the most pro-American leader in the Western world" and that "a Harper victory will put a smile on George W. Bush's face." Another ad asserted that Harper was "very popular with right-wingers in the U.S."[74] Martin also criticized the Americans directly. In the days before the campaign began, the prime minister accused the US of a "breach of faith" over softwood lumber.[75] Once the campaign was under way, he lectured the Americans on their failure to ratify the Kyoto Protocol: "I say there is such a thing as a global conscience, and now is the time to listen to it."[76] The US ambassador, David Wilkins, inadvertently helped Martin along by saying publicly that real friends do not constantly criticize each other and that "Canada never has to tear down the United States to build itself up."[77] The prime minister's response was indignant: "I am not going to be dictated to as to the subjects that I should raise. I will make sure that Canada speaks with an independent voice now, tomorrow, and always, and you should demand nothing less from your prime minister."[78] The comments were the last rites for Martin's earlier promise of a more sophisticated approach to Canadian–American relations and were not enough to stop his party's defeat in the election.

The major damage to the relationship had sprung from the US decision to ignore the advice of its close allies and to invade Iraq on the pretense that the country had weapons of mass destruction. The American reprimand of Canada for staying out of the war and the treatment of Iraqi prisoners further scarred the image of the Bush administration in Canadian eyes. Martin's own actions reflect the changed mood in Canada. The prime minister was not anti-American but a politician attuned to public opinion, believing he could win votes by attacking the United States and by associating the Conservatives with Americans on the political right.

# Since 2006

Changes in personnel fundamentally altered the relationship between Ottawa and Washington, which had soured in the years after the invasion of Iraq. After the Conservatives won the election of 2006, Stephen Harper became prime minister. Then in 2009, Barack Obama, who was enormously popular in Canada, became president of the United States. Polls showed a decline in Canadian hostility toward the United States, an illustration of the resiliency of the relationship.

When Harper was leader of the opposition, he made it clear that his outlook differed substantially from that of Paul Martin and Jean Chrétien on both domestic and foreign policy. Harper was critical of Chrétien's decision to stay out of Iraq and promised a foreign policy based on conservative values. While still leader of the opposition, Harper stepped back from his support for the Iraq war as it became increasingly unpopular in Canada. In office, Harper's policies on Canadian–American relations have not differed substantially from those of his two immediate predecessors. He has not pushed for closer military relations between the two countries. His government has kept a healthy distance from the United States, while working to improve trade relations and border security. If there is a difference, it is that Harper has put more emphasis than Chrétien or Martin on promoting energy exports from his home province of Alberta.

For the Harper government, trade and security remained the two key items on the Canada–US agenda. The two converged on the issue of border management. Since 2006, Canada and the United States have continued to work to improve border infrastructure and to cooperate in dealing with cross-border crime. More than 300,000 people cross the border every day, with 8,000 trucks travelling across the Windsor–Detroit border, the busiest of the crossing points. In 2012, Canada announced it would build a new six-lane bridge to handle the traffic between Windsor and Detroit, the crossing point for one-quarter of all Canadian–American trade.[79]

Canada and the US have been moving ever so slowly toward a North American trade and security perimeter. People and goods entering Canada or the United States from overseas might eventually face the same regulations, go through the same customs facilities, and answer questions posed by a Canadian or a US official employed by a joint border security agency. The two countries intend to exchange information instantaneously about travellers entering or exiting either country, including biometric data. At the same time, the governments are working to harmonize regulations in a host of areas—agriculture, food, transportation, health, the environment, among others—to make it easier for companies to do business in both countries.

Energy remains crucial. Ninety per cent of Canada's energy exports go to the United States, and about one-quarter of US petroleum imports come from Canada.[80] The Harper government has made it a high priority to convince the US to grant a permit for the construction of the Keystone XL pipeline to transport oil from the Alberta oil sands to markets in the United States. The US has an interest in a secure supply of petroleum, and Canada in selling resources to the United States. Much to the prime minister's frustration, President Obama has been delaying a decision on whether to approve the project because of concerns about the environmental impact of the pipeline.

## Summary

Throughout the Chrétien and Martin years, Canada clung to multilateralism as American officials backed away from that approach to solving international problems. The US supported the idea of eliminating landmines and bringing war criminals to justice—and did much to advance those causes—but would not be tied down to multilateral treaties that might constrain the country in the future. At odds with the United States over cultural policy, Canada attempted a multilateral solution that turned out to be no solution at all when the US refused to take part and remained free to retaliate against Canada if it pleased.

When the US was attacked on 11 September 2001, Canadians were helpful and supportive. Without hesitation, Canada joined the fight against the al Qaeda terrorists and the Taliban regime that sheltered them in Afghanistan. But Iraq was another matter. For Canadians, the United States was abusing its power and acting like a bully. Many Canadians lashed out at the United States, but it was really the Bush administration that angered them. Later, after Bush left office, anti-American sentiment in Canada all but disappeared.

The conflicts between Canada and the United States are always more noticed than the steady, incremental, healthy cooperation. The period since 1993 has been marked by many disagreements, yet the relationship remained sturdy. Bilateral trade continued to be crucial to the two countries, as their economies have become more closely linked. Since the 1990s, free trade has been widely accepted, despite irritations over issues such as softwood lumber. The two countries are distinct, but at the same time they share many basic values—values that endure despite a desire on the part of some Canadians to exaggerate the differences between Canadians and Americans.

## Beyond the Book

1.  In cases where Canada and the United States are at odds, such as over magazines or softwood lumber, is there anything Canadian officials can do if the Americans will not back down?
2.  Why did Canadian views of the US rebound so quickly after George W. Bush left office? What does that say about the Canadian–American relationship?

3.  What are the benefits and costs for a Canadian party leader who tries to harness anti-American sentiment?

## Further Reading

Much of what we know about Canadian–American relations in the Chrétien and Martin years comes from memoirs and biographies of the key actors. Chrétien has contributed two volumes of memoirs, both ghostwritten by journalist Ron Graham: *Straight from the Heart* (Toronto: Key Porter, 1985); and *My Years as Prime Minister* (Toronto: Alfred A. Knopf, 2007). The first has little to say about the United States, but offers a window into Chrétien's character and politics. Also valuable is the perceptive book by Chrétien's closest adviser for more than 30 years: Eddie Goldenberg, *The Way It Works: Inside Ottawa* (Toronto: McClelland and Stewart, 2006). Journalist Lawrence Martin provides a critical view in a lively two-volume biography: *Chrétien: The Will to Win* (Toronto: Lester, 1995); and *Iron Man: The Defiant Reign of Jean Chrétien* (Toronto: Viking, 2003). Chrétien's first trade minister, Roy MacLaren, offers his account in *The Fundamental Things Apply: A Memoir* (Montreal and Kingston: McGill–Queen's University Press, 2011). For Paul Martin, see the book ghostwritten by Paul Adams: *Hell or High Water: My Life in and out of Politics* (Toronto: McClelland and Stewart, 2008). The best sources on Martin's election campaigns are both edited by Jon H. Pammett and Christopher Dornan: *The Canadian General Election of 2004* (Toronto: Dundurn, 2004); and *The Canadian Federal Election of 2006* (Toronto: Dundurn, 2006).

For the American side of the Canada–US relationship, one learns little from Bill Clinton's *My Life* (New York: Alfred A. Knopf, 2004), a tedious, almost day-by-day, account of his presidency, which has nothing interesting to say about Canada. Fortunately, two ambassadors have published their recollections of the Chrétien and Martin years: James J. Blanchard, *Behind the Embassy Door: Canada, Clinton and Quebec* (Toronto: McClelland and Stewart, 1998); and Paul Cellucci, *Unquiet Diplomacy* (Toronto: Key Porter, 2005).

Several volumes in the *Canada Among Nations* series are invaluable for this period. The examination of the Axworthy agenda by Norman Hillmer and Adam Chapnick is the most helpful part of Fen Osler Hampson, Norman Hillmer, and Maureen Appel Molot, eds., *Canada Among Nations, 2001: The Axworthy Legacy* (Toronto: Oxford University Press, 2001). The chapter by Molot and Hillmer on the "Diplomacy of Decline" and Andrew Cohen's on Canadian–American relations stand out in Norman Hillmer and Maureen Appel Molot, eds., *Canada Among Nations, 2002: A Fading Power* (Toronto: Oxford University Press, 2002). In David Carment, Fen Osler Hampson, and Norman Hillmer, eds., *Canada Among Nations, 2003: Coping with the American Colossus* (Toronto: Oxford University Press, 2003), every chapter speaks to relations between the North American neighbours. The two most closely linked to this book's themes are Stephen Azzi and Tamara Feick on the Cultural Diversity Convention and Inger Weibust on the Kyoto Protocol. When reading David Carment, Fen Osler Hampson, and Norman Hillmer, eds., *Canada Among Nations 2004: Setting Priorities Straight* (Montreal and Kingston:

McGill–Queen's University Press, 2005), pay particular attention to the editors' chapter on smart power, Philippe Lagassé's on defence policy, Robert Bothwell's on the "fire and ice" thesis, and Graham Fraser's superb overview of Chrétien's foreign policy.

On the human security agenda, see Lloyd Axworthy, *Navigating a New World: Canada's Global Future* (Toronto: Alfred A. Knopf, 2003). Critical assessments can be found in Fen Osler Hampson and Dean F. Oliver, "Pulpit Diplomacy: A Critical Assessment of the Axworthy Doctrine," *International Journal* 53, no. 3 (Summer 1998): 379–406; Kim Richard Nossal, "Pinchpenny Diplomacy: The Decline of 'Good International Citizenship' in Canadian Foreign Policy," *International Journal* 54, no. 1 (Winter 1998–9): 88–105; and David A. Lenarcic's first-rate and pro-vocative book, *Knight-Errant? Canada and the Crusade to Ban Anti-Personnel Land Mines* (Toronto: Irwin, 1998). Joseph S. Nye Jr, explains his ideas in *Soft Power: The Means to Success in World Politics* (New York: PublicAffairs, 2004). On the decline of the Canadian military, foreign service, and aid programs in the Chrétien years, see Andrew Cohen's eloquent *While Canada Slept: How We Lost Our Place in the World* (Toronto: McClelland and Stewart, 2003).

On the wars in Afghanistan and Iraq, see Janice Gross Stein and Eugene Lang, *The Unexpected War: Canada in Kandahar* (Toronto: Viking, 2007). The book is me-ticulously detailed and benefits from extensive interviews with decision makers and from Lang's experience as chief of staff to two defence ministers, which also turns out to be the book's main weakness: too often the minister's enemies become the authors' foes as well. Jennifer Welsh's idealistic book, *At Home in the World: Canada's Global Vision for the 21st Century* (Toronto: HarperCollins, 2004), has much to say about Afghanistan and Iraq. More detail on Canada's decision not to go to Iraq can be found in Don Barry, "Chrétien, Bush, and the War in Iraq," *American Journal of Canadian Studies* 35, no. 2 (Summer 2005): 215–45.

On continental defence, see Joseph T. Jockel, *Canada in NORAD, 1957–2007: A History* (Montreal and Kingston: McGill–Queen's University Press, 2007); and Philippe Lagassé, "A Common 'Bilateral' Vision: North American Defence Cooperation, 2001–2012," chapter 10 in *Game Changer: The Impact of 9/11 on North American Security*, edited by Jonathan Paquin and Patrick James (Vancouver: UBC Press, 2014). The Ballistic Missile Defense story is mapped out in Paul H. Chapin, "The Real Story of Canada and BMD," *Ottawa Citizen*, 26 April 2013, A13; James G. Fergusson, *Canada and Ballistic Missile Defence, 1954–2009: Déjà vu All Over Again* (Vancouver: UBC Press, 2010); and Patrick Lennox, *At Home and Abroad: The Canada–US Relationship and Canada's Place in the World* (Vancouver: UBC Press, 2009).

Little has been written on Stephen Harper's approach to Canadian–American Relations. Adam Chapnick provides an excellent early assessment in "A Diplomatic Counter-Revolution," *International Journal* 67, no. 1 (Winter 2011–12): 137–54. Canada's leading political columnist, Paul Wells, has written the best book-length examination of the prime minister, one that offers insights on the Conservative gov-ernment's policies toward the United States: *The Longer I'm Prime Minister: Stephen Harper and Canada, 2006–* (Toronto: Random House, 2013). Also important is

Geoff Hale, *So Near Yet So Far: The Public and Hidden Worlds of Canada–US Relations* (Vancouver: UBC Press, 2012).

Michael Adams outlines his views on the growing gap between Canadian and American values in a book co-authored with Amy Langstaff and David Jamieson: *Fire and Ice: The United States, Canada and the Myth of Converging Values* (Toronto: Penguin, 2003). The most sustained rebuttal can be found in Edward Grabb and James Curtis, *Regions Apart: The Four Societies of Canada and the United States* (Toronto: Oxford University Press, 2005).

# Conclusion

―――――᧽―――――

## Similarities and Differences

Canadians and Americans usually emphasize their divergences. Living next to a colossus, Canadians have long struggled to define their own identity, and an easy way of doing so was to characterize Canada as *not American*, a sentiment that often became *better than American*. For Peter C. Newman, Canada's leading journalist in the 1960s and 1970s, the difference between the two countries was that Canadians had "respect for law and order, regard for civil rights, abhorrence of mob rule and gangsterism (whether practiced at the bottom or the top of the social scale)."[1] For Americans, national identity came from being the exceptional nation, the country that had pioneered the principles of liberty and democracy, and had a mission to spread them to the world. Recognizing a strong likeness with Canada undermined the sense that the United States was special.

But the similarities have always far outweighed the differences. Despite what they may have said, the Loyalists were far more American than British. They brought American customs and culture with them to Quebec and Nova Scotia, while often maintaining their family and business ties across the border. Even as they proclaimed their loyalty to the British Crown, they helped build a new country that was remarkably like the United States. Their systems of education and land ownership were American. They had to use the British political system, but the Loyalists still maintained remarkably American political attitudes. They valued democracy, equality (or at least equality of white men), and the separation of church and state—all ideas that put them at odds with late eighteenth-century Britain, where the majority could not vote, a landed aristocracy dominated society, and only members of the Church of England could hold public office.

After the War of 1812, British officials set out to make the colonies British, not just in name but also in fact. They encouraged British immigration while they expelled or harassed American immigrants, denied them citizenship, and prevented them from teaching in schools. Later generations of Canadians proclaimed that their country was British, but this was an artificial construct, created to serve the interests of the mother country. The idea of a British Canada was agreeable to the large numbers of British immigrants who arrived in the nineteenth century, but less so to the subsequent waves of continental Europeans and Asians. In any case, a "British" identity never stopped Canadians from borrowing aspects of the American political structure. A federal system, paid legislators, and the decennial redrawing of electoral boundaries were all ideas that came from south of the border and were alien to British political practice.

The North American environment was usually a more powerful force than efforts to maintain a British identity, particularly in the West. Canadians copied American homestead policy and survey practices. Governments in Ottawa—whether Liberal or Conservative—worked to lure American settlers because conditions were similar on both sides of the line and Americans knew the techniques and technology required to farm in Canada. Common circumstances also led to the growth of similar protest movements on both sides of the border in the early twentieth century.

Among the indigenous people, the similarities were particularly pronounced. For generations after the border was drawn, Aboriginal people moved back and forth as if it did not exist. The Metis lived and hunted in both Canada and the United States. Their leader, Louis Riel, might have been a key figure in Canadian history, but he was also a US citizen. Later, in the 1960s and 1970s, Aboriginal activists on both sides of the border emphasized their common bonds, feeling more Aboriginal than Canadian or American.

Often the celebrated differences between the two countries do not distinguish them very much at all. Canadians believe that they live in a more just nation. They decried McCarthyism in the United States in the 1950s, while the Canadian government quietly removed alleged communists from their jobs and discriminated against homosexuals on the dubious grounds that they were security risks. Canadians have been convinced that their country has treated Aboriginal people better than the US had. It is true that there were fewer violent conflicts in Canada, but both countries pursued the same policies of assimilation that ultimately left Aboriginal people dispossessed and destitute. As much as Canadians boast about having a tolerant and inclusive country, their history is marked by prejudice. They have often forgotten that slavery existed in Canada and that Upper Canada only abolished the practice after six northern US states had already done so. The Underground Railroad, a proud part of Canada's history, was in fact more American than Canadian. After the abolition of slavery, parts of Canada imposed racial segregation, as did large parts of the US. In the late nineteenth and early twentieth centuries, both the Canadian and US governments worked to restrict immigration from Asia on racial grounds. During the Second World War, the two countries forcibly removed individuals of Japanese descent from the West Coast.

Many great symbols of Canada were at least partly American. US businessmen, managers, and surveyors were central to the construction of the

Canadian Pacific Railway. The Mounties adapted to the Western environment by abandoning their British hats, saddles, and guns for American ones. The Calgary Stampede was created by an American imitating the summer celebrations in the cattle-raising parts of the United States.

When there have been tensions between the two countries, they were often caused by a Canadian sense that the Americans were disloyal to common North American values. McCarthyism in the 1950s violated the rights of the accused. The violent assaults on black civil rights protestors in the 1950s and 1960s dishonoured the principle of equality. The war in Vietnam was a clear betrayal of the commitment to peace and self-determination.

The civil rights movement and the war in Vietnam led to much criticism of the United States in the 1960s and 1970s. Some of this was anti-Americanism, with large numbers of Canadians lashing out at anything and anyone from south of the border. But in another sense, Canadian critiques of the United States reflected a common North American experience. Both Canadians and Americans objected to the US government's hypocrisy, its failure to live up to its proclaimed ideals. On both sides of the border, protestors came from similar backgrounds, pursued similar causes, and used similar slogans and protest techniques.

Historian Frank Underhill exaggerated when he said that the Canadian was "the first anti-American, the model anti-American, the archetypal anti-American, the ideal anti-American as he exists in the mind of God."[2] Anti-Americanism, when it has existed in Canada, has been of the low-grade variety, more whine than rage. Canadians will grumble about the United States, make snide comments about American attitudes toward guns and health care, but will not take to the streets to chant "death to America" or cheer the terrorists who attack American targets. Sometimes the effort to distance Canada from the United States is little more than a pose. Most Canadians do not strive to be less like Americans as much as they work to reassure themselves and others that they are not American. This contradiction—wanting the benefits of being American while rejecting the United States—is crucial to understanding the perennial Canadian identity crisis.

English Canada's self-image could be seen clearly in 2000 in, of all things, a beer ad. Molson's Brewery ran a highly popular 60-second advertisement, known as "The Rant," on television and in cinemas. A young man, later nicknamed Joe Canadian, walked onto a stage and began talking into a microphone, greeting the audience with a casual "Hey." He then enumerated the factors that made Canada distinct, starting hesitatingly but becoming more passionate as he proceeded. Some of the items on the list were fundamental, such as the use of the French language in Canada and the political differences between the two countries. But others bordered on the banal: "A tuque is a hat! A chesterfield is a couch! And it is pronounced zed—not zee—*zed*!" The ad became surprisingly popular, and Joe began to perform The Rant live at hockey games, where he would bring the crowd to its feet. In Toronto, Joe "generated the kind of fist-in-the-air ovation usually reserved for goals scored in sudden-death," according to an American journalist.[3] The Rant showed that Canadians loved those things, big or small, that differentiated them from the Americans. Deep in the Canadian psyche, the differences are treasured, nurtured, and exaggerated.

None of this is to say that Canada and the United States are the same. They *are* distinct countries. For instance, the difference between parliamentary democracy and a presidential system has had a profound impact on the development of the two polities. In Canada, the prime minister's party usually controls a majority of the seats in the House of Commons, where party discipline is strictly enforced. As a result, a Canadian prime minister typically speaks not only for the government, but also for the legislature. Such is not the case for the US president, who deals with an independent Congress that often travels in its own direction, as it did when investigating communists in government in the 1950s. Frequently, the US Senate has refused to ratify treaties, leaving the United States out of the League of Nations, the Kyoto Protocol, and the International Criminal Court, and delaying the development of the St Lawrence Seaway for more than 20 years. Lester Pearson's government was able to implement a national health-care program in the late 1960s, but not so for successive American presidents. President Harry Truman tried and failed in the 1940s and 1950s, as did Bill Clinton in the 1990s. In 2010, Congress passed a watered-down bill to reduce the number of Americans with no medical coverage under the existing mixed private/public system, but millions remained uninsured.

Two regions pull the countries apart. One-quarter of Canada's population resides in Quebec, a province with a French-speaking majority, a distinct culture, and a different legal system. The US South, depending on how it is defined, is home to about one-third of the country's population and tends to be more conservative than the rest of the United States. Traditional attitudes toward religion, ethnicity, and the role of government are more likely to prevail in the South than further north or west.

## The Politics of the Relationship

Public distrust of the United States has shaped Canadian politics. Pierre Trudeau felt pushed into measures to assert Canadian control over Arctic waters. Prime Minister Paul Martin gave every indication that he was going to sign on to the US Ballistic Missile Defense program, until shifting public opinion scared him away. Running against the Americans has frequently proven fruitful for Canadian politicians. John A. Macdonald won the election in 1891, in part because he promised to keep Canada's distance from the United States, as did Robert Borden in 1911 and John Diefenbaker in 1957 and 1958. But the political algebra has changed since Diefenbaker's triumphs. He tried to harness anti-American sentiment again in 1963 and failed. The same happened to John Turner in 1988: a campaign that relied on a Canadian desire for economic independence from the US came up short. Paul Martin lost the Liberal majority in 2004 and then his government in 2006, despite doing his best to establish himself as Canada's defender against the threats of George W. Bush's America.

The many conflicts between the governments in Ottawa and Washington are not easy to characterize. Often, the problem is a clash of incompatible interests, as has been the case over the Northwest Passage. Sometimes the Canadian leadership is unreasonable, as it was in the late Diefenbaker years when a paranoid prime minister was determined to put President Kennedy in his place, despite the harm it might do to Canadian interests. At other times, the US administration must take most of the blame. President George W. Bush was, as Canadians thought, wrong about the war in Iraq. It was sensible for Canadians to stay out of that conflict without being told in exaggerated terms that they had let down a friend whose security was at stake.

As much as the Canadian public might gain satisfaction from a direct confrontation with the United States over contentious issues, an adversarial approach has seldom benefitted Canada. Diefenbaker did nothing to advance Canada's interests by quarrelling with Kennedy. Trudeau's government could not secure Canada's position on the Northwest Passage by fighting the issue in public. The Chrétien government gained little in its efforts to secure Canadian cultural policy by appealing to like-minded countries in the face of opposition from the United States. Even when Ottawa's position is bolstered by rulings of international bodies, as was the case with softwood lumber, Canada will have a hard time winning in open and direct conflict with the Americans.

For the most part, Canadian leaders have advanced their country's interests more effectively by pursuing good relations in Washington than by openly clashing with American leaders. Mackenzie King outperformed Pierre Trudeau in advancing Canadian interests with the Americans; Brian Mulroney got more of what he wanted in Washington than Diefenbaker did—even if Mulroney's approach was pilloried by nationalists at home. More often than not, the best approach is a cooperative one, where a negotiated settlement serves the interests of both sides and no one keeps score to see who "won" and who "lost."

The same principles apply to the United States. American leaders have gained little through public conflict with Canada. US officials took a risk in 1963 by contradicting Prime Minister John Diefenbaker and might well have caused a backlash against the United States. Through an emissary, John Kennedy offered to provide public support to Lester Pearson in the 1963 election, but the Liberal campaign chair, Walter Gordon, responded that the president should keep quiet lest he make Pearson look like the American candidate. Similarly, right after George W. Bush publicly urged Canada to join the Ballistic Missile Defense system, Prime Minister Paul Martin told him that Canada was "a lot further away than we were five minutes ago" from taking part.[4] Bush did not understand that Canadian politicians are always wary about getting too close to the United States, and cannot be seen as taking orders from Washington. US officials are wise to act cautiously, lest they stir up Canadian nationalism.

It is striking that conflicts between the governments have never led to long-term damage in the relationship. After the American war in Vietnam ended in 1973, Canadian confidence in the United States quickly returned. The two governments argued over Canada's decision to prevent Taiwanese athletes from competing under the name *China* at the 1976 Olympic Games in Montreal; the Americans were upset, some even suggesting a boycott of the event, but the wounds healed quickly and the Americans used the same arguments against the Taiwanese just four years later at the winter Olympics in Lake Placid. Similarly, public opinion of the US and relations between the two governments recovered as soon as George W. Bush left office in 2009. Ottawa and Washington are pulled together by similar values, common economic interests, and the necessity of securing the North American continent, factors that cannot be cancelled out by short-term spats or personality conflicts.

So similar are political values that often the two governments travel in parallel paths without any coordination between them. Both countries enacted national prohibition during the First World War, remained wary of involvement in international affairs in the 1920s, adopted New Deal policies to resuscitate the two economies during the Great Depression, lauded appeasement in the 1930s, pursued a policy of limited liability in the early days of the Second World War, and forced citizens of Japanese descent to abandon their homes on the West Coast during the war.

## The Economics of the Relationship

The United States began as a small agricultural economy, but quickly became an economic powerhouse. Canada benefitted from the Reciprocity Treaty of 1855–66 and from American entrepreneurs who developed railways, the lumber industry, and other sectors of the Canadian economy. Largely because of its proximity to the United States, Canada became affluent in the twentieth century. By the 1920s, the United States had the largest national economy in the world, was the largest foreign investor in Canada, and served as Canada's main trading partner. Canada could sell to a resource-hungry America and had access to the American capital and technology necessary to develop the domestic economy. From time to time, Ottawa tried—and failed—to broaden Canada's trade to reduce the country's dependence on the American market. Certainly, diversification makes sense, but Canada will always be reliant on the American economy.

Canada's challenge was how to benefit from American affluence without joining the US, a debate that raged from the 1840s until the 1990s, when Canadians decided that they could maintain their independence even as their economy became integrated with that of their powerful neighbour. Free trade, the subject of bitter political debate from before Confederation to the 1980s, is now accepted by all but a few critics, most of whom are outside the political mainstream.

In Canada, economic nationalism has rarely been about the best interests of the nation as a whole. The National Policy grew less from Macdonald's judgment about the country's economic needs than his failure to obtain a trade agreement with the United States and his realization that he could use the tariff as a political weapon against his opponents. The policy resulted in widespread foreign investment in Canada, bemoaned by later generations of nationalists, and tensions between the Canadian centre and the periphery, as Ontario and Quebec industrialized at the expense of the poorer areas of the country. Western Canadians, for instance, generally opposed the policy because it meant they would have to purchase expensive products from Ontario rather than more suitable and affordable items from across the border. Trudeau's National Energy Program similarly promoted the interests of those parts of Canada that were net consumers of energy over those that were net producers, at a significant cost to national unity. Nor was there anything particularly national about so-called nationalist policies to restrict foreign investment. Those Canadians, like Brian Mulroney and Jean Chrétien, who came from small towns where American firms were the major employers did not see foreign investment as a threat to their identity, but rather as a necessity for survival. Toronto accountants, professors, and novelists could decry foreign investment at little or no cost to themselves, but it was not easy for an electrician in Baie-Comeau or a machinist in Shawinigan Falls to do so.

A special economic relationship made sense for both sides. The Hyde Park agreement of 1941 bailed out the Canadian economy, but it helped the US too. A Canadian balance of payments crisis was not in the best interests of the US, because the war effort required that Canadian industry continue to pump out munitions for the allies. The 1963 interest equalization tax and the 1971 Nixon Shock should not have applied to Canada, not because

Canada deserved special treatment as the best friend of the United States, but because the United States damaged its own economic interests by imposing those measures on Canada.

## The Politics of Security

In the nineteenth century, there was deep distrust between the United States and the colonies that would become Canada. Canada's only significant security threat came from south of the border. American forces invaded during the American Revolution and the War of 1812, and the US government did little to stop the Fenian attacks of the 1860s and 1870s. Tensions along the border threatened to erupt into war until the last disputed portion of the line was finalized in 1903 with the settlement of the Alaska Boundary Dispute. Because the Canada–US border had been settled through negotiation, not war, it has proved one of the most resilient boundaries in the world.

By the 1930s, the threat for both Canada and the United States came from across the oceans. Franklin Roosevelt might have been the first president to realize that American security depended on a secure Canada, leading to his 1938 pledge in Kingston, Ontario, that the US would defend Canada against outside aggression. At the same time, his Canadian counterpart, Prime Minister William Lyon Mackenzie King, realized that national sovereignty—and national self-respect—demanded that Canada contribute to, and have a say in, its own defence. King pledged that Canada would defend itself, so that Canadian territory could not be used by a third country to launch an attack on the United States. In 1940, he eagerly joined Roosevelt's proposed Permanent Joint Board on Defence, allowing Canadian and American military officials to plan jointly for the defence of the continent.

The principle of the joint defence of North America was further developed in the North American Air Defence Command (NORAD) agreement, in which Canada and the US pledged to work together to protect the two countries against bomber or missile attacks. Critics, particularly in the late 1960s and early 1970s, suggested that Canada had lost some of its sovereignty by agreeing to this arrangement. Yet staying out of NORAD would have done nothing to advance Canadian interests, even if it might have eased Canadian fears about being swallowed by the United States. As Paul Martin said, when he was arguing in favour of Canadian participation in Ballistic Missile Defense, "You want to talk about sovereignty? My sovereignty says you don't send missiles up over my airspace unless I'm there."[5]

The terrorist attacks of 11 September 2001 changed the US perception of homeland security. Now Americans realized that terrorists might cross the border from Canada to strike at US targets. For both governments, a longstanding challenge became a pressing problem: How could they keep the border open to trade and legitimate visitors but closed to terrorists and criminals? The solution has been closer integration and cooperation. In the early years after the al Qaeda attacks, the two countries did much to share information and beef up border security, while creating programs to allow cargo trucks and businesspeople to bypass lines at the border. The process of harmonization continues, though it has lost some of the urgency that it once had.

# Culture and Cultural Policy

Culture comprises all the aspects of human experience that are not genetic: language, clothing, cuisine, architecture, sports, and art. In these areas, Canada and the United States are remarkably similar. In fact, people who live near the border usually have more in common with those just across the line than with fellow citizens on the other side of the country. Seattle's culture is closer to that of Vancouver than it is to that of Miami. The residents of St Stephen, New Brunswick, feel much more at home in Calais, Maine, than they do in Blainville, Quebec, or Grand Prairie, Alberta. This is natural, a reflection of the geography that binds the two countries.

Every generation of Canadians has lamented the Americanization of Canada, not realizing how American Canada was from its moment of birth. Long before Canadians could watch American television programs, they flocked to American films. Before they could listen to American music on the radio, they watched American plays at the theatre and read American novels and magazines. For decades, Canadians have regretted the way US teams dominate the National Hockey League, not aware that before hockey, Canada's national sport was baseball, played according to New York rules.

The concern over American cultural influences often focuses on the mass media. Throughout the twentieth century and into the twenty-first, Canadians have legitimately believed that the survival of a Canadian identity has depended, at least in part, on the existence of Canadian television programs, films, popular music, and magazines. Given the high cost of these endeavours and the relatively small size of the Canadian market, it was difficult for cultural producers in Canada to compete with the Americans. They could only do so if the government intervened, creating quotas for the broadcasting of Canadian music or television programs, subsidizing Canadian film, or taxing American magazines. Without these measures, there would have been very little Canadian content in the mass media.

Yet sometimes Canadian cultural policy has advanced the economic interests of Canadian owners and not Canadian content, a point American officials have made vigorously. When the US won the magazine case before the World Trade Organization (WTO) in 1997, the country's trade representative hailed the decision because it would prevent Canada "from using 'culture' as a pretext for discriminating against imports."[6] The law requiring that split-run magazines be printed in Canada might well have benefitted Canadian printers, but did nothing to advance the country's culture. The measures preventing foreigners from buying TV stations might protect domestic owners from competition, but do not increase the amount of Canadian content, which is regulated by the Canadian Radio-television and Telecommunications Commission (CRTC).

Canadian cultural policy has continued to be protectionist, while Canadian and US trade policies have been moving, for the better part of a century, toward the free flow of goods and services across the border. This led to the unresolved culture–trade quandary: How can Canada protect or promote domestic culture while honouring its trade agreements? Sheila Copps attempted to solve this problem through the Cultural Diversity Convention, but at best won a symbolic victory. Subsequent ministers of Canadian heritage have had no more success in resolving the issue.

## Final Words

No one on earth is more like an American than a Canadian. The two people share many values: freedom, democracy, equality, and the market economy. They have different political systems, but they share some essential elements: federalism, the separation of church and state, and a written constitution that protects individual rights. More often than not, the interests of the two countries intersect. Both have a vital stake in North American security, in protecting the environment, in promoting peace abroad. The two countries quibble frequently—they might even have the occasional public spat—but they maintain their relationship and reconcile their differences, because they share the same values and it is in their best interests to get along.

# Notes

## Preface

1. T. Watson Smith, *History of the Methodist Church within the Territories Embraced in the Late Conference of* *Eastern British America*, vol. 2 (Halifax: S.F. Huestis, 1877), 67.

## Chapter 1

1. L.F.S. Upton, *The Loyal Whig: William Smith of New York and Quebec* (Toronto: University of Toronto Press, 1969), 53.
2. Elizabeth Mancke, *The Fault Lines of Empire: Political Differentiation in Massachusetts and Nova Scotia, c. 1760–1830* (New York: Routledge, 2005), 11.
3. John Bartlet Brebner, *New England's Outpost: Acadia before the Conquest of Canada* (New York: Columbia University Faculty of Political Science, 1927).
4. Emily P. Weaver, "Nova Scotia and New England during the Revolution," *American Historical Review* 10, no. 1 (October 1904): 55.
5. David Brion Davis and Steven Mintz, *The Boisterous Sea of Liberty: A Documentary History of America from Discovery through the Civil War* (New York: Oxford University Press, 1998), 144.
6. John Bartlet Brebner, *The Neutral Yankees of Nova Scotia: A Marginal Colony during the Revolutionary Years* (New York: Columbia University Press, 1937), 160.
7. Donna J. Spindel, "Anchors of Empire: Savannah, Halifax, and the Atlantic Frontier," *American Review of Canadian Studies* 6, no. 2 (Autumn 1976): 102, n. 42.
8. An Act for the Better Securing the Dependency of His Majesty's Dominions in America upon the Crown and Parliament of Great Britain, 6 Geo. 3, c. 12 (1766). This legislation is usually known as the Declaratory Act.
9. Davis and Mintz, *Boisterous Sea of Liberty*, 151.
10. Ernest Clarke, *The Siege of Fort Cumberland, 1776: An Episode in the American Revolution* (Montreal and Kingston: McGill–Queen's University Press, 1995), 3.
11. John Bartlet Brebner, *North Atlantic Triangle: The Interplay of Canada, the United States and Great Britain* (1945; Toronto: McClelland and Stewart, 1966), 56.
12. Wendell Phillips Garrison and Francis Jackson Garrison, *William Lloyd Garrison, 1805–1879: The Story of His Life Told by His Children*, vol. 1, *1805–1835* (New York: Century, 1885), 7.
13. Brebner, *Neutral Yankees*, 311.
14. Mancke, *Fault Lines of Empire*, 78.
15. William B. Hamilton, "Society and Schools in Nova Scotia," chapter 5 in *Canadian Education: A History*, edited by J. Donald Wilson, Robert M. Stamp, and Louis-Philippe Audet (Scarborough, Ontario: Prentice–Hall, 1970), 89–90.
16. *The Writings of George Washington*, vol. 3, *1775–1776*, edited by Worthington Chauncey Ford (New York: G.P. Putnam's Sons, 1889), 127.
17. Alan Taylor, *The Civil War of 1812: American Citizens, British Subjects, Irish Rebels, and Indian Allies* (New York: Alfred A. Knopf, 2010), 23.

18. James W. St G. Walker, *The Black Loyalists: The Search for a Promised Land in Nova Scotia and Sierra Leone, 1783–1870* (1976; Toronto: University of Toronto Press, 1992), 46.

19. Fred Landon, *Western Ontario and the American Frontier* (Toronto: Ryerson, 1941), 134.

20. David V.J. Bell, "The Loyalist Tradition in Canada," *Journal of Canadian Studies* 5, no. 2 (May 1970): 22.

21. Larry Diamond, "A Giant Among Teachers: An Appreciation of the Original 'Political Man'," *Hoover Digest*, 2007, no. 1., www.hoover.org/publications/hoover-digest/article/6041, viewed 20 May 2012.

22. Seymour Martin Lipset, *Continental Divide: The Values and Institutions of the United States and Canada* (New York, Routledge, 1990), 1.

23. "An American Farmer," *Aurora* [Philadelphia], 18 June 1813, quoted in Taylor, *Civil War of 1812*, 3.

24. Taylor, *Civil War of 1812*, 8.

25. George C. Herring, *From Colony to Superpower: U.S. Foreign Relations since 1776* (New York: Oxford University Press, 2008), 116.

26. Taylor, *Civil War of 1812*, 6.

27. George Dangerfield, *The Era of Good Feelings* (New York: Harcourt, Brace, 1952), 40.

28. A.L. Burt, *The United States, Great Britain, and British North America: From the Revolution to the Establishment of Peace after the War of 1812* (New York: Russell and Russell, 1961), 322.

29. Gerald M. Craig, *Upper Canada: The Formative Years, 1784–1841* (Toronto: McClelland and Stewart, 1963), 74.

## Chapter 2

1. Elijah Leonard, *A Memoir* (London, Ontario: n.p., 1874?), 10.

2. Kathy Bockus, "Prime Minister Opens New Crossing," *Saint Croix Courier*, 12 January 2010. I heard the story many times when I worked for the member of Parliament for Carleton–Charlotte, the riding that included St Stephen. There is no contemporary evidence to support the story and no reason to believe that British military officials would have allowed the gunpowder to be given to the enemy. It is possible that some leftover gunpowder crossed the border many years after the war, and that this event became warped each time the story was retold until it became a wartime, not a postwar, event.

3. David A. Wilson, *The Irish in Canada*, Canada's Ethnic Groups booklet no. 12 (Ottawa: Canadian Historical Association, 1989), 5; J.M. Bumsted, "Americans," pp. 183–99 in *Encyclopedia of Canada's Peoples*, edited by Paul Robert Magocsi (Toronto: University of Toronto Press, 1999), 185.

4. Alexis de Tocqueville, *De la Démocratie en Amérique*, vol. 2 (Brussels: Louis Hauman, 1835), 483; Patrick Shirreff, *A*

*Tour through North America; Together with a Comprehensive View of the Canadas and the United States* (Edinburgh: Oliver and Boyd, 1835), 95–6; John Robert Godley, *Letters from America*, vol. 1 (London: John Murray, 1844), 201–2.

5. Robert Gourlay, *Statistical Account of Upper Canada, Compiled with a View to a Grand System of Emigration*, vol. 2 (London: Simpkin and Marshall, 1822), 422.

6. Thomas Chandler Haliburton, *The Clockmaker; or, The Sayings and Doings of Samuel Slick of Slickville*, first series, fourth edition (London: Richard Bentley, 1838), 89; *The Attaché; or, Sam Slick in England*, vol. 1 (London: Richard Bentley, 1843), 261; *The Clockmaker; or, The Sayings and Doings of Samuel Slick, of Slickville*, second series (Philadelphia: Carey, Lea, and Blanchard, 1838), 101.

7. V.L.O. Chittick, *Thomas Chandler Haliburton ("Sam Slick"): A Study in Provincial Toryism* (New York: Columbia University Press, 1924), 358.

8. Francis B. Head, *A Narrative* (London: John Murray, 1839), 75.

9. John George Lambton, Earl of Durham, *The Report and Dispatches of the Earl of Durham* (London: Ridgways, 1839), esp. 191, 230.

10. Arthur to Col. J.F. Love, 6 March 1839, in *The Arthur Papers: Being the Canadian Papers, Mainly Confidential, Private and Demi-Official of Sir George Arthur, KCH*, edited by Charles R. Sanderson, vol. 2 (Toronto: Toronto Public Libraries and University of Toronto Press, 1957), 75.

11. Winfield Scott, *Memoirs of Lieut.-General Scott, LLD*, vol. 2 (New York: Sheldon and Company, 1864), 334.

12. Cephas D. Allin and George M. Jones, *Annexation, Preferential Trade, and Reciprocity* (Toronto: Musson, [1912]), 384.

13. Elgin to Lord Grey, 23 April 1849, pp. 346–50 in *The Elgin–Grey Papers, 1846–1852*, edited by Arthur G. Doughty, vol. 1 (Ottawa: Dominion Archives, 1937), 349.

## Chapter 3

1. George Brown, "Anti-Slavery Demonstration" speech to the annual meeting of the Anti-Slavery Association, 24 March 1852, pp. 252–61 in *The Life and Speeches of the Hon. George Brown, edited by Alexander Mackenzie* (Toronto: Globe Printing, 1882), 260.

2. J.M.S. Careless, *Brown of the Globe*, vol. 2, *Statesman of Confederation, 1860–1880* (Toronto: Macmillan, 1963), 252.

3. "The Coloured Population of Canada," *Globe*, 21 March 1849.

4. Robin W. Winks, *The Blacks in Canada: A History*, 2nd ed., Carleton Library Series no. 192 (Montreal and Kingston: McGill–Queen's University Press, 1997), 494; Michael Wayne, "The Black Population of Canada West on the Eve of the American Civil War: A Reassessment Based on the Manuscript Census of 1861," *Histoire Sociale/Social History* 28, no. 56 (November 1995): 469–70.

5. Laurier commenting on a speech by Goldwin Smith, 14 November 1904, Canadian Club of Ottawa, in *Addresses Delivered before the Canadian Club of Ottawa, 1903–1909*, edited by Gerald H. Brown (Ottawa: Mortimer Press, 1910), 80.

6. S.G. Howe, *The Refugees from Slavery in Canada West: Report to the Freedmen's Inquiry Commission* (Boston: Freedmen's Inquiry Commission, 1864), 43, 45.

7. Richard J. Hinton, *John Brown and His Men* (New York: Funk and Wagnalls, 1894), 505.

8. W.L. Morton, "British North America and a Continent in Dissolution, 1861–71," *History* 47, no. 160 (January 1962): 146.

9. "The Hostility of Canada—The Anglo-Rebel Alliance," *New York Times*, 16 December 1864, 4.

10. P.B. Waite, *Life and Times of Confederation: Politics, Newspapers, and the Union of British North America* (1962; Toronto: Robin Brass Studio, 2001), 29.

11. John A. Macdonald to Edward Watkin, 27 March 1865, quoted in Waite, *Life and Times of Confederation*, 329.

12. Janet Ajzenstat et al., eds., *Canada's Founding Debates* (Toronto: Stoddart, 1999), 281.

13. Donald Creighton, *John A. Macdonald*, vol. 2, *The Old Chieftain* (Toronto: Macmillan, 1955), 81.

14. Allan Nevins, *Hamilton Fish: The Inner History of the Grant Administration* (New York: Dodd, Mead and Company, 1937), 490.

# Chapter 4

1. Richard Gwyn, *Nation Maker*, vol. 2 of *Sir John A. Macdonald: His Life, Our Times* (Toronto: Random House, 2011), 427.

2. John F. Finerty, *War-Path and Bivouac: The Conquest of the Sioux* (Chicago: n.p., 1890), 25. This quotation is often misattributed to Big Bear.

3. *The Queen vs. Louis Riel, Accused and Convicted of the Crime of High Treason: Report* (Ottawa: n.p., 1886), 158–9.

4. J.M. Bumsted, "Louis Riel and the United States," *American Review of Canadian Studies* 29, no. 1 (Spring 1999): 29.

5. Blair Stonechild, *The New Buffalo: The Struggle for Aboriginal Post-Secondary Education in Canada* (Winnipeg: University of Manitoba Press, 2006), 19.

6. Martin Robin, *The Rush for Spoils: The Company Province, 1871–1933* (Toronto: McClelland and Stewart, 1972), 44.

7. *Debates of the House of Commons of the Dominion of Canada*, 2nd session, 4th Parliament, vol. 8, 5 April 1880, 1052.

8. Augustus Bridle, "Sir William Van Horne," in *Sons of Canada: Short Studies of Characteristic Canadians*, by Augustus Bridle (Toronto: J.M. Dent and Sons, 1916), 199.

9. Robert Bruce Shepard, "American Influence on the Settlement and Development of the Canadian Plains" (PhD thesis, University of Regina, 1994), 104.

10. *Fifth Census of Canada, 1911*, vol. 2 (Ottawa: Census Office, 1913), 376–7.

11. Clifford Sifton, "The Immigrants Canada Wants," *Maclean's*, 1 April 1922, 16.

12. W.D. Scott, "Immigration and Population," in *Canada and its Provinces: A History of the Canadian People and Their Institutions*, edited by Adam Shortt and Arthur G. Doughty, vol. 7 (Toronto: Glasgow, Brook, 1914), 555–6.

13. *Official Report of the Debates of the House of Commons of the Dominion of Canada*, 1st session, 12th Parliament, vol. 104, 15 February 1912, 3154.

14. Russell W. Fridley, "When Minnesota Coveted Canada," *Minnesota History* 41, no. 2 (Summer 1968): 77.

15. *Official Debates of the House of Commons of the Dominion of Canada*, 4th session, 4th Parliament, vol. 12, 12 May 1882, 1477.

16. F.H. Leacy, M.C. Urquhart, and K.A.H. Buckley, eds., *Historical Statistics of Canada*, 2nd ed. (Ottawa: Statistics Canada, 1983), series E44. In 1905, the average worker on the production (as opposed to supervisory or clerical) side of the manufacturing industry in Canada earned $375.

17. J. Castell Hopkins, *Canadian Annual Review of Public Affairs, 1907* (Toronto: Annual Review Publishing, 1908), 392. (This quotation is often misattributed to R.B. Bennett.)

18. James S. Woodsworth, *Strangers within Our Gates, or Coming Canadians* (Toronto: F.C. Stephenson, 1909), 190–1.

19. R. Bruce Shepard, "Plain Racism: The Reaction against Oklahoma Black Immigration to the Canadian Plains," *Prairie Forum* 10, no. 2 (Autumn 1985): 369.

20. Order-in-Council PC1324, 12 August 1911, reprinted in R. Bruce Shepard, *Deemed Unsuitable* (Toronto: Umbrella, 1997), x.

21. Julian Sher, *White Hoods: Canada's Ku Klux Klan* (Vancouver: New Star Books, 1983), 49–50; Martin Robin, *Shades of Right: Nativist and Fascist Politics in Canada, 1920–1940* (Toronto: University of Toronto Press, 1992), 33, 43–4.

22. W.L. Morton, *The Progressive Party in Canada* (Toronto: University of Toronto Press, 1950), 39.

23. Leacy, Urquhart, and Buckley, eds., *Historical Statistics of Canada*, series M228.

# Chapter 5

1. The quotation and the description of Macdonald's coffin are from "Lying in State: Arrangements for the Premier's Funeral," *Montreal Daily Witness*, 8 June 1891, 3.

2. Convention between Great Britain and Russia, signed at St Petersburg, 28/16 February 1825, in *A Complete Collection of the Treaties and Conventions, and Reciprocal Regulations, at Present Subsisting between Great Britain and Foreign Powers, and the Laws, Decrees, and Orders-in-Council, concerning the Same, so Far as They Relate to Commerce and Navigation . . .* , vol. 3 (London: Henry Butterworth, 1841), 362–66.

3. Norman Penlington, *The Alaska Boundary Dispute: A Critical Reappraisal* (Toronto: McGraw–Hill Ryerson, 1972), 37, 124–7.

4. Roosevelt to John Hay, 10 July 1902, from *The Theodore Roosevelt Treasury: A Self-Portrait from His Writings*, compiled and with an introduction by Hermann Hagedorn (New York: G.P. Putnam's Sons, 1957), 170–1.

5. Charles Callan Tansill, *Canadian–American Relations, 1875–1911* (New Haven: Yale University Press, 1943), 224.

6. Anthony Steel, "The British Empire and the United States of America, 1870–1914," chapter 9 in *The Cambridge History of the British Empire*, vol. 3, *The Empire–Commonwealth, 1870–1919*, edited by E.A. Benians, James Butler, and C.E. Carrington (Cambridge: Cambridge University Press, 1959), 319.

7. "Position of the Minority," *New York Times*, 21 October 1903.

8. George W. Smalley, *Anglo–American Memories* (New York and London: G.P. Putnam's Sons, 1911), 270–1.

9. C.P. Stacey, *Canada and the Age of Conflict: A History of Canadian External Policies*, vol. 1, *1867–1921* (Toronto: University of Toronto Press, 1984), 98.

10. Kurkpatrick Dorsey, *The Dawn of Conservation Diplomacy: U.S.– Canadian Wildlife Protection Treaties in*

the *Progressive Era* (Seattle: University of Washington Press, 1998), 4.

11. O.D. Skelton, "General Economic History, 1867–1912," in *Canada and Its Provinces: A History of the Canadian People and Their Institutions*, edited by Adam Shortt and Arthur G. Doughty, vol. 9 (Toronto: Edinburgh University Press, 1913), 153; Canada, *Report of the Department of Trade and Commerce for the Fiscal Year Ended June 30, 1905* (Ottawa: Department of Trade and Commerce, 1906), 15.

12. Canada, *Report of the Minister of Agriculture of the Dominion of Canada for the Calendar Year 1882* (Ottawa: Department of Agriculture, 1883), no. 14 in *Sessional Papers, First Session of the Fifth Parliament of the Dominion of Canada*, vol. 10 (Ottawa: Parliament, 1883), 161; Robert Bruce Shepard, "American Influence on the Settlement and Development of the Canadian Plains" (PhD thesis, University of Regina, 1994), 144; T.D. Regehr, *Remembering Saskatchewan: A History of Rural Saskatchewan* (Saskatoon: University of Saskatchewan Extension Division, 1979), 31.

13. J.H. Dales, "'National Policy' Myths, Past and Present," *Journal of Canadian Studies* 14, no. 3 (Autumn 1979): 94.

14. *Debates of the House of Commons of the Dominion of Canada*, 1st session, 4th Parliament, vol. 6, 28 March 1879, 794.

15. *Debates of the House of Commons of the Dominion of Canada*, 5th session, 3rd Parliament, vol. 4, 7 March 1878, 862.

16. Joseph Pope, *Memoirs of the Right Honourable Sir John A. Macdonald, G.C.B., First Prime Minister of the Dominion of Canada* (Toronto: Musson Book Company, [1894]), 774, 777.

17. R.E. Hannigan, "Reciprocity 1911: Continentalism and American Weltpolitik," *Diplomatic History* 4, no. 1 (Winter 1980): 1.

18. *Congressional Record*, 61st Congress, 3rd Session, 14 February 1911, vol. 46, 2520.

19. J. Castell Hopkins, *The Canadian Annual Review of Public Affairs, 1911* (Toronto: Annual Review Publishing, 1912), 30.

20. Robert Laird Borden, *His Memoirs*, vol. 1, *1854–1915*, edited by Henry Borden, abridged ed., edited by Heath Macquarrie, Carleton Library no. 46 (Toronto: McClelland and Stewart, 1969), 142.

21. "Monster Meeting Protested against Reciprocity Pact," *Hamilton Spectator*, 22 February 1911, 11.

22. Paul Stevens, introduction to *The 1911 General Election: A Study in Canadian Politics*, edited by Paul Stevens (Toronto: Copp Clark, 1970), 2.

23. Library and Archives Canada, Diary of William Lyon Mackenzie King, 26 September 1911, www.collectionscanada.gc.ca/databases/king, viewed 5 June 2012.

24. Leon E. Truesdell, *The Canadian Born in the United States* (New Haven: Yale University Press, 1943), 10; Alan A. Brookes, "Canadians, British," in *Harvard Encyclopedia of American Ethnic Groups*, edited by Stephan Thernstrom (Cambridge, Massachusetts: Belknap Press, 1980), 192–3.

25. Wilfrid Laurier to Edward Blake, 29 December 1891, in "Laurier and Blake, 1891–2," a selection of correspondence collected and introduced by Frank H. Underhill, *Canadian Historical Review* 24, no. 2 (June 1943): 135–55.

26. Goldwin Smith, *Canada and the Canadian Question* (Toronto: Hunter, Rose, 1891), 265.

27. Goldwin Smith, *The Political Destiny of Canada* (Toronto: Willing and Williamson, 1878), 71.

28. Frank H. Underhill, *The Image of Confederation* ([Toronto]: Canadian Broadcasting Corp., [1964]), 27.

29. Stephen Leacock, "Greater Canada: An Appeal," *University Magazine*, April 1907, 133.

30. Carl Berger, *The Sense of Power: Studies in the Ideas of Canadian Imperialism, 1867–1914* (Toronto: University of Toronto Press, 1970).

31. I am grateful to Anthony Michel, whose research has shown that independence was a seriously debated topic, one that historians have largely neglected. See Anthony P. Michel, "The Nile Voyageurs: Recognition of Canada's Role in the Empire, 1884–1885," PhD thesis, Carleton University, 2012.

32. "Mr. Cattanach on Imp. Fed," *Globe*, 27 February 1889, 6.

33. "Mercier Visits Washington," *New York Times*, 13 April 1893, 2.

34. "Our English Relations," *New York Times*, 1 March 1871.

35. "Restless Canada," *Atlanta Constitution*, 4 December 1889, 4.

36. "Canadian Agitation for Independence," *Chicago Daily Tribune*, 13 February 1890, 4.

37. Alan Metcalfe, *Canada Learns to Play: The Emergence of Organized Sport, 1807–1914* (Toronto: McClelland and Stewart, 1987), 98.

38. Archibald MacMechan, "Canada as a Vassal State," *Canadian Historical Review* 1 (December 1920): 350.

39. Peter Morris, *Embattled Shadows: A History of Canadian Cinema, 1895–1939* (Montreal and Kingston: McGill–Queen's University Press, 1978), 26.

40. Lady Gay [Grace Denison], "Between You and Me," *Toronto Saturday Night*, 26 May 1894, 7.

41. Lady Gay, "Between You and Me," 8 January 1898, 8.

42. F.H. Leacy, M.C. Urquhart, and K.A.H. Buckley, eds., *Historical Statistics of Canada*, 2nd ed. (Ottawa: Statistics Canada, 1983), series E175–177.

43. John Crispo, *International Unionism: A Study in Canadian–American Relations* (Toronto: McGraw–Hill, 1967), 14.

## Chapter 6

1. Margaret Prang, *N. W. Rowell: Ontario Nationalist* (Toronto: University of Toronto Press, 1975), 361.

2. John MacCormac, "Rowell Stirs Assembly with Straight Talk," *Montreal Gazette*, 9 December 1920, 1, 15.

3. J.L. Granatstein, *Yankee Go Home? Canadians and Anti-Americanism* (Toronto: HarperCollins, 1996), 70.

4. Robert Laird Borden, *His Memoirs* (Toronto: Macmillan, 1938), vol. 2, 772–3.

5. N.W. Rowell, "Canada and the Empire, 1884–1921," chapter 30 in *The Cambridge History of the British Empire*, vol. 6, *Canada and Newfoundland*, edited by J. Holland Rose, A.P. Newton, and E.A. Benians (Cambridge: Cambridge University Press, 1930), 710.

6. C.P. Stacey, *Mackenzie King and the Atlantic Triangle* (Toronto: Macmillan, 1976), 30.

7. George A. Drew, "Salesmen of Death: The Truth about War Makers," *MacLean's*, 1 August 1931, 3–4, 30, 32, 34.

8. "Must Take Peace Seriously Massey Warns Kiwanians," *Toronto Daily Star*, 12 June 1934, 2.

9. Claude Bissell, *The Young Vincent Massey* (Toronto: University of Toronto Press, 1981), 264–91.

10. *The Treaty of Peace and the Covenant of the League of Nations as Negotiated between the Allied and Associated Powers and Germany* (Philadelphia: John C. Winston, 1920), 48.

11. *Official Report of the Debates of the House of Commons of the Dominion of Canada*, 3rd session, 13th Parliament, vol. 139, 11 September 1919, 230.

12. Jeffrey D. Brison, *Rockefeller, Carnegie, and Canada: American Philanthropy and the Arts and Letters in Canada* (Montreal and Kingston: McGill–Queen's University Press, 2005), 7.

13. Carl C. Berger, "Internationalism, Continentalism, and the Writing of History: Comments on the Carnegie Series on the Relations of Canada and the United States," in *The Influence of the United States on Canadian Development: Eleven Case Studies*, edited by Richard A. Preston (Durham, NC: Duke University Press, 1972), 35.

14. R, "Neighbors: A Canadian View," *Foreign Affairs* 10, no. 3 (April 1932): 422.

15. S. Delbert Clark, "The Positive Content of Canadian National Life," in *Canada and Her Great Neighbor: Sociological Surveys of Opinions and Attitudes in Canada concerning the United States*, edited by H.F. Angus (Toronto: Ryerson Press, 1938), 245.

16. Stacey, *Mackenzie King*, 1–2.

17. Thomas G. Paterson, et al., *American Foreign Relations: A History*, vol. 2, *Since 1895*, 7th ed. (Boston: Wadsworth, 2010), 120.

18. "Report of Inter-Imperial Relations Committee," in *Imperial Conference, 1926: Summary of Proceedings* (London: His Majesty's Stationery Office, 1926), 14.

19. George M. Wrong, "Relations with the United States," in *Canadian Annual Review of Public Affairs, 1923* (Toronto: Canadian Review, 1924), 84.

20. James R. Allum, "'An Outcrop of Hell': History, Environment, and the Politics of the *Trail Smelter* Dispute," chapter 1 in *Transboundary Harm in International Law: Lessons from the Trail Smelter Arbitration*, edited by Rebecca M. Bratspies and Russell A. Miller (Cambridge: Cambridge University Press, 2006), 14.

21. Mary Vipond, *The Mass Media in Canada*, 4th ed. (Toronto: James Lorimer, 2011), 30.

22. Mary Vipond, "Canadian Nationalism and the Plight of Canadian Magazines in the 1920s," *Canadian Historical Review* 58, no. 1 (March 1977): 43–4.

23. Vipond, *Mass Media*, 38.

24. Graham Spry, "The Canadian Broadcasting Issue," *Canadian Forum*, April 1931, 247.

25. Peter Mellen, *The Group of Seven* (Toronto: McClelland and Stewart, 1970), 110.

26. Stacey, *Mackenzie King*, 1.

27. A.E. Safarian, *The Canadian Economy in the Great Depression* (Toronto: McClelland and Stewart, 1970), 103, 106, 115.

28. *Canada Year Book 1922–23* (Ottawa: Dominion Bureau of Statistics, 1924), 481, 483; *Canada Year Book 1932* (Ottawa: Dominion Bureau of Statistics, 1932), 427, 429, 433, 435.

29. Frederic H. Soward, "The Canadian Elections of 1930," *American Political*

*Science Review* 24, no. 4 (November 1930): 998.

30. John MacCormac, "Roosevelt Visit Links 3 Nations," *New York Times*, 1 August 1936, 5.

31. Chester Bloom, letter to John W. Dafoe, in *The Bennett New Deal: Fraud or Portent?*, edited by J.R.H. Wilbur (Toronto: Copp Clark, [1968]), 98.

32. Herridge to Bennett, 12 April 1934, in *The Bennett New Deal*, 69.

33. William Lyon Mackenzie King, diary entry, 11 November 1935, Library and Archives Canada, www. collectionscanada.gc.ca/databases/king/.

34. "3 Nations Reap Trade Benefit," *Montreal Gazette*, 18 November 1938, 9.

35. C.P. Stacey, *Canada and the Age of Conflict: A History of Canadian External Policies*, vol. 2, *1921–1948: The Mackenzie King Era* (Toronto: University of Toronto Press, 1981), 231.

## Chapter 7

1. For descriptions of that day, see Arthur Milnes, ed., *In Roosevelt's Bright Shadow: Presidential Addresses about Canada from Taft to Obama in Honour of FDR's 1938 Speech at Queen's University* (Montreal and Kingston: McGill–Queen's University Press, 2009); "First Visit of Roosevelt to Ontario Marked by Enthusiasm at Kingston," *Ottawa Evening Citizen*, 18 August 1938, 1; Felix Belair Jr, "Aims at Dictators: 'We Won't Stand Idly By', He Says in Extending Monroe," *New York Times*, 19 August 1938, 1, 3. The text of the speech is chapter 5 of *In Roosevelt's Bright Shadow*.

2. W.L. Mackenzie King, *Canada at Britain's Side* (London: MacMillan, 1941), 170.

3. Canada, House of Commons, *Official Report of the Debates*, 12 November 1940, 57. King also used that phrase as the title when he had the two speeches published in pamphlet form: *The United States and Canada: Reciprocity in Defence* (Ottawa: King's Printer, 1939).

4. "Refugee Committee," *Time*, 4 April 1938, 12.

5. Theodore S. Hamerow, *Why We Watched: Europe: America, and the Holocaust* (New York: W.W. Norton, 2008), 31.

6. Erik Eckermann, *World History of the Automobile* (Warrendale, PA: Society of Automotive Engineers, 2001), 120.

7. United States, Department of State, *Peace and War: United States Foreign Policy, 1931–1941* (Washington, DC: United States Government Printing Office, 1943), 438.

8. Hadley Cantril, ed., *Public Opinion, 1935–1946* (Princeton: Princeton University Press, 1951), 385.

9. Library and Archives Canada, William Lyon Mackenzie King Diary, 12 November 1938, www.collectionscanada .gc.ca/databases/king.

10. Irving Abella and Harold Troper, *None is Too Many: Canada and the Jews of Europe, 1933–1948* (Toronto: University of Toronto Press, 2012), xx.

11. F.H. Underhill, "Canadian Foreign Policy in the 1920s," in *Canada and the Organization of Peace* (Toronto: Canadian Institute of International Affairs, 1935), 64.

12. C.P. Stacey, *Canada and the Age of Conflict: A History of Canadian External Policies, vol. 2, 1921–1948: The Mackenzie King Era* (Toronto: University of Toronto Press, 1981), 216.

13. Secretary of State Cordell Hull to US Ambassador in London Joseph Kennedy, 28 September 1938, in *Foreign Relations of the United States, Diplomatic Papers, 1938*, vol. 1, *General* (Washington: Department of State, 1955), 688.

14. Bruce Hutchison, *The Incredible Canadian, A Candid Portrait of Mackenzie King: His Works, His Times, and His Nation* (New York: Longmans, Green, 1952), 250.

15. C.P. Stacey, *Arms, Men, and Governments: The War Policies of*

*Canada, 1939–1945* (Ottawa: Department of National Defence, 1970), 9.

16. Library and Archives Canada, Mackenzie King Diary, 20 April 1941, www.collectionscanada.gc.ca/databases/king.

17. Library and Archives Canada, Mackenzie King Diary, 17 February 1944, www.collectionscanada.gc.ca/databases/king.

18. Leslie Roberts, *The Mackenzie* (New York: Rinehart, 1949), 239.

19. W.L. Morton, review of *William Lyon Mackenzie King*, vol. 2, *The Lonely Heights, 1924–1932*, by H. Blair Neatby, *Canadian Historical Review* 45, no. 4 (December 1964): 320–1.

20. Donald Creighton, *The Forked Road: Canada, 1939–1957* (Toronto: McClelland and Stewart, 1976), 43, 44.

21. J.W. Pickersgill and D.F. Forster, *The Mackenzie King Record*, vol. 3, *1945–1946* (Toronto: University of Toronto Press, 1970), 60.

22. J.L. Granatstein, *How Britain's Weakness Forced Canada into the Arms of the United States* (Toronto: University of Toronto Press, 1989), 32.

23. Some writers quote much higher figures, but these include individuals who were not residents of the United States, such as seamen on foreign ships docked in American ports and enemy aliens from Latin America who were interned in the United States.

# Chapter 8

1. All quotations in this introduction are from Igor Gouzenko, *This Was My Choice: Gouzenko's Story* (Toronto: J.M. Dent and Sons, 1948), 302–23. See also John Sawatsky, *Gouzenko: The Untold Story* (Toronto: Macmillan, 1984).

2. Ralph S. Brown, Jr, *Loyalty and Security: Employment Tests in the United States* (New Haven: Yale University Press, 1958), 182.

3. United States Senate, Committee on Expenditures in the Executive Departments, Subcommittee on Investigations, *Employment of Homosexuals and Other Sex Perverts in Government*, interim report, 81st Congress, Document No. 241 (Washington: Government Printing Office, 1950), 19.

4. Robert Winters, "Civil Service Homosexuals Fired as 'Security Risks'," *The Gazette* [Montreal], 23 February 1985, A4.

5. Reg Whitaker and Gary Marcuse, *Cold War Canada: The Making of a National Insecurity State, 1945–1957* (Toronto: University of Toronto Press, 1994), 181–2.

6. Whitaker and Marcuse, *Cold War Canada*, 187.

7. James L. Kenny and Andrew Secord, "Public Power for Industry: A Re-Examination of the New Brunswick Case, 1940–1960," *Acadiensis* 30, no. 2 (Spring 2001): 102.

8. Library and Archives Canada, William Lyon Mackenzie King Diary, 30 March 1948, www.collectionscanada.gc.ca/databases/king.

9. "Special Message to the Congress Urging Action on the St Lawrence Seaway," 28 January 1952, in *Public Papers of the Presidents of the United States: Harry S. Truman, 1952–53* (Washington: National Archives and Records Service, 1966), 126.

10. See the high levels of trust toward the Soviets in polls conducted in both Canada and the United States before the Gouzenko affair and the sudden change in opinion afterward. Hadley Cantril, ed., *Public Opinion, 1935–1946* (Princeton: Princeton University Press, 1951), 369–71; "The Quarter's Polls," *Public Opinion Quarterly* 10, no. 2 (summer 1946): 264–5.

11. Robert S. Prince, "The Limits of Constraint: Canadian–American Relations and the Korean War, 1950–51," *Journal of Canadian Studies* 27, no. 4 (Winter 1992–3): 147.

12. "North Atlantic Treaty," appendix 2 in *Time of Fear and Hope: The Making of the North Atlantic Treaty, 1947–1949*, by Escott Reid (Toronto: McClelland and Stewart, 1977), 264.

13. Denis Stairs, *The Diplomacy of Constraint: Canada, the Korean War, and the United States* (Toronto: University of Toronto Press, 1974), 9.

14. Lester B. Pearson, *Mike: The Memoirs of the Right Honourable Lester B. Pearson, vol. 2, 1948–1957* (Toronto: University of Toronto Press, 1973), 138.

15. Blair Fraser, *The Search for Identity: Canada, 1945–1967* (Garden City, New York: Doubleday, 1967), 98.

16. Pearson, *Mike*, 180.

## Chapter 9

1. Frank A. Tinker, "I'm Leaving Canada . . . and I'm Glad," *Maclean's*, 1 December 1954, 20–1, 48, 50–1, 54–5.

2. "US Students Are Surprised by Antagonism," *Globe and Mail*, 16 April 1956, 3.

3. *House of Commons Debates: Official Report*, 3 December 1953, 596.

4. *House of Commons Debates: Official Report*, 23 November 1953, 237.

5. "McCarthy: Curiosity in Politics," *Ottawa Journal*, 26 November 1953, 6.

6. "McCarthy Effigy Burned," *Montreal Gazette*, 7 November 1953, 2.

7. Library and Archives Canada (LAC) Heeney Papers, MG30 E144, vol. 2, Heeney Diary, 7 July 1955.

8. "Drew Suggests 4-Point Plan for US Firms," *Globe and Mail*, 20 March 1956, 40; "Unless US Economic Ties Shattered Canada's Future Lost, Drew Warns," *Hamilton Spectator*, 20 March 1956, 7; Joseph Barber, *Good Fences Make Good Neighbors: Why the United States Provokes Canadians* (Toronto: McClelland and Stewart, 1958), 119.

9. *House of Commons Debates: Official Report*, 15 March 1956, 2184.

10. LAC, Lester B. Pearson Papers, MG 26 N9, vol. 11, Mar.–Sept. 1956 file, "Some Aspects of Canadian–American Relations," speech to the Canadian Club, Montreal, 27 March 1956.

11. LAC, C.D. Howe Papers, MG27 III B20, vol. 164, file 89-2 (70), "Public Policy and Economic Expansion," speech to Hamilton Chamber of Commerce, 23 April 1956.

12. "US Envoy Belittles Peril of Control of Resources," *Globe and Mail*, 17 April 1956, 1, 10; "Triangle at Ottawa," *Saturday Night*, 12 May 1956, 5.

13. House of Commons, Standing Committee on External Affairs, *Minutes*, 17 April 1956, 36.

14. Royal Commission on Canada's Economic Prospects, *Final Report* (Ottawa: The Commission, 1957), 389–90.

15. *House of Commons Debates: Official Report*, 4 April 1957, 3059.

16. Knowlton Nash, *History on the Run: The Trenchcoat Memoirs of a Foreign Correspondent* (Toronto: McClelland and Stewart, 1984), 56.

17. LAC, Lester B. Pearson Papers, MG 26 N6, vol. 12, Walter Gordon file, "Notes for Mike," 18 April 1958.

18. Donald Creighton, "Canada and the Cold War," in *Towards the Discovery of Canada: Selected Essays* (Toronto: Macmillan, 1972), 245; Charles Taylor, *Radical Tories: The Conservative Tradition in Canada* (Toronto: Anansi, 1982), 35.

19. *House of Commons Debates: Official Report*, 24 March 1955, 2352.

20. Peter C. Newman, "Who *Really* Owns Canada?" *Maclean's*, 9 June 1956, 11.

21. "Says Govt. Too Timid with US," *Ottawa Citizen*, 11 April 1957, 7.

22. H. Basil Robinson, *Diefenbaker's World: A Populist in Foreign Affairs* (Toronto: University of Toronto Press, 1989), 168.

23. Knowlton Nash, *Kennedy and Diefenbaker: Fear and Loathing across the Undefended Border* (Toronto: McClelland and Stewart, 1990), 96–7.

24. Nash, *Kennedy and Diefenbaker*, 11, 12.
25. Nash, *Kennedy and Diefenbaker*, 14.
26. Canadian Institute of Public Opinion, "Poll, Too, Shows More Women Favor Nuclear Arms Than Men," *Toronto Daily Star*, 27 December 1962, 5.
27. "United States and Canadian Negotiations Regarding Nuclear Weapons," Department of State press release no. 59, 30 January 1963, in *Foreign Relations of the United States, 1961–1963*, vol. 13, *Western Europe and Canada* (Washington: United States Government Printing Office, 1994), 1195.
28. Donald M. Fleming, *So Very Near: The Political Memoirs of the Honourable Donald M. Fleming*, vol. 2, *The Summit Years* (Toronto: McClelland and Stewart, 1985), 588.
29. *House of Commons Debates: Official Report*, 31 January 1963, 3289.
30. *House of Commons Debates*, 31 January 1963, 3315.
31. Patrick Nicholson, *Vision and Indecision* (Don Mills, Ontario: Longmans, 1968), 232; Donald M. Fleming, *So Very Near: The Political Memoirs of the Honourable Donald M. Fleming*, vol. 2, *The Summit Years* (Toronto: McClelland and Stewart, 1985), 598; Nash, *Kennedy and Diefenbaker*, 261.
32. George Grant, *Lament for a Nation: The Defeat of Canadian Nationalism* (Toronto: McClelland and Stewart, 1965), 4–5, 12.
33. Taylor, *Radical Tories*, 148.
34. Charles Ritchie, *Storm Signals: More Undiplomatic Diaries, 1962–1971* (Toronto: Macmillan, 1983), 48.
35. Michael Patrick Grady, "The Canadian Exemption from the United States Interest Equalization Tax" (PhD thesis, University of Toronto, 1973), 94; Gerald Wright, "Cooperation and Independence: Canada's Management of Financial Relations with the United States, 1963–1968" (PhD thesis, Johns Hopkins University, 1976), 143.
36. Nash, *Kennedy and Diefenbaker*, 92.
37. Ritchie, *Storm Signals*, 52.
38. *DesRosiers Automotive Yearbook, 2000* (Don Mills, Ontario: DesRosiers Automotive Consultants, 2000), 190.
39. Lester B. Pearson, *Mike: The Memoirs of the Right Honourable Lester B. Pearson*, vol. 3, *1957–1968* (Toronto: University of Toronto Press, 1975), 125. External Affairs Minister Paul Martin has a different memory of the event. In his version, Johnson called the prime minister "Drew Pearson," confusing him with the Washington journalist. Paul Martin, *A Very Public Life*, vol. 2, *So Many Words* (Ottawa: Deneau, 1985), 395.
40. John English, *The Worldly Years, 1949–1972*, vol. 2 of *The Life of Lester Pearson* (Toronto: Alfred A. Knopf, 1992), 360.
41. Paul Litt, "The Massey Commission, Americanization, and Canadian Cultural Nationalism," *Queen's Quarterly* 98, no. 2 (Summer 1991): 377.
42. Frank Underhill, "Notes on the Massey Report," *Canadian Forum*, August 1951, 102.
43. Isaiah Litvak and Christopher Maule, *Cultural Sovereignty: The Time and Reader's Digest Case in Canada* (New York: Praeger, 1974), 30.
44. Royal Commission on Publications, *Report* (Ottawa: Queen's Printer, 1961), 4.
45. Royal Commission on National Development in the Arts, Letters and Sciences, *Report* (Ottawa: King's Printer, 1951), 50.
46. For the Canadian figure, see Ted Magder, *Canada's Hollywood: The Canadian State and Feature Films* (Toronto: University of Toronto Press, 1993), 137. A quick check of some of the top American films of 1967 (*In the Heat of the Night, Bonnie and Clyde, The Graduate, Guess Who's Coming to Dinner*) shows that they all had budgets between $2 million and $4 million. See Tino Balio, *United Artists: The Company that Changed the Film Industry* (Madison: University of Wisconsin Press, 1987), 187; Stephen Prince, "The Hemorrhaging of American Cinema: *Bonnie and Clyde*'s Legacy of Cinematic Violence," in *Arthur Penn's* Bonnie and Clyde,

edited by Lester D. Friedman (Cambridge: Cambridge University Press, 2000), 134; J.W. Whitehead, *Appraising* The Graduate*: The Mike Nichols Classic and Its Impact in Hollywood* (Jefferson, North Carolina: McFarland, 2011), 16; James Robert Parish, *Katharine Hepburn: The Untold Story* (New York: Advocate Books, 2005), 263.

47.  Manjunath Pendakur, *Canadian Dreams and American Control: The Political Economy of the Canadian Film Industry* (Toronto: Garamond, 1990), 155.

48.  Victor Levant, *Quiet Complicity: Canadian Involvement in the Vietnam War* (Toronto: Between the Lines, 1986), 55.

49.  Edelgard Mahant and Graeme S. Mount, *Invisible and Inaudible in Washington: American Policies toward Canada* (Vancouver: UBC Press, 1999), 49.

50.  J.L. Granatstein and David J. Bercuson, *War and Peacekeeping from South Africa to the Gulf: Canada's Limited Wars* (Toronto: Key Porter, 1991), 205.

51.  Charles Ritchie, "The Day the President of the United States Struck Fear and Trembling into the Heart of Our PM," *Maclean's*, January 1974, 42; Ritchie, *Storm Signals*, 82–3.

52.  Lawrence Martin, *The Presidents and the Prime Ministers, Washington and Ottawa Face to Face: The Myth of Bilateral Bliss, 1867–1982* (Toronto:

Doubleday, 1982), 2. I am grateful to Lawrence Martin, who identified Charles Ritchie as his source for this quotation.

53.  Pearson, *Mike*, 143.

54.  Ritchie, *Storm Signals*, 80.

55.  Sam Houston Johnson, *My Brother Lyndon* (New York: Cowles, 1970), 135.

56.  Task Force on the Structure of Canadian Industry, *Foreign Investment and the Structure of Canadian Industry* (Ottawa: Privy Council Office, 1968), 91.

57.  M.J. Arlen, "Living-Room War," *New Yorker*, 15 October 1966, 200–2.

58.  "Is the US a 'Sick Society'? Yes, Say Nearly 4-in-10 People," *Gallup Report*, 12 October 1968.

59.  Ian Lumsden, ed., *Close the 49th Parallel Etc: The Americanization of Canada* (Toronto: University of Toronto Press, 1970).

60.  Walter Gordon, "The War in Vietnam," speech to the Sixth Arts and Management Conference of Professional Women, 13 May 1967, appendix 8 in *A Political Memoir* (Toronto: McClelland and Stewart, 1977), 363–9.

61.  Canadian Institute of Public Opinion, "US Investment Not Needed," *Ottawa Citizen*, 12 February 1972, 7.

62.  Frank Underhill, foreword to *Nationalism in Canada*, edited by Peter Russell (Toronto: McGraw–Hill, 1966), xix.

## Chapter 10

1.  Richard Rohmer, *Ultimatum* (Markham, Ontario: Clarke, Irwin, 1973); Richard Rohmer, *Exxoneration* (Toronto: McClelland and Stewart, 1974).

2.  Dave Billington, "Exxageration: A Base National Fantasy," review of *Exxoneration*, by Richard Rohmer, *Montreal Gazette*, 26 October 1974.

3.  John Herd Thompson and Stephen J. Randall, *Canada and the United States: Ambivalent Allies*, 4th ed.

(Montreal and Kingston: McGill–Queen's University Press, 2008), 222; J.L. Granatstein, *Yankee Go Home? Canadians and Anti-Americanism* (Toronto: HarperCollins, 1996), 180.

4.  Dawn Rae Flood, "A Black Panther in the Great White North: Fred Hampton Visits Saskatchewan, 1969," paper to the Canadian Historical Association, June 2013. I am grateful to Dr Flood for sharing her paper with me before it is published.

5. Mike Boone, "Stokely Preaches Violent Revolution," *McGill Daily*, 15 October 1968, 1–2, 6.

6. J.A. Wainwright, "'New Skin for the Old Ceremony': Canadian Identity Revisited," *Essays on Canadian Writing* 63 (Spring 1998): 64.

7. Canada, *House of Commons Debates*, 14 February 1969, 5517–8.

8. Gordon Sinclair, *Will Gordon Sinclair Please Sit Down* (Toronto: McClelland and Stewart, 1975), 163–4.

9. Sinclair, *Please Sit Down*, 165; "Hot 100," *Billboard*, 9 February 1974, 56; "RPM Top Singles," *RPM Weekly*, 23 February 1974, 20.

10. Ray Smith, "Cape Breton Is the Thought Control Center of Canada," in *The New Romans: Candid Canadian Opinions of the US*, edited by Al Purdy (Edmonton: Hurtig, 1968), 30.

11. Heather Robertson, "Confessions of a Canadian Chauvinist Pig, *Maclean's*, April 1975, 96.

12. Vern Harper, *Following the Red Path: The Native People's Caravan, 1974* (Toronto: NC Press, 1979), 9–10.

13. The circulation figures are on the front page of most issues. The 85,000 figure comes from *Akwesasne Notes*, early spring 1977.

14. Dennis Banks with Richard Erdoes, *Ojibwa Warrior: Dennis Banks and the Rise of the American Indian Movement* (Norman: University of Oklahoma Press, 2004), 64.

15. Canada, Department of Indian Affairs and Northern Development, *Statement of the Government of Canada on Indian Policy, 1969* (Ottawa: Queen's Printer, 1969), 11.

16. Betty Friedan, *The Feminine Mystique* (London: Victor Gollancz, 1963), 282.

17. Kay MacPherson, "The Seeds of the Seventies," *Canadian Dimension*, June 1975, 41.

18. Richard M. Nixon, *Six Crises* (Garden City, New York: Doubleday, 1962), 117.

19. John English, *Citizen of the World*, vol. 1 of *The Life of Pierre Elliott Trudeau* (Toronto: Alfred A. Knopf, 2006), 138.

20. Lawrence Martin, *The Presidents and the Prime Ministers, Washington and Ottawa Face to Face: The Myth of Bilateral Bliss, 1867–1982* (Toronto: Doubleday, 1982), 242.

21. "The President's News Conference of September 16, 1971," in *Public Papers of the Presidents of the United States: Richard Nixon, 1971* (Washington: National Archives and Records Service, 1972), 957.

22. Robert Bothwell, "Thanks for the Fish: Nixon, Kissinger, and Canada," chapter 15 in *Nixon in the World: American Foreign Relations, 1969–1977*, edited by Fredrik Logevall and Andrew Preston (Oxford: Oxford University Press, 2008), 309, 314.

23. John Hay [J.H.], "Still Sleeping with an Elephant," *Maclean's*, 26 January 1981, 20.

24. John English, *Just Watch Me*, vol. 2 of *The Life of Pierre Elliott Trudeau, 1968–2000* (Toronto: Alfred A. Knopf, 2009), 169; Henry Kissinger, *The White House Years* (Boston: Little, Brown, 1979), 383.

25. See, for example, Bothwell, "Thanks for the Fish," in *Nixon in the World*, 315; English, *Just Watch Me*, 166, 168, 169, 170–1.

26. Kissinger, *The White House Years*, 383.

27. Pierre Trudeau, "Address of Prime Minister Trudeau to the National Press Club, March 25, 1969," in *Canadian–American Summit Diplomacy, 1923–1973: Selected Speeches and Documents*, edited by Roger Frank Swanson (Toronto: McClelland and Stewart, 1975), 275. According to Richard Goff et al., since the 1920s and 1930s, Mexican leaders frequently compared their position next to the United States to that of a mouse sleeping next to an elephant. See *The Twentieth Century and Beyond: A Brief Global History*, 7th ed. (Boston: McGraw Hill, 2008), 132.

28. Pierre Elliott Trudeau, *Memoirs* (Toronto: McClelland and Stewart, 1993), 219.

29. Ivan L. Head and Pierre Elliott Trudeau, *The Canadian Way: Shaping Canada's Foreign Policy, 1968–1984*

(Toronto: McClelland and Stewart, 1995), 28.

30. J.L. Granatstein and Robert Bothwell, *Pirouette: Pierre Trudeau and Canadian Foreign Policy* (Toronto: University of Toronto Press, 1990), 18.

31. Bruce Hutchison, *The Unfinished Country: To Canada with Love and Some Misgivings* (Vancouver: Douglas and McIntyre, 1985), 90.

32. The most rigorous estimates can be found in John Hagan, *Northern Passage: American Vietnam War Resisters in Canada* (Cambridge, Massachusetts: Harvard University Press, 2001), 35, 195, 241; and Renée G. Kasinsky, *Refugees from Militarism: Draft-Age Americans in Canada* (New Brunswick, New Jersey: Transaction Books, 1976), 5, 80. The chart on p. 294 of the Kasinsky book suggests that there were about 27,000 draft-age American male immigrants to Canada more than usual in the years from 1965 to 1974. Others may have come in illegally and might not have been recorded in the figures, though there would have been little reason to enter illegally after May 1969, when Canada announced it would not consider military status when deciding whether to admit immigrants.

33. English, *Just Watch Me*, 213.

34. John S. Odell, *US International Monetary Policy: Markets, Power, and Ideas as Sources of Change* (Princeton, New Jersey: Princeton University Press, 1982), 263.

35. In 1971, Canada's total exports amounted to $17.82 billion, of which $11.683 billion went to the United States. F.H. Leacy, M.C. Urquhart, and K.A.H. Buckley, eds., *Historical Statistics of Canada*, 2nd ed. (Ottawa: Statistics Canada, 1983), series G427, G428.

36. Granatstein and Bothwell, *Pirouette*, 67.

37. Martin, *The Presidents and the Prime Ministers*, 247–8.

38. Richard Nixon, "Address to a Joint Meeting of the Canadian Parliament, April 14, 1972," in *Public Papers of the Presidents of the United States: Richard Nixon, 1972* (Washington:

National Archives and Record Service, 1974), 537.

39. "Wither Waffle?" *Canadian Dimension*, April 1971, 24.

40. Don McQueen, "The Waffle Lives On," *Commentator*, June 1971, 15.

41. Philip Resnick, *The Land of Cain: Class and Nationalism in English Canada, 1945–1975* (Vancouver: New Star Books, 1977), 147.

42. Alastair W. Gillespie with Irene Sage, *Made in Canada: A Businessman's Adventures in Politics* ([Montreal]: Robin Brass Studio, 2009), 144–5.

43. "Canadian Development Corp. Wins Solid Public Support," *Toronto Daily Star*, 23 January 1971, 13.

44. Mitchell Sharp, "Canada–U.S. Relations: Options for the Future," *International Perspectives*, special issue, Autumn 1972, 13.

45. Robert Bothwell, *Canada and the United States: The Politics of Partnership* (Toronto: University of Toronto Press, 1992), 110.

46. Martin, *The Presidents and the Prime Ministers*, 255.

47. Robert Bothwell, "Thanks for the Fish," in *Nixon in the World*, 314.

48. Robin Mathews, "Mathews Replies to Petch's Statistical Defence for Hiring US Profs—What Are You Doing about It?" *The Chevron* [University of Waterloo], 26 September 1969, 19.

49. Albert L. Danielsen, *The Evolution of OPEC* (New York: Harcourt Brace Jovanovich, 1982), 160.

50. Jim Stott, "Alberta Will Fight National Oil Policy," *Calgary Herald*, 15 September 1973, 21.

51. Citibank advertisement, *New York Times*, 31 January 1980, A15; Greyhound advertisement, *Gazette* [Montreal], 14 February 1980, 42; Greyhound advertisement, *Toronto Star*, 15 February 1980, A11.

52. A Canadian Petroleum Association poll showed that 84 per cent of respondents favoured the move toward a 50 per cent Canadian ownership of the oil and gas industry. A Gallup poll reported that 64 per cent would support a goal of 75 per cent Canadian ownership. G. Bruce Doern and Glen Toner, *The*

Politics of Energy: The Development and
Implementation of the NEP (Toronto:
Methuen, 1985), 107–8.

53. Ronald Reagan, "Remarks at the
Annual Convention of the National
Association of Evangelicals in
Orlando, Florida, March 8, 1983,"
in Public Papers of the Presidents of the
United States: Ronald Reagan, 1983, vol.
1 (Washington: National Archives and
Records Service, 1984), 364.

54. Trudeau, Memoirs, 329.

55. John Brecher with Eleanor Clift and
Andrew Szende, "Hands Across the
Border," Newsweek, 23 March 1981, 39.

56. Don Jamieson, No Place for Fools,
vol. 1 of The Political Memoirs of
Don Jamieson, edited by Carmelita
McGrath (St. John's: Breakwater,
1989), 11.

57. Granatstein and Bothwell, Pirouette, 371.

58. Michael T. Kaufman, "Top US Official
Quoted as Ridiculing Trudeau," New
York Times, 23 December 1983, A9.

59. Ronald Reagan, The Reagan Diaries,
edited by Douglas Brinkley (New York:
HarperCollins, 2007), 205.

60. Ian Urquhart, "The Welcome Wagon,"
Maclean's, 1 November 1976, 40p.

61. Urquhart, "The Welcome Wagon," 40p.

## Chapter 11

1. Mordecai Richler et al., "Oh Canada!
Patriotic or Apathetic? Canadians
Ponder Their Native Land," Maclean's,
1 July 1994, 42; J.L. Granatstein,
Yankee Go Home? Canadians and Anti-
Americanism (Toronto: HarperCollins,
1996), 251.

2. Brian Mulroney, Memoirs, 1939–1993
(Toronto: McClelland and Stewart,
2007), 21.

3. Peter C. Newman, The Canadian
Revolution, 1985–1995: From Deference to
Defiance (Toronto: Viking, 1995), 231.

4. Lawrence Martin, "Tories Take
the Gloves Off: Mulroney Rejects
'Inexperience' Tag as Clark Joins Attack,"
Globe and Mail, 3 June 1983, 1, 8.

5. Mulroney, Memoirs, 231.

6. John Urquhart, "An Outspoken US
Friend in Ottawa," Wall Street Journal,
24 September 1984, 32.

7. Brian Mulroney, "New Climate for
Investment," extracts from a speech
to the members of the Economic
Club, New York, 10 December 1984,
document 41 in Canadian Foreign
Policy, 1977–1992: Selected Speeches
and Documents, edited by Arthur
E. Blanchette (Ottawa: Carleton
University Press, 1994), 69.

8. Mulroney, Memoirs, 367.

9. Ronald Reagan, An American Life
(New York: Simon and Schuster,
1990), 388; Ronald Reagan, The
Reagan Diaries, edited by Douglas

Brinkley (New York: HarperCollins,
2007), 309; George Bush and Brent
Scowcroft, A World Transformed (New
York: Alfred A. Knopf, 1998), 62.

10. Stephen F. Knott and Jeffrey L.
Chidester, At Reagan's Side: Insiders'
Recollections from Sacramento to the
White House (Lanham, Maryland:
Rowman and Littlefield, 2009), 170.

11. Derek H. Burney, Getting It Done:
A Memoir (Montreal and Kingston:
McGill–Queen's University Press,
2005), 100.

12. Linda Diebel, "FIRA, Again, Is Under
Fire. It's Too: (1) Soft. (2) Tough. (3)
Don't Know." Montreal Gazette, 17
March 1984, D1, D4.

13. "51% Support for Free Trade is High
Point in Economic Rating," Montreal
Gazette, 29 July 1985, B6.

14. William Johnson, "Canada Must Act
on Free Trade, Macdonald Says,"
Globe and Mail, 19 November 1984, 1.

15. Mike Duffy, "Canada–US Free
Trade Talks: 'You Are a Hack!'" The
National, CBC-TV, 22 September
1987, CBC Digital Archives, http://
www.cbc.ca/archives/categories/
economy-business/trade-agreements/
canada-us-free-trade-agreement/you-
are-a-hack.html; "Reisman Calls Star
'a Rag', Tells Reporter He's 'a Hack',"
Toronto Star, 23 September 1987, A4.

16. Marci McDonald, Yankee Doodle
Dandy: Brian Mulroney and the

*American Agenda* (Toronto: Stoddart, 1995), 227.

17. Paul Litt, *Elusive Destiny: The Political Vocation of John Napier Turner* (Vancouver: UBC Press, 2011), 375–6.

18. "Encounter/88," CBC Television news special, 25 October 1988, CBC Archives, http://www.cbc.ca/archives/categories/politics/elections/leaders-debates-1968-2011-arguing-for-canada/leaders-debate-1988.html.

19. Michael Adams, Donna Dasko, and James Matsui, "Liberals Move Ahead of PCs in Wake of Leaders' Debates," *Globe and Mail*, 1 November 1988, A1.

20. Robert Mason Lee, *One Hundred Monkeys: The Triumph of Popular Wisdom in Canadian Politics* (Toronto: Macfarlane Walter and Ross, 1989), 216.

21. Graham Fraser, "Klan Remark Draws Hot Retort from Mulroney," *Globe and Mail*, 4 November 1988, A10.

22. Graham Fraser, *Playing for Keeps: The Making of the Prime Minister, 1988* (Toronto: McClelland and Stewart, 1989), 367.

23. Lee, *One Hundred Monkeys*, 228.

24. Fraser, *Playing for Keeps*, 413.

25. Stephen Azzi, "Debating Free Trade," *National Post*, national edition, 14 January 2006, A22.

26. For a summary of the literature on the impact of the trade agreements on Canada, see Richard G. Harris, "The Economic Impact of the Canada–US FTA and NAFTA Agreements for Canada: A Review of the Evidence," in *NAFTA@10*, edited by John M. Curtis and Aaron Sydor (Ottawa: Department of Foreign Affairs and International Trade, 2006), 9–42.

27. Lou Cannon, *President Reagan: The Role of a Lifetime* (New York: PublicAffairs, 2000), 102–3.

28. Bill Prochnau, "The Watt Controversy," *Washington Post*, 30 June 1981, A1.

29. "Environmentalists: More of a Political Force," *Business Week*, 24 January 1983, 85.

30. "Acid Rain No Big Deal: US Energy Secretary," *The Gazette* [Montreal], 21 June 1986, A8.

31. *Canada–United States Air Quality Agreement: Progress Report 2012* (Ottawa and Washington: International Joint Commission, 2012), 1.

32. Stephen F. Knott and Jeffrey L. Chidester, *At Reagan's Side: Insiders' Recollections from Sacramento to the White House* (Lanham, Maryland: Rowman and Littlefield, 2009), 170.

33. Knott and Chidester, *At Reagan's Side*, 171.

34. Mulroney, *Memoirs*, 350.

## Chapter 12

1. Jim Farrell, "Canadian Commander 'Over the Moon'," *Ottawa Citizen*, 29 January 2002, A8.

2. "Nearly Every Canadian Investor Affected by US Trade Agreement," *Financial Post*, 23 November 1935, 12.

3. Jean Chrétien, "Closing Remarks," in *Finding Common Ground: The Proceedings of the Aylmer Conference*, edited by Jean Chrétien (Hull, Quebec: Voyageur, 1992), 245.

4. Tad Szulc, "Don't Take Canada for Granted," *Parade Magazine* (insert in the *Washington Post*), 20 February 1994, 5.

5. Tim Harper, "PM's Private Jabs at Clinton Go Public: Didn't Know Mike was Live," *Toronto Star*, 10 July 1997, A1, A28.

6. Jean Chrétien, *My Years as Prime Minister* (Toronto: Alfred A. Knopf, 2007), 100.

7. *Creating Opportunity: The Liberal Plan for Canada* (Ottawa: Liberal Party of Canada, 1993), 24.

8. Barrie McKenna, "Deadline Scrapped for NAFTA Rule Changes," *Globe and Mail*, 2 September 1995, B1, B5.

9. "What the Governments Had to Say," *Toronto Star*, 3 December 1993, A27.

10. Clyde H. Farnsworth, "After Criticism by US, Mulroney Jabs Back," *New York Times*, 8 March 1992, 15.

11. James J. Blanchard, *Behind the Embassy Door: Canada, Clinton and Quebec* (Toronto: McClelland and Stewart, 1998), 238.

12. Edward Greenspon and Anthony Wilson-Smith, *Double Vision: The Inside Story of the Liberals in Power* (Toronto: Doubleday, 1996), 327.

13. Blanchard, *Behind the Embassy Door*, 248.

14. Lloyd Axworthy, *Navigating a New World: Canada's Global Future* (Toronto: Alfred A. Knopf, 2003), 34.

15. Joseph S. Nye Jr, *Bound to Lead: The Changing Nature of American Power* (New York: Basic Books, 1990), 31–2.

16. Lloyd Axworthy, "Why 'Soft Power' Is the Right Policy for Canada," *Ottawa Citizen*, 25 April 1998, B6.

17. Bruce Wallace, "Axworthy's 'Soft Power'," *Maclean's*, 13 July 1998, 29.

18. "Landmine Facts," *Vancouver Sun*, 29 November 1997, H1.

19. Fen Osler Hampson and Dean F. Oliver, "Pulpit Diplomacy: A Critical Assessment of the Axworthy Doctrine," *International Journal* 53, no. 3 (Summer 1998): 388.

20. Hampson and Oliver, "Pulpit Diplomacy," 379–406.

21. Kim Richard Nossal, "Pinchpenny Diplomacy: The Decline of 'Good International Citizenship' in Canadian Foreign Policy," *International Journal* 54, no. 1 (Winter 1998–9): 93.

22. Prosper Bernard, Jr, "Canada and Human Security: From the Axworthy Doctrine to Middle Power Internationalism," *American Review of Canadian Studies* 36, no. 2 (Summer 2006): 241.

23. Andrew Cohen, *While Canada Slept: How We Lost Our Place in the World* (Toronto: McClelland and Stewart, 2003), 85–6.

24. Cohen, *While Canada Slept*, 47.

25. *For an Extra $130 Bucks . . . Update on Canada's Military Crisis, a View from the Bottom Up: Report of the Standing Committee on National Security and Defence* (Ottawa: The Senate, 2002), 11.

26. Stephen J. Randall, "Great Expectations: America's Approach to Canada," chapter 15 in *Transnationalism: Canada–United States History into the 21st Century*, edited by Michael D. Behiels and Reginald C. Stuart (Montreal and Kingston: McGill–Queen's University Press, 2010), 284.

27. Caroline E. Mayer, "FCC Chief's Fears: Fowler Sees Threat in Regulation," *Washington Post*, 6 February 1983, K1, K6.

28. Graham Fraser, "Barshefsky Sees Magazine Ruling as Trade Weapon," *Globe and Mail*, 30 January 1997, B13.

29. Peter C. Newman, "Let's Not Play Pluto to Mickey Mouse," *Maclean's*, 8 April 1996, 44.

30. Jean-Yves Nau and Claire Tréan, "Bioéthique et culture, nouveaux espaces diplomatiques," *Le Monde*, 24 October 2003, 20.

31. Paul Wells, "How Our Leader Reacted," *National Post*, 20 September 2001, A1.

32. Bruce Campion-Smith, "'Best' Friends to US on Worst Day," *Toronto Star*, 12 September 2006, A10.

33. Jim DeFede, *The Day the World Came to Town: 9/11 in Gander, Newfoundland* (New York: HarperCollins, 2002), 6–7.

34. Paul Cellucci, *Unquiet Diplomacy* (Toronto: Key Porter, 2005), 13.

35. Graham Thompson and Tim Naumetz, "Chrétien, Dallas Hosts Exchange Plaudits," *Ottawa Citizen*, 29 November 2001, A9

36. "Jean Chrétien: Visit Underscores Canada's Importance," *Dallas Morning News*, 28 November 2001.

37. Hugh Winsor, "Dispelling Myth about Canada as Terrorist Portal," *Globe and Mail*, 4 December 2001, A10.

38. George W. Bush, "Remarks Following Discussions with Prime Minister Jean Chretien of Canada," 24 September 2001, in *Public Papers of the Presidents of the United States: George W. Bush, 2001* (Washington: National Archives and Records Administration, 2003), vol. 2, 1155.

39. Sheldon Alberts, "PM under Fire over 'Shocking' Remarks," *National Post*, 13 September 2002, A1, A7.

40. Robert Sheppard, "Keeping Our Distance: We're Sympathetic but Not

Really Close to Americans," *Maclean's*, 31 December 2001, 26–7; "Since Sept. 11: The Responses Show How Terrorism and War Have Left Their Mark," *Maclean's*, 31 December 2001, 38–9.

41. Tim Harper, "Tightening the Canada–U.S. Border," *Toronto Star*, 8 October 2001, A1, A10.

42. George W. Bush, "Address before a Joint Session of the Congress on the United States Response to the Terrorist Attacks of September 11," 20 September 2001, in *Public Papers of the Presidents of the United States: George W. Bush, 2001* (Washington: National Archives and Records Administration, 2003), vol. 2, 1142.

43. Allan Thompson, "Canada to Chart Own Course, Graham Vows," *Toronto Star*, 22 January 2002, A6.

44. Anthony Wilson-Smith, "Chaos vs. Conspiracy," *Maclean's*, 20 January 2003, 4.

45. Robert Fife, "Powell Hints Mulroney's Style Worked Better," *National Post*, 25 November 2002, A5.

46. "Question Period Round Table," *Question Period*, CTV Television, 8 September 2002.

47. Eddie Goldenberg, *The Way it Works: Inside Ottawa* (Toronto: McClelland and Stewart, 2006), 287.

48. Mike Trickey and Robert Fife, "Calling Bush a 'Moron' Should Cost PM's Aide Her Job: Alliance," *Ottawa Citizen*, 22 November 2002, A1.

49. Paul Cellucci, "Canadian Position on Iraq Unchanged," diplomatic cable, 16 January 2003, wikileaks.org/cable/2003/01/03OTTAWA178.html.

50. "We'll Help, but Um . . . Ah . . . : The View from Elsewhere," *The Economist*, 15 February 2003, 23–6.

51. Janice Gross Stein and Eugene Lang, *The Unexpected War: Canada in Kandahar* (Toronto: Viking, 2007), 77.

52. Daniel Leblanc, "Parrish Says She Regrets Remark Made 'in the Heat of the Moment'," *Globe and Mail*, 27 February 2003, A1.

53. Shawn McCarthy, "Dhaliwal Joins Chorus in His Caucus against Bush,"

*Globe and Mail*, 20 March 2003, A12. On Cellucci's response see Sheldon Alberts, "Anti-US Rhetoric Risky, Cellucci Warns Party Leaders," *Ottawa Citizen*, 1 December 2005, A4.

54. Paul Cellucci, "We Are Family," *Policy Options*, May 2003, 13.

55. Paul Cellucci, "Canada–US Security Relations—Getting Past Iraq," diplomatic cable, 22 April 2003, wikileaks.org/cable/2003/04/03OTTAWA1123.html.

56. Jeff Sallot, "Bush Lied to Justify Iraq War, Canada Right to Stay Out: Poll," *Globe and Mail*, 15 March 2004, A1, A6.

57. Brian Bethune, "BestSellers," *Maclean's*, 29 September 2003, 52.

58. Michael Adams with Amy Langstaff and David Jamieson, *Fire and Ice: The United States, Canada and the Myth of Converging Values* (Toronto: Penguin, 2003), 3.

59. Adams with Langstaff and Jamieson, *Fire and Ice*, 4, 39.

60. Edward Grabb and James Curtis, *Regions Apart: The Four Societies of Canada and the United States* (Toronto: Oxford University Press, 2005).

61. Shawn McCarthy, "Bypass UN if Necessary, Martin Says," *Globe and Mail*, 1 May 2003, A1.

62. Jeff Sallot, "Ottawa to Move on Missile Defence," *Globe and Mail*, 30 May 2003, A4.

63. Anne Dawson, "Canada Must Be Able to Defend North," *National Post*, 29 April 2003, A6.

64. Robert Fife, "Canadians Want Missile Defence: Poll," *National Post*, 11 February 2004, A7.

65. Charles Gordon, "Hold That Writ, Mr. Martin," *Ottawa Citizen*, 1 May 2004, B6.

66. Elizabeth Thompson, "Canadians Oppose Missile Shield," *National Post*, 5 November 2004, A5.

67. Paul Martin, *Hell or High Water: My Life in and out of Politics* (Toronto: McClelland and Stewart, 2008), 387.

68. Paul Cellucci, "Martin Government Expected to Announce This Week It Will Not Sign on to BMD: It's All

about Domestic Politics," diplomatic cable, 24 February 2005, www.
wikileaks.org/plusd/cables/05OT-
TAWA572_a.html.

69.  Heather Scoffield and Campbell
Clark, "Martin Waves the Flag," *Globe
and Mail*, 24 May 2004, A1, A4.

70.  Janice Tibbetts, "When You're in
Doubt, Bash the Americans," *Ottawa
Citizen*, 26 May 2004, B1.

71.  Jane Taber, "PM Rebukes Parrish for
New Insult to US," *Globe and Mail*, 26
August, 2004, A7.

72.  "Parrish Offers Her Thoughts on
America's Re-Election of George W.
Bush," *National Post*, 4 November
2004, A13.

73.  Susan Riley, "Much Hypocrisy over
Parrish," *Ottawa Citizen*, 19 November
2004, A14.

74.  Daniel Leblanc, "Just How Accurate
Are Liberal Attack Ads?" *Globe and
Mail*, 12 January 2006, A7.

75.  Shawn McCarthy, "PM Links
Softwood Dispute to Energy," *Globe
and Mail*, 7 October 2005, A1.

76.  Peter Gorrie and Peter Calamai,
"Martin Fails to Budge US," *Toronto
Star*, 8 December 2005, A6.

77.  Daniel Leblanc and Gloria Galloway,
"US Tired of Canadian Attacks on
Environment, Trade Policies," *Globe
and Mail*, 14 December 2005, A1.

78.  Campbell Clark and Gloria Galloway,
"Martin Cranks Up Nationalist
Rhetoric," *Globe and Mail*, 15
December 2005, A1.

79.  Government of Canada, "Canada–US
Shared Border: Key to Security and
Prosperity," 5 July 2013,
www.can-am.gc.ca/relations/border
_frontiere.aspx?lang=eng; Transport
Canada, "Government of Canada
Welcomes Presidential Permit for
Detroit River International Crossing,"
press release, 12 April 2013,
www.tc.gc.ca/eng/mediaroom/
releases-2013-h043e-7125.html.

80.  Government of Canada, "Energy
Relations," 5 July 2013, www.
can-am.gc.ca/relations/energy-energie.
aspx?lang=eng.

## Conclusion

1.  Edward Cowan, "Canada: Economic
Nationalism," *New York Times*, 7
February 1971, section 3, 1, 14.

2.  J.L. Granatstein, *Yankee Go Home?
Canadians and Anti-Americanism*
(Toronto: HarperCollins, 1996), 8.

3.  Steven Pearlstein, "I'm Me and Damn
Proud of It," *Washington Post*, 28 April
2000, A24.

4.  Janice Gross Stein and Eugene
Lang, *The Unexpected War: Canada in
Kandahar* (Toronto: Viking, 2007),
164.

5.  Anne Dawson, "Canada Must Be Able
to Defend North," *National Post*, 29
April 2003, A6.

6.  Stephen Azzi and Tamara Feick,
"Coping with the Cultural Colossus:
Canada and the International
Instrument on Cultural Diversity,"
chapter 6 in *Canada Among Nations
2003: Coping with the American
Colossus*, edited by David Carment,
Fen Osler Hampson, and Norman
Hillmer (Toronto: Oxford University
Press, 2003), 106.

# Index